Happy inquests!

Chris Morris

13.10.10

CORONERS' COURTS

A GUIDE TO LAW AND PRACTICE

REPORTABLE DEATHS: A BRIEF GUIDE

A death should be referred to HM Coroner if either:

- the cause of death is unknown;
- it cannot readily be certified as being due to natural causes;
- the deceased was not attended by the doctor during his last illness or was not seen within the last 14 days or viewed after death;
- there are any suspicious circumstances or history of violence;
- the death may be linked to an accident (whenever it occurred);
- there is any question of self-neglect or neglect by others;
- the death has occurred or the illness arisen during or shortly after detention in police or prison custody (including voluntary attendance at a police station);
- the deceased was detained under the Mental Health Act;
- the death is linked with an abortion;
- the death might have been contributed to by the actions of the deceased (such as a history of drug or solvent abuse, self injury or overdose);
- the death could be due to industrial disease or related in any way to the deceased's employment;
- the death occurred during an operation or before full recovery from the effects of an anaesthetic or was in any way related to the anaesthetic (in any event a death within 24 hours should normally be referred);
- the death may be related to a medical procedure or treatment whether invasive or not;
- the death may be due to lack of medical care;
- there are any other unusual or disturbing features to the case;
- the death occurs within 24 hours of admission to hospital (unless the admission was purely for terminal care);
- it may be wise to report any death where there is an allegation of medical mismanagement;

This note is for guidance only, it is not exhaustive and in part may represent desired local practice rather than the statutory requirements. If in any doubt contact the coroner's office for further advice.

CORONERS' COURTS

A GUIDE TO LAW AND PRACTICE

Second edition

Christopher Dorries

OXFORD

UNIVERSITY PRESS

OXFORD
UNIVERSITY PRESS

Great Clarendon Street, Oxford OX2 6DP

Oxford University Press is a department of the University of Oxford.
It furthers the University's objective of excellence in research, scholarship,
and education by publishing worldwide in

Oxford New York

Auckland Cape Town Dar es Salaam Hong Kong Karachi Kuala Lumpur
Madrid Melbourne Mexico City Nairobi New Delhi Shanghai Taipei Toronto

With offices in

Argentina Austria Brazil Chile Czech Republic France Greece
Guatemala Hungary Italy Japan Poland Portugal Singapore
South Korea Switzerland Thailand Turkey Ukraine Vietnam

Oxford is a registered trade mark of Oxford University Press
in the UK and in certain other countries

Published in the United States
by Oxford University Press Inc., New York

British Library Cataloguing in Publication Data

Data available

Library of Congress Cataloging in Publication Data

Data available

ISBN 978-1-84-174246-5

9 10 8

Typeset by Hope Services (Abingdon) Ltd
Printed in Great Britain
on acid-free paper by
the MPG Books Group

For Christine, Leanne and Martin

In memory of Nigel Bruce Thompson who died aged 33 in the North Tower of
the World Trade Centre on 11 September 2001.
Nigel was the son of Norman and Pat Thompson. Norman served as a coroner's
officer in the Sheffield jurisdiction for 25 years.

FOREWORD

Like so many aspects of our legal system, coroners are gearing up for reform. But what is so extraordinary about the recommendations delivered by a Home Office review in June 2003 is that they would amount to the biggest changes to coroners that we have seen in more than 800 years.

As Christopher Dorries tells us in Chapter 1, the first legislation to define the coroner's role in investigating sudden deaths was the Statute of Westminster in 1275. 'It is sometimes argued,' he says, 'that this was both the first and last defining legislation, as everything that followed, including the present law, has been a consolidation in one form or another.' No other institution in our legal system has survived unchanged for so long.

But now, if the review team's recommendations are accepted, coroners will be put on to a modern statutory footing. Part-time coroners will at last be abolished, reducing the number from about 130 in England and Wales to just 60. Coroners will be appointed and funded in the same way as other judges, rather than by local authorities as they are now.

A hierarchy will be set up, headed by a chief coroner. Circuit judges or High Court judges will preside over the most sensitive inquests, such as those involving major transport accidents. Bereaved relatives will have greater involvement in the process, perhaps with publicly funded legal representation. Under a Family Charter, relatives will have new rights to challenge decisions by coroners—for example, to order a post-mortem examination in the face of religious objections, or not to order one despite family concerns.

But all that must still be some years off—if it happens at all. In the meantime, coroners and those who work with them must make sense of the current law with all its limitations and of procedures that are often vague or discretionary. One problem is that coroners are independent of each other and of everyone else, leading to much inconsistency across the country. This book should help to spread best practice, to the benefit of all.

Most of us will encounter coroners only rarely, at times of great stress and emotion. By explaining just what a coroner can and cannot do, Mr Dorries has provided valuable guidance for those who may suffer a sudden and unexpected bereavement, explaining when an inquest may be held and what procedures will be followed.

He is also to be commended for throwing a shaft of light onto what the Home Office review team called a 'forgotten service'. If nothing more, it should remind ministers that there is an urgent need for reform.

Realistically, it will take some years to introduce legislation and bring it into effect. In the meantime, there is still plenty that can be done if the Home Office is serious about improvement. As Mr Dorries notes, more money could be spent on training coroners and their staff. The Coroners' Rules could be updated. And a Coronial Council could be set up to supervise reforms.

But in order to plan for the future you have to understand the present. The Home Office should buy a copy of this book for everyone involved in creating a system of coroners' courts fit for the twenty-first century. And the rest of us will find it pretty handy too.

September 2003   Joshua Rozenberg

ACKNOWLEDGEMENTS

I should like to express my sincere gratitude to those who have helped with one or more aspects of this text including Steve Bates, Emma Beazley, Ginny Belson, Dr Rob Bisset, Mark Blake, Nick Bracken, Mike Burgess, Ann Chalmers, Denis Clark, Judith Cooke, Nick Dean, Peter Dean, Natalie Dix, Professor Paul Griffiths, Veronica Hamilton-Deeley, Diane Hallatt, John Harthman, John Hudson, Steven Jones, Debbie Large, Professor Sebastian Lucas, Selina Lynch, Gillian Mansell, Nigel Meadows, Mr S. Adler, Graham Owen, Brian Patterson, Dr Roy Palmer, Gemma Pearce, Andre Rebello, Vic Round, Richard Sturt, Phil Trendall, Professor James Underwood, Jacquie Vallis, Dick Venables, Lisa Voden-Decker, Ali Warner and my wife Christine.

My particular thanks are due to Robert Forrest, David Hinchliff, Chris Johnson, and Howard McCann, who gave generously of their time to read and comment upon drafts, and Meg Zawadzki at Oxford University Press who has been a (patient) source of encouragement throughout.

I should also record my thanks to those who work with me, Julie Atkinson, Janet Betts, Donald Coutts-Wood, Linda Dale, Pauline Davison, Keith Hollingsworth, Michelle Jordan, Graham Marsden, Judith Naylor, and Stella Nicholson, for their help and support through a difficult time.

PREFACE

The first edition of this work was not intended as a textbook for coroners or their officers, nor was it meant for those who need to argue detailed points of procedure in court. These functions are dealt with to greater effect by *Jervis on Coroners*, long regarded as the standard text on the subject. That the book actually found a market amongst those working in the system on a daily basis came as a genuine surprise to me and I am most grateful to the many coroners and officers who have encouraged me to a second edition.

In preparing the new edition (which is a substantial rewrite) I have again tried to keep difficult issues simple. If the book is useful as a guide to point the reader in the right direction then it will have served its intended purpose, but the reader must accept that this 'simplistic' approach to law inevitably loses something in the translation.

At the same time I have tried to throw some light on the difficult and commonly misunderstood points of law that arise, such as neglect. As the case law becomes more complex, and in some cases more self-contradictory, this has not been an easy task. Indeed, the amendment of coronial law and practice in the last five years is nothing short of staggering in comparison to the previous rate of change. The list might include a widened definition of 'unnatural', the problems of Article 2, and a complete change in the direction of the neglect verdict, not to mention the transformation in practice following Alder Hey. It seems hard to believe that when the first edition was published in 1998, disclosure was almost unheard of and even the bereaved might not have been given access to the autopsy report until after the inquest.

But all this is likely to be dwarfed by changes in the next five years. I have deliberately avoided comment on the proposals current at the time of going to press; that is not the role of a text such as this. In any event, it is still difficult to foresee the exact nature of the changes that will occur and there can be little more futile than earnest comment on a particular proposal that the reader now realizes never came to fruition! But two things are clear—considerable change is necessary and those changes must be properly funded. We have an opportunity to create a workable and well-respected system that should not be wasted. At the same time, the current system has developed as it has over the last couple of decades for good reason and it might be a mistake to throw the baby out with the bathwater.

Returning to the text, after an initial chapter introducing the coroner the book has again been structured, so far as possible, to follow events in chronological order. This brings its own complications, for the law and practice consist of many intertwined threads, but I have tried to let the reader deal with one issue at a time. Two final chapters deal with the separate subjects of disaster and treasure.

Once again I have described the work of the coroner in a broad-based manner to reflect the considerable divergence in practice and procedure from jurisdiction to jurisdiction. These variations arise from the relatively small amount of legislation and case law, together with the traditional independence of coroners and the substantial discretion afforded them in their inquiries. There are more than 120 coroners and probably almost as many (correct) ways of approaching an inquest. The reader will therefore have to accept that many of the points and interpretations put forward are the author's personal view and may not necessarily find complete favour in the local coroner's court. The fact that each coroner is entitled to his or her own approach to both law and practice, and to the exercise of a wide measure of discretion, cannot be overemphasized.

Although I have tried to 'de-gender' the text so far as practicable, lady readers will have to forgive the remaining references to the coroner (and others) with the male pronoun. I beg in my defence the general rule at law that *he* includes *she* etc.

In similar vein, to maintain readability it has been necessary on occasions to refer to 'properly interested persons' at an inquest as 'parties'. Many will correctly point out that these terms are not interchangeable and that 'parties' is a word more suited to adversarial proceedings. I hope that I will be excused on the basis of 'author's licence'.

Sheffield
1 October 2003

Christopher Dorries

CONTENTS—SUMMARY

CONTENTS

Contents

TABLE OF CASES

TABLES OF LEGISLATION

UK Statutory Instruments

European Legislation

TABLE OF ABBREVIATIONS

ACPO	Association of Chief Police Officers
CPS	Crown Prosecution Service
ECHR	European Convention on Human Rights
FAI	Fatal Accident Inquiry
FLO	Family Liaison Officer
HRA	Human Rights Act 1998
HSE	Health and Safety Executive
JCSB	Jury Central Summoning Board
MCCDs	medical certificate as to cause of death
nvCJD	new variant CJD
PCA	Police Complaints Authority
PVS	persistent vegetative state
RIDDOR	Reporting of Injuries, Diseases and Dangerous Occurrences Regulations 1995
SIM	Senior Identification Manager
SIO	Senior Investigating Officer

1

THE CORONER

The coroner was the people's judge, the only judge the people had the power to appoint. The office has been specially instituted for the protection of the people.[1]

This chapter gives the reader background knowledge of the office of coroner and an understanding of the coroner's role within the legal system. It includes:

- the history of the office;
- the development of modern legislation;
- the independence of the coroner;
- appointment and immunities;

---

[1] Dr Thomas Wakley (Coroner 1839–1862).

- arrangements for finance; and
- the role of the coroner's officer.

1.01 Introduction

The office of coroner, as we now understand it within the English legal system, is virtually unique even though medico-legal officials known by the title 'coroner' exist in a number of countries.

Many nations had the English legal system imposed during the days of Empire and thus acquired the office of coroner. However, just as the work of the coroner has changed out of all recognition in this country over the last 150 years, the overseas coroners developed their own roles in different directions. In many countries 'coroners' are now actually medical examiners, more akin to our forensic pathologist. Even Scotland, with its separate laws, has nothing similar to the English (and Welsh) coroner.[2]

As a judicial officer, the coroner is almost unique within our own legal system, having the role of an 'inquisitor' rather than simply presiding over court proceedings.

An understanding of the modern coroner and inquest requires a knowledge of the long history of the office, which predates the rest of today's judicial system. Some readers may also appreciate an understanding of the more unusual facets of the coroner's appointment, administration, and unique independence.

The Office of Coroner

1.02 Creation of the Office

The first real evidence of the office of coroner dates back to the reign of Richard I in 1194, although there are indications that the post might have earlier origins. As a Norman, Richard was primarily interested in his rights to Saxon England only as a source of money.

Richard took action to consolidate his hold upon the undeveloped country through control of the administration of justice and at the same time seized the opportunity to raise money, so creating an official who had both financial and judicial responsibilities. Until then justice had largely depended upon the whim of the feudal lords and the King's Sheriffs, who were generally corrupt and inefficient.

---

[2] Although Scotland did have coroners in pre-Reformation times.

The Articles of Eyre[3] issued in September 1194 first outlined the Office of Coroner in a form containing elements recognizable today and decreed:

> In every County of the King's Realm should be elected three Knights and one Clerk to keep the pleas of the Crown.

In Latin the title was *custos placitorum coronae*[4] and it is not difficult to see how the post-holder became known as the 'crowner' and subsequently 'coroner'. The office was responsible for examining cases of sudden death but also dealt with a much wider range of tasks on behalf of the Crown.

The coroner was elected by a meeting of the Freemen of the County, fostering independence of established authority. The unique independence of the coroner remains a key feature of the modern inquest system and an important safeguard for society.

The Medieval Coroner   1.03

The role of the early coroner was that of an independent and reliable revenue collector for the Crown, acting as a check on the power of the Sheriffs and Feudal Lords. The office was unpaid and the requirement of knighthood implied a man of stature with significant financial resources.

The most important task for the coroner was the investigation of sudden death, a potent source of revenue for the Crown. There was a rigid procedure upon the finding of a body and any failure to follow this exactly was punishable by a fine.

In this early period much of the justice system was taken up with compensation for the victim or the raising of revenue for the Crown. The object causing death, known as a deodand, would often form part of this financial aspect. One of the earliest functions of the coroner was to monitor this process and make sure that the Crown received it's proper share.

The coroner was also required to keep records of the financial benefits accruing to the King from the administration of justice. Whilst not generally responsible for the actual seizure of sureties and possessions from convicted felons and outlaws, the coroner had to ensure that such monies were properly taken and held until the King's Justices visited the area on circuit. This would occur infrequently, commonly every seven years. On the arrival of the court, the Coroner's Rolls (ie records) would be presented and the administration of justice could proceed.

The role of the King's Justices at that time was more than simple punishment of offenders. Justice was a form of general taxation upon the inhabitants. One

---

[3] Articles were a pronouncement of royal powers.
[4] 'Keeper of the Pleas of the Crown.'

example was the 'murdrum'[5] fine, imposed originally by William the Conqueror to protect his fellow Normans in an unfriendly Saxon environment. When a violent or unexpected death occurred, the person finding the body was responsible for raising the 'hue and cry'. This would bring the death to the attention of the coroner, who would ride out immediately to where the body lay and gather a jury of men from the area. Unless it could be *proven* that the body was that of a Saxon the deceased would be presumed to be Norman. The coroner would record details of the event and the murdrum would eventually be imposed upon the locality. This punishment was invariably harsh and proved a valuable source of revenue to the Crown.

1.04 Early Duties

Consequently the coroner has always had a specific role in the investigation of violent or unexplained death. The coroner had to attend and make inquiries before the body could be removed for burial.

Although it was not intended that the coroner should sit as a judge to dispense justice, this became a common occurrence. The Magna Carta of 1215 curtailed the practice by proclaiming;

> No sheriff, constable, coroner or other of our bailiffs, shall hold the pleas of the Crown.

Besides keeping accurate records, in order that no-one would escape paying the sums due, the early coroner had a variety of other duties. These included dealing with suspects and criminals who had taken sanctuary within a church. Sanctuary provided only temporary refuge but one way to escape justice permanently was to 'abjure the realm'. This meant making a confession to the coroner in a formal procedure at the end of the 40 days' sanctuary. The coroner would then arrange seizure of the man's land and goods, pending the next visit of the Justices. The criminal, wearing sackcloth and carrying a cross, had to leave the country by an allotted port, at least until the crime was forgotten. Sanctuary was abolished in 1624.

Strangely, the early coroner was also connected with the barbaric practice of trial by ordeal. The suspected criminal would have to prove innocence by a task such as picking up a red hot bar without suffering any burns, the principle being that God would protect the innocent from harm. The coroner would be present to record details of the event and preserve any forfeited property for the Crown.

As society became more civilized, the emphasis of the coroner's role changed to that of a medico-legal witness viewing victims of crime, from ravished women to

---

[5] Said to be the origin of the present day word 'murder'.

those alleging a wounding. The coroner had to bear witness and record injuries so that this evidence could be presented to the King's Justices in due course. The coroner also took sureties from those suspected of the crime to ensure that they appeared to answer the allegations. Since they frequently failed to appear, this was another good source of income for the Crown.

In 1275 the Statute of Westminster was passed, the first enactment to set out the duties of the coroner. It is sometimes argued that this was both the first and last defining legislation, as everything that followed, including the present law, has been a consolidation in one form or another.

The development of an improved and more regular system of justice[6] eventually led to a great decline in the importance of the coroner. By 1500 the only significant task left for the coroner was the investigation of sudden death.

Development of the System   1.05

The Coroner's Act[7] of 1751 was the first effort to provide a realistic reward for the duties of the office and also allowed for the removal of a neglectful coroner. However, there remained considerable disagreement between coroners and the authorities over whether particular cases merited an inquest, and therefore payment. The minutes of Doncaster Town Council[8] record a number of instances where the coroner's fees were considered and rejected including a decision in 1843:

> It was ordered that the coroner's charge of £2.6s.8d. on the inquest held on the body of Mrs Sarah Hall be not allowed, the coroner not having taken a view of the body as by law required.

The coroner held an important position within the county as regards law and order, a situation not without peril. In 1832 Thomas Badger, coroner for the Rotherham and Sheffield district of Yorkshire was called upon to read the formal terms of the Riot Act from the steps of Sheffield Town Hall during a terrible disturbance which ended in the deaths of six rioters. The rioters then set upon Badger who received a severe beating, although he survived to serve another 31 years in office.[9]

The increasing complexity of society necessitated proper records of births and deaths, resulting in the Births and Deaths Registration Act of 1836. As the desirability of inquiries into the circumstances of a death became apparent, the role of the coroner began to grow in importance once more. The Act provided that there

---

[6] The Justice of the Peace Act 1360 established the early magistracy.

[7] 25 Geo 11 c29.

[8] Jenny Moran, 'By the instigation of the Devil: The Doncaster Coroner's Records' in Elliot, B. (ed) *Aspects of Doncaster No 1* (1997, Wharncliffe Publishing Limited).

[9] Obituary of Thomas Badger from the records of a local newspaper.

could be no burial without either a registrar's certificate or a coroner's order and required the coroner to inform the registrar of the verdict in all inquests.

In the same year legislation[10] was passed giving coroners power to require a doctor to perform an examination and/or attend at court to give evidence as to the cause of death. From this time onwards the coroner's inquiry could properly be regarded as a medico-legal investigation with at least the prospect of increased detection of homicide.

The appointment of the coroner by way of an election continued. The Lowe Committee in 1860[11] recommended that the process should be as similar as possible to the election of a Member of Parliament.[12]

The gradual transition in the eighteenth century from feudalism to the development of early industrialization was also bringing a reconstruction of the law. As the possibilities of unnatural death increased, so the value of the coroner became more apparent and the coroner's court developed as a forum at which wider issues concerning conditions and liability could be raised following an individual death.

1.06 Modern Developments

The modern coroner is a product of the County Coroners Act of 1860 and the Coroners Act of 1887. These Acts established a system of payment for coroners and to some extent clarified their role in relation to the investigation of certain classes of death. The 1887 Act consolidated earlier law into the structure for our present system, removing the traditional prominence of the Crown's financial interests and emphasizing the modern concept of an investigation into the cause and circumstances of a death. The Act also prohibited the holding of inquests in public houses, a development marking a more judicial approach to the investigative process.

The increasing sophistication of society brought new challenges for the coroner. In August 1886 Mrs Bridget Driscoll became the first victim of the motor car when she died from head injuries having been struck down near the gateway of Crystal Palace in London. At the inquest, the coroner expressed the hope that such an event should never occur again.[13]

---

[10] An Act to provide for the Attendance and Remuneration of Medical Witnesses at Coroner's Inquests: 1836.

[11] Parliamentary Select Committee on the Office of Coroner 1860.

[12] In 1826, rival candidates for a jurisdiction in the East Riding of Yorkshire brought nearly 2,000 freeholders to the Castle Yard at York for the election. The following year in Lincoln, candidates organized torchlight processions led by bands through crowded streets.

[13] Approximately 3,500 deaths now occur on British roads each year.

The Local Government Act of 1888 abolished the election of coroners by the freeholders of the county, providing instead that they be appointed by the local authority (see section 1.15 below).

By 1926 the police service had developed sufficiently to take full responsibility for investigating homicides. The Coroners (Amendment) Act of 1926 reduced the coroner's duties in the detection of crime by requiring an adjournment of the inquest until the conclusion of indictable criminal proceedings. This moved the focus of the coroner's work to the non-homicidal, but nevertheless 'sudden or violent death', with which we are familiar today. However, the coroner still retained the power to commit a person for trial on a charge of murder, manslaughter or infanticide.

The 1926 Act also introduced a requirement for the coroner to have a legal or medical qualification.

The number of coroner's jurisdictions was significantly reduced over a period of time, the Wright Committee of 1936[14] having observed that many part-time coroners, because of the small size of their jurisdictions, had little experience in the conduct of their duties. It was suggested that this should be remedied by merging small jurisdictions. At that time there were 309 coroners, by 1962 this had been reduced to 254;[15] and by 2003 there were only 128 jurisdictions (see section 1.27 below).

The Brodrick Committee, appointed in 1965 to review death certification and the role of coroners, discussed the issue of criminal liability and commented that the inquisitorial nature of the proceedings placed a suspected person at considerable disadvantage.[16]

Unfortunately, although both Wright and Brodrick had recommended significant changes, their reports were largely shelved.

The Last 30 Years   1.07

Concern was renewed in 1975 when a coroner's jury named the missing Lord Lucan as guilty of the murder of his children's nanny. The anachronism was removed by the Criminal Law Act 1977 which excluded the question of criminal liability from the purposes of the inquest. This brought to an end the coroner's major role in the detection of crime and removed, except in cases of contempt, the coroner's power of committal.

---

[14] Departmental Committee on Coroners 1936 (Cmnd 5070).
[15] Memorandum on the Coroners System 1962: Coroner's Society of England and Wales.
[16] Report of the Committee on Death Certification and Coroners: Sept 1971 (Cmnd 4810).

The Act also replaced the verdicts of murder, manslaughter, and infanticide by the single verdict of 'unlawfully killed', emphasizing the neutral role of the inquest. The number of inquests in which juries must be summoned was also substantially reduced, most noticeably in cases of road traffic deaths.

The Coroners Act of 1980 made one change of great significance to the everyday work of the coroner. Previously, jurisdiction over a body had been gained by actually viewing it, a remnant of the medieval necessity for the coroner to ride out and view the body *in situ* before it could be taken for burial. With the continual increase in reported deaths[17] this became impractical, and the modern concept of jurisdiction arising purely from the presence of a body lying within the coroner's geographical area was introduced.

The current legislation governing the role of the coroner takes the form of the 1988 Coroners Act (the Act) and the 1984 Coroners Rules[18] (the Rules).

1.08 Review of the Coroner System

In January 2001 the Home Office ordered a fundamental review of the coroner and death certification systems (the Review) under the chairmanship of Mr Tom Luce. Announcing the Review Team membership in July 2001 the Home Office Minister said:

> Coroner arrangements and the inquest system have laboured for many years under antiquated legal provisions which were never designed to meet the demands of today's society.

> Public expectations, both in terms of public service and the product of coroners' inquiries, have run well ahead of what coroners can currently deliver. This fundamental overhaul is essential if we are to modernise the coroner system, in line with our plans to reform the criminal justice system.

The Review was welcomed by coroners who currently make a system work which has not been subject to a major revision since the reign of Queen Victoria. The Government promised 'a root and branch review' to help modernize the arrangements and ensure the needs of the 21st century are met.

The Review report[19] was published in June 2003 declaring that:

> . . . neither the certification nor the investigation system is 'fit for purpose' in modern society. Both need substantial reform.

---

[17] Reported deaths rose from 53,000 in 1920 to 201,000 in 2002, amounting to nearly 38 per cent of all registered deaths. The number of inquests dropped from 31,500 in 1920 to 22,700 in 1997. Since then there has been a general upward trend and the 2002 figure was 26,400 inquests, amounting to approximately 13 per cent of the total deaths reported to coroners. *Home Office Statistical Bulletin* Issue 06/03.

[18] Subordinate legislation made under the provisions of the earlier Coroners Act of 1980.

[19] Death certification and investigation in England, Wales and Northern Ireland; the report of a fundamental review. June 2003 Cm 5831.

But the report went on to say:

> We agree that the people working within the system often manage to produce better results than could reasonably be expected from the obsolete and flawed structures through which they work. It is to their credit that things are not worse. The challenge now is to provide structures which support them better and give the public services which reliably safeguard their interests.

The full report is available on the Home Office website.[20] It is not the function of this text to consider the proposals in detail, particularly as the final outcome of the Review and the Shipman Inquiry (see below) remains unclear at the time of going to press. However, a summary of the proposals is shown at Table 1.1.

Table 1.1. Summary of proposals from Fundamental Review of death certification and investigation

A consistent professional service based on full-time leadership:
- a national jurisdiction, within the responsibility of the Lord Chancellor;*
- a Chief Coroner plus an Inspectorate to monitor standards;
- a Rules Committee to promote consistency and respond to changing needs;
- reduction to about 60 full-time coroners' jurisdictions based on police areas;
- additional part-time deputies as caseload demands;
- structured and mandatory training;
- a statutory basis for the Service with necessary powers.

Consistency of service to families:
- audit of timeliness in completion of investigation and inquests;
- a statement of families' right to specified information;
- a right to formal review of decisions to order or refuse an autopsy;
- proper links with bereavement services;
- a mechanism for complaints.

Appointment in each area of a Statutory Medical Assessor (SMA) to:
- bring a new dimension of medical expertise into the coroner service;
- support and audit the death certification process;
- support the coroner in death investigation;
- supervise cases involving death from natural disease;
- choose and support 'second certificants';
- create appropriate links with public health and other safety networks.

* Now the Department for Constitutional Affairs

Some elements of the Review proposals are difficult to reconcile with the findings of the Shipman Inquiry. It will take the government until early 2004 to consider what parts (if any) of the two reports should be implemented and to formulate a policy. In the meantime, a Coroner Reform Team has been set up within the

---

[20] www.homeoffice.gov.uk/justice/legalprocess/coroners/index.html. Also available on the www.official-documents.co.uk website. Volume 2 of the report, containing a number of research papers etc, can be found at www.homeoffice.gov.uk/docs2/cofundrev.html.

Home Office to take forward reform of the coronial and certification systems, when Ministers have completed this process. This will include interim improvements pending legislation.

It may take up to two years for consultation in the usual way and the enactment of legislation, so it would seem optimistic to expect any significant statutory changes before the spring of 2006. However, the transitional arrangements suggested by the Review may well start to have relevance during the validity of this text and are shown at Table 1.2.

Table 1.2. Extract from suggestion for transitional arrangements: Coroner Review

The Review suggested that the following 'worthwhile changes' could be made in advance of new legislation and hoped that there would be clear progress on each by June 2004:

- Doctors working within the NHS Strategic Health Authorities or Health Departments to be allocated to work in an advisory capacity with the Registration Service and local coroners, to begin the process of auditing and supporting the death certification process.
- The existing Coroners Rules to be reviewed in the light of the Report's recommendations on the outcomes, conduct, and scope of inquests.
- The Registration Service, the Home Office, and the Chief Medical Officer to give guidance on the use of autopsies in the light of the Report recommendations.
- A new charter of standards for service to families to be produced and recommended on an advisory basis, pending introduction of new powers to give statutory force.
- Training programmes for Coroners' Officers to be introduced with some support from central funds. The development of new training arrangements for coroners to be started.
- Informal piloting of death certification changes.
- The Coronial Council to be appointed on an informal basis to oversee progress with the reforms.

The Shipman Inquiry

Harold Shipman was convicted of the murder of 15 patients in January 2000. Shortly thereafter the Health Secretary announced an independent inquiry to establish what changes to the current system were necessary to safeguard patients in the future. It was originally intended that the inquiry would be held in private although the report made public. Following a judicial review of this decision, the Health Secretary announced in September 2000 that the inquiry would be held in public under the terms of the Tribunals of Inquiry (Evidence) Act 1921. Dame Janet Smith DBE was appointed Chair. Phase One of the inquiry reported in the summer of 2002 on how many patients Shipman killed and by what means.

Phase Two of the inquiry undertook to look at different aspects of practice to ensure that such events could not reoccur. Stage One dealt with the police investigation of March 1998 which had not found evidence of wrongdoing by Shipman. Stage Two looked at death and cremation certification, including the role of the coroner, and the reporting and investigation of sudden death.

The Stage Two report was published in July 2003 and can be found on the inquiry website at www.the-shipman-inquiry.org.uk.

The inquiry has made substantial proposals for change which, to some extent, do not accord with the proposals of the Coroner Review. For example, the Statutory Medical Assessor's role is rejected in favour of a medical coroner system which would receive reports of all deaths.

The main function of the judicial coroner would be the conduct of inquests and the direction of the preceding investigation, without being responsible for the collection of evidence as at present. In addition, the judicial coroner would direct the more complex investigations into the circumstances of deaths where an inquest was not envisaged. In cases where both medical and circumstantial investigations were required, the two coroners would work together, each applying their professional expertise to the problem. It is suggested that rather fewer judicial coroners would be required than at present, operating from regional rather than local offices.

As with the Review report, some transitional proposals may be considered in the short term and are shown at Table 1.3.

Table 1.3. Extract from suggestion for transitional arrangements: Shipman Inquiry

19.137	The Home Office should provide funding and support for improved training for coroners, in conjunction with the Judicial Studies Board. New practices should be introduced into coroner's offices, for example allowing for greater involvement of the relatives of the deceased. Improved methods of investigation could be introduced, so that, for example, a coroner need not accept the opinion of a pathologist in isolation but would consider it in the context of other evidence. Coroners could develop and promulgate protocols for the work of coroner's officers. Recruitment policies could be changed to reflect the relevance of medical knowledge and experience to the work of the coroner's officer.
19.138	Funding should be provided for better pathology services with increased use of histology and toxicology. Coroners should ensure that pathologists provide full reports but that the opinions expressed are limited to the scope of their expertise. A pathologist should not be expected to act as an 'all purpose' medical expert to the coroner.
19.139	Training should be provided for coroner's officers and coroner's liaison officers. The work of the Coroner's Officers Association should be funded, supported, and expanded upon. The Association should be encouraged to develop protocols of good practice.

The Independence of the Coroner

1.10 Importance of Independence

The coroner remains an independent judicial officer, responsible to the Crown, who can be removed from office only by the Lord Chancellor or the courts for misconduct. The autonomy of the office is a key element in the investigation of death and an important safeguard for society. Overt independence is a corner-stone of the inquest, for the coroner may need to investigate a death involving almost any recognized authority—police, government, NHS, or local council.

Nonetheless, coroners cannot operate in a vacuum and need administrative support as well as the manpower and investigative abilities of the police. Inevitably there must be a link with central government, particularly as the Act requires action or approval by the Secretary of State on certain issues. However, it is important that the provision of these services is carried out in such a way that the coroner remains unconstrained in both actions and decisions.[21]

1.11 The Local Authority

Before the County Councils Act of 1888 the coroner had to negotiate financial arrangements with the Justices for the area. This was unsatisfactory and the 1888 Act made attempts to regularize the position. In doing so it placed the coroner, as a judicial officer, in the unique position of obtaining a salary and the expenses of office through the local authority.

That local authorities are responsible for appointing and funding the coroner may give rise to the misconception that the coroner is an employee of the authority. Having appointed the coroner, the local authority has no further control over the post-holder and little influence on the way in which the work is undertaken.

Providing the coroner is acting properly, the expenses cannot be denied or challenged.[22] The system is well established in practice but the success with which it operates varies considerably between districts. Finance of the coroner is further discussed at sections 1.24 *et seq.*

The local authority are responsible for providing the coroner with administrative staff and accommodation. Quite apart from the considerations of independence or finance, this gives rise to a number of difficulties discussed at section 1.26.

---

[21] For example, in 1982 a whole-time coroner was said to have appeared as an expert forensic witness for the police in a criminal prosecution. The Secretary of State and Lord Chancellor expressed concern that a coroner, as a judicial officer, should engage in any activity which may give rise to a suspicion of partiality in the exercise of his judicial duties or raise doubts as to his independence. See also section 1.22 following.

[22] See section 1.24.

Central Government   1.12

Whilst the Lord Chancellor[23] can remove a coroner for misbehaviour, he plays no special part in administration other than in a general way as head of the judiciary.

The Home Office is the government department mostly concerned with coroners, providing the necessary link with central government where approval of the Secretary of State is needed and acting as a focus for contact with coroners. The Home Office deals with:

- approval of the appointment of coroners in certain jurisdictions under s 1(2);[24]
- making or approving alterations in coroner's districts under s 4;[25]
- making an order allowing the holding of an inquest in the absence of a body under s 15(2);[26]
- setting down prescribed fees for post-mortem examinations and the attendance of witnesses under s 24(1);[27]
- setting the fees payable to coroners for the supply of depositions and other documents under s 24(3);[28]
- the coroner's annual return furnished under s 28;[29]
- dealing with parliamentary questions and complaints from the public;[30]
- informing coroners as to relevant legislation and giving unofficial advice;
- facilitation of training courses;
- regular liaison with the Coroners' Society of England and Wales.

Nonetheless, the Home Office is always careful to point out that coroners are independent judicial officers, with a responsibility to the Crown rather than government, and that ministers have no authority to intervene or comment upon the way in which a coroner conducts inquiries in any individual case.

Coroners' Service Model Charter   1.13

In 1999 the Home Office provided coroners with a model charter[31] intended to promote broad consistency in the way the service is delivered in different jurisdictions. It was accepted that each jurisdiction had a background of different

---

[23] See section 1.16 with regard to the changes in this office.
[24] See section 1.15.
[25] See section 1.29.
[26] See section 2.11.
[27] See sections 1.25 and 10.04.
[28] By virtue of rule 57—see section 10.13.
[29] See section 10.05.
[30] See section 1.16 below.
[31] Home Office Circular 46/1999. The Model Charter is available on the Home Office website at www.homeoffice.gov.uk/ccpd/corchart.htm.

circumstances, workloads, and support arrangements, necessitating local management and decisions. Consequently a model charter which could be adapted to local conditions was thought to be the most effective manner of achieving stability in service delivery.

The charter is a mixture of information and suggested service standards, eg time limits for certain actions, provision of post-mortem reports prior to inquest etc. It has no statutory basis.

Qualification and Appointment

1.14 Qualification

To be appointed as coroner an applicant must have been qualified as a solicitor, barrister or medical practitioner for a minimum of five years.[32] In reality, experience of nearer 20 years will be required. Comparatively few medical practitioners are now appointed coroner[33] and, of those that are, many (but not all) have a legal qualification as well.[34]

By s 1(2) of the Act, the approval of the Secretary of State is required for the appointment of a coroner within London or the metropolitan districts.

The medically qualified coroner gives rise to an interesting anomaly under the Courts and Legal Services Act 1990. Section 76 of this Act prohibits holders of full-time judicial office[35] from a wide range of legal work on the basis that some conflict of interest could arise. Although coroners are included within the list of persons so affected, it seems not to have been considered that the post-holder might be a doctor. Such a coroner has the ability to take on additional medical work—with every prospect of even greater conflict of interest. The same Act also lists coroners amongst those eligible for appointment as a Circuit Judge, giving rise to the theoretical possibility that a coroner with only a medical qualification could be so appointed.

---

[32] Section 2 of the Act as amended by s 71 of the Courts and Legal Services Act 1990.

[33] As at July 2003 there are about 123 coroners of whom a relatively small number (about 18) hold a medical qualification—but more than half of these are also legally qualified. Of the 26 whole time coroners, eight are medically qualified.

[34] Prior to 1926, the only requirement for a coroner was to be a 'fit person' which led to some strange appointments. In 1819 Thomas Mandall, a plumber, was appointed coroner of Strafforth and Tickhill (Rotherham) and combined this duty with his family business for the next 31 years. In Doncaster, the charter of Edward IV for the borough (1467) authorized whoever held the position of Mayor to act as coroner, a power which was not abolished until the Municipal Corporations Act of 1835.

[35] Defined by Schedule 11 of the Act.

The coroner is no longer required to live within the jurisdiction. In earlier times, when ownership of land within the appropriate area was a qualification for appointment, some coroners are said to have fulfilled this by the ownership of burial plots. Whether this was a macabre sense of humour or simply a cheap and effective way of meeting the qualification must remain a matter of conjecture.

Persons holding office as a local authority councillor or who have held such office within the previous six months cannot be appointed as a coroner.

Appointment   1.15

Although coroners hold freehold office under the Crown, by s 1 of the Act they are chosen by the members of the local authority, in effect the local population still electing their coroner at one remove. However the power of the local authority is simply to appoint the coroner and they do not have the power to impose any special conditions upon the term of office.

In practice local authorities often seek an assurance from shortlisted candidates for a whole-time appointment that they will not hold any other type of employment. This would avoid the anomaly under the Courts and Legal Services Act 1990 referred to above. However the validity of any such supposed restriction by a local authority must be dubious and is probably unenforceable.

The practicalities of appointment create many difficulties. As a local authority may only appoint a new coroner once in 20 years there is rarely a local precedent. The members of the local authority sitting on the appointment panel will inevitably have a limited understanding of the role of the coroner or the qualities necessary in such a person. For this reason it is common that a senior member of the Council of the Coroner's Society of England and Wales is present at the appointment panel in an advisory capacity.

The appointment procedures differ from area to area. Some local authorities will take care to place an advertisement in the major legal periodicals whilst others are content to keep the matter more local. Some appointments involve presentations and technical interviews over lengthy periods whilst others are made on the basis of a comparatively short interview. This disparity in procedure probably reflects the confusion that local authorities have in their dealings with the coroner.

Under s 1 of the Act, the appointment is made by the 'relevant council'. If tradition is properly followed the decision as to who should be appointed is made only by the elected councillors and not by their paid officers.

Within London and the metropolitan districts, the approval of the Secretary of State is required under s 1(2) before the local authority appoint their preferred candidate.

The coroner is appointed to a particular jurisdiction. Most counties will be divided into two or more coroner's districts but under s 4(5) of the Act each of the coroners has the powers of coroner for the whole county. Coroners appointed to any district in Wales have the powers of a coroner for the whole of Wales.

It is now common for a person appointed as coroner, particularly to a whole-time appointment, to have had some experience as a deputy or assistant deputy.

1.16 Removal from Office

The Lord Chancellor has power under s 3(4) of the Act to remove a coroner from office for inability or misbehaviour in the discharge of his duty. He also has a common law power to dismiss a coroner for neglect of duty. Given the limited number of coroners this procedure is extremely rare. However, in a letter to all coroners (November 2000) the Lord Chancellor made it plain that a conviction for driving whilst over the prescribed limit would normally be regarded as sufficient to merit removal.

Modern practice seems to be that any allegation with a prima facie case for dismissal would be investigated by the Home Office on behalf of the Lord Chancellor. No form of hearing generally takes place (although there have been exceptions in recent times) but the decision of the Lord Chancellor is presumably open to judicial review by an aggrieved coroner.

In June 2003 the government announced the intended abolition of the Office of Lord Chancellor as soon as a package of reforms was in place. The Lord Chancellor's Department is now known as the Department for Constitutional Affairs. It has not yet been decided how the Lord Chancellor's disciplinary role will devolve, a consultation document[36] has listed various options. These include involvement of the Lord Chief Justice (effectively the Lord Chancellor's replacement as Head of the Judiciary) and/or a lay involvement, possibly through the Judicial Appointments Commission.

By s 3(6) of the Act, a court convicting a coroner of corruption, wilful neglect of duty or misbehaviour under s 3(5) may remove him from office in addition to a fine and/or imprisonment for up to two years.

Any member of the public is entitled to raise a complaint against a coroner, although there are relatively few. Some complaints arise from a fundamental misunderstanding of the coroner's role, the bereaved occasionally holding expectations of an inquest that the law will not allow the coroner to fulfil.[37]

The general retirement age for a coroner is 70 although this can be extended.

---

[36] 'Constitutional Reform: a new way of appointing judges' (July 2003).
[37] Rules 36 and 42—see sections 7.02 and 9.12 *et seq* for a more detailed discussion.

Resignations 1.17

A coroner can resign the office at any time but the resignation does not take effect until accepted by the appointing local authority. Presumably it follows that a coroner should remain in office until a successor is appointed and takes up post, which may be several months. It is difficult to see how this could be enforced in practice.

Salary Arrangements 1.18

Under Schedule I of the Act, the coroner is paid an annual salary by the relevant council at a rate fixed by agreement between the coroner and that authority. This gives the misleading picture of the coroner working for the council, and of each coroner negotiating with the local authority. This latter point was taken (unsuccessfully) in the judicial review of the Hillsborough Disaster inquest[38] where it was alleged that this must lead to a conflict of interest in a case where the local authority has involvement. However, the reality is that salary negotiations take place nationally under a Joint Negotiating Board.

The coroner's salary is therefore paid by the local authority, out of the Council Tax Collection Fund, although the expenses of maintaining the coroner's office are taken into account when the government's contribution to the authority (the Revenue Support Grant) is set.

Part-time Coroners 1.19

Most coroners attend to their duty on a part-time basis as the number of deaths within the jurisdiction is below the 'whole-time caseload' of approximately 2,000 deaths per year.[39] Most part-time coroners are solicitors in private practice and use the facilities of their own office for the administrative work. Thus in some areas it might be that an inquest would be opened (or occasionally even concluded) with the participants gathered round a desk in the solicitor's office.[40]

The salary scales for coroners contain specific provision for the payment of part-time coroners according to their annual caseload. There should also be agreement between the coroner and the relevant local authority as to reimbursement of the operational expenses per death—ie cost of secretarial assistance, office overheads and the like. The figure which local authorities are prepared to pay by way of reimbursement varies considerably from area to area. While some coroners are truly reimbursed their operating costs there are many where the office of coroner is directly subsidized by the partnership in which the coroner practices.

---

[38] *R v HM Coroner for South Yorkshire ex p Stringer* (1993) 158 JP 453.
[39] Although there are several part-time coroners whose caseload perpetually exceeds 2,000 by some margin.
[40] But the hearing must still be open to the press and public if they wish to attend.

1.20 Deputies

By s 6(1), a coroner is required to appoint a deputy and may also appoint an assistant deputy. It is now widely accepted that there is no bar to the appointment of two or more assistant deputies. The power of appointment lies with the coroner rather than with the local authority but the Act also requires that the person appointed is approved by the Chair of the relevant council. This presumably infers a right to refuse approval although it is difficult to see on what grounds this might be justified.

Any person appointed as deputy or assistant deputy must be qualified to act as coroner in their own right (ie must be legally or medically qualified with a minimum of five years post-qualification experience).[41]

Section 7 states that the deputy may act only if the coroner is absent through illness, some other lawful or reasonable cause, or is disqualified from hearing that particular case. The assistant deputy may act in similar circumstances only where the deputy coroner is not available. On the face of it this seems quite restrictive.

However, this issue was considered in the 2002 case of *Commissioner of Police for the Metropolis*.[42] The High Court had ordered that a new inquest be held into the incident known as the Deptford fire.[43] The coroner asked for clarification of s 7, pointing out that to deal with a case lasting several months without a deputy being allowed to continue the normal work would be virtually impossible, let alone unfair to the other relatives kept waiting for an inquest. The court held that:

> ... the section is ... perfectly capable of bearing the meaning of 'lawful absence from performance of his normal duties', for example because of the carrying out of other coronial work. Such an interpretation is consistent with the objectives of the statute, which must include the just and expeditious disposal of the work of the coroner.

When acting on the coroner's behalf, the deputies have the same jurisdiction as the coroner and will sign documents in their own names.

Remuneration of a deputy coroner is provided for by a complex calculation that converts the actual jurisdiction caseload into a notional figure for a part-time jurisdiction. There is no specific provision for payment to an assistant deputy but it is commonplace, where the two deputies share the workload, that the deputy's salary is divided proportionately.

A deputy coroner may resign at any time or have the appointment revoked by the coroner. This revocation cannot take effect until a successor has been appointed

---

[41] Section 6(4) as amended by s 70 of the Courts and Legal Services Act 1990.

[42] *Commissioner of Police for the Metropolis v HM Coroner [Inner London South]* (2003) All ER 585.

[43] Which occurred in 1981 with the loss of 13 lives.

and approved by the Chair of the relevant council. There is no such restriction on the revocation of an assistant deputy's appointment as there is no statutory requirement for this post to be filled.

Coroner of the Queen's Household   1.21

The tradition of a separate coroner having exclusive jurisdiction in respect of inquests into the death of persons within the limits of any of the Queen's palaces is perpetuated by s 29 of the Act.

The Coroner of the Queen's Household is appointed by the Lord Steward. The limits of jurisdiction are defined as 'any court, garden or other place within the curtilage of the palace or house but not further'.

The jury at an inquest held by the Coroner of the Queen's Household consists of Officers of the Household rather than members of the general public.

The Courts and Legal Services Act 1990   1.22

By s 75 of the Courts and Legal Services Act 1990, a whole-time coroner (being one of the holders of office listed in Schedule 11 of the Act) is prohibited from:

- providing any advocacy or litigation services in any jurisdiction;
- providing any conveyancing or probate services;
- practising as a barrister, solicitor, public notary or licensed conveyancer;
- practising as an advocate or solicitor in Scotland;
- acting for remuneration as an arbitrator or umpire.

This comprehensive ban on extraneous legal work for holders of full-time judicial office is plainly designed to prevent any conflict of interest or similar situation arising. Of course, no such ban could ever be applied to the holders of a part-time appointment who have to be particularly aware of the possibility of an allegation of bias or improper conduct.[44] The Law Society's Guide to the Professional Conduct of Solicitors[45] sets out the following:

> A solicitor who is a coroner or deputy or assistant deputy coroner should not appear on behalf of a client before a coroner's court for the area or district for which he or she is appointed. Nor should such a solicitor (or any partner or employee of the solicitor) act professionally in any civil or criminal proceedings resulting from a death where the solicitor has held an inquest into the circumstances of such a death. Further, since the coroner acts in a judicial capacity, such a solicitor must make arrangements for another person to carry out an inquest into the death of a person

---

[44] It is reported that a solicitor/coroner (part-time) was called before the Solicitors Disciplinary Tribunal in 1995 and reprimanded for opening an inquest as coroner and later acting as advocate for an interested party, although having first transferred the case to another jurisdiction.

[45] *Guide to the Professional Conduct of Solicitors*, (1999) 8th edition at para 15.06. Law Society Publications: www.guide.lawsociety.org.uk.

where it might be thought that some bias could arise out of his or her personal or professional connection with the deceased or with a near relative of the deceased.

The question of bias generally is dealt with more fully at section 7.25.

As noted earlier, s 75 is concerned with holders of judicial office of all types and does not have regard for the prospect that a coroner may be medically rather than legally qualified. Thus there is no bar to a medically qualified coroner undertaking any medical work, even within the jurisdiction. Good sense would obviously dictate that caution needs to be applied.

1.23 Immunities

Historically the coroner was entitled to various privileges or immunities. These included immunity from arrest on civil (as opposed to criminal) process when engaged in the course of coronial duties.[46] However civil arrest is virtually unknown in modern times. Perhaps of more significance for the moment is the coroner's ineligibility for jury service[47] but this is likely to be changed in the 2003 Criminal Justice Act.

Of greater importance is the general rule that no action will lie against a judge for any matter done by him in the exercise of judicial functions—in this context the definition of judge includes a coroner. Thus no action for libel can be taken against a coroner in respect of anything said during an inquest. There is no test of reasonableness or good faith for this immunity but it does not extend beyond the court door or the end of the actual proceedings. Of course this immunity in no way protects a coroner from judicial review or the disciplinary powers of the Lord Chancellor.[48]

It is likely that a coroner carrying out an administrative function (deciding within the office which cases require a post-mortem and/or inquest) is immune from civil proceedings for a decision made in good faith. This contrasts sharply with practice in the United States where a coroner may be sued for the decision to autopsy a body which ultimately reveals only a natural cause of death.

Financing and Staffing

1.24 Payments by Councils

The issue of costs incurred by the coroner has caused problems for several centuries. It continues to provoke furore from time to time, particularly as the overall budget for local authorities has diminished in real terms year by year.

---

[46] *Callaghan v Twiss* (1847) 9 Irish Law Reports 422.

[47] Jury Act 1974 s 1 Schedule 1—but this is to be altered in the latter part of 2003.

[48] See section 1.16.

Section 27 of the Act provides that within four months of paying any fee, allowance, or disbursement, the coroner shall lay a full account before the relevant council. The council may examine the coroner on oath as to such accounts and, upon being satisfied as to their correctness, must pay to the coroner any sum due out of the general rate fund. However, it is now more common (and perhaps considerably more efficient) for an account of fees to be delivered to the local authority each month. The authority then make appropriate payments directly to the pathologist or witness etc.[49]

In the modern climate of financial accountability it is hardly surprising that local authority officers look for coroners to cut their 'budget' in the same way as any other area. Such demands have to be met with a reminder that as independent judicial officers, responsible only to the Crown, coroners are not bound by the local authority or subject to any budget, reducing or otherwise. It would be wholly improper for a coroner to be influenced in decisions by thoughts of whether funds could run to a post-mortem examination or an inquest. Equally, as a guardian of public money, the coroner must not act in a profligate or insensitive manner.

Section 104 of the Access to Justice Act 1999 inserts a new section into the Coroners Act 1998 (s 27(a)). This requires the responsible local authority to indemnify the coroner against certain costs or damages incurred, or ordered to be paid in the course of legal proceedings. Effectively this closed a loophole by which local authorities could refuse to meet costs incurred in judicial review cases.

Types of Payment   1.25

The fees commonly paid out by a coroner may be summarized briefly as follows:

- fees for post-mortem examinations, including those requiring 'special skills' for which a different rate is paid;[50]
- fees for special examinations—ie those requiring a person (not necessarily a doctor) with particular qualifications or experience (eg toxicology);
- fees for medical witnesses attending court—fees agreed between the BMA and the Home Office are set down for payment to medically qualified witnesses called to court. The exact fee varies according to the length of time the witness is away from their normal place of work;

---

[49] The total direct cost of the coroner service in 1995/96 was £38m of which mortuary charges were £11m and pathology fees £12m. Coroner's salaries amounted to £4m. However, a conservative estimate of the total cost (including less direct costs such as coroner's officers salaries met by the police) was said to be £48m which would give an average cost per death reported of approximately £250. *Home Office Research Study 181* (1998).

[50] Distinguish a 'post-mortem requiring special skills' (eg potential homicide) from a 'special examination' (eg toxicology). The Secretary of State, when setting the appropriate fees under s 24 allows a much higher fee for a post-mortem requiring special skills.

- witness or jury expenses providing compensation for travel, loss of earnings, or other expenses incurred because of attendance at court;
- fees for reports from expert witnesses—exceptionally the coroner may seek the advice of an expert witness (medically qualified or otherwise) on a particular point and would thus incur a fee for the preparation of a report in addition to attendance of the expert at court.

The fees for post-mortem examinations plus allowances for witness and jury expenses are set down by regulation[51] and updated from time to time.

1.26 Staffing

Staffing arrangements vary widely between jurisdictions, dependent not only upon the caseload but also the different practices that have developed in each area over the years. In each jurisdiction there will be administrative staff and at least one coroner's officer (ie those carrying out the day to day handling of investigations into deaths on behalf of the coroner). However, in practice there may be no clear dividing line between these two types of work.

The role of the coroner's officer, and issues of civilianization, are more fully discussed at section 1.30 *et seq* below.

The administrative staff in a coroner's jurisdiction are usually employees of the local authority or, in a smaller area, may be the staff of the legal office where the coroner practices. The coroner's officers might also come from the local authority, or may either be serving police officers or police civilian employees. This raises two difficulties. First, given the ambiguous links with the local authority and the police, exercising day to day control over staff who are neither employed by or responsible to the coroner can create problems. Secondly, the coroner may have to run an office with personnel from two very different organizations, often with divergent structures, hours, and facilities, and even dissimilar I.T. equipment.

Coroners' Districts

1.27 Statistics

The Home Office Statistical Bulletin[52] for 2002 refers to 535,400 deaths in England and Wales of which 37.6% (201,400) were reported to coroners. Post-mortems were held in 117,700 cases and there were 26,400 inquests.

---

[51] Sections 24 and 25.
[52] Home Office Statistical Bulletin issue 06/03.

The same bulletin lists 128 coroners' jurisdictions in England and Wales.[53] The Coroner Review Report in June 2003 (see section 1.08) refers to 123 coroners[54] of whom 23 are whole-time.[55] The apparent discrepancy arises from coroners who hold two or more adjoining districts.

The great majority of part-time coroners are solicitors in private practice with caseloads ranging between 200 and 2,000 reported deaths a year. A Home Office Research Study (181) in 1998 found that in 33 jurisdictions the coroner dealt with a significant part of the administrative work from home.

Historically, lack of communication and travel facilities led to each jurisdiction being relatively compact. To a large extent this remains the case, although there have been numerous amalgamations in the last 50 years.[56] In many jurisdictions, the population is not large enough to generate the 2,000 deaths that would justify a whole-time appointment. Approximately one in five coroner's jurisdictions has less than 600 deaths reported annually and half deal with fewer than 900 cases per year. Although a few districts see less than 200 deaths, some whole-time coroners deal with more than 4,000 and two regularly have more than 5,000 deaths reported.

Division of a County   1.28

Each jurisdiction forms part of a county (or in a few cases the whole of a county) but in some areas the county council no longer exists. Accordingly, one of the City or Metropolitan Borough Councils within the county is designated as the 'relevant council' for the appointment and funding of the coroner.[57] This authority recovers a proportion of its expenditure from the other councils within that jurisdiction.

Section 4(5) of the Act makes clear that where a county is divided into coroner's districts, each coroner, although appointed to a particular district, is able to act as coroner for the whole administrative area. In practice this means that should the police or a transplant co-ordinator need to refer a matter urgently they can contact an adjoining coroner within the same county, if neither the first coroner nor deputies are available immediately.

---

[53] Excluding the Coroner for the Queen's Household but including the Isles of Scilly where just seven deaths were reported.

[54] Although a figure of 136 districts is also mentioned within the document.

[55] The figure of 26 whole-time coroners is also commonly given. It is a little difficult to be precise because more than one part-time coroner has two jurisdictions, effectively giving a whole-time position. In any event, between them, the whole-time coroners deal with approximately half the reported deaths in England and Wales.

[56] See section 1.06.

[57] The Coroners' Districts (Designation of Relevant Councils) Order 1985.

1.29 Alteration of Coroners' Districts

Section 4 of the Act gives the Secretary of State (ie the Home Secretary) power to divide, amalgamate, or otherwise alter a coroner's district. Further, a local authority may submit a draft order for an alteration for the Secretary of State's approval under s 4(2). The Local Government Reorganisation (Amendment of Coroners Act 1988) Regulations 1996 have led to some geographical changes in coroners' jurisdictions but did not generally bring about the anticipated merger of districts.[58] Nonetheless, there have been a number of mergers in the last five years.

It has been argued that a reduction in the number of coroner's jurisdictions, by amalgamation, would lead to more whole-time coroners with a consequent increase in expertise and commitment. The opposing view is that part-time coroners provide a valuable local service at a realistic level of cost.

The Coroner's Officer

1.30 Introduction

There is no statutory provision for this post. The duties of the coroner's officer have evolved in different jurisdictions over many years, and the way in which the task is performed now differs markedly between areas. Nonetheless, the importance and responsibility of the coroner's officer should not be overlooked.

Coroner's officers are likely to experience considerable emotional pressure in their work. Whilst the coroner is generally insulated from direct contact with grieving relatives, and has the formality of the court as support, the officer may spend the entire day dealing with telephone calls or visits from the suddenly and traumatically bereaved. The post therefore calls for a strong, yet tactful and empathetic character.

1.31 Civilianization

Traditionally the coroner's officer has been an experienced police officer on permanent secondment, but recent civilianization of police administrative posts has also affected coroners. Generally the civilian coroner's officer remains an employee of the police authority, but in some areas the post has been transferred into local authority responsibility.

The Association of Chief Police Officers has maintained for some time that the Police Service should not be providing and paying for coroner's officers. Local

---

58 Although this has happened to a small extent in Wales.

authorities have shown some acceptance of this point in principle but there remains widespread disagreement about funding.

The Home Office set up a working party to examine the role of coroner's officers which reported in 2002. The report[59] provided a helpful overview of the work undertaken by officers without seeking to reach any conclusion about responsibility for the post or make recommendations. The government has decided that general changes to present arrangements would not be justified in advance of the outcome of the Review.

The nature of the coroner's work is particularly complex and much will be unfamiliar to a police officer. This presents a considerable challenge to the new officer who must spend much time understanding medical phraseology, and gaining experience generally, before being able to have a meaningful conversation with a doctor reporting a death.

Manner of Work
1.32

A coroner with a large jurisdiction may have a number of officers dealing with different geographical areas. In some jurisdictions the officer is personally responsible for attending the scene of a sudden death, taking initial details and making arrangements for the removal of the body. Where necessary there will be a search made for evidence (eg suicide note). If there are suspicions about the death, police colleagues would immediately be called in to perform a more detailed investigation. However, in routine cases it is generally sufficient for the officer to obtain an understanding of the circumstances surrounding the death, and the basic medical history, particularly whether the deceased has seen a doctor in recent weeks. The officer may then liaise with the deceased's GP to establish whether the doctor is able to issue a medical certificate of cause of death.

In other jurisdictions, the officer will spend the day within the office, receiving reports from hospital doctors, GPs, and uniform or CID officers about sudden deaths. Dependant upon experience, the officer might discuss each individual case with the coroner or may be given authority to make some routine decisions within carefully set criteria.

The issue of delegating decision making to coroner's officers was the subject of comment in the 2001 Redfern report[60] which suggested that the decision to order a post-mortem examination should only be taken by the coroner personally after proper inquiries. The response of the Coroners' Society was that this was an

---

[59] Report on the provision of coroner's officers: August 2002, distributed in Home Office Circular 46/2002.

[60] *Report of the Inquiry into the Royal Liverpool Children's Hospital NHS Trust*, sometimes known as the Alder Hey Report: January 2001. www.rlcinquiry.org.uk.

impracticable view which, if followed to the letter, would bring the system grinding to a halt. Whilst it was accepted that responsibility would always remain with the coroner, certain strictly limited matters could and should be delegated to appropriately instructed officers acting within the coroner's directions. Obviously this delegation could not extend to judicial (as opposed to administrative) functions. It was also noted that there are many other examples of statutory duties placed upon office-holders which are inevitably discharged by responsible junior officers.

In deaths necessitating a post-mortem examination, the officer will liaise with the pathologist and the mortuary, this may include arrangements for a formal identification of the body. In cases not proceeding to inquest the officer will prepare the appropriate disposal form for the coroner to sign. All of this involves much liaison with the relatives of the deceased, sometimes made more difficult by disagreement between different elements of the family. The officer must be capable of explaining the cause of death given by the pathologist or certifying doctor in terms that the relatives can understand.

The officer will also be in regular contact with funeral directors, registrars, or the press, and may well be responsible for arranging the jury when required.

If the death necessitates an inquest, the officer will either take, or arrange for, statements from witnesses. In due course the officer will prepare a statement for the coroner to use at the opening of the inquest, setting out the result of the initial inquiries and confirming that a proper identification of the body has been made.

At a later stage the officer will ensure that all relevant information is available for the coroner to choose which witnesses are required at the inquest. Arrangements will then be made to ensure those witnesses are told of the date, as well as relatives and other interested parties. Finally, at the inquest itself the officer will organize the court for the coroner, acting as both clerk and usher.

The Coroner's Officers Association[61] has been formed in recent years and has attracted a sizeable membership. The Association has held a number of training sessions and seminars, the first national effort to provide education or standards for officers.

The University of Teesside[62] has developed a programme of studies for the coroner service. The University now offers Certificates in Professional Development (coroner's law and procedure) and Fundamental Medicine, both specifically for

---

[61] The Secretary of the Coroner's Officers Association is Mrs Ali Warner, Hailsham Police Station, George Street, Hailsham, East Sussex BN27 1AB. Telephone: 01323 414067.

[62] Centre for Applied Socio-Legal Studies, Teesside University, Middlesbrough TS1 3BA: details are on the University website www.tees.ac.uk under short courses. Telephone Judy Flynn: 01642 342333.

coroner's officers. A Masters degree programme in Medico-Legal Death Investigation will be introduced from September 2004.

Summary

- The office of coroner dates back to at least 1194, but the duties of the post have changed greatly over time.
- Coroners may be legally or medically qualified, but a significant majority are now legally qualified.
- There are approximately 123 coroners in England and Wales but only about 26 are whole-time, many of the remainder being solicitors in private practice who attend to the coroner's work on a part-time basis.
- The coroner, whilst appointed by and financed through the local authority for historical reasons, is an independent judicial officer holding office under the Crown and can be dismissed only by the Lord Chancellor.
- The coroner's officer may be a serving police officer or a civilian.

2

JURISDICTION

An inquest ought to be held in every case of violent or unnatural death, and in cases of sudden death where the cause of death is unknown, and also where, though the death is apparently natural, reasonable suspicion of criminality exists.
Recommendation of the Lowe Committee 1860[1]

This chapter explains the basis upon which a coroner takes jurisdiction over a body. The chapter will deal with:

- the statutory basis of the coroner's jurisdiction;
- the problems of territorial jurisdiction;
- the meaning of 'death';
- the problems arising in persistent vegetative state cases;
- the definition of 'unnatural'.

---

[1] Parliamentary Select Committee on the Office of Coroner chaired by Robert Lowe in 1860.

2.01 Introduction

The coroner's powers to inquire into the circumstances of a death are wide ranging. Nonetheless, it would be wrong for any authority to have unlimited ability to invade the privacy of individuals, or distress relatives with unjustified demands for a post-mortem examination. Thus the right to inquire (ie jurisdiction) must ultimately be limited by statute.

In this context 'jurisdiction' has a number of distinct meanings:

- that there is a body;
- that the body lies within the coroner's territorial jurisdiction;
- that it is a death of the type into which the coroner must inquire.

2.02 The Legislation

The coroner's powers to acquire jurisdiction over a body are set out in s 8(1) of the Coroners Act 1988 (the Act) which provides that:

8(1) Where a coroner is informed that the body of a person (the deceased) is lying within his district and there is reasonable cause to suspect that the deceased—

(a) has died a violent or unnatural death
(b) has died a sudden death of which the cause is unknown
(c) has died in prison or in such a place or in such circumstances as to require an inquest under any other act

then whether the cause of death arose within his district or not the coroner shall as soon as practicable hold an inquest into the death of the deceased either with, or subject to sub-section (3) below, without a jury.[2]

Many cases will be reported to the coroner which, at first appearance, fall within s 8(1). However, initial inquiries by the coroner's officers, or a post-mortem examination ordered under s 19, will often show that the death does not fall within the section.[3] No inquest will be held and the coroner will issue a certificate allowing the death to be registered in the normal way.[4]

2.03 Exceptions to Jurisdiction

If the deceased held diplomatic immunity it seems that this extends to any inquiry by a coroner into the death, although such immunity can be waived by the foreign government.

A member of a designated visiting military force (generally Commonwealth, European and US services) is not exempt from the coroner's inquiry into his/her

---

[2] For a discussion about the requirement for a jury see section 8.03 *et seq.*
[3] Only about 13 per cent of cases reported to coroners actually require an inquest.
[4] For a detailed explanation of this subject refer to section 4.19 *et seq.*

death but an inquest may only be held by authority of the Secretary of State, which would not usually be given.[5]

All other citizens of any nation who lie within the coroner's district are subject to the provisions of s 8 of the Act.

The Body of a Person

Introduction   2.04

In most instances the presence of a body, and the necessity for a coroner's inquiry, will be all too apparent. On other occasions, the finding of major human parts will be substantial evidence that a body exists. However a number of practical problems can arise, in particular with human remains of great age, remnants of a body, or a foetus.

Human Remains   2.05

By s 8 of the Act, the coroner's jurisdiction only arises when 'the body of a person is lying within his district'. However, not all finds referred to the coroner might actually amount to 'a body' or turn out to be of relevance.

It is not uncommon for the police to receive a report that a body has been discovered by someone digging in the ground. Occasionally the remains turn out to be human and prompt a major police investigation. More commonly, a preliminary investigation by forensic pathologists or anthropologists will show that the bones have come from an animal. Very occasionally it will transpire that the dig has unearthed a former cemetery or burial ground, again such remains are unlikely to be of significance to the coroner.

There is no time limit on the holding of an inquest and in theory a coroner would be required to take jurisdiction in respect of ancient human remains, if there were grounds to suspect that the death had been unnatural. In reality it might be inappropriate to expend public funds on a death which had obviously occurred so long ago that there was no prospect of a meaningful investigation—in practice this is likely to mean any death occurring outside living memory.

Remnants of a Body   2.06

Another potential problem is whether the discovery of partial human remains constitutes 'a body' for the purpose of jurisdiction under s 8.[6] The test must be

---

[5] Section 7 of the Visiting Forces Act 1952; see also Home Office Circular 54/1981 which generally requires the coroner to refer all such cases to the Secretary of State to enable a direction on whether or not to hold or resume an inquest.

[6] See also section 2.11 concerning the situation where no body exists.

whether the quantity of remains found is sufficient to prove death. For example, death may be regarded as apparent where a head is found but the same cannot necessarily be said of finding an arm or leg. The latter might, for example, be an amputated limb lost from normal hospital disposal procedures. Much would depend upon the surrounding circumstances: fragments of human tissue at the site of an aircrash may be convincing evidence of death, but would be far from certain proof if discovered by themselves on the ground.

In the rare event that parts of the same body are found lying over two jurisdictions, the coroners involved would agree between themselves as to who should take the case, most probably on the basis of where the death is likely to have occurred.

2.07 Foetus

The most difficult question about the presence of 'a body' in terms of the coroner's jurisdiction may come from the death of a foetus, which can arise through premature birth or abortion. Whilst it would be rare for problems to arise from a premature birth (for the 'death' is usually due to natural causes) the situation may be more complex with an abortion.

Until recently the general weight of medical opinion was that a child born before the end of the 24th week of pregnancy was non-viable, ie although the foetus might show some brief signs of life it was never capable of independent existence. Thus, because an abortion or miscarriage up to the 24th week could not produce a child capable of separate existence, it was not a matter for the coroner. This was recognized in the definition of a stillborn child under s 41 of the Births and Deaths Registration Act 1953 as amended in 1992:[7]

> ... one which has issued forth from its mother after the twenty-fourth week of pregnancy and which did not at any time after being completely expelled from its mother breathe or show any other signs of life.

However, medical expertise and technology has pushed back the start of viability to around 22 weeks; at this age abortion is legal. This raises problems with the foetus aborted at 23 weeks which then shows signs of life.

Such a case raises profound ethical problems for the medical staff involved which are outside the remit of this text. There are no easy answers and the coroner will take great care to obtain the fullest information before deciding whether there is a body over which to take jurisdiction.

---

[7] The Still-Birth Definition Act 1992.

Death   2.08

It must be established that the body is actually dead. Surprisingly, there is no legal definition of death[8] but problems normally only arise in this connection when a patient is ventilated on a life support machine due to an irrecoverable coma. This may be relevant to the coroner if organ transplantation is envisaged.

The standard practice in such situations[9] is for brain stem function tests to be carried out at least three hours apart by two different, suitably experienced doctors. These tests, essentially a check upon fundamental reflexes, will not be performed until the doctors are satisfied that:

- there are no drugs remaining within the body which might interfere with the patient's ability to function; *and*
- all reversible causes of coma (eg hypothermia) have been excluded; *and*
- the chemistry of the body is essentially normal so that there is no artificial inhibition of the brain stem reflexes.

The question then arises as to when death occurs. It can be argued that the patient should be regarded as dead once the first tests have shown a failure to respond, the second test merely being confirmatory. However, some would contend that as it is established practice for there to be a second test, that death should only be regarded as certain at that stage.

As a practical issue, the doctors treating the patient may prefer to regard death as occurring when the irreversible coma set in, but this is not supportable in law.

Persistent Vegetative State   2.09

The situation concerning 'persistent vegetative state' (PVS) patients is rather different. Here the higher parts of the brain dealing with more sophisticated tasks, such as conscious movement and thought, have failed irreversibly but the patient is not dead as the brain stem and the basic reflexes still function.

Many PVS patients (although not all) will have the origins of their condition in a traumatic event and ultimately their death will be reported to the coroner. In some cases there have been allegations that medical treatment allowed the patient to die in contravention of the law and it is possible that the inquest can be caught up in questions of whether proper practice was followed.

---

[8] In medical terms death might be defined as 'an irreversible cessation of cardiac and respiratory functions'.
[9] 'Criteria for diagnosis of brain death', *BMJ*, 1976, 1187–1188. See also: 'Criteria for the diagnosis of brain stem death', *J Roy Col Phys*, 1995, 29, 381–382.

The law on this remains set out in the case of Tony Bland.[10] Although the facts are generally well known, the ruling of the court is not always clearly understood.

Tony Bland was injured at the Hillsborough Disaster in April 1989. He suffered irreversible brain damage and for a number of years lay in a persistent vegetative state. His condition caused great distress to his parents and those who had to nurse him. Expert opinion was that there was no hope of recovery. On the other hand, the physical functions of the young man's body could continue for many years, provided that he was artificially fed.

The Airedale NHS Trust took the case before the High Court for a Declaration. The decision of the Court (upheld by the Court of Appeal and the House of Lords in turn) was that it was proper *in this case* for the feeding to be withdrawn, thus allowing the patient to die. It was made clear that this was not a general licence for doctors to take such decisions upon themselves and that a Declaration of the Court would be needed in individual cases. This has happened in a small number of cases since.[11]

The decision in *Bland* was on a different basis to the normal rule of medical ethics; that there is no requirement to actively treat a patient who would not benefit from that treatment, or where such treatment is not in the interests of the patient. Rather, this case was about the continuance of routine matters such as feeding. Doctors have a common law duty to provide nourishment, warmth, and shelter to those in their care. Deliberate failure to do so can ordinarily lead to a criminal prosecution, the judgment in the *Bland* case effectively protected the medical staff from such repercussions.

More recently the High Court has had to consider the implications of the European Convention on Human Rights[12] for withdrawal of hydration and nutrition to PVS patients. In brief, the court held that the cessation of treatment in the context of PVS did not contravene Article 2 (the right to life) nor did the process of withdrawal of the nutrition and hydration in those circumstances contravene Article 3 (inhuman or degrading treatment).[13]

2.10 Switching off Ventilators

From time to time coroners are approached for 'permission' to turn off a patient's ventilator or allow a patient to die. The coroner has no power to make a decision on these issues. Whilst such approaches are inevitably well meaning the coroner is

---

[10] *Airedale NHS Trust v Bland* [1993] 1 All ER 821.

[11] The High Court subsequently issued a Practice Direction [1996] 4 All ER 766. This refers to Royal College of Physicians guidelines but in the more recent case of *NHS Trust A v H* [2001] 2 FLR 501 the court considered a case which did not wholly meet the criteria.

[12] See section 4.41 *et seq.*

[13] *NHS Trust A v M and NHS Trust B v H* [2001] HRLR 12.

placed in a difficult position. The coroner's jurisdiction only starts with a dead body and there is no power to absolve a doctor from responsibility for action or inaction concerning a live patient.

Further, it is unlikely that every facet of the case would be brought to light in a telephone conversation lasting only a few minutes. Whilst the coroner may be able to remind the doctor of general principles or make some suggestions based upon experience of similar cases, this is a situation where a great deal of caution must be exercised by both parties to the conversation.

If No Body Exists   2.11

Where a death is believed to have occurred, but the body no longer exists or cannot be recovered, the coroner may make an application under s 15 of the Act to the Secretary of State for permission to hold an inquest in the absence of a body.[14]

A number of criteria must be met before the Secretary of State can consider exercising such a power:

- There must be some evidence that a death had actually occurred, it is insufficient for there merely to be suspicion of a death on the disappearance of an individual.[15]
- The death must have occurred in or near the coroner's jurisdiction.[16] The words 'in or near' were said in the 1988 case of *Healey*[17] to mean a short distance or close proximity, and needed applying in a common-sense manner. Where a body is lost at sea, current Home Office practice remains that this will be interpreted as within the 12-mile territorial limit.
- The body must have been destroyed or lie in a place from which it cannot be recovered. The author would maintain that in some instances the inability to recover the body does not prevent the certainty of it lying within the coroner's jurisdiction, thus negating the requirement for the Secretary of State's permission in the first place.[18]
- The death must obviously occur in circumstances where an inquest is appropriate.

---

[14] For example, where a body had been cremated but circumstances subsequently came to light necessitating an inquest.

[15] Although it might be that the circumstances are sufficiently clear to be persuasive, eg upon a conviction for murder. Such a case occurred in the author's jurisdiction, the Secretary of State eventually gave permission under s15 but only after all normal avenues of appeal had been exhausted by the defendant.

[16] It is not generally sufficient that the body is brought into the applicant coroners' jurisdiction prior to cremation.

[17] *R v East Sussex Coroner ex p Healey* (1988) 1 All ER 30.

[18] Although there might be cases where the death took place within a coroners' district but the body was taken abroad for the funeral. It is thus not 'recoverable' if the coroner subsequently learns of circumstances which require the holding of an inquest (see also section 2.26).

Whilst the coroner would not normally have any discretion about holding an inquest upon a violent or unnatural death, it seems that there is a discretion as to whether to apply for permission to the Secretary of State. However, if there is reasonable cause to suspect that a death has occurred in circumstances where an inquest would normally be held, it is difficult to see what justification there would be for a refusal to apply. The Secretary of State also has discretion whether to grant the request. Both coroner and Home Office must exercise discretion according to judicial principles.

The Home Office has expressed the view that where a coroner has considered a case under s 19 of the Act (ie by post-mortem examination and Form B[19]) it would be unnecessary for a s 15 application to be made if later information (after cremation) showed an inquest was required.[20] This is presumably because the body still existed at the time the coroner first dealt with the case. However, in contrast a s 15 application would be needed if the coroner had only considered the case by the Form A procedure[21] (no post-mortem); that is not a statutory procedure and the coroner has never taken jurisdiction.[22]

Territorial Considerations

2.12 Deaths at Sea or in the Air

As the coroner's jurisdiction arises from the presence of a body, rather than where the death occurred, such cases are less problematical than might be thought. If a body is washed up on the shore, the death will be investigated by the coroner for that district. If several persons are lost from one vessel and washed up in different places, the coroners involved may agree between themselves so that there is only one inquest (see section 2.13). Other issues will arise if a body is known to be lost at sea but has not been recovered (see section 2.11).

Similarly, the landing of an aircraft brings a body into that coroner's jurisdiction, no matter where the aircraft might have been when the death occurred. However,

---

[19] See section 4.20.

[20] The Home Office has also taken the view that if a coroner reached a decision to hold an inquest, but the body is cremated before possession can be taken, that an inquest may be held without the necessity for a s15 application.

[21] See section 4.19.

[22] In the case of *R v Inner North London Coroner ex p Touche* [2001] QB 1206 the Court of Appeal said that the body must remain in existence at the time of the decision to hold the inquest. However, this was a case dealt with under the non-statutory Form A procedure (see section 4.19) although a hospital post-mortem then took place with the consent of the family. The Home Office view seems to be that taking jurisdiction for a post-mortem examination and subsequent Form B is different.

a single body being returned from abroad will usually be dealt with in the jurisdiction where it is to be buried or cremated in due course.

Territorial Transfers

Section 14 of the Act allows a coroner who has prima facie jurisdiction, but who believes it expedient for the inquest to be dealt with elsewhere, to request another coroner to take the case. Such transfers are common and might occur, for instance, where a person is injured in an accident within one jurisdiction but is then transferred to a specialist hospital unit within another area before death.

Similarly, where several people have died in an incident abroad and their bodies are repatriated to different places, it would usually be agreed that one coroner would deal with all of the deaths, often the coroner at the point of entry. Examples of this have been seen following the deaths of armed forces personnel whose bodies were returned into the country at RAF Abingdon.

There are provisions for the Secretary of State to make a direction in the unlikely event that coroners disagree on a request for transfer.

Several queries commonly arise about s 14 transfers:

- There is no necessity for the deceased to be moved, the coroner taking jurisdiction can act in the absence of the body. However the request and acceptance between the coroners must be made in writing.
- The coroner accepting jurisdiction will, under s 16(9), be responsible for any fees and expenses (eg post-mortem fee) incurred by the coroner originally holding jurisdiction.
- It is less clear whether s 14 allows the transfer of a case once the inquest has actually been opened by the first coroner. Whilst opinions vary, the author would argue that the wording of s 14(1) is sufficiently broad to allow this.

By s 22 of the Act the coroner may also move a body into 'an adjoining district' for the purpose of a post-mortem examination without affecting jurisdiction over the case. All that is necessary (self-evidently) is the permission of the person or authority by whom the receiving mortuary is provided.

If the definition of 'adjoining' is taken in the common meaning of 'touching, next to or having a common boundary' it would seem that s 22 should not be used to move a body between districts that do not fulfil this condition. This may be troublesome with cases of suspicious death where the increasing complexity of the examination sometimes requires a mortuary with particular facilities. In a rural area the nearest such mortuary might be several districts away. However, at least one dictionary defines 'adjoining' as 'very near to'. Certainly this is an area of the legislation that will need attention in any forthcoming changes.

2.14   Deaths Abroad

One of the more remarkable responsibilities of the coroner is to hold inquests upon those who have died abroad but whose bodies have been repatriated for funeral. By s 8 of the Act (see section 2.02), jurisdiction comes from the body lying within the coroner's district and it is irrelevant where the death occurred.[23] Provided that the coroner has reason to believe that the person might have met a violent, unnatural, or sudden death of unknown cause (ie the normal s 8 requirement) the current interpretation is that there must be an inquest.[24]

Such deaths can present serious problems for the coroner. Many countries, even those within Europe, take little care to examine the circumstances of a death once suspicious circumstances have been ruled out. It is unlikely that many statements will be taken and the police report on (say) a road death might reveal little detail. Any post-mortem examination carried out may fall below standards normally encountered in this country. Quite commonly the internal organs will not have been returned to the body meaning that a further autopsy upon return is rarely straightforward. Even if the internal organs are left, embalming for transportation will have contaminated the body fluids, rendering toxicology largely useless.

Whatever records exist abroad will be difficult to obtain and, if provided at all, are likely to be without translation. The attendance of witnesses from overseas is generally impracticable and in any event the coroner has no power to enforce their attendance.

Taking all of these difficulties into account, some inquests on deaths abroad leave significant unanswered questions.[25] However, other such inquests fulfil a useful function, with the coroner obtaining information from foreign authorities[26] that the relatives would never have acquired on their own. On some occasions the witnesses (or a number of them) are resident in the UK, having perhaps been on holiday with the deceased when the death occurred.

2.15   Deaths in Scotland

If a body is returned to England or Wales in circumstances falling within s 8(1), an inquest would be required. However, if the Procurator Fiscal has completed

---

[23] *R v West Yorkshire Coroner ex p Smith* [1983] QB 335.

[24] See section 2.15 regarding the return of a body from Scotland.

[25] The Report of the Fundamental Review of Death Certification and Investigation (see section 1.08) recommends at para 11.76 that the coroner should hold a discretion on whether to hold a public inquest into deaths abroad but should offer the bereaved help with their inquiries in other cases.

[26] The Foreign and Commonwealth Office can be extremely helpful in obtaining copies of documents from overseas authorities: International Legal Matters Unit, Consular Directorate, Foreign & Commonwealth Office, King Charles Street, London SW1A 2AL.

inquiries and issued the certificates necessary for burial/cremation, there is no practical necessity for the coroner to be informed of the presence of the body. Nonetheless, a common law obligation remains to inform the coroner so that an inquest may be held.

A Home Office Circular[27] suggests that it may not be appropriate to hold an inquest if the death has been the subject of a fatal accident inquiry (FAI) in Scotland. Jervis[28] disagrees with this view, pointing out that the body will usually be returned to this jurisdiction before any FAI can take place (and often before any decision is made as to whether one will ever be held). In any event, an FAI is comparatively rare, being held only where the deceased died as a result of an incident at work, whilst in custody, or where the death is a matter of public interest.[29] In any other case that falls within the ambit of s 8(1), the author would suggest that the requirement for an inquest is clear.

Statutory Jurisdiction

Having established that there is a body lying within the coroner's jurisdiction, it must then be considered whether the death might fall within one of the three categories under s 8(1) of the Act requiring the coroner to hold an inquest, ie reasonable cause to suspect that the deceased;

- has died a violent or unnatural death;
- has died of sudden death of which the cause is unknown;
- has died in prison or in such a place or in such circumstances as to require an inquest under any other Act.

Sufficient Grounds for Inquiry   2.16

Once a death has been reported to the coroner, inquiries will be made to establish whether there is reasonable cause to suspect that the case might fall within these criteria. A post-mortem examination is often an important part of the inquiry but there may be other elements such as the obtaining of statements from witnesses.

The Act requires the coroner to hold an inquest on the basis of 'reasonable cause to suspect'.[30] This could be described as a relatively low threshold but that is not to say that the coroner has to react to every unsubstantiated allegation by holding

---

[27] Home Office Circular 94/1985.
[28] Matthews (ed), *Jervis on Coroners* (12 edn, 2002: Sweet and Maxwell) at para 18.04.
[29] Section 1, Fatal Accident and Sudden Deaths Inquiry (Scotland) Act 1976.
[30] See *Terry v Craze (HM Coroner for East Sussex)* [2002] QB 312 where the Court of Appeal confirmed an earlier Divisional Court decision that because a diagnosis of an industrial disease 'could not be completely ruled out' this did not amount to reasonable cause to suspect that the death was unnatural.

an inquest.[31] However, the coroner is not strictly bound by what might be admissible evidence at this stage. The decision-making process is considered further at section 4.11 *et seq.*

The 1992 *Thomas* case (see section 2.19 below) made clear that there is no general discretion for a coroner to hold an inquest in the public interest, either a case falls within s 8(1), where an inquest is mandatory, or it does not.

It may now help to consider the individual components of s 8(1) in some detail.

2.17 Violent Death

A violent death is usually easy enough to recognize, at least if some thought is given to the chain of causation.[32] If the death flows from any sort of traumatic event, accidental or deliberate, self-induced or otherwise, the death clearly falls within the meaning of 'violent or unnatural'. There is no requirement that the violence was intended and no time limit within which the death must occur.

2.18 Unnatural Death

There is no statutory definition of natural or unnatural.[33] A death from a natural cause might be defined as the normal progression of a natural illness without any significant element of human intervention.[34]

Unnatural[35] death was defined in 1884 as 'a reasonable suspicion that there may have been something peculiar in the death; that it may have been due to other causes than common illness'.[36] In more modern times it was suggested that an unnatural death might mean one which was 'wholly or partly caused, or accelerated, by any act, intervention or omission other than a properly executed measure intended to prolong life'.[37]

Deaths from a heart attack or bronchopneumonia are obvious examples of natural causes. However, if the heart attack is 'caused' by the deceased having been left bound and gagged for many hours by a burglar one might take a different view. Similarly, if the pneumonia is caused by prolonged immobilization after a fall results in a fractured bone, the illness clearly has its origin in an unnatural event.

---

[31] *R v Inner North London Coroner ex p Touche* [2001] QB 1206: see section 2.20 below and in particular the final quote from Simon Brown LJ therein.

[32] See section 4.04 for an explanation of 'the chain of causation'.

[33] For a discussion of natural causes in the context of verdicts refer to sections 9.15, and in the context of the decision-making process refer to sections 4.11 *et seq.*

[34] The Coroners' Benchbook suggests a definition of death from natural causes as 'the result of a naturally occurring disease running its [full] course'.

[35] Dictionary definitions of unnatural include; 'abnormal, contrary to nature, artificial' (OED) and 'not in accordance with or determined by nature' (UltraLingua).

[36] *R v Price* (1884) 12 QBD 247.

[37] Herbert H. Pilling, 'Natural and unnatural deaths', *Medicine, Science & the Law*, April 1967.

Inevitably there are cases which fall on the dividing line and are difficult to categorize. The man with a cardiac history who has his heart attack shortly after a minor scuffle in a pub may be regarded as a death due to 'natural causes' but his relatives could have some difficulty appreciating the point.

The definition of 'unnatural' is of great significance to the question of jurisdiction as this is the main 'trigger' in the requirement to hold an inquest under s 8 of the Act. Such is the importance and complication of this definition that the Court of Appeal has considered the matter twice in the last decade. Some understanding of the judgment in both cases (only briefly set out here) is necessary.

The *Thomas* Case   2.19

The 1992 *Thomas* case[38] considered the definition of 'unnatural'. The deceased, a young woman, suffered a severe and prolonged asthma attack. An ambulance was called four times without success because of a fault in the system. By the time she arrived at hospital some 40 minutes had passed and she could not be revived. Evidence was given that, had she arrived within a more reasonable time span, survival was a distinct possibility. The death was reported to the coroner who, after post-mortem examination, refused to hold an inquest on the basis that 'status asthmaticus' is a natural cause of death.

The family applied for judicial review of this decision, seeking an order that the coroner must hold an inquest. It was claimed that a death from a naturally occurring disease became 'unnatural' within the meaning of s 8 when it could, and should, have been prevented by the performance of a duty owed to the deceased by another. It was argued that the delay had been a substantive factor in the death and might justify a verdict of 'natural causes aggravated by lack of care'.[39]

The High Court agreed with this submission and allowed the judicial review. However, the Court of Appeal overturned the ruling saying that asthma was a natural and common cause of death which was not turned into an unnatural event by the late arrival of the ambulance. Further, it was held that this particular death could not be considered unnatural on the basis of 'natural causes aggravated by lack of care' as the deceased had not been in the care of the ambulance service at the material time.[40]

---

[38] *R v Poplar Coroner ex p Thomas* [1993] QB 610, sub nom: *R v HM Coroner for Greater London ex p Thomas*.

[39] 'Aggravated by lack of care' was the forerunner of the current verdict 'contributed to by neglect' introduced by the Jamieson case in 1993—see section 9.24.

[40] Modern case law (see section 9.25) no longer requires the deceased to have been in the care of the third party, instead using a concept of 'someone in a dependent position' which is rather wider and might, in some circumstances, include a person dependent upon an ambulance service for help.

However, the comments of Lord Justice Simon Brown (who gave the third judgment) were an important marker for the future. Whilst not overtly dissenting from his colleagues, the learned judge argued that there would be circumstances in which a natural death could be turned into unnatural by causes that are secondary but not necessarily irrelevant:

> Why should [the coroner] not sometimes find death to be the result of two causes, either one of which could serve to make it unnatural.

> I do not suggest that the coroner was bound to take that view here. But there will be occasions when in my judgement that will be the only proper approach. Take a medical condition between the extremes—neither a condition like strangulated hernia or ectopic pregnancy which clearly ought never to result in death and which, if it does, will result in an inquest, but nor a condition as serious as this deceased's asthma with its considerable natural mortality rate; assume then that consequent upon some clear failure of the emergency services, the condition, unusually, proves fatal. Would not common-sense dictate that this was an unnatural death?

The learned judge went on to say that he would perhaps have regarded this very case as unnatural if the late arrival of the ambulance had constituted a more extreme failure of the service than the facts actually supported.

Jervis perhaps described the true situation succinctly in saying that Miss Thomas had not died of status asthmaticus so much as *untreated* status asthmaticus.[41]

In the 1997 Divisional Court case of *Benton*[42] there was further consideration of what might amount to an unnatural death (although in the context of verdicts) and it was held that:

- where a patient was suffering from a potentially fatal condition, and the medical intervention (even if wrongly given) merely failed to prevent the death, the proper verdict was 'natural causes' as it was the underlying condition which had caused the death;
- where there was a failure to give medical treatment to such a patient, even negligently, this would still amount to a death from natural causes (but see section 9.24 *et seq* concerning neglect);
- if the patient was not suffering from a life-threatening condition but the treatment (for whatever reason) caused death, the proper verdict was accident or misadventure, unless there was a question of unlawful killing.

This perhaps followed the majority decision in *Thomas*,[43] ie a natural illness remains a natural cause of death despite intervening circumstances. But the

---

[41] Now to be found in *Jervis on Coroners* (12th edition) at para 8.22 but this comment was first made (somewhat ahead of the *Touche* case) in the 4th Supplement to the 11th edition at para 8.20.

[42] *R v Birmingham Coroner ex p Benton* (1997) 162 JP 807. Some have argued that this case was decided very much on its facts and that a different view might be taken today. Nonetheless, the decision does fit moderately comfortably with *Touche*—see section 2.20 and further comment in 2.21.

[43] See n 38 above.

phrase 'potentially fatal condition' perhaps also encompassed the minority view of Simon Brown LJ; that intervening circumstances may make the death unnatural if the illness was not one where death would normally be expected.

The *Touche* Case   2.20

The death of Mrs Laura Touche in 1999 gave rise to further consideration in the Court of Appeal of what amounted to an unnatural death. Mrs Touche died from a cerebral haemorrhage, the result of severe hypertension, possibly secondary to eclampsia following delivery of twins by caesarean section. It was subsequently ascertained that her blood pressure had not been monitored in the immediate post-operative phase, medical evidence suggesting that if she had been properly monitored the death would probably have been avoided.

Although the death was reported to the coroner, this was in such terms that no concerns were aroused and an inquest was considered unnecessary.[44] Some time later the family asked that an inquest be held but this was refused on the basis (following the *Thomas* decision) that there was no reasonable cause to suspect the death was unnatural.

At the subsequent judicial review, medical evidence described the failure to monitor as 'astonishing' and the level of neglect as 'starkly apparent'. It was said to be likely that more prompt identification and treatment of Mrs Touche's hypertension would have prevented her cerebral haemorrhage.

The court found in favour of the family and an inquest was ordered to be held. The coroner appealed and the matter was heard in the Court of Appeal in March 2001.[45] On this occasion the senior of the three judges was Simon Brown LJ (who had given the third opinion in the *Thomas* case).

The court refused the coroner's appeal saying firstly that even if the death was strictly due to natural causes it may also have been contributed to by neglect. Thus even within the *Thomas* judgment, the death could not be described as natural and therefore required an inquest:

> Upon such material as is presently available to the coroner he could not properly have decided otherwise than that there is reasonable cause to suspect that Mrs Touche's death was (a) at least contributed to by 'neglect' (narrowly defined as by Jamieson) and thus (b) unnatural (as would necessarily follow from Thomas).

The court then went on to consider the wider issue. Simon Brown LJ questioned whether many today would find the majority view in *Thomas* entirely satisfactory.

---

[44] The coroner issued a Form A (see section 4.19) and a hospital post-mortem (ie with the consent of the family rather than on the order of the coroner) subsequently took place.

[45] *R v Inner North London Coroner ex p Touche* [2001] QB 1206; also [2001] 2 All ER 752.

He suggested that the court's approach to causation had changed in the intervening period.

> When deciding . . . whether or not for s 8(1)(a) purposes a death is unnatural, one should be considering why Parliament has included this category of deaths amongst those into which an inquest must be held. What is it about unnatural deaths that call for an inquest? Is there not a powerful case for saying that an inquest should be held whenever a wholly unexpected death, albeit from natural causes, results from some culpable human failure? Or, more strictly, whenever the coroner has reasonable grounds to suspect that such is the case. Such deaths prompt understandable public concern and surely no small part of the coroner's function is to carry out an appropriate investigation to allay such concern.

Later in the judgment the court held:

> Undoubtedly there will be cases which fall outside the category of 'neglect' and yet appear to call for an inquest on the basis already indicated, namely cases involving a wholly unexpected death from natural causes which would not have occurred but for some culpable human failure. It is a combination of their unexpectedness and culpable human failing that allow them to happen which to my mind makes such deaths unnatural. Deaths by natural causes, though undoubtedly they are, they should plainly never have happened and in that sense are unnatural.
>
> An inquest will, of course, be held only if the coroner has reasonable cause to suspect such a combination of circumstances. That does not mean that he will have to make detailed investigations into every hospital death.

2.21 Conclusion

The *Touche* case widened the definition of an unnatural death[46] beyond that previously contained in *Thomas*. Whilst it might already have been apparent that the prospect of a natural death contributed to by neglect would be 'unnatural' within s 8 of the Act, it is now clear that a wholly unexpected death from natural causes resulting from some culpable human failure will also qualify.

It seems to the author that the 'wholly unexpected' criteria is an important issue (that could easily be overlooked), maintaining the requirement of both *Thomas* and *Benton* that only a death from a normally survivable illness could amount to an unnatural event in appropriate circumstances.

The author doubts that the *Touche* case need be seen as wholly overruling *Benton* but clearly that case must now be read in the light of the later (Court of Appeal) case.

The conclusion may be that each case must still be treated on its individual merits—a reasonable prospect of an event amounting to an unnatural cause must be investigated and, if it *might* be substantiated, an inquest held. The practical

---

[46] *Jervis on Coroners* (12th edition) uses a very descriptive phrase at para 5.54: 'It is now clear that unnatural death is wider than death from unnatural causes'.

difficulty is how the coroner is to investigate such a prospect quickly enough. A decision must generally be taken either to dispose of the case by certificate or to open an inquest within only a few days of the death. It is presumably neither practical nor the correct approach to delay a decision on whether to hold an inquest until various independent medical reports etc, have been sought—but equally the coroner must remain cautious of opening an inquest merely on the basis of unsubstantiated allegations of poor care.

For further discussion of the decision-making process on this point see section 4.11 *et seq.*

Unnaturally Contracted and Rare Diseases   2.22

There are inevitably some diseases which, although natural in one sense, are acquired by an unnatural means. Examples might include HIV or hepatitis which arises from an infected blood transfusion. Such cases will normally merit an inquest.

For some time there was confusion as to whether a natural but rare disease might be 'unnatural' by its very rareness.[47] This confusion was exacerbated by the judgment in *Thomas*[48] where Simon Brown LJ had made reference to the need for an inquest in deaths from legionnaires' disease because of the great rarity of such cases. However, in the *Touche*[49] judgment it became clear that the learned judge felt somewhat misled by the submission of counsel in the former case and that legionnaires' disease should be regarded as unnatural for entirely different reasons:

> In *Thomas* we were given to understand that inquests are held into these deaths because 'it is regarded, on a broad view, as unnatural that a person should die of an extremely rare disease'. Now we are told that such inquests are held because 'the disease is caused by the mechanical spraying of infected water into the atmosphere'. This act is unnatural and may be unlawful and the disease is seen as occurring unnaturally—unlike hypertension which occurs very naturally indeed. The holding of an inquest in such cases has nothing to do with the fact that the death may be rare.

This supported a clear statement in the original (Divisional Court) decision on *Touche* that where the cause of death is known and is natural, the coroner is not entitled to hold an inquest simply because the cause is rare.

There have been differing views as to whether deaths from 'new variant CJD' (nvCJD) should be regarded as unnatural and thus require an inquest.[50] If nvCJD

---

[47] Some definitions of unnatural include phrases such as 'unusual' or 'at variance with what is natural, usual or expected' (OED).

[48] *R v Poplar Coroner ex p Thomas* (n 38 above).

[49] *R v Inner North London Coroner ex p Touche* (n 45 above).

[50] Compare deaths from CJD contracted from human growth hormone which are clearly unnatural as they arise from a medical treatment.

is to be regarded as an unnatural cause of death, this cannot be because it is rare but only because of the argument that it may result from an unnatural infection of meat in the human food supply arising from human intervention or activity. It may be thought that this latter point remains unclear.

2.23   Sudden Death of Cause Unknown

Sudden death is a term which, in the author's view, can lead to confusion. One must assume that the legislation actually meant 'unexpected'.

Further complications arise from the phrase 'of which the cause is unknown'. Many unexpected deaths referred to the coroner can be ascribed to a natural cause with reasonable certainty, but the attending doctor remains unclear as to exactly *which* natural cause is involved. For example, there seems likely to have been a cardiac event of some nature but was it a heart attack, a long-standing blood supply problem, or a burst vessel?

The system of death registration does not permit the use of vague terms such as 'natural causes' or 'heart failure' and thus such deaths form a large part of the coroner's caseload,[51] albeit inevitably dealt with by the coroner on certificate rather than inquest, following a post-mortem examination.[52]

2.24   Prison and Police Deaths

The only occasion where the coroner has automatic jurisdiction in a death overtly due to natural causes arises under s 8(1)(c) of the Act which requires an inquest if a person[53] dies 'in prison or in such a place or in such circumstances as to require an inquest under any other Act'.[54] The actual cause of death is irrelevant, such is the concern about a fatality in prison that the coroner has an obligation to inquire into the death. The inquest must be held before a jury.[55] A death in any form of legal detention may also now have implications arising from Article 2 ECHR.[56]

In addition, the 1989 case of *ex p Linnane*[57] made clear that a death also fell within these requirements if the deceased died in hospital having been transferred from some form of custody.

---

[51] For a more detailed discussion of s 19 of the Act see section 5.05 below.

[52] This topic is covered in detail at section 4.20 *et seq.*

[53] The legislation refers to the death of a *person* rather than a *prisoner* and the proper interpretation of this would include prison staff or visitors dying within the prison—surely not what Parliament intended?

[54] In practical terms there is no other legislation likely to have an effect under this sub-section.

[55] Section 8(3) of the Act, as to which see section 8.03 below.

[56] Article 2, European Convention on Human Rights, given effect in UK law by the Human Rights Act 1998. See section 4.43.

[57] *R v HM Coroner for Inner North London ex p Linnane* [1989] 1 WLR 395.

Surprisingly, the Act makes no similar requirement for an inquest on a death due to natural causes in police custody yet requires a jury if such an inquest is to be held. However, Home Office Circular 109/1982 indicated the Secretary of State's view that it was desirable for an inquest to be held (with a jury) in all cases of death occurring in any form of legal custody, even though the death may have occurred in hospital or elsewhere and even though it may have been due to natural causes. This view contrasts rather strangely with the clear ruling of the Court of Appeal expressed in both *Thomas* and *Touche* (above) that the coroner has no discretion on whether to hold an inquest, either a death is due to an unnatural cause or it is not.

The death from natural causes of a patient detained under the Mental Health Act would not automatically be regarded as a death in custody.[58]

Functus Officio   2.25

Recent cases have considered further the point at which a coroner ceases to have jurisdiction by virtue of having concluded an interest in the case.

It has always been clear that once an inquest has been concluded the coroner cannot reopen the case except by order of the High Court—see section 10.06 *et seq.* Equally, it has long been accepted that, subject to the continued presence of a body, the coroner may reconsider an initial decision not to inquire into a death. The Form A procedure (see section 4.19) is merely an administrative notification to the registrar that an inquest is considered unnecessary and cannot be binding upon the coroner in any way.

What *had* been a matter of difficulty was whether a decision not to hold an inquest following a post-mortem under s 19 of the Act (the Form B procedure: see section 4.20), could be reconsidered, and an inquest then held, if there was subsequently reason.

The Court of Appeal considered this in the 2001 case of *Terry v Craze*[59] and rejected an argument that the s 19 procedure was alike to an inquest, being based upon a medical investigation and coronial decision. It was held that the s 19 procedure does not take the place of an inquest and that the coroner was not *functus officio* as a result. The coroner's approach to fresh evidence should simply be whether there was *now* reasonable cause to suspect the deceased had died an unnatural death. It was unnecessary to talk in terms of 'a change of circumstances of some significance' or 'powerful evidence' as the question (under s 8(1) of the Act) would remain the same for the coroner throughout.

---

[58] *R v Northamptonshire Coroner ex p Wilson* (unreported: 24 July 2002); see also section 8.07.
[59] *Terry v Craze (HM Coroner for East Sussex)* [2002] QB 312. Sometimes known as *Terry v East Sussex Coroner*.

However, unless the body was buried within the coroner's jurisdiction, it may still be necessary to make an application to the Secretary of State for permission to hold an inquest in the absence of a body—see section 2.11 above.

2.26 Removal out of England and Wales

Another circumstance in which a death, even if apparently due to natural causes, falls within the coroner's remit is where the relatives seek to take a body out of the country.[60] Before a body may be removed from England and Wales the formal consent of the coroner is required under the Removal of Bodies Regulations 1954. This prevents any attempt to thwart a coroner's investigation and allows sufficient time to examine the basic circumstances of the death.

If, having allowed removal of the body, the coroner subsequently learns of cause to hold an inquest then an application could be made to the Home Office under s15 of the Act on the basis that the body is now irrecoverable or destroyed (see section 2.11). Obviously there may still be evidential difficulties as to the cause of death and circumstances if no post-mortem examination took place before the removal.

Summary

- The coroner's jurisdiction arises from the presence of a body within the geographical district, if the case may fall within s 8 of the Coroners Act.
- Section 8 requires an inquest to be held if there is a reason to suspect the death may have been violent, unnatural, of unknown cause, or occurred in a prison.
- A death from a natural cause which was either contributed to by neglect or, being wholly unexpected, was brought about at least in part by a culpable human failure may be considered unnatural for the purposes of s 8.
- Bodies returned to this country for disposal following a death abroad also fall within the coroner's jurisdiction.

---

[60] For further discussion of this topic refer to section 4.31 below.

3

REPORTING DEATHS

If any man be found killed, and another be found near him, with the knife or another weapon in his hand all bloody, wherewith he killed him, the coroner shall be presently fetched, and in his presence the felon shall upon testimony of those who saw the felony done, be judged to death.
Brittons Treatise 1291

This chapter deals with issues on the reporting of deaths to the coroner, including:

- who has the duty to report;
- which cases need to be reported;
- problems arising from deaths involving a medical procedure;
- some common mistakes.

Introduction   3.01

Before registration of a death and disposal of the body can take place there must either be:

- a properly issued medical certificate[1] as to cause of death from a doctor;[2] or
- a certificate from the coroner after appropriate investigations.

The evolution of this 'fail-safe' system[3] ensures that the circumstances of every death are subject to scrutiny and in particular that violent, unnatural, or unexplained sudden deaths are given a full medico-legal investigation. But the system stands or falls on the co-operation, understanding, and integrity of the medical profession. The safeguards are of little value if those involved with deaths on a day to day basis have no clear knowledge of which cases need to be referred to the coroner, or if they fail to live up to what might reasonably be expected of them. Unfortunately, research[4] and investigation on doctor's knowledge of which cases need to be referred has shown an alarming lack of understanding.

The 2001 Redfern Inquiry[5] noted that there was generally a clouded view amongst doctors of what the coroner's jurisdiction required and 'a lack of precision in the minds of clinicians as to when a death is strictly reportable to the coroner'.

The issues of death certification and reporting of deaths are obviously closely linked and there is a likelihood of significant change to both areas in the next few years. The Home Office Fundamental Review of the coroner system and the Shipman Inquiry (see sections 1.08 and 1.09) have addressed these areas in detail but it is likely to be some time before any major changes take effect.

3.02   The Problem

A prime reason for confusion may be the lack of clear statutory guidelines, for there is no specific legislation requiring a doctor to report particular deaths to the coroner.[6] Further, the limited amount of time presently given to the legal aspects of medicine within the undergraduate medical syllabus fails to equip a junior doctor for the complexities of death certification and the coronial system.

Some measure of this confusion was shown in answers given by undergraduate medical students to questions on reporting a death. One student declared that the coroner needed to be informed of 'all crimes that were accidents' whilst another was in favour of reporting 'all deaths which have occurred within the previous twenty-four hours'. Whilst these may be extreme examples, it is certainly the case

---

[1] As to which see section 4.02 *et seq*.

[2] See reg 41 of the Births and Deaths Regulations 1987 referred to in section 3.10.

[3] Burton, Chambers, and Gill, *Coroners Inquiries: a guide to law and practice* (Kluver Law, 1985).

[4] Start et al, 'Clinicians and the coronial system: ability of clinicians to recognise reportable deaths', *BMJ* (1993), 306, 1038–41 and also Start et al, 'General practitioners' knowledge of when to refer deaths to a coroner', *British Journal of General Practice* (1995) 45, 191–93.

[5] *Report of the Inquiry into the Royal Liverpool Children's Hospital NHS Trust*, sometimes known as the Alder Hey Report: www.rlcinquiry.org.uk.

[6] Compare this to s 7 of the Coroners Act (Northern Ireland) 1959 referred to in section 3.03.

that many doctors, whether newly qualified or experienced, have difficulty recognizing some categories of reportable death[7] and suffer misconceptions about those categories that they do recognize. Nor is it always appreciated that the certification and proper reporting of deaths[8] are legal matters upon which doctors do not hold any measure of discretion.[9]

However, in 1996 the Deputy Chief Medical Statistician at the Office for National Statistics (formally OPCS) issued written guidance to doctors on referral to coroners for the first time. This document was subsequently revised in 1997[10] and is set out in full at Appendix 1. A copy of the guidance is also now sent out with each new book of medical certificates as to cause of death (MCCDs). The advice underlines the importance both of correct death certification and referral where appropriate,[11] setting out a table of which deaths to refer.

Death certification in general is outside the scope of this text but is referred to briefly in section 4.02 *et seq*. However, to some extent a proper understanding of death certification and referral to the coroner go hand in hand. Unfortunately, a paper published in 2002 by Swift and West[12] reports that standards of death certification are also far from ideal. The study examined one thousand completed MCCDs and found only 55 per cent to a minimally acceptable standard. Nearly 10 per cent were completed poorly, being illogical or inappropriately completed. This study took place within a large teaching hospital where one might have hoped that standards would be better than commonly encountered elsewhere.

The Duty to Report a Death

The Necessity to Report   3.03

There is no specific statutory requirement in England and Wales for members of the public to inform the coroner of deaths which might fall within s 8 of the Act. The sole statutory obligation rests with the Governor of a prison who must inform the coroner of the death of an inmate.[13]

---

[7] Start et al: see n 4 above.

[8] Even if only by the supply of a correctly completed medical certificate to the registrar who must then inform the coroner in appropriate cases—see section 3.10.

[9] See *R v Sood* [1998] 2 Cr. App. R 355 where a GP was convicted of making a false declaration for knowingly giving incorrect details on a medical certificate as to cause of death.

[10] The 1997 guidance also makes the valuable point that a voluntary referral to the coroner (as opposed to the registrar identifying the case under regulation 41—see section 3.10) allows an opportunity for the doctor to explain the reason for the referral to the relatives in person.

[11] Circular letter to all doctors dated 1 July 1996, revised and re-issued 1 July 1997.

[12] Swift and West, 'Death Certification; an audit of practice entering the 21st century', *J. Clin Pathol* (2002) 55, 275–9.

[13] This applies, through various statutes, to all types of military and civil detention or imprisonment, eg rule 29(2) Young Offenders Institute Rules 2000.

This contrasts with Northern Ireland where, by s 7 of the Coroners Act (Northern Ireland) 1959 there is a duty[14] to inform the coroner of a death by misadventure, violence, unfair means, negligence, misconduct, malpractice, or in circumstances requiring investigation, or from any cause other than natural illness treated by a doctor within the last 28 days.[15] Similarly, the relevant New Zealand legislation[16] imposes a statutory duty on medical staff to inform the coroner (via the police) when death occurs during or as a result of a medical/surgical procedure.

In Scotland, although there is no statutory requirement, the Crown Office issues specific guidance for doctors on which deaths should be reported to the Procurator Fiscal. This is reproduced at Table 3.3 on page 69.

The lack of clear legislation in England and Wales means that the citizen must find a way through an unsatisfactory jumble of common law and limited statutory duties. It may also put the doctor in a difficult position when relatives argue against a referral to the coroner in a borderline case.

3.04 Sources of Referrals

Deaths may be referred or reported to the coroner from a wide range of sources. A high proportion[17] will be referred by the medical profession. The majority of the remainder will be referred by the police who have been called to a sudden death. A small but significant proportion (about 2 per cent) are referred by the Registrar of Deaths under the statutory obligation of regulation 41[18] where the registrar is unable to accept a doctor's certificate as to cause of death. A few cases are referred to the coroner by relatives dissatisfied with medical treatment or suspicious of the circumstances in which a death has occurred. Undertakers also occasionally refer cases to the coroner having become concerned at circumstances surrounding the body or because of matters raised by relatives.[19]

The category of cases referred by relatives (admittedly small) can cause its own difficulties because such a report often only arises sometime after the death. Thus the body may have already been disposed of without opportunity for a post-mortem examination.

---

[14] This duty falls upon doctors, registrars, undertakers, occupiers of houses, or persons in charge of institutions or premises where the deceased resided and is subject to criminal penalty under s 10 of the same Act.

[15] Section 8 imposes a strict duty upon the police whenever a dead body is found or an unexpected or unexplained death occurs.

[16] Section 4, Coroners Act (New Zealand) 1988.

[17] A random sample in the author's jurisdiction suggests about 60 per cent.

[18] Births and Deaths Regulations 1987—see section 3.10.

[19] For example, an undertaker becomes alarmed by substantial and excessive bedsores or is made aware that relatives had tried to call a doctor but were refused a visit.

Common Law Duty upon all Citizens **3.05**

Coroner's legislation has long provided that the coroner shall 'examine on oath concerning the death all persons who tender evidence as to the facts of the death and all persons having knowledge of those facts whom he considers it expedient to examine'.[20] This presupposes that, in some manner, the coroner will first become aware of the death and its true circumstances so that the relevant witnesses may be called.

Thus for many years there has been a common law duty[21] upon all citizens to give information which may lead to the coroner having notice of circumstances requiring the holding of an inquest.[22] The original duty was to give immediate notice, ie 'whilst the body is fresh and whilst it remains in the same situation as when death occurred' because if reporting were delayed it would be 'a nuisance and may infect people'. Whilst a delay may no longer present the health hazard of earlier days, it is still important that the report be given promptly. If not, vital evidence may be lost or the funeral might be delayed, causing additional trauma for the relatives.

Even if the body has been disposed of, the duty remains, for the Act enables the coroner to hold an inquest where a body has been destroyed or is irrecoverable, on a direction from the Secretary of State (see section 2.11).

The ancient origins of this duty have led to it being questioned.[23] The author would argue that whilst coronial legislation retains its present format, unsatisfactory as that may be, it is clear that the common law duty upon the public to bring forward information must still exist. To hold otherwise would be to render valueless the whole 'fail-safe system' of scrutinizing deaths in this country. In any event, mere age does not render laws defunct, eg Justice of the Peace Act 1361 which is still used regularly in Magistrates' Courts.

Common Law and Statutory Offences **3.06**

This duty raises a common law offence of obstructing the coroner, whether by disposing of a body before the coroner can inquire, or otherwise acting to frustrate or prevent an inquest.[24] However, criminal sanction could probably only be taken

---

[20] Now s 11(2) Coroners Act 1988.

[21] *R v Clerk* (1702) 1 Salk 377.

[22] Knapman and Powers, *The law and practice on coroners* (Chichester: Barry Rose, 1985).

[23] Leadbetter and Knight, 'Reporting deaths to the coroner', *BMJ* (1993) 306: 1018.

[24] See *Jervis on Coroners* (12th edition) at para 5.17 which quotes a number of cases over the last century, the most recent of which is 2001. In a 1998 case the defendant was sentenced to three years imprisonment for obstructing the coroner by concealing a body in his flat despite being asked twice by the police to assist in tracing the deceased. *R v Godward* [1998] 1 Cr App C (S) 385.

where the failure to report was part of a deliberate attempt to obstruct the coroner in the exercise of his duty.[25, 26]

An agreement between several people to conceal the true facts of a death from the coroner might amount to a statutory conspiracy.

Offences of perverting the course of justice can be committed in respect of inquest proceedings but could probably only relate to acts intended to mislead the inquest itself[27] rather than any failure to report a death and thus avoid an inquest in the first place.

The Births and Deaths Registration Act 1953 places a duty upon a 'qualified informant' to give the registrar particulars required to be registered concerning the death. Failure to do so is a criminal offence. The particulars might obviously include information giving rise to an inquest and the registrar will inform the coroner under reg 41 of the Births and Deaths Regulations 1987.[28]

The phrase 'qualified informant' covers a surprisingly wide range but in practice will usually be a close relative of the deceased. As the true circumstances of a dubious death may be concealed from such a person, the value of this legislation (from the coroner's point of view) is limited.

3.07 NHS Responsibilities

The common law and statutory duties are not imposed upon doctors[29] especially, but relate to all citizens. Nonetheless, the 1997 case of *Clegg*[30] is deserving of mention.

Miss Clegg died following admission to hospital from an aspirin overdose. At the inquest the coroner was not aware that the girl's treatment during her twelve hours in hospital had been inappropriate. An independent NHS review of the treatment later found that she had been 'assessed incorrectly, investigated and monitored

---

[25] *R v Purcy* (1933) 149 LT 432 (concealing a body).

[26] A 1993 publication suggested that 18 per cent of junior doctors admitted they would alter what they knew to be the true cause of death in order to avoid involving the coroner or further distress to relatives. Maudsley and Williams, 'Death certification by house officers and general practitioners—practice and performance', *J Public Health Med* (1993) 15, 192–201.

[27] 'An act has such a tendency [ie to pervert the course of public justice] if it gives rise to the possibility that it will mislead a tribunal concerned with public justice and might cause a miscarriage of justice. Public justice is any judicial proceedings which might arise from the death of [the patient] including an inquest, civil or criminal proceedings.' *R v Sinha*, Times Law Reports, 13 July 1994, where a doctor had falsified records to make it appear that he was not at fault for a death.

[28] See section 3.10.

[29] Compare New Zealand where, under the Coroners Act 1988, there is a statutory duty to report deaths during or as a result of medical or surgical procedures to the coroner.

[30] *R v HM Coroner for Wiltshire ex p Clegg* (1996) 161 JP 521.

inadequately[31] and treated poorly'. The High Court later commented that it was beyond doubt that this was known at the time of the inquest by persons within the hospital but no one had thought to inform the coroner.

In a letter quoted at the judicial review[32] the Chief Executive of the NHS said that there was no specific guidance for staff on giving evidence to the coroner and that they were simply expected to do what the law requires; that is to answer the questions which are asked truthfully. This was criticized by the court which suggested that the NHS should give appropriate guidance to staff.

Subsequently the Chief Medical Officer wrote a letter to all doctors (CMO's Update 20/98) with clarification:

> The Select Committee on Public Administration earlier this year stressed the need for clinicians to disclose all relevant information to the coroner to ensure a fully informed decision on cause of death. Whilst there is no specific duty on clinicians to do this, all those who have information which could help coroner's inquiries should disclose it voluntarily and not only when requested. The GMC has updated and the UKCC will shortly be publishing amended professional guidance emphasising the need to inform the coroner.

The amended GMC guidance[33] now states:

> [32] . . . you must assist the coroner . . . by responding to enquiries and by offering all relevant information to an inquest or inquiry into a patient's death. Only where your evidence may lead to criminal proceedings being taken against you are you entitled to remain silent.[34]

The UKCC (now the Nursing and Midwifery Council) did not amend their guidance but stated publicly that all practitioners have a duty to co-operate with coroners.

Pathologists undertaking a hospital (ie consent) autopsy should be aware of the guidelines of the Royal College of Pathologists[35] which state:

> Where it appears to the pathologist, whether from the clinical history or from additional findings at autopsy, that the death should be reported to the coroner, the

---

[31] Compare the later *ex p Touche* case (see section 2.20) where a failure to monitor was the subject of much consideration.

[32] The parents were seeking a fresh inquest, but the High Court felt it inappropriate to order a new hearing in view of the lapse of time (four years), the fact that there had been a detailed investigation and that the deficiencies were identified publicly.

[33] General Medical Council, *Good Medical Practice* (September 2001), available from General Medical Council, 178 Gt Portland Street, London, W1W 5JE.

[34] The author would suggest it is abundantly clear that the reference to a right to silence relates to a formal setting, such as a police interview under caution or the protection within r 22 of the Coroners Rules 1984 (see section 7.40.1) and should not be taken as tacit approval of a failure to reveal the true circumstances when a death is reported just because one's own position may be in jeopardy.

[35] Royal College of Pathologists, *Guidelines on Autopsy Practice* (2002) para 3.8, www.rcpath.org.

pathologist should ensure that this is done to permit the coroner the opportunity to assume jurisdiction.

3.08 Statutory Requirements upon a Doctor

The only statutory duty for a doctor comes under s 22 of the Births Deaths and Registration Act 1953 which requires;

> . . . a registered medical practitioner attending a person in his last illness to sign and transmit to the Registrar of Births and Deaths a certificate in the proper form stating, to the best of his knowledge and belief, the cause of death.

Thus technically speaking, a doctor fulfils the regulation by issuing a medical certificate as to the cause of death and sending it (usually via the relatives) to the registrar, even if it is known (and made plain on the certificate) that the death is unnatural and will require referral to the coroner—but see section 3.09 below as to recognized practice.

It is important to understand that the medical certificate as to cause of death (MCCD) is a legal document and the doctor is obliged to certify the true cause of death to the best of his/her knowledge and belief. If a doctor were to give a cause of death that they knew to be untrue, charges of perjury[36] and making a false declaration[37] could follow.

In *R v Sood*[38] the Court of Appeal upheld the conviction of a doctor for making a false declaration contrary to the Perjury Act 1911 by deliberately completing an MCCD knowing that it contained false details as to when he had last seen the patient. The court said that the motive for making the statement, and whether or not there was an active intention to deceive, were essentially irrelevant, the vice being the abuse of the occasion and the likely perpetuation of falsehood in relation to matters of public record. The court emphasized that such an offence could not be regarded as a mere technicality, the qualification and status of the doctor meaning that his declaration would be readily accepted.

The Court of Appeal endorsed the remarks of the sentencing judge at Crown Court:

> The declaration that you make so far as someone's death [is concerned] is very important indeed . . . let us hope it is going to become clear that if other doctors think that it is merely a matter of form or technicality they will learn now that it is not so and that it is a matter of grave substance.

It has been said that even giving a technically correct cause of death, but deliberately completing the certificate in a way which does not make clear to the registrar

---

[36] Section 4 of the Perjury Act 1911.
[37] Section 37 Births and Deaths Registration Act 1953.
[38] *R v Sood* [1998] 2 Cr App R 355.

the circumstances necessitating a referral, could amount to an obstruction of the coroner by preventing an inquest.[39, 40]

A doctor is also said to be under a duty to alert the police or some other proper authority to the fact that a death has arisen from a criminal offence particularly where evidence is likely to be lost if the authorities are not advised in time.[41]

Recognized Practice

3.09

Whilst there is no specific legal duty upon a doctor, it is the proper and accepted practice to ensure that the coroner is informed where appropriate, and a doctor knowing of such a case will refer the matter direct to the coroner's office. This is recognized not only in the 1997 advice from the Deputy Chief Medical Statistician[42] but also by advice to doctors actually contained within the booklet of medical certificates of cause of death. The 1997 advice is now sent out with each booklet.

Failure by doctors to recognize reportable deaths can have serious consequences for the relatives of the deceased. As soon as the registrar sees the certificate, or asks the most basic questions of relatives, the registration must be refused and the matter referred to the coroner.[43] This may necessitate the relatives travelling to the coroner's office, dashing their expectations of a simple end to the administrative side of the death. Only now are they to learn that a post-mortem examination might be required and possibly even an inquest.

Beyond any understandable annoyance, the relatives' faith in the doctor, and any assurances given that everything possible was done for the deceased, will have taken something of a blow. Some relatives may now believe that the doctor was trying to cover up an error, others will assume mere incompetence. This all flows from the doctor's ignorance of which cases need referring to the coroner.

The situation might be even worse, for the relatives are under no obligation to go immediately to the registrar and might have put funeral arrangements in hand. The coroner's late involvement could mean that the funeral must be postponed. At the very least the body may have to be removed from a Chapel of Rest back to the mortuary for examination.

---

[39] James and Leadbetter, 'The use of personal health information in the coroner's inquiry', *Journal of Royal College of Physicians of London* (1997) 31(5), 509.

[40] See also *Jervis on Coroners* (12th edition) at paras 5.16–5.17 which gives a list of criminal authorities on the subject of obstructing the coroner etc.

[41] This is quoted in *Jervis on Coroners* (12th edition) at 5.34, referring to a 1914 judgment circulated to all coroners with the authority of the Lord Chief Justice.

[42] See section 3.02 and Appendix 1.

[43] Regulation 41 of the Births, Deaths and Marriages Regulations 1987—see section 3.10.

Quite apart from any legal obligation, the author would suggest in the strongest terms that doctors have a simple duty to ensure that matters concerning referral to the coroner are '**right first time every time**'.

3.10 Regulation 41—The Registrar's Obligation

Instances of failure to report are regularly picked up by every Registrar of Births and Deaths. Although it is not the registrar's duty to investigate, many will have an informal discussion with the relatives whilst preparing to register and it may become apparent that the doctor's certificate is not soundly based. About 2 per cent of referrals come from the registrar because of faulty certification by a doctor, usually a failure to recognize potential industrial disease or that the death was an indirect result of simple trauma.

The registrar's duty to report deaths to the coroner is set down by regulation 41 of the Registration of Births and Deaths Regulations 1987 which is set out at Table 3.1 below.

Table 3.1. Regulation 41, Registration of Births and Deaths Regulations 1987

41(1) Where the relevant registrar is informed of the death of any person he shall, subject to paragraph (2), report the death to the coroner on an approved form if the death is one:

- in respect of which the deceased was not attended during his last illness by a registered medical practitioner
- or in respect of which the Registrar:
  - has been unable to obtain the delivery of a duly completed certificate of cause of death or
  - has received such a certificate with respect to which it appears to him from the particulars contained in the certificate that the deceased was not seen by the certifying medical practitioner either after death or within 14 days before the death
- or the cause of which appears to be unknown
- or which the Registrar has reason to believe to have been unnatural or caused by violence or neglect or by abortion, or to have been attended by suspicious circumstances;
- or which appears to the registrar to have occurred during an operation or before recovery from the effects of an anaesthetic
- or which appears to the registrar from the contents of any medical certificate of cause of death to have been due to industrial disease or industrial poisoning.

By regulation 41(2) the registrar must refrain from registering any death:

- which he has himself reported to the coroner; *or*
- which to his knowledge it is the duty of some other person or authority to notify to the coroner; *or*

- which has been notified to the coroner

until he has received a coroner's certificate after inquest[44] or a notification from the coroner[45] that he does not intend to hold an inquest.

If the registrar gives the coroner notification under regulation 41, it is for the coroner to make inquiries and this task should not be avoided by asking the registrar to make direct contact with the certifying doctor.[46]

The Anomaly of Regulation 41   3.11

Although the wording of regulation 41 is difficult to understand, the author would suggest that there is particular cause for concern about the provision which allows a doctor who has treated the patient in their last illness, but not seen them within the last 14 days, to certify the cause of death if the body is viewed. There seems to be little logic in this so-called 'alternative procedure'. The author understands that registrars are advised by the Office of Population, Census and Surveys (OPCS) to accept a certificate from a doctor in circumstances where the patient was seen up to 12 months before death if the body has been viewed after death. This raises a number of issues:

- What is the point of a coroner refusing to accept certification by a GP after (say) three months if a certificate would have been accepted by the registrar just for the sake of the doctor taking a brief look at the body?
- The purpose of such a viewing after death must be open to question. Presumably the doctor is only confirming that the named individual is dead? The doctor *may* be able to confirm identification but there is no requirement for a close examination of the body externally and the author understands that this is rarely performed. Thus the viewing would not even rule out a grossly suspicious death. Admittedly, it *might* reveal obvious signs such as bruises, dehydration, or bedsores but surely this is a rather 'hit and miss' system for identifying homicide or abuse?
- In what way does viewing the body after death assist the doctor in determining the cause of death?

Nonetheless, it is worth making the point that regulation 41 is the *only* statutory explanation or guidance to expand on the coroner having reasonable cause to suspect that the death was violent or unnatural under s 8(3)(1)(a) of the Act.

---

[44] Form 99 referred to at section 10.02.
[45] Coroners Form A or B, referred to at sections 4.19–4.20.
[46] Home Office Circular 28/2003.

3.12 Written Advice

Whilst there is no legislation that a doctor can turn to for a clear explanation of what is required, there is official written advice available. Each medical certificate as to cause of death bears an explanation on the reverse that:

> The coroner needs to consider all cases where:
>
> * the death might have been due to or contributed to by a violent or unnatural cause (including an accident)
> * or the cause of death cannot be identified
> * or the death might have been due to or contributed to by drugs, medicine, abortion or poison
> * or there is reason to believe that the death occurred during an operation or under or prior to complete recovery from an anaesthetic or arising subsequently out of an incident during an operation or anaesthetic.

Each booklet of death certificates contains a page of advice about completion, including a copy of regulation 41 (see above). Additionally, as set out at section 3.02, there is now clear written advice from the Deputy Chief Medical Statistician.[47]

Despite the ready availability of this written advice, the subject matter is not easily comprehensible. Indeed, the legislation pertaining to disposal of the dead was described as 'anachronistic, ambivalent and ambiguous' in 1986.[48] This is not an area upon which much time is spent in the medical school syllabus—but even less time is spent upon the English/Welsh coronial system in the medical schools of Germany and Spain, a significant factor in view of the free interchange of doctors between member states of the European Community. Perhaps one answer to this is for medico-legal subjects to be included in the syllabus of British postgraduate examinations which are commonly taken by doctors from many other countries.

Ability to Recognize

Two studies, in which the author assisted, highlighted the inability of both hospital clinicians and general practitioners to recognize some categories of reportable deaths.[49]

---

[47] See also Appendix 1, this advice is also sent out with each booklet of MCCDs.

[48] Leadbetter and Knight 'Anomalies and ambiguities in the disposal of the dead', *Journal of the Royal College of Physicians of London* (1986) 20(4), 273.

[49] Start et al. (1993) n 4 above, 1038–41. Start et al (1995) n 4 above, 191–193.

Hospital Deaths 3.13

The first paper, on hospital deaths, showed that individual clinicians at all grades had a variable appreciation of the different categories of cases which should be reported to the coroner, with consultants consistently performing worse than their junior staff. When asked to assess medical histories and whether the resulting death should have been reported, anything up to 60 per cent were wrong in individual cases. Not all doctors reported the cases involving death in police custody, crime, suicide, or industrial disease. Many seemed unaware that all deaths resulting from an accident are reportable to the coroner, no matter how long has elapsed between the injury and the death.

General Practice 3.14

In a second study involving general practitioners, only 3 per cent recognized all those deaths which should have been reported for further investigation. More than 15 per cent of doctors were unable to identify half the reportable cases and others held disturbing misconceptions in relation to the coronial system. These could have a wide range of outcomes from serious crime going undetected to loss of industrial pension or other appropriate compensation for relatives. Two respondents indicated that recording a natural cause of death would be preferable to reporting a suicide in order to avoid possible financial loss to the family. It would appear that some doctors believe they have discretion over which deaths must be reported to the coroner.

Conclusion 3.15

Both studies highlight many features of the coronial system which are poorly understood by the medical profession and recommend that:

- continuing medical education should regularly address medico-legal subjects with the participation of pathologists and the coroner's office; *and*
- coroners should provide hospital doctors and general practitioners with a regularly updated guide to indications for referral.

In the absence of new legislation, it would seem that the answer lies primarily in education and close liaison with the coroner's office. This was also recognized within the report of the Home Office Review of Death Certification (September 2001) which recommended that more emphasis be placed on the training of doctors in death certification procedures. It is also clear that the Coroner Review and the Shipman Inquiry (see sections 1.08 and 1.09) have addressed these issues thoroughly but it now remains to be seen what changes are put in place.

Reportable Deaths

3.16 Practical Guidance

The present requirements for reporting deaths to the coroner are a muddle of legislation, common law and varying advice. This is most unsatisfactory and in an effort to provide doctors in his own jurisdiction with some clear guidance the author prepared the list set out at the front of this book, and repeated at Table 3.2 below. With one or two minor amendments this has found a general measure of favour amongst coroners in the Yorkshire region.

Table 3.2. Reportable deaths: a brief guide

A death should be referred to HM Coroner if either:

- the cause of death is unknown;
- it cannot readily be certified as being due to natural causes;
- the deceased was not attended by the doctor during his last illness or was not seen within the last 14 days or viewed after death;
- there are any suspicious circumstances or history of violence;
- the death may be linked to an accident (whenever it occurred);
- there is any question of self-neglect or neglect by others;
- the death has occurred or the illness arisen during or shortly after detention in police or prison custody (including voluntary attendance at a police station);
- the deceased was detained under the Mental Health Act;
- the death is linked with an abortion;
- the death might have been contributed to by the actions of the deceased (such as a history of drug or solvent abuse, self injury or overdose);
- the death could be due to industrial disease or related in any way to the deceased's employment;
- the death occurred during an operation or before full recovery from the effects of an anaesthetic or was in any way related to the anaesthetic (in any event a death within 24 hours should normally be referred);
- the death may be related to a medical procedure or treatment whether invasive or not;
- the death may be due to lack of medical care;
- there are any other unusual or disturbing features to the case;
- the death occurs within 24 hours of admission to hospital (unless the admission was purely for terminal care);
- it may be wise to report any death where there is an allegation of medical mis-management.

This note is for guidance only, it is not exhaustive and in part may represent desired local practice rather than the statutory requirements. If in any doubt contact the coroner's office for further advice.

The list is merely the author's own interpretation of statute and (hopefully) common sense combined, it is of course possible to find exceptions or arguments in many of the categories. However, it is hoped that the following notes will clarify some of the more difficult issues:

The death cannot readily be certified as being due to natural causes[50]   **3.16.1**

The issue is quite straightforward—if the doctor does not know the cause of death to be natural disease the coroner must be notified.[51] However two points need to be stressed. First, the doctor should be completely happy that *only* natural causes are involved, if there is any reason for doubt then it is for the coroner to make a decision on the matter, not the doctor. Secondly, research has shown[52] that doctors frequently fall into the trap of looking only at the immediate cause of death. Bronchopneumonia is a natural cause, but if it has arisen through immobility following trauma, the sequence of events plainly contains factors which require the coroner to be informed. The doctor must therefore think the sequence of causation through carefully—which may even mean referring to notes from before the patient came into his/her care.

The deceased was not attended by the doctor during his last illness or was neither seen   **3.16.2**
within the last 14 days or viewed after death

However obvious the cause of death, under regulation 41 of the Births and Deaths Regulations 1987 (see section 3.10) a doctor's MCCD is only acceptable if he/she has attended the patient for his last illness and *either* saw him within the 14 days prior to death *or* viewed the body after death. The reader may query what practical use there is in the doctor viewing after death if the patient has not been seen for several months—see section 3.11.

The doctor who attended the patient and who now wishes to certify must be one and the same. Whilst there is no formal definition of 'last illness' there must be a clear link between the reason for the attendance and the stated cause of death. It may be reasonable to say in this context that the doctor should have 'seen and assessed' the patient with regard to what is now said to be the cause of death.

Many coroners will be prepared to extend the 14-day period and allow the doctor to certify, backed up by a coroner's certificate to the registrar on Form A.[53] Exactly how much this time limit might be extended differs from case to case and coroner to coroner.

---

[50] See section 2.19 and section 9.15 for discussion on the meaning of 'natural causes'.
[51] 1962 Memorandum on the Coroners System—issued by the Coroners Society of England and Wales.
[52] Start et al (1993) n 4 above, 1038–41. Start et al (1995) n 4 above, 191–193.
[53] For a discussion of coroner's forms see section 4.19 *et seq.*

3.16.3   *There are any suspicious circumstances . . .*

If the circumstances contain *any* element of concern it is a matter for the coroner to make a decision rather than the doctor. The doctor may not be in possession of all the facts that a coroner's investigation could reveal and should not try to make a decision on whether the suspicious circumstances are relevant.

3.16.4   *. . . or history of violence*

Whilst there must be some element of common sense involved, it can be dangerous for doctors to assume that they have been told all the circumstances where a history of violence is suspected. This will be a matter for the coroner rather than the certifying doctor.

3.16.5   *The death may be linked to an accident (whenever it occurred)*

It is a common error for doctors to believe that deaths arising from an accident are only of interest to the coroner if there are some suspicious circumstances. It is an equally common error to believe that the accident must lead to the death within a year and a day.[54] In fact there is no time limit and the coroner is interested in any trauma no matter how innocent or accidental it was. Coroners frequently have to deal with deaths (usually involving paralysis) where the actual injury was sustained in an accident many years before. Once again, it is incumbent upon the certifying doctor to think carefully through the sequence of causation. Death arising from an osteoporotic fracture should still be referred but may not result in an inquest.[55]

3.16.6   *If there is any question of self-neglect or neglect by others*

It is vital that the coroner be told immediately of any death which may have arisen from neglect by a person with a duty to care for the deceased, whether hospital, nursing home, or relatives. However, self-neglect can be more difficult to categorize—there are many instances where the elderly fail to accord themselves proper treatment for one reason or another. Bearing in mind that a patient is entitled to refuse medical treatment, it must be a matter of common sense for the doctor to decide whether the issue is sufficient to report.

3.16.7   *The death has occurred in police or prison custody*

The coroner will need to hold an inquest before a jury if a person dies in prison, whatever the cause. Strangely, this includes staff and visitors, not just prisoners. Inevitably, many who become ill in custody will be moved to hospital before the

---

[54]   This previously related to the period in which an assault victim must die if the assailant was to be charged with murder but has now been abolished.

[55]   Local practice on reporting of osteoporotic fractures may vary—for further discussion of deaths following such a fracture see section 3.18 and section 9.15.3.

death occurs but an inquest is still required.[56] Deaths following detention or action by the police should be referred in a similar way.

The deceased was detained under the Mental Health Act

3.16.8

A death during detention under the Mental Health Act[57] for treatment does not *of itself* require an inquest by law—there are no provisions identical to those for prison custody deaths. However, it is plainly in the public interest that the death of any person who is not at liberty must be investigated and deaths of such patients should be referred to the coroner, whatever the suspected cause.

The death might have been contributed to by the actions of the deceased himself

3.16.9

Some doctors are reluctant to report a potential suicide for fear of distress and possible financial loss to the family.[58] However a doctor holds no such discretion and should consider that, in extreme circumstances, an agreement not to report such a death might be construed as conspiracy to defraud an insurance company.

This heading covers more than suicides. If the doctor is aware of a history that may be relevant to the death it becomes a matter for the coroner to investigate further. Nonetheless, it is worth stating that chronic (as opposed to acute) alcohol abuse is now a legitimate natural cause of death, certified by the doctor rather than requiring referral.

The death could be due to industrial disease or related to employment

3.16.10

This will most commonly relate to coal mining or asbestos-related diseases although there are a number of other industries that may need consideration in particular areas.

Some lateral thinking may be required as to whether a particular cause of death could be related to the deceased's employment.[59] Doctors should remember that most respiratory diseases (however expressed) in a person who has worked as an underground miner for 20 years or more now constitute an industrial disease.[60] The opportunity for a spouse to claim compensation or some form of industrial pension may be lost forever, in the absence of a post-mortem examination, if the disease process is not thought through with some care.[61]

---

[56] Home Office Circulars 35/1969 and 23/1981 indicate the Secretary of State's view that it is desirable for an inquest to be held (with jury) even where the death has occurred in hospital. See also *R v HM Coroner for North London ex p Linnane* [1989] 1 WLR 395.

[57] The Mental Health Act 1983 contains a number of provisions for the compulsory detention of a patient to allow assessment and treatment.

[58] Start et al, see sections 3.13–3.16 above.

[59] See sections 5.38 and 9.21 for further consideration of industrial diseases.

[60] The Social Security (Industrial Injuries) (Prescribed Diseases) Amendment (No 2) Regulations 1993.

[61] The proportion of verdicts of 'industrial disease' returned by coroners has doubled in the last 10 years and in 2002 amounted to 2,653 verdicts. Home Office Statistical Bulletin 06/03.

3.16.11 *The death was during an operation or was in any way related to the anaesthetic*

The statutory basis for the first part of this is set out at section 3.10. There is no def-inition of 'full recovery' from an anaesthetic but it is suggested that the question should be asked 'would the death have occurred at this moment in time had it not been for the operation, procedure or anaesthetic?' The list suggests (without a statutory basis) that it is appropriate to refer any death within 24 hours of an oper-ation or procedure but this certainly does not negate the requirement to report where the death occurs much later but is still thought to relate to the procedure.

3.16.12 *The death may be related to a medical procedure or treatment, invasive or not*

Covering much the same ground as the previous point, this provides a reminder that it is not purely an operation which can lead to a reportable death. A death aris-ing from medical treatment of any sort must be reviewed by the coroner. There will obviously be many circumstances where the patient dies despite the treatment rather than because of it, but ultimately it may be in the doctor's own interest to err on the side of caution and report.

3.16.13 *The death may be due to lack of medical care*

Undoubtedly it is difficult and embarrassing for a doctor to report facts which may show fault on the part of colleagues but there is certainly no ethical protec-tion open to a doctor who chooses not to do so. Indeed, the doctor might end up in an even more difficult position than those originally involved if a deliberate decision to cover up a death is made. See section 3.19 *et seq* below.

3.16.14 *The death occurs within 24 hours of admission (unless purely for terminal care)*

There is certainly no statute to support this suggestion and some coroners choose not to apply it. No doubt it is now easier with modern technology for a doctor to reach a diagnosis within 24 hours of the patient being admitted to hospital, but in the author's experience this rule tends to disclose a number of cases which needed reporting but would not otherwise have come to the coroner's attention.

3.16.15 *It may be wise to report a death involving an allegation of medical mis-management*

There is no statutory requirement for a doctor to report a case simply because there is a complaint, so long as it is clear that the circumstances are not relevant to the death or that the complaint has no factual basis at all. In considering this, some thought must be given to the circumstances defining an 'unnatural death' in the case of *Touche*—as to which see section 2.20 above.

However, it would also be wise to bear a number of points in mind. The com-plainant presumably believes that the death is due to other than natural causes. Secondly, an independent post-mortem is likely to put an end to such allegations once and for all. Finally, if the doctor fails to report the case but it is later brought to the attention of the coroner by another, some difficult questions may be asked, particularly if the post-mortem examination shows the allegations to be correct. See section 3.19 *et seq* below.

Old Age   3.17

There is no specific requirement upon a doctor to report a death that genuinely arises from old age. Advice in the booklet of medical certificates as to cause of death (MCCDs) suggests this wording (or senility) is only acceptable if a more specific cause of death cannot be given and the patient is aged over 70. Surprisingly, earlier references to 'gradual failure' and 'deterioration' are not currently included, although the author understands that advice may soon be issued suggesting that there must be a witnessed deterioration over some time.

Many might argue that 70 is too early a starting point. The Shipman Inquiry[62] suggests that 80 is more appropriate, but only where there is a positive diagnosis, eg a slow general decline preceding death.[63] It is inappropriate to use this cause merely because there is an absence of any other diagnosis.

The author would suggest that some caution must be exercised here. Where the certifying doctor is unsure, it may be wise to discuss the case with the coroner's office.

Osteoporosis   3.18

One area that is often a source of misunderstanding and confusion is the issue of deaths following a fracture due to osteoporosis—sometimes known as brittle bone disease. This disease affects a large proportion of elderly women[64] and can, at its most severe, lead to the fracture of bones caused by little more than an awkward twist or stumble. Frequently the fracture will be to the neck of the femur, where the thigh fits in to the pelvis in a form of socket that is susceptible to wear. The relative immobility of the patient following such a fracture can often lead to bronchopneumonia and death, despite the best efforts of medicine.

At first glance, such cases are just another form of trauma and require an inquest. However, many coroners take the view that whilst some minor trauma may have occurred, the real culprit is the disease.

If the disease is truly the only factor of any significance involved then it is right to treat this as a natural death. The question must be asked 'would a relatively

---

[62] Vol 3, chapter 17 at paras 169 and 174. See section 1.09 above.

[63] This does seem to be reflected in the use of the phrase; in 1999 there were 556,118 deaths of all ages of which 13,473 were certified as 'old age'. Only 60 of these were under 75 and only 414 were under 80, whereas 3,762 were over 95. Just over 5 per cent of those dying aged 80 or more were certified as 'old age'. Source: ONS.

[64] Less commonly this affects elderly men, in a comparatively small number of cases it affects younger people.

healthy bone have been expected to break in these circumstances?' Clearly, if the aged person fell 20 feet from a balcony, osteoporosis is irrelevant.

Whilst registrars may accept such a 'qualified fracture' as part of the cause of death on a doctor's certificate, they will often check that the coroner has no interest in the case. In general, it would be wise for any doctor wanting to issue a certificate on the basis of an osteoporotic fracture to speak with the coroner's office before-hand. Any suggestion of a push or other 'assault' would necessitate urgent referral.

3.19 Reporting Medical Deaths

The fact that a death has to be reported to the coroner should not be seen by doctors as either a professional insult or a tacit admission of negligence. It should also be remembered that the mere referral of a death to the coroner does not inevitably mean that there will be an inquest and may not even mean that there will be a post-mortem.[65] Coroners are well aware of the reality that some patients will die 'on the table' simply because their bodily systems are too damaged by disease.

It is absolutely essential that the doctor reporting the death is wholly familiar with the patient's care, otherwise relevant information may go unrecognized and thus undisclosed.

Finally, doctors must also bear in mind that the definition of 'unnatural' in connection with a death in hospital has widened in recent years. A coroner is now required to hold an inquest where there has been an unexpected death from natural causes which is contributed to by some culpable human failure, in this context omission being as relevant as commission.[66] See section 2.19 *et seq* above.

3.20 Comparison with the Scottish Requirement

Possibly the clearest explanation of when a 'medical death' should be referred to the coroner comes from a document prepared by the Crown Office in Scotland. The Procurator Fiscal, effectively the Scottish prosecution agency, is also respons-ible for overseeing inquiries into particular deaths and as such takes reports of deaths in some ways similar to the coroner. Although the legal system in Scotland is wholly different, the guidance set out could equally well apply in England and Wales.

The relevant sections of the advice published are set out in Table 3.3 below.

---

[65] Post-mortem examinations were held on about 58 per cent of deaths reported to coroners in 2002. Inquests were held on around 13 per cent of deaths reported. Home Office Statistical Bulletin 06/03.

[66] For example where the patient's death was contributed to by a failure to monitor in a routine way with a consequential loss of opportunity to provide timely treatment (*R v Inner North London Coroner ex p Touche* [2001] QB 1206).

Table 3.3. Deaths under medical care in Scotland

Certain deaths associated with the provision of medical care should be reported to the Procurator Fiscal. Most deaths under medical care represent an unfortunate outcome where every reasonable care has been taken, but they may result from acts of either negligent commission or omission on the part of medical or para-medical staff, or may be associated with criminality. It is the duty of the Procurator Fiscal to enquire into deaths which fall into the following categories, which are not to be regarded as exhaustive, viz:

- deaths which occur unexpectedly having regard to the clinical condition of the deceased prior to his receiving medical care;
- deaths which are clinically unexplained;
- deaths seemingly attributable to a therapeutic or diagnostic hazard;
- deaths which are apparently associated with lack of medical care;
- deaths which occur during the actual administration of general or local anaesthetic.

'Medical care' includes surgical, anaesthetic, nursing or any other kind of medical care and these deaths may be the result of medication (oral, parenteral, including inhalation), or of diagnostic or therapeutic procedures (operations, investigations, x-ray procedures, etc).

Where a patient has died in such circumstances the Procurator Fiscal must be informed without delay. The responsibility for notification lies with the doctor concerned in the care of the patient or the doctor called in at the time of death. The Procurator Fiscal should be notified by telephone or otherwise as soon as possible after the occurrence.

The forensic pathologist and/or the independent specialist adviser will require to direct his attention to the following points, viz:

- whether the patient was properly and sufficiently examined before the procedure;
- whether all due precautions were observed in the performance of the procedure and the selection and administration of any anaesthetic or medication;
- whether there were any factors present which could have been discovered indicating that the procedure would be attended with special risk to life.

A Simplified Guide to Reportable Deaths   3.21

Whilst the list shown in Table 3.2, and referred to above, is relatively comprehensive it is also somewhat complex and daunting for those acquiring their first knowledge of the subject. The author now uses a shorter list for teaching purposes which simply divides suggested reportable deaths into six categories:

- cause is unknown;
- not treated in last 14 days;
- cause may be unnatural (with some examples);
- deceased was under detention;

- known complaint about medical treatment;
- other unusual or disturbing features.

Whilst there are obvious dangers in oversimplification this may be a rather more digestible format for the medical student or newly qualified. The list continues to show deaths that *should* be referred rather than purely those that *must* be referred.

Conclusion

3.22 Common Errors

Some of the most common errors amongst doctors in relation to coroners' referrals are already set out in the comments on the list of reportable deaths at section 3.16. However, it is worth emphasizing the following points:

- Deaths resulting from industrial disease are frequently not recognized as reportable, particularly if there is a long interval between conclusion of the employment and the death.
- Similarly, domestic accidents in which elderly people have fallen commonly go unreported where there is a significant interval between the event and the death.
- Many certifying doctors consider only the eventual cause of death rather than giving sufficient thought to the sequence of events leading to the death.
- There is no limit of time between the traumatic event and the death in terms of necessity for referral.
- Chronic (as opposed to acute) alcohol abuse is no longer an indication for referral.
- The definition of industrial disease has changed in recent years and now includes chronic obstructive airways disease, chronic bronchitis, or emphysema etc, in a person who worked underground as a miner for 20 years or more.
- A decision not to refer a case because of potential distress to relatives or embarrassment to colleagues is misguided and cannot be justified in law.
- Whilst pathologists and coroner's officers are always happy to advise doctors on referral, the advice given can only be correct if the referring doctor has recognized and disclosed all of the relevant information
- Referral should be by a doctor who has a good knowledge of the patient. It is unwise to delegate the task to another with little or no understanding of the case, or to someone who is too junior to appreciate the proper implications of the facts.

Sources of Advice   3.23

Whilst the complications of this area of law are many, and the training currently offered doctors is minimal, help is nearly always at hand. Pathologists tend to have a much better understanding of death certification and local coroner's practice than their clinical colleagues. Coroner's officers are also well placed to offer realistic advice. A phone call to either can save hours of aggravation later, both for the doctor and for the relatives of the deceased.

Summary

- The 'fail safe' system of death registration in this country will only be effective if doctors recognize those cases which need reporting to the coroner.
- In considering the medical cause of death, careful attention should be paid to the sequence of causation.
- Relatives of the deceased may be considerably inconvenienced, or even suffer financial loss, if doctors fail to report appropriate deaths promptly.
- The certification and proper reporting of deaths are legal matters upon which doctors do not hold any measure of discretion.
- If in doubt, doctors should ask the coroner's officer for advice.

4

DECISIONS AND INQUIRIES

Wherefore the King our Sovereign Lord by the assent of his Lords Spiritual and Temporal and the Commons in this present parliament assembled and by authority of the same, ordaineth that upon a request made to a coroner to come and inquire upon the view of any person slain drowned or otherwise dead by misadventure, the said coroner shall diligently do his office upon the view of the body.
An Act concerning coroners 1509[1]

[1] From an Act regulating the conduct of coroners made at the time of Henry VIII—coroners had refused to conduct inquiries into non-felonious (ie misadventure) deaths as they did not receive the thirteen shillings and fourpence fee otherwise paid.

The public perception of the coroner's work centres around the inquest. In reality, whilst inquests may be the higher profile part of the work, nearly 90 per cent of the coroner's caseload comprises deaths that do not require a hearing. The coroner's decisions outside the courtroom affect far more people than those made in the course of an inquest and it is essential that those decisions are made on a sound basis and (now) with proper regard for the effects of the Human Rights Act 1998.

This chapter examines the coroner's administrative role[2] and in particular:

- issues relating to the certification of death;
- the variety of decisions open to the coroner;
- the basis upon which those initial decisions are made;
- disposal without inquest by the coroner's Form A and B;
- burial, cremation and removal of bodies;
- suspicious deaths;
- an overview of the Human Rights Act 1998.

4.01 Introduction

When a death is reported to the coroner there are effectively only three options: taking no investigative action, ordering a post-mortem and/or holding an inquest. However, the framework in which these decisions must take place is complex and difficult to summarize concisely. By splitting the topic into the component parts: death certification; the procedural decisions which may be made; the procedures involved; and the formalities of disposal, it is hoped that the subject will become a little clearer.

Death Certification

4.02 Certifying Deaths—A Confusion of Terminology

The terminology used in the certification of death is often misunderstood and as a result widely misused. Those not within the medical profession may benefit from a short explanation.

---

[2] Sometimes known as the 'executive' or 'ministerial' function of the coroner.

When a body is found, a doctor (or commonly now a paramedic) will attend and confirm that life is extinct or confirm the fact of death. Although this is obviously an important matter, there are no formalities involved, in particular there is no formal document certifying the patient to be dead.[3] The only record of the event may be entries by those present in their own notes. However, it is customary to record the exact time at which this procedure is carried out, so confusingly the deceased may be referred to as having been certified dead at a stated time.

Any doctor called to the locus may not have seen the patient before, particularly if a police surgeon or deputizing doctor, and will not therefore be in a position to know the medical cause of death.

However, if the deceased's own GP attends and the necessary criteria are fulfilled,[4] this doctor may be able not only to confirm that death has occurred but also to give a medical certificate of cause of death (MCCD).[5] Confusingly, this is often referred to as a death certificate, even by coroners and doctors.

The doctor will ensure this certificate is sent to the Registrar of Deaths, usually by handing it to the relatives. On receipt of the MCCD, the registrar will register the death and give a Certified Copy of an Entry[6] which is the document most properly referred to as a formal death certificate.

To add to the confusion, in cases where an inquest is held the procedure is somewhat different. No MCCD will be issued, instead the coroner will supply an Interim Certificate as to the Fact of Death[7] under rule 30 of the Coroners Rules 1984 (the Rules). The interim certificate is not a death certificate, nor can it be used to register the death.[8]

It is sometimes mistakenly believed that once the inquest has been concluded the coroner will supply a 'death certificate'. In reality the coroner issues a certificate on Form 99 to the registrar, stating the facts found at the inquest.[9] When the registration has taken place the registrar will supply the formal Certified Copy of an Entry to anyone making application.

---

[3] Although in some areas a paramedic will issue a short form confirming that they have carried out the recognition of death protocol.

[4] The criteria are briefly set out in section 4.03 but see Chapter 3 for a more detailed examination of which deaths should be referred to the coroner.

[5] Under the Births and Deaths Registration Act 1953 in a form prescribed by the Registration of Births and Deaths Regulations 1987.

[6] A certified copy of an entry in the Register of Deaths, pursuant to the Births and Deaths Registration Act 1953.

[7] See Table 7.3 on page 202 for an example.

[8] However many insurance companies and statutory bodies will accept the coroner's interim certificate to enable legal formalities to be started.

[9] See section 10.02.

4.03   Issue of Papers for Registration and Disposal by a Doctor

Referral of deaths to the coroner is dealt with in greater detail at Chapter 3 but it is appropriate to set out briefly the circumstances in which a GP or hospital doctor can issue papers leading to the registration of the death and disposal of the body. About two-thirds of all deaths will fall into this category, meaning that doctors form an important part of the 'fail safe system' of death registration.[10]

A doctor can properly issue a certificate as to cause of death if:

- he/she is satisfied that they can state the correct cause of death; *and*
- the cause of death is entirely natural; *and*
- he/she has attended the patient for their last illness;[11] *and either*:
    - such attendance was during the previous 14 days, *or*
    - he/she has viewed the body after death.[12]

If the deceased is to be buried, the doctor does not have to issue any papers in respect of the disposal. However, if cremation is desired a number of further complications arise, as to which see section 4.29.

The report of a Home Office Review of Death Certification was published in September 2001, this being intended to complement rather than compete with the Fundamental Review of death certification and investigation and the Shipman Inquiry (see sections 1.08 and 1.09). Nonetheless, this report now appears somewhat overshadowed by the more in-depth studies and, although there will undoubtedly be changes in the near future, it is impossible at the time of writing to say what these will be.

4.04   The Chain of Causation

Detailed advice on the completion of the MCCD is outside the remit of this work but some readers may appreciate a brief explanation of the issues involved. Those requiring a further account are referred to the standard works on this subject including Professor Bernard Knight's 'Legal Aspects of Medical Practice'.[13]

---

[10]   So called because without a valid medical certificate or evidence of a coroner's inquiry (Form B or inquest) the death cannot be registered nor the body disposed of, thus *every death* will be subject to scrutiny: Burton, Chambers and Gill, *Coroners Inquiries: a guide to law & practice* (1985, Kluver Law).

[11]   This phrase is not defined satisfactorily in any statute or text book. It can probably be taken to mean no more than 'that which the patient died of' or that the death must be compatible with the illness for which the doctor was previously attending.

[12]   The question may be asked how a doctor viewing in this manner can accurately state a cause of death if they have not seen the patient for several months. Some anomalies of this legislation are discussed at section 3.11.

[13]   Knight, *Legal Aspects of Medical Practice*, (5th edition, 1992: Churchill Livingstone).

In writing the MCCD, the doctor is required to certify the cause of death, to the best of his/her knowledge and belief. However, setting out the chain of causation leading to death in the format[14] of 1a, 1b, 1c, and II causes a great deal of confusion to those not thoroughly familiar with the system.[15]

Under 1a the doctor will insert the disease or condition directly leading to death. This is the immediate cause of death such as bronchopneumonia or myocardial infarction. The doctor should be careful not to use phraseology which is merely 'a mode of dying' (eg cardiac arrest) rather than an actual cause of death.

At 1b the doctor will give any other disease or condition which led to the immediate cause of death. In the examples quoted above, this might be immobility which led to the bronchopneumonia, or coronary atheroma leading to the myocardial infarction.

If there is a further link in the sequence of causation which led to the matter referred to in 1b, then this will be recorded in 1c. For example, the bronchopneumonia might have been caused by immobility which was itself caused by dementia. There is no provision for a 1d.

The most widely misunderstood section is Part II. This is meant to be a record of other significant conditions which have contributed to the death but are not related to the disease or condition causing it. For example, diabetes is a well-known background factor in the formation of coronary atheroma, thus the diabetes can contribute to the death without directly causing it. Unfortunately, some think that Part II requires a list of every other disease that the deceased suffered at the time of death.

The Decision to Inquire

The legal definition of the coroner's jurisdiction (ie the right to inquire into a death) is closely examined in Chapter 2.[16] This section examines issues surrounding the decision on whether a case is appropriate for inquiries by the coroner, whilst that following deals with the decision to hold an inquest based upon those initial inquiries.

---

[14] The MCCD format used in England and Wales may seem slightly awkward but accords with that recommended by the World Health Organisation in the 9th Revision of the International Classification of Diseases. This allows cross-border comparability of cause of death data.

[15] A study published in 2002 suggests that despite increased undergraduate education on the point, death certification continues to be poorly performed. A study of 1000 certificates completed in a large teaching hospital showed only 55 per cent completed to a minimally acceptable standard, nearly 10 per cent were illogical or inappropriately completed. Swift and West, 'Death Certification; an audit of practice entering the 21st century', *J Clin Pathol* (2002) 55, 275–279.

[16] The individual components of the coroner's right to assume jurisdiction into a death are discussed at section 2.16 *et seq*.

Delegation of decision making by coroners to their officers is considered at section 1.32.

4.05 Introduction

Whilst the many deaths referred to coroners[17] inevitably include a number which did not need reporting, or which are quickly recognized as natural (see section 4.07), the coroner's jurisdiction more properly arises under s 8(1) of the Coroners Act 1988 where:

- the body is lying within the coroner's district; *and*
- there is reasonable cause to suspect that either:
  - the death was violent or unnatural, *or*
  - was a sudden death of unknown cause, *or*
  - the death occurred in a prison.

If the initial information suggests that one of these criteria might be met then the coroner must enquire further:

- If there is reasonable cause to suspect from the outset that the death was violent, unnatural or occurred in a prison etc, the coroner must proceed to hold an inquest.[18]
- If the cause of death is unknown (which might include a case where the question of violent/unnatural is unclear[19]) the coroner will order a post-mortem examination to establish the cause and, so far as practicable, the circumstances:
  - if the examination confirms a violent or unnatural cause of death, or if the cause remains unknown, the coroner must hold an inquest;
  - if the examination establishes a natural cause of death the coroner's interest in the case will terminate and the registrar will be notified by the appropriate form.[20]

4.06 Lack of Information

Much depends upon the quality of the information given. If a reporting doctor either does not recognize, or fails to disclose, all relevant information the whole decision-making exercise is flawed.[21] The same might be said where the officer taking the report for the coroner is inexperienced and cannot recognize relevant factors.

---

[17] Approximately 201,400 in 2002.
[18] Although a post-mortem examination will commonly be ordered for evidential purposes under s 20.
[19] *R v Greater Manchester Coroner ex p Worch and Brunner* [1988] QB 513.
[20] Under the Form B procedure, as to which see section 4.20.
[21] See section 3.07 for the doctor's duty to disclose all relevant information voluntarily.

Quite often, the full facts are not readily available for a variety of reasons. It may be possible to obtain more information quickly from other sources[22] and the coroner must then make an initial decision as to how to proceed with the case.

It is almost inevitable that the coroner will still be working on partial information at this stage because obtaining full details and written reports from all those involved would usually take several weeks. Instead, the initial decision will usually have to be made by the coroner within the first two or three working days of the death. This difficulty is considered further in the context of the decision to hold an inquest at section 4.11.

Referrals not Requiring a Post-mortem Examination   4.07

A significant proportion of deaths are reported to the coroner where the doctor is actually prepared to issue an MCCD for the registrar. The referral may nonetheless take place because either:

- the doctor wants advice as to whether the case needs reporting;
- the doctor wants advice as to the correct wording to put on the certificate;
- the doctor could otherwise issue an MCCD but has not seen the deceased within the last 14 days.

There are also cases where the death is referred by an accident and emergency doctor who has had insufficient time to make a diagnosis but inquiries of the deceased's GP then reveal that they would be able to issue an MCCD.

Although the circumstances must always be considered on a case by case basis, there is usually no requirement for the coroner to intervene further in such deaths and the reporting doctor will be advised to issue the MCCD.

Recording Cases that do not Require Further Investigation   4.08

Practice varies as to how such cases will be dealt with administratively. The coroner has two choices:[23]

- issue a notification to the registrar on Form A,[24] confirming that the death has been reported and that it is considered unnecessary to take any further action;
- record the case as a 'no further action' without issuing a Form A.

---

[22] Which if at all possible should include contact with the family, see section 5.15.
[23] Presumably the third choice is not bothering to record the query at all, but in the author's view that is not an acceptable option for the reasons set out.
[24] See section 4.19.

Form A must be used where the case falls within regulation 41 of the Births and Deaths Regulations 1987[25] otherwise the registrar will be forced to reject the doctor's certificate and refer the case to the coroner again.

In other cases, the author would argue that it is generally better for a Form A to be issued, unless the referral merely relates to the wording to be used on the certificate, or the circumstances really did not need reporting at all. Otherwise there is no way of ensuring that the cause given by the doctor to the coroner's office is the same as that given to the registrar.

Whether Form A is used or not, the author maintains a strong view that it is necessary for *all* inquiries or reports, from whatever source, to be recorded for the following reasons:

- Home Office Circular 28/2003 notes it as good practice to record any inquiry about the need to report a death;[26]
- unless all reports are fully recorded, it would be difficult to disprove a later incorrect claim from an unscrupulous doctor that a death was referred;
- the coroner's annual return to the Home Office (see section 10.05) includes the number of NFA (no further action) cases. Comparisons of totals becomes meaningless if some jurisdictions record every case and others do not.

Much is sometimes made of the apparent anomaly between different coroner's jurisdictions on the percentage of cases subject to autopsy. For example, Jurisdiction A autopsies 50 per cent of reported deaths whereas in Jurisdiction B it is 80 per cent—therefore B appears to undertake a great many 'unnecessary' autopsies. But if A records all cases referred, even for informal advice, whilst B records only those cases where some active intervention is necessary, the statistical base is radically different.[27]

4.09 Referrals where the Cause of Death is Unknown

The coroner's statutory powers to order a post-mortem or special examination under s 19 or s 20 of the Act are discussed fully at sections 5.05–5.07.

---

[25] Which in these circumstances would generally be that the doctor had not seen the patient in the last 14 days—see section 3.10.

[26] Including the advice or decision taken, the name of the registrar or doctor making the referral, the details of the person making the record and the date.

[27] For example, A records 4000 reported deaths of which 2000 (50 per cent) are autopsied. B has a similar number of calls but the officers only record the 2500 where some active intervention takes place, from these 2,000 (80 per cent) are autopsied. The same criteria have been used to decide which cases go to post-mortem but the figures look wholly different. For this reason, until common recording criteria are established, it is much better to compare autopsy rates on a per head of population basis.

On the face of it, if the cause of death is unknown, the case falls within s 8(1) and an inquest will be necessary. However, the coroner will order an examination under s 19, which may show that an inquest is unnecessary by establishing a natural cause of death.

In most cases it will be apparent from an early stage that the cause is likely to be natural, the question being the exact cause of that natural death. An accurate cause is necessary for registration[28] and in the absence of a doctor able or willing to issue a medical certificate, the coroner will have little choice other than to order an examination.[29]

It may be wise for coroners to ensure that inquiries made by their officers prior to the decision on an autopsy, and the reason for the examination, are recorded.

Deaths which are Clearly Violent or Unnatural   4.10

If the death is obviously due to trauma such as a road traffic collision, fall from height, or drowning, it is clear that an inquest must be held under the provisions of s 8(1) of the Act. Nonetheless a post-mortem examination (and potentially special examinations[30]) will normally be held by virtue of s 20 to provide evidence as to the cause of death and see whether there are any other circumstances relevant to the incident (eg the driver of a car in a collision has been suffering a stroke at the time, or is under the influence of drugs).[31]

The Decision to Hold an Inquest

The complexities surrounding the coroner's legal right to assume jurisdiction over a body are examined in Chapter 2. The previous section dealt with the coroner's decision on whether to make inquiries into a death. Having received information on the basis of those inquiries, the coroner must then decide if an inquest is to be held.

Introduction   4.11

By s 8(1) of the Act, an inquest *must* be held where the coroner is informed that the body of a person is lying within the district and there is reasonable cause to suspect that the deceased:

---

[28] In some countries it is considered sufficient to certify that death is due to 'natural causes' but this has never been acceptable under the Registration Acts here.

[29] It has been suggested that coroners have 'a routine and unfocused resort to the post-mortem' (see section 5.04) but the real issue is that without a doctor prepared to certify, the coroner has no option but to order the post-mortem.

[30] See section 5.07.

[31] See section 5.06 for some examples of the unexpected issues that may be revealed in this situation.

- has died a violent or unnatural death; *or*
- has died a sudden death of which the cause is unknown; *or*
- has died in prison or in such a place or in such circumstances as to require an inquest under any other Act.

The great majority of deaths are either plainly due to a natural cause or clearly arise from a grossly unnatural (and sometimes violent) event such as a traffic collision or suicide. Similarly, although few in number, cases where the cause of death remains unknown after proper inquiries or where a death has occurred in prison[32] tend to be self-evident. Thus in most cases the decision to hold an inquest is not problematic.

However, the coroner may face more equivocal circumstances which will need careful consideration of both the facts and law:

- a natural cause where the death might have been contributed to by neglect;[33]
- a wholly unexpected death from natural causes resulting from a culpable human failure;[34]
- a patient suffering from a life-threatening condition where, because of a failure in medical treatment, the death was not prevented;[35]
- a natural death becoming unnatural by causative or intervening events;[36]
- a natural disease brought about by the deceased's employment;[37]
- unnaturally arising diseases;[38]
- a death where considerations of Article 2 ECHR[39] arise—although this would usually fall into one of the other categories.

4.12 Extent of Inquiries before the Decision is Made

Often the decision on whether or not to hold an inquest must be made quickly. Relatives are (understandably) awaiting the release of the body so either the issue of a Form A/B or the opening of an inquest is needed.

Whilst there must be careful consideration of the known facts, there is usually no question of being able to arrange detailed reports about every aspect of the

---

[32] See section 8.03 for the somewhat extended definition of a prison death.

[33] See section 9.24 *et seq* on the subject of neglect verdicts.

[34] Described as a death that 'should plainly never have happened'. *R v Inner North London Coroner ex p Touche* [2001] QB 1206. See section 2.20.

[35] *R v Birmingham Coroner ex p Benton* (1997) 162 JP 807. See section 2.19.

[36] See section 2.19 *et seq.*

[37] For example, emphysema is commonly an entirely natural disease but in a person who has worked underground as a coal miner for 20 years it will be regarded as an industrial disease and is 'unnatural'. See section 9.21.

[38] For example, HIV arising from infected blood or CJD contracted from the human growth hormone. See section 2.22.

[39] Article 2 European Convention on Human Rights (the right to life) given effect in UK domestic law by the Human Rights Act 1998. See section 4.43 and section 9.30 *et seq.*

circumstances or a full independent opinion on some difficult medical point. It may be possible for initial inquiries to be made by the coroner's officer or police to see if there is a realistic basis for any untoward suggestion made. It may also be possible to get brief advice on relevant points from the pathologist, but there will probably be insufficient time for much beyond that.

In any event, the Act requires the coroner to hold an inquest if 'there is reasonable cause to suspect'[40] that any of the criteria set out in the section are met, which presumably leaves the decision threshold at a simple level, although still requiring more than a mere unsubstantiated allegation that there is something unnatural about the death.

The coroner must also be careful of what is in effect 'holding an inquest behind closed doors' by making detailed inquiries and then deciding that the death is natural. It can be argued that if there is a need for *detailed* inquiries to decide this in the first place[41] then the 'reasonable cause to suspect' test for an inquest is satisfied. Thus the proceedings should be opened and then the results of the coroner's subsequent investigations dealt with in the normal open way at the hearing. This is a difficult point where the needs of individual cases will vary according to the circumstances.

Basis of the Decision   4.13

To understand the basis upon which the coroner should make a decision as to whether a case requires an inquest under s 8(1), it is important to distinguish two quite different concepts:

- the pathologist giving a natural cause of death on the limited basis of the pathological evidence;
- the coroner's decision that, taking all the known circumstances into account, there is nothing to suggest that the death might be unnatural.

Thus the coroner is entitled to decide that an inquest is necessary, despite a natural cause of death in the pathologist's report, if other circumstances give rise to a reasonable suspicion that there is something unnatural about the death. This is supported by the 1996 case of *Weeks*,[42] where the court held:

> Thus, in practical terms, when a coroner is informed of a death within his jurisdiction, he must consider all the relevant material before him and ask whether he has reasonable cause to suspect that the deceased died a violent or unnatural death or a

---

[40] It might be argued that this is a lower level than 'reasonable cause to believe'.

[41] A clear distinction must be made here between the detailed inquiries envisaged in the text involving experts or protracted police inquiries and the normal (but nonetheless rigorous) investigation of the circumstances before a decision as to an inquest is made.

[42] *R v HM Coroner for South District of Greater London ex p Weeks* (unreported) QBD 6 December 1996.

sudden death the cause of which is unknown. If he does have cause to suspect, he must hold an inquest. The test is one of objective fact. The matters that fall to be considered are not limited to admissible evidence.

Thus the coroner must take into account all relevant facts including any representations which are made. Any decision must be made on judicial principles and for clearly definable reasons.

The coroner's decision as to whether a death should be dealt with by the Form A or B procedure, or be subject to an inquest, is an administrative one—albeit undertaken by a judicial officer. There is no provision for this decision to be made in a court setting. There is no form of appeal against a decision by a coroner but an aggrieved party may seek judicial review of the coroner's action. For a brief discussion of judicial review see section 10.06 *et seq.*

4.14 The Question of Discretion

The question then arises as to whether the coroner has a discretion to hold an inquest (eg in the public interest) where the cause of death is wholly natural and does not therefore fall within s 8(1).

In the 1992 case of *Thomas*[43] the Court of Appeal held that there is no general discretion for a coroner to hold an inquest in the public interest. Either a case falls within s 8(1), where an inquest is mandatory, or it does not. Of course, the decision as to whether a given set of facts amount to an unnatural death involves the exercise of a degree of judgement but that is different to 'discretion'.

However, this contrasts with advice given by the Home Office[44] on deaths from natural causes in police custody, where the coroner is urged to hold an inquest despite there being no provision for this in the legislation—see section 8.04.

Ancillary Decisions

4.15 Organ Donation and Transplants

One area of decision making in which coroners frequently become involved is little appreciated by those outside the medical profession—it is necessary to seek the coroner's consent before removing organs from a transplant donor if the donor's death will need referral to the coroner.[45]

---

[43] *R v HM Coroner for Inner London ex p Thomas* (1993) 2 WLR 547.
[44] Home Office Circular 109/1982.
[45] It is often the case that a donor's death will be reportable, donors are commonly young, fit people who have suffered a catastrophic trauma, such as a road collision, leaving them on a ventilator.

The person in lawful possession of the body (usually a hospital administrator at this stage) may give authority, under s 1(2) of the Human Tissue Act 1961, for organ removal, subject to there being no known objection made by the deceased in his lifetime or a surviving relative. But s 1(5) of the same Act states:

> 1(5) Where a person has reason to believe that an inquest may be required to be held on any body or that a post-mortem examination of any body may be required by the coroner he shall not, except with the consent of the coroner:
> (a) give an authority under this section in respect of the body or
> (b) act on such an authority given by any other person.

This can bring an interesting if semantic point: the coroner only has jurisdiction once a death has occurred but the necessary speed with which transplant donation must be completed makes it inevitable that the coroner is asked to consent before the patient 'dies'.[46]

The coroner will wish to establish the basic facts from the transplant co-ordinator or referring doctor and in particular will want to be assured that there are no suspicious circumstances surrounding the death.[47] This may necessitate immediate inquiry of the police to establish whether they are aware of the incident leading to the death and what their inquiries have revealed.

If there are no potential criminal aspects to the death, it is unlikely that organ donation would be obstructing the coroner's purposes and immediate consent would normally be given. Nonetheless there will occasionally be non-suspicious but still unnatural deaths where donation of a particular organ may prevent the pathologist answering relevant questions for the inquest. This becomes a balancing act of the different public interests involved although there will be a natural preference to allow donation if at all possible; some liaison with the pathologist and perhaps the family may be necessary.

Home Office Circular 65 of 1977 advised coroners that as impartial legal officers they should not refuse permission on grounds of ethical or moral judgements.

There are significant complications where the death might be due to a criminal act such as murder or manslaughter.[48] These are considered in further detail at section 4.38.

---

[46] See section 2.08 for discussion on the meaning of 'death' and brain stem function tests.

[47] It is not uncommon for reporting doctors to be somewhat vague on this point which may need probing, but this is hardly surprising. The doctors making a referral will probably not be those who were involved when the patient was first admitted and will be reliant on what their colleagues wrote in the notes. Secondly, they will have been more concerned with treating the patient's injuries than establishing how they arose in the first place.

[48] A potential charge of causing death by dangerous driving might not always lead to difficulty in this regard but the circumstances of each individual case will need to be considered carefully.

4.16   Power of Exhumation

On rare occasions the coroner must decide whether it is appropriate to direct an exhumation. By s 23 of the Act a coroner may order by warrant[49] the exhumation of a body lying within their district if it appears that an examination of the body is necessary either:

- for the purpose of the coroner's own functions in holding an inquest or inquiring into the death; or
- for the purpose of criminal proceedings (instituted or contemplated) in respect of that death or another connected death.[50]

Coroners exhumations are extremely rare, on average only four nationally each year.[51]

4.17   Removal out of England

If it is desired to remove a body from England and Wales[52] for disposal, the coroner's authority is required, whether or not the death was due to natural causes. This effectively prevents a body being removed to thwart an inquiry by the coroner or police and is also some measure of control against the transmission of infection.

In deciding such applications, which are often made as a matter of urgency out of normal office hours, the coroner will primarily be concerned to rule out any prospect of suspicious circumstances. Obviously, where the cause of death is unknown or where an inquest may be necessary the coroner will also require an autopsy to be held before release of the body, as with any other case.

There are considerable practical difficulties in the expectation that coroners will provide a 'seven day a week' service to deal with such requests. There is no statutory requirement for this[53] nor are coroners generally given the support services by way of necessary deputy cover. A great deal of assistance is actually provided to applicants on a goodwill basis but there are also significant practical problems in organizing appropriate investigations at weekends or public holidays.

---

[49] For which a suitable form is suggested in Schedule 4 of the Rules.

[50] Note that the power only arises in respect of inquiries into *a death*; thus in a case where a grave had been disturbed (but refilled) and the head of the corpse stolen, the coroner did not have power to exhume the remainder of the body under s 23, for the exhumation was really to check that the head belonged to that corpse rather than to investigate the death; the Home Secretary had to give consent under the provisions of the Burial Act 1857.

[51] Taking the period 1993–2002; Home Office Statistical Bulletin 06/03.

[52] Being the legal jurisdiction in which coroners operate.

[53] Rule 4 only requires that a coroner shall at all times hold himself ready to undertake, either by himself or his deputies, any duties in connection with *inquests and post-mortem examinations*. See also *Jervis on Coroners* (12th edition) at para 3.03.

The procedural issues relating to such applications are dealt with at section 4.31.

Procedural Matters

Introduction   4.18

By s 19(3) of the Act, if a post-mortem examination has been made and the coroner is then satisfied that an inquest is unnecessary, a certificate must be sent to the registrar stating the cause of death disclosed by the pathologist.

Whilst there is no similar statutory requirement for a notification to the registrar that the coroner is concluding inquiries without a post-mortem examination or inquest, there is obviously a practical requirement for some form of certificate.

There is no statutory format for either of these certificates but the Registrar General has for many years provided coroners with forms of an acceptable type. Form 100A (see Table 4.1 below) refers to deaths where there has been no post-mortem, Form 100B (see Table 4.2 below) to those cases where a post-mortem has taken place but no inquest is to be held.

As a practical point, these forms are sometimes referred to as Pink Form A or B, even though Form A has not been coloured pink for a number of years.

Form 100A Procedure   4.19

If, after consideration of the circumstances, the coroner decides that a post-mortem and inquest are unnecessary because the (natural) cause of death is evident, a Form A (see Table 4.1 below) will be issued notifying the registrar accordingly. This sets out the cause of death as certified by the deceased's doctor and states that the coroner does not consider it necessary to hold an inquest.

The deceased's doctor will still issue the medical certificate of cause of death and ensure this is transmitted to the registrar, usually by handing it in an envelope to the relatives of the deceased.[54] The certificate should bear reference[55] to the fact that the case has been referred to the coroner—otherwise the registrar may not know that a Form A should also be available.

---

[54] There has been much criticism of the fact that the relatives may not be aware of the cause of death stated by the doctor until the envelope is opened by the registrar. Death certification and investigation in England, Wales and Northern Ireland; the report of a Fundamental Review; at Chapter 2, para 4 f. See section 1.08.

[55] Puzzlingly the medical certificate of cause of death requires this information twice—in exactly the same terms on front and reverse.

Table 4.1. Form A

NOTIFICATION TO THE REGISTRAR BY THE CORONER that he does not consider it necessary to hold an inquest	To be completed by Registrar	
FORM A - NO POST-MORTEM HELD	Register No.	
	Entry No.	

To the _____ Registrar of Births and Deaths

PARTICULARS OF THE DECEASED

Name and Surname

Sex

Age (or Date of Birth)

Date of Death

Place of Death

Cause of Death   I (a)

        (b)

        (c)

        II

(Where this notification relates to a stillborn child, this should be stated)

CORONER'S CERTIFICATE

The circumstances connected with the death of the above person have been reported to me and I do not consider it necessary to hold an inquest

Date

Signed

Name

Appointment

Jurisdiction

INSTRUCTIONS TO REGISTRAR OVERLEAF

Form 100A

SB30/4 1/93 R

It is important that, having agreed the terms in which the cause of death will be certified, the doctor uses the same phraseology in the certificate. If not, the registrar will be faced with inconsistent documents and will have to delay registration until the coroner is contacted and a replacement form obtained. This could cause difficulty for the relatives.

When the registrar has the two documents together the death can be registered. It is now common for registrars to accept a Form A by fax from the coroner (but not a Form B).

One problem with the current Form A system relates to cremation. The medical referee of a crematorium does not get a copy of the form and, if told that a death has been reported to the coroner, will not know what cause of death was given— or even if the death was actually reported.

Form 100B Procedure   4.20

If the post-mortem examination discloses a natural cause of death, so that an inquest is not required, the coroner will sign a Form B (see Table 4.2 below) which states that an inquest is unnecessary.[56] The Form B replaces the medical certificate of cause of death that would otherwise be issued by the doctor and instead certifies the cause of death found at the post-mortem examination.

The original (not a fax) of this form will be required by the registrar when the informant attends to register the death.[57] Thus the form may be collected from the coroner's office by relatives of the deceased or, in more rural areas, might be sent to the registrar by post.

Additional Information   4.21

On occasions the coroner is made aware by the pathologist that the initial cause of death given at post-mortem may be subject to revision following histology.[58] It is clear that the cause of death will remain natural, the further examination only providing additional information as to the exact cause or origin of a disease.[59]

In such cases the coroner will continue with the Form B procedure, releasing the body in the normal manner, but will note on the form that a histological or bacteriological[60] examination is to be made. This will cause the Registrar of Births

---

[56] But this does not prevent the matter being examined further if there is reason. See section 2.25 as to when the coroner becomes 'functus officio'.

[57] See section 4.27.

[58] The study of sections of tissue under a microscope—see sections 5.31 and 5.36.

[59] This contrasts with the situation in which the autopsy does not reveal a cause of death at all so a special examination (such as toxicology) is required—here the coroner must open an inquest.

[60] See section 5.31 as to whether a s 19 autopsy allows a bacteriological examination to be made despite the wording of the Form B.

Table 4.2. Form B

NOTIFICATION TO THE REGISTRAR BY THE CORONER that he does not consider it necessary to hold an inquest	To be completed by Registrar
	Register No.
FORM B · POST-MORTEM held under Section 19 of the Coroner's Act 1988	Entry No.

To the _____ Registrar of Births and Deaths

PARTICULARS OF THE DECEASED

Name and Surname

Sex

Age (at Date of Birth)

Place of Death

Handwritten notes overlaid:

NOTIFICATION TO THE REGISTRAR —
form 100A no PM — no inquest

form 100B PM — inquest.

form A — HMC may NEVER HAVE
TAKEN POSSESSION.
form B — WILL HAVE TO UNDERTAKE PM

Address

Is a histological or bacteriological examination to be made?

Date

Signed

Name

Appointment

Jurisdiction

INSTRUCTIONS TO REGISTRAR OVERLEAF

Form 100B
SB29/5 1/93

and Deaths to dispatch a further form to the coroner on which it is shown whether the stated cause of death has been changed.

In any event, it may be wise for the coroner to establish a system to ensure that any promised additional information (or final report) is actually supplied by the pathologist.

Statistics   4.22

Although the long-term trend has been upwards, the number of deaths reported to coroners has remained steady for several years at around 201,000.[61] The proportion of all deaths occurring which were reported to coroners was 37.6 per cent in 2002 reflecting a steady rise.

Post-mortem examinations were ordered on 58 per cent of reported deaths in 2002, a fall of 10 per cent since 1995. This proportion has been in slow decline since the 1970s when it was at about 88 per cent. If cases requiring an inquest are excluded, then only 53 per cent of the remaining deaths were subject to an autopsy.

Inquests were held on 13 per cent of reported deaths, the highest percentage for at least 30 years. This equates to 4.9 per cent of the total number of deaths occurring.

Although Form B cases (after post-mortem examination) form the greater part of the coroner's workload, Form A cases (no post-mortem) are a substantial factor and continue to increase.[62] An analysis by the Home Office of coroner's annual returns shows that 99 per cent of such non-inquest cases are concluded within one week.

As a percentage of deaths referred to coroners	1997	2002
Form A procedure	35.2%	41.2%
Form B procedure	52.8%	45.8%
Inquest held	12.0%	13.0%

---

[61] It seems a strange coincidence that the total number of deaths reported to coroners in each of the years 1999–2002 was within 100 of 201,300.

[62] Deaths reported to coroners in England and Wales 2002: Home Office Statistical Bulletin 06/03.

Release of the Body

4.23 The Coroner's Right to Possession

The basic principle at common law is that there is no property in a body, that is to say that a body cannot be owned[63] or be regarded as the property of another.[64] However, the right to take possession of the body is a different concept.

If the death has been dealt with under the Form A procedure, the coroner may never have taken possession of the body. However, if the coroner needs to take possession, whether to undertake a post-mortem examination or to ensure that it is not otherwise interfered with, it is clear that there is an absolute right to do so at common law:

> . . . the coroner's authority over the physical control of the body arises as soon as he decides to hold an inquest and lasts at common law until the inquest itself is determined.[65]

The exercise of this power is of course susceptible to judicial review, so a coroner who refused to release a body may have this action reviewed by the High Court and, where appropriate, an order for release might be made.

In the vast majority of cases the coroner will be anxious to release the body to those lawfully entitled at the earliest opportunity. Generally this will be immediately the post-mortem examination has been completed or, in appropriate cases, once the inquest has been opened.[66]

4.24 Disputes

The question of who is entitled to receive the body can be difficult. In the vast majority of cases no problem arises but occasionally there is disagreement between two factions of a family and the coroner must then consider the legal position carefully.

If the deceased has made a will it is the personal representatives (the executors) who have the legal duty to dispose of the body and therefore presumably the better claim.[67] The executor's power is derived from the will and they have rights conferred upon them from the time of the death. If the deceased was without a will then the person first entitled to apply for a Grant of Letters of

---

[63] *Dobson v N Tyneside Health Authority* [1996] 4 All ER 474.

[64] Thus a body cannot be stolen within the meaning of the Theft Act 1968. So when a body was unlawfully taken from a mortuary as part of a gangland vendetta the culprits could only be charged with theft of the shroud in which the body was wrapped.

[65] *R v Bristol Coroner ex p Kerr* [1974] 2 All ER 719.

[66] See section 5.34 for further discussion on the release of the body.

[67] *Dobson v N Tyneside Health Authority* (n 63 above).

Administration[68] is a surviving spouse. However, the rights of an administrator do not start until Letters of Administration are actually granted by the court.

In general terms a partner or companion, ie the so-called common law spouse of the deceased, can be in a difficult situation. Unless a will exists the common law spouse has few direct rights, however long the cohabitation has been, and may take second place to blood relations who may not have seen the deceased for years. This situation is beginning to change with Article 8 ECHR[69] giving recognition of private and family life to a broad range of unions.

It may take all the diplomacy of the coroner's officer to effect a sensible compromise in such disputes. Very occasionally the situation will progress further and those disagreeing will continue to demand that the body should be released only to them. It is not for the coroner to choose between rivals in this manner and they must come to an agreement or have the civil courts make an order. From a practical point of view it may be better to gain consent that the coroner release the body to an undertaker pending a decision being made by the various parties.[70] Cases which go as far as a court order are rare.

Criminal Cases   **4.25**

In criminal cases the issue of releasing the body becomes more difficult. Although there is no statutory authority, it is well-established practice to allow the medical advisors of a person charged with the killing to conduct a second post-mortem examination. This is dealt with in greater detail at section 4.37 and section 5.12 below.

Deceased without Relatives or Funds   **4.26**

It is not uncommon for a body to be found in circumstances where no relatives can be identified or where no one will take responsibility for funeral costs. In such cases, or where the deceased's estate is without funds to meet undertakers' charges etc, the local authority has a statutory responsibility under the Public Health (Control of Diseases) Act 1984 to provide a simple funeral, usually by burial.

---

[68] The probate order giving rights to deal with the estate of the deceased.

[69] Article 8, European Convention on Human Rights (the right to private and family life) given effect in UK domestic law by the Human Rights Act 1998—see section 4.45.

[70] Eg *R v Inner S London Coroner ex p Brinson* (unreported, The Times, 18 July 1995); the wife and mistress of the deceased both demanded possession of the body. The coroner let the parties argue their case before the High Court, which eventually persuaded them to instruct an undertaker jointly.

Disposal of the Body

Whilst disposal of a body is usually by burial or cremation, there is no statute requiring that either must take place. Bodies may also be removed from the country for disposal.

[Handwritten: REGISTRATION - IN THE CASE OF AN INQUEST TO BE HELD - ITS CARRIED OUT AFTR - FORM 99]

4.27 Registration

All deaths occurring within England and Wales must be reported to the Registrar of Births and Deaths who will register the death in the manner required by the Registration of Births and Deaths Act 1953.[71] Other than where an inquest is to be held, the notification must take place within five days of the death. This responsibility falls upon 'the informant' who will usually be a relative of the deceased, although this may be someone living in the same house or looking after the deceased during his life.[72]

Where the death has been reported but a Form A[73] is issued (because no post-mortem examination was held) the MCCD will be given to the informant by the certifying doctor and taken to the registrar. The coroner's Form A[73] will also be sent to the registrar.

If the coroner has ordered a post-mortem examination, but subsequently no inquest is to be held, the coroner's Form B[73] will be collected by the informant and taken to the registrar. This replaces the doctor's MCCD in these circumstances.

Where an inquest is to be held, the death cannot be registered until the coroner's proceedings are concluded.[74] By s 11(7) of the Act, the coroner is obliged to supply the registrar with a certificate on Form 99 within five days of the inquest, setting out the date of hearing, the verdict, and particulars of the deceased.[75]

---

[71] Some significant reforms to the manner of registration, although not the requirement for registration to take place, are proposed by the government following the 2002 White Paper, *Civil Registration: Vital Change*. It will be possible to register deaths by phone and on-line, it is also intended that the registered cause of an individual death will become private information with limited availability. The required legislative changes (under powers within the Regulatory Reform Act 2001) are expected to be completed by the end of 2004.

[72] See section 4.19.

[73] See section 4.20.

[74] Although the coroner will issue an interim certificate of the fact of death which may assist the relatives in dealing with the deceased's affairs in the meantime, as to which see sections 4.02 and 7.16.

[75] See section 10.02.

Burial   **4.28**

There is no statutory requirement for a body to be buried in a properly authorized place, it is perfectly in order to bury one's spouse in the garden—provided that all other necessary legal formalities have been completed first.[76]

Burial attracts comparatively few formalities so far as the coroner is concerned. In cases dealt with under Form A or Form B it is the registrar who will issue a certificate allowing disposal by burial.[77] The coroner will issue a burial order[78] only where an inquest is opened.[79]

Cremation   **4.29**

The practicalities of cremation are complex. The formalities will differ according to whether a post-mortem has taken place and whether an inquest is to be held.

Cases without post-mortem or inquest   **4.29.1**

In a case where the coroner has issued a Form A the death must first be registered. The registrar will issue a certificate allowing disposal.[80] The executor or nearest relative of the deceased must then make an application for cremation in the prescribed manner.[81]

This is an intricate procedure involving an application from the relative, and certificates from the deceased's own doctor and an independent doctor. The papers are examined by the medical referee of the cremation authority.

Despite the complexities, this system has been heavily criticized by the recent reviews (see sections 1.08 and 1.09) as providing insufficient safeguard against homicide.

Inquest and post-mortem cases   **4.29.2**

If a post-mortem examination has taken place, or an inquest has been opened, the application for cremation is still necessary[82] but the medical certificates are not. Instead the coroner will issue a certificate on Cremation Form E. The medical referee's consent is still required.

---

[76] Including a burial register. See A. Nicholson, 'Grave concerns deny the departed eternal rest' *Sunday Telegraph*, 27 February 1994 at page 18.

[77] Certificate for the Disposal of the Body by Burial or Cremation, under the Births and Deaths Registration Act 1926.

[78] A form is suggested by the Coroners Rules, Schedule IV, form 21.

[79] If there is to be an inquest, registration of the death will not have taken place at the time of the burial and thus the coroner's order is a practical requirement.

[80] See n 77.

[81] Form A of the schedule to the Cremation Regulations 1930.

[82] Regulation 7(1) of the Cremation Regulations 1930.

4.29.3 *Cremation of body parts*

The Cremation Amendment Regulations 2000 make provision for the cremation of parts of a body removed and retained at autopsy, the body having been previously subject to burial or cremation. The pathologist or other authority holding the body parts must certify that the coroner no longer needs the parts to be retained.

4.30 Bodies Returned from Abroad

Even though the death occurred abroad the coroner's obligation to investigate (and possibly hold an inquest) may still arise if the body is returned to this country, dependent upon the circumstances of the death.[83]

The formalities surrounding the disposal will differ according to whether burial or cremation is intended and whether there is a post-mortem examination or inquest:

Burial: no post-mortem or inquest:	Only Registrar's Certificate of no liability to Register is required
Burial: post-mortem but no inquest:	Only Registrar's Certificate of no liability to Register is required
Burial: inquest to be held:	Coroner issues Burial Order
Cremation: no post-mortem or inquest:	Registrar's Certificate of no liability to Register required, followed by application for cremation and probably Secretary of State's authorization
Cremation: post-mortem but no inquest:	Coroner issues Cremation Form E
Cremation: inquest to be held:	Coroner issues Cremation Form E

4.31 Removal out of England and Wales

A person intending to remove a body from England and Wales must give notice in the proper form[84] to the coroner within whose jurisdiction the body is lying. Whilst it is preferable for the death to have been registered (unless, of course, an inquest is to be held) this is not a legal requirement.

The coroner must then make inquiries into the death and consider whether a post-mortem examination or an inquest are required. The decision-making process is considered at section 4.17.

The coroner will acknowledge the intention to remove the body.[85] This will state that either:

---

[83] See section 2.14.
[84] This is Form 104rev set out in the Removal of Bodies Regulations 1954 Schedule 1.
[85] Form 103 of the Removal of Bodies Regulations 1954 Schedule 2.

- the coroner is satisfied no further inquiries are necessary and that the body may be moved at any time thereafter; or
- the body can be removed after the expiration of four clear days from the day on which notice was received by the coroner unless a lawful direction to the contrary is given in the meantime.

Should circumstances require, the coroner may direct within the four-day period that the body is not to be removed as further inquiries or examination are needed.[86] Removal of a body in contravention of the Removal of Bodies Regulations 1954 is a criminal offence.

A problem with the current system is that the coroner has no way of knowing whether the person making application to remove the body has authority to do so from the true next of kin. It has been suggested that the removing undertaker should provide the coroner with an authority from the next of kin and confirmation that they do not know of any objection to the removal.

Suspicious Deaths

Introduction 4.32

For many years the coroner had a duty to investigate who was guilty of criminal involvement in a death. As society developed a more sophisticated system of criminal investigation, the coroner's role in suspicious deaths diminished. By 1977 the ability of the coroner to commit for trial was regarded as an anachronism and the Criminal Law Act of that year abolished this power.

Although the public perception is rather different, suspicious deaths are a very small part of the coroner's work. There were 866 deaths initially recorded as homicide by the police in 2001/02, which is approximately 1 in every 232 deaths reported to coroners. Inevitably there will be a greater number initially regarded as suspicious but the percentage of the coroner's caseload remains slight. Nonetheless, these are difficult and high profile cases which can raise complex issues.

The coroner and the police maintain a coexistent right of inquiry. This may be easier to understand on the basis that the police investigate the crime whilst the coroner inquires into the body.

Coroners generally make it plain that they have no wish to interfere with a police inquiry. For example, they would rarely visit the scene of a suspicious death. However, the coroner retains a number of rights and duties which must continue alongside the obligations of the police.

---

[86] *R v Bristol Coroner ex p Kerr* [1974] 2 All ER 719.

4.33 Notification of the Death

The right to possession of a body rests with the coroner, not with the police (see section 4.23). With the right to possession must come a right to prompt notification[87] of the death from the police force involved.[88]

Further, in theory at least, the coroner's authority is required before the body may be removed from where it is found. This stems not only from s 22 of the Act but also from the right to view and inquire before removal enshrined in ancient law, certainly going back to the Statute of Westminster in 1275. This is a right that most coroners are happy to delegate to the police, both for suspicious and non-suspicious deaths.

The police do not have power to order a post-mortem examination, even with a suspicious death.[89] This is vested solely in the coroner[90] (see section 5.05). It follows that if the police need to have the body examined by a forensic pathologist as a matter of urgency there must be liaison with the coroner first. Indeed, it is only the coroner who has the right to choose which pathologist is instructed.[91] It is thus more than mere courtesy that the coroner is told of the investigation promptly by a senior officer[92] involved in the case.

4.34 Examination of a Scene, or of the Living

The coroner's power is to make an examination of the dead. There are occasions before a death has occurred when it is necessary to have a forensic pathologist examine the scene or the dying victim (generally to view marks that may soon fade or to give the police immediate advice on the direction of injuries etc). In one sense, this is not an issue for the coroner as there is as yet no body. However, some common sense is necessary (from both sides) for two reasons. Such a matter will almost inevitably relate to a death at some stage and it seems a necessary courtesy that the coroner should be told what is to happen. Secondly, and more impor-

---

[87] The Murder Investigation Manual (ACPO) acknowledges this at pages 93, 108 and 231. However, in most non-suspicious deaths this notification can be adequately given at the start of the next business day.

[88] Occasionally there are difficulties in deciding whether the British Transport Police (BTP) or the local force should be dealing with a death that has occurred on railway land. For example, was the victim killed elsewhere and laid on the track to destroy evidence and make the death look like a suicide? See s 53 British Transport Police Commission Act 1949 and Home Office Circular 25/2002 (protocol that BTP will investigate murders on railway land).

[89] Murder Investigation Manual (n 87 above) at pages 62, 93 and 231.

[90] Apart from the medical referee at a crematorium who has a largely theoretical power in appropriate circumstances.

[91] Although by rule 6(1)(b) the coroner must consult with the police before making this decision. See section 4.35 below.

[92] This is not a task to be delegated to a control room operator or junior officer with little direct knowledge of the circumstances, the Murder Investigation Manual (n 87 above) at page 108 places the responsibility on the senior investigating officer.

tantly, the police will presumably want the same pathologist to examine the body after death, and that choice does fall within the coroner's remit (see below).

On a practical point, in the author's experience events can go badly wrong as regards examination of those not yet dead. If asking a forensic pathologist to go to a hospital and view the dying, it is *essential* to make sure that the doctors in the hospital know and accept the necessity for this. It is grossly discourteous to a clinician trying to treat a patient for a forensic pathologist to walk onto the ward uninvited, in expectation of the death.

Such confusions have occurred because of a breakdown in communication, both police and pathologist thinking the other has organized events, and neither actually does so. Whilst there is no rule as to who should co-ordinate this, a great deal of ill-will is engendered if nobody does.

The Right to Choose the Pathologist   **4.35**

By rule 6, the coroner should consult the Chief Officer of Police when choosing the pathologist to carry out a post-mortem examination in a suspicious death. However, the coroner is not bound by the views of the police. This can lead to difficulty if the coroner considers it appropriate to instruct a forensic pathologist other than one with whom that police force have a standing contract for the provision of advice.[93] In extreme cases this can mean that the pathologist whom the police wish to instruct must stand and watch the coroner's chosen pathologist carry out the examination.[94] Few would regard this as an acceptable situation.

Who can Attend the Post-mortem?   **4.36**

At first glance this seems unlikely to become a vexed question in a suspicious death but it can cause difficulties in certain circumstances.

Rule 7 gives a detailed list of who can attend or be represented at the examination.[95] Whether the post-mortem examination is 'routine' or relates to a possible homicide is irrelevant in this regard.

Although most persons who have a right to be informed of the time and place of the examination are not allowed to attend themselves, they may nominate a doctor to attend. Thus a relative of the deceased, under suspicion of causing the death, would theoretically be entitled to have a doctor present to report back to him.

---

[93] The 1989 Wasserman Report, from a working party examining the provision and funding of forensic pathology, suggested contractual arrangements between police forces and forensic pathology departments.
[94] By rule 8, a person attending the post-mortem examination must not interfere.
[95] See sections 5.15 and 5.24.

Rule 7(2)(c) indicates that where the death occurred in a hospital then 'the hospital' are allowed to send a representative to the post-mortem.[96] This may be a problem if the death is thought to have been caused by the gross negligence of a doctor. The clinician involved could be nominated by the hospital to be present at the post-mortem.

Although rule 8 specifically prohibits interference with the examination there may be yet more difficulties. If the pathologist asks the surgeon a question during the examination,[97] in front of police officers, does this amount to an interview within the meaning of the Police and Criminal Evidence Act—is any answer to be written down in case it has relevance at a later trial?

The simple answer may be that although the hospital has a right to nominate someone to attend the examination, the coroner should not allow this to be a person whose conduct may have amounted to a criminal act, see also s 20(3) of the Act.

4.37 The Second Post-mortem

There is no statutory authority for those who stand accused to request a post-mortem examination on their own account, although case law and practice now recognize this as inevitable.[98] Failure to accord an opportunity for a second post-mortem could result in a judicial review of the coroner's decision and may create difficulties for the prosecution in the Crown Court. Second examinations are considered in greater detail at section 5.12.

A second autopsy may take some time to arrange for various reasons, indeed there may be no defendant arrested. The coroner is caught between the rights of a prospective defendant and the victim's family who have not only suffered a loss but now have to endure delay and the indignity of further examinations upon the body. There is no easy answer.

A 'memorandum of good practice' agreed by the Home Office[99] with representatives of other interested groups (eg ACPO and the Law Society) deals with a range of issues on second examinations but has also gone some way to avoiding undue delay. In particular, where no one has been charged with a suspected homicide within 28 days of the death the coroner will commission a second autopsy by another pathologist. This will be available to any subsequent defendant but would

---

[96] See also s 20(3) of the Act.

[97] Which would certainly be commonplace in the ordinary circumstances of a clinician attending the post-mortem examination of a patient.

[98] *R v Bristol Coroner ex p Kerr* [1974] 1QB 652 and *R v HM Coroner for Greater London ex p Ridley* [1985] 1 WLR 1347. See also Home Office Circular 30/1999.

[99] Home Office Circular 30/1999; Memorandum of good practice re: early release of bodies in cases of suspicious death.

normally also be disclosed to the police. In the event that the first and second examinations differ in their conclusion, the coroner will order a third.

Unfortunately, in seeking to avoid delay in other circumstances where a person has been charged, the memorandum relies in large measure on the ideal that the initial coroner's autopsy report (from the forensic pathologist) will be made available to all parties within 14 days of the examination, a time limit which can rarely be met.

Transplant Cases   4.38

By s 1(5) of the Human Tissue Act 1961, the coroner's consent to transplantation must be obtained if there is reason to believe an inquest may be required.[100] Whilst there is no specific provision in respect of deaths involving criminal culpability, these will obviously fall within the provision as 'requiring an inquest'.

The coroner will always wish to approve transplantation unless there is good reason to the contrary. However, in criminal cases some organs that might otherwise be transplanted may be required as evidence in relation to the death.[101] It must be remembered here that the coroner will be as much concerned with allowing the prosecution to be in a position to *disprove* any spurious allegations later put forward by the defendant as with strict proof of the cause of death.

To achieve any measure of organ donation in such instances will require liaison between the coroner and the forensic pathologist (to gain medical advice on what can be donated), and the police (to find out which organs might be relevant to the incident). The police will sometimes wish to liaise with the Crown Prosecution Service, and will need to inform the defence solicitor of the situation.[102]

Each of these organizations has an opportunity to make representations. But the decision must ultimately rest with the coroner. It is usually possible to allow some donation to take place but coroners must err on the side of caution if there is a possibility of a particular organ having evidential relevance.

Transplant cases can be very difficult and complex. The coroner needs the maximum possible warning of such cases where a victim of crime seems likely to die.

---

[100] This is dealt with in further detail at section 4.15.

[101] For example, in a case of suffocation there may be petechiae (tiny haemorrhages) on the surface of various organs and on the eyelids. Removal of the cornea might damage the area around the eyelid or lead to allegations that the petechiae arose from another reason, so would also have to be refused.

[102] Guidance on this for police officers was published by the ACPO Crime Committee in August 1994. It is summarized in the Murder Investigation Manual (n 87 above) at page 94.

4.39 Opening and Adjourning the Inquest—Section 16

By s 16 of the Act (see Table 4.3 below), where the coroner is informed[103] that a person has been charged with one of the specified offences[104] relating to the death, the inquest must be adjourned to await conclusion of the criminal proceedings at the Crown Court.[105] The coroner will issue a certificate under s 16(4) on Form 121 allowing the family to register the death and obtain a death certificate.

However, the coroner will still open an inquest to take formal evidence of identification. Where possible the coroner will also be given evidence of the cause of death. Ideally the court will be told that both police and defence have no objection to the release of the body.

Such an adjournment would only relate to indictable proceedings before the Crown Court. If a person faces a summary offence connected to the death (eg

---

Table 4.3. Section 16: Adjournment of inquest in certain cases

(1) If on an inquest into a death the coroner before the conclusion of the inquest—
    (a) is informed by the clerk of a magistrates' court under section 17(1) below that some person has been charged before a magistrates' court with—
        (i) the murder, manslaughter or infanticide of the deceased;
        (ii) an offence under section 1 or 3A of the Road Traffic Act 1988 (dangerous driving or careless driving when under the influence of drink or drugs) committed by causing the death of the deceased; or
        (iii) an offence under section 2(1) of the Suicide Act 1961 consisting of aiding, abetting, counselling or procuring the suicide of the deceased; or
    (b) is informed by the Director of Public Prosecutions that some person has been charged before examining justices with an offence (whether or not involving the death of a person other than the deceased) alleged to have been committed in circumstances connected with the death of the deceased, not being an offence within paragraph (a) above, and is requested by the Director to adjourn the inquest, then subject to subsection (2) below, the coroner shall in the absence of reason to the contrary, adjourn the inquest until after the conclusion of the relevant criminal proceedings, and, if a jury has been summoned, may, if he thinks fit, discharge them.

---

[103] The coroner's power to adjourn is when informed by the clerk of the Magistrates' Court (under requirements in s 17) that some person has been charged before a Magistrates' Court with one of the specified offences. However s 51 of the Crime and Disorder Act 1998 abolished committal from the lower court for indictable only offences, so no-one will now be 'charged before a Magistrates' Court' with relevant matters. An amendment to the Criminal Justice Bill at the House of Lord's Committee stage is promised for late 2003.

[104] Murder, manslaughter, infanticide, causing death by dangerous driving or by careless driving whilst under the influence of drink/drugs, aiding and abetting suicide. The coroner can also be asked to adjourn where there is another offence committed in circumstances connected with the death.

[105] See section 7.17.

(2) The coroner—
  (a) need not adjourn the inquest in a case within subsection (1)(a) above if, before he has done so, the Director of Public prosecutions notifies him that adjournment is unnecessary; and
  (b) may in any case resume the adjourned inquest before the conclusion of the relevant criminal proceedings if notified by the Director that it is open to him to do so.
(3) After the conclusion of the relevant criminal proceedings, or on being notified under paragraph (b) of subsection (2) above before their conclusion, the coroner may, subject to the following provisions of this section, resume the adjourned inquest if in his opinion there is sufficient cause to do so.
(4) Where a coroner adjourns an inquest in compliance with subsection (1) above, he shall send to the registrar of deaths a certificate under his hand stating, so far as they have been ascertained at the date of the certificate, the particulars which under the 1953 Act are required to be registered concerning the death.
(5) Where a coroner does not resume an inquest which he has adjourned in compliance with subsection (1) above, he shall (without prejudice to subsection (4) above) send to the registrar of deaths a certificate under his hand stating the result of the relevant criminal proceedings.
(6) Where a coroner resumes an inquest which has been adjourned in compliance with subsection (1) above and for that purpose summons a jury (but not where he resumes without a jury, or with the same jury as before the adjournment):
  (a) he shall proceed in all respects as if the inquest had not previously begun; and
  (b) subject to subsection (7) below, the provisions of this Act shall apply accordingly as if the resumed inquest were a fresh inquest.
(7) Where a coroner resumes an inquest which has been adjourned in compliance with subsection (1) above:
  (a) the finding of the inquest as to the cause of death must not be inconsistent with the outcome of the relevant criminal proceedings;
  (b) the coroner shall supply to the registrar of deaths after the termination of the inquest a certificate under his hand stating the result of the relevant criminal proceedings; and
  (c) the provisions of section 11(7) above shall not apply in relation to that inquest.
(8) In this section 'the relevant criminal proceedings' means the proceedings before examining justices and before any court to which the person charged is committed for trial.

careless driving) it is important that the inquest is heard first to preserve the coroner's right to refer the matter further to the Crown Prosecution Service under rule 28 (see section 7.38).[106] The importance of this has been underlined recently in the case of *Stanley*[107] where it was said that any decision by the CPS *not* to proceed with an indictable offence 'must be regarded as provisional' pending the

---

[106] *Re Beresford* [1952] 36 Cr App R 1. *Smith v DPP & anor* (2000) 164 JP 96.
[107] *R v HM Coroner for Inner North London ex p Stanley*, EWHC 1180 Admin.

conclusion of the inquest.[108] This recognizes that the inquest may reveal facts justifying an indictable charge, but if summary proceedings are already concluded it may be impossible for the prosecution to take the matter further.

4.40 Resuming the Inquest

Once the Crown Court proceedings are concluded the coroner may resume the inquest under s 16(3) if there is sufficient cause to do so. The decision 'is of a highly discretionary character'.[109]

It is unusual for an inquest to be resumed if there has been a substantive hearing about the death in the Crown Court.[110] The general test might be whether the facts of the death have been adequately aired in public.[111] The coroner will also have in mind the requirement of s 16(7)(a), that the findings[112] of any resumed inquest cannot be inconsistent with the verdict in the Crown Court.[113]

The 2003 case of *Hurst*[114] held that the coroner must also consider whether the circumstances of the death engages the procedural requirement to investigate under Article 2 ECHR[115] and may be compelled to resume the inquest where this is so.

If the coroner decides that it is unnecessary to resume the inquest, the registrar will be notified of this on Form 121.

The subject of criminal proceedings, adjournments, and subsequent inquests is dealt with further at section 7.17.

---

[108] See also the case of *R v DPP ex p Manning and Melbourne* (2000) 3 WLR 463 where it was said that if a jury returned a verdict of unlawful killing at an inquest implicating an identifiable person 'the ordinary expectation would naturally be that a prosecution would follow'. If summary offences have been heard before the inquest this may be more difficult.

[109] *R v Inner West London Coroner ex p Dallaglio* [1994] 4 All ER 139.

[110] One of the few recent examples is the Selby rail crash inquest—the coroner took the view that the criminal trial had been solely concerned with whether a motorist fell asleep at the wheel etc and did not deal with other important issues relating to the deaths.

[111] See *R (application of Southall Black Sisters) v HM Coroner for West Yorkshire* [2002] EWHC 1914 Admin, where the court also took into account that the family of the deceased did not want the inquest reopening and that there was little prospect of anything other than an open verdict.

[112] The section actually refers to the 'cause of death' which, taken literally, might refer just to the medical cause of death. However, it is generally regarded as illogical to interpret the requirement as meaning anything other than the *whole* of the findings of the inquest.

[113] Although a not guilty verdict in the Crown Court might only mean that the defendant was not guilty of the killing, so may not necessarily preclude an unlawful killing verdict on the basis that another was involved—much will depend on the circumstances, as to which see *R v Home Secretary ex p Weatherhead* (1996) 160 JP 627.

[114] *Hurst v HM Coroner Northern District of London* [2003] EWHC 1721 Admin where the coroner was ordered to resume. However a contrary decision was made in the *Southall Black Sisters* case (n 111 above) on broadly similar facts.

[115] See sections 4.43, 7.06, and 9.30.

Human Rights

The Human Rights Act 1998 gave effect in UK law to the European Convention on Human Rights (ECHR). It was not immediately obvious what the effect would be on coroner's law and practice. It has now become clear that there are significant consequences, most particularly with regard to the investigation of deaths under the provisions of Article 2, but the full impact is not yet plain, particularly as a major case awaits a decision from the House of Lords as this text goes to print.

This is a complex subject and any detailed study is outside the scope of this text. What follows is a short introduction to the topic[116] which is also briefly considered elsewhere in the context of particular issues. Engagement of Article 2 in relation to the scope of the inquest is dealt with at section 7.06, and in the context of verdicts of system neglect at section 9.30 *et seq.*

Those wanting a more detailed analysis of this area in relation to inquests are referred to *Jervis* (12th edition) at Chapter 21: *Inquests: A Practitioner's Guide*[117] at Chapter 18; or the advice from counsel contained within Volume 2 of the Fundamental Review as Report 3.[118]

The Human Rights Act 1998   4.41

The ECHR is a treaty of the Council of Europe, drafted in the late 1940s to avoid a repetition of the abuses of human rights that took place during the Second World War. Although the UK ratified the Convention in 1951 it was not adopted in UK domestic law and it was not until 1966 that the aggrieved were able to petition the European Court of Human Rights at Strasbourg. Since then the UK has frequently had to defend itself against charges of infringing Convention rights and has sometimes changed domestic law to give effect to decisions of the European Commission and Court of Human Rights.

In October 2000 the Human Rights Act 1998 (HRA) gave effect to the ECHR in domestic law. Whilst this does not make decisions of the European Court and Commission of Human Rights binding in domestic law, it does include strong provisions in relation to the interpretation of Convention rights:

---

[116] I am grateful to Mr Dennis Clark from the University of Teesside for his assistance with this section.

[117] Thomas, L, Friedman, D, and Christian, L, *Inquests: A Practitioner's Guide* (2003, Legal Action Group Books; www.lag.org.uk).

[118] Submission from Tim Owen QC and Danny Friedman; Report 3, Volume 2; Death Certification and Investigation in England, Wales and Northern Ireland, the Report of a Fundamental Review. See section 1.08.

- courts are now required to take account of decisions of the European Court[119] when determining questions in relation to Convention rights; and

- courts must interpret existing legislation in a manner compatible with the Convention rights.

4.42 Interpretation of Convention Rights

Section 2(1) of the HRA requires that any court or tribunal determining a question in connection with a Convention right must take into account, inter alia, judgments, decisions, declarations, and advisory opinions of the European Court of Human Rights.

This requires courts to take account of Strasbourg decisions regardless of the identity of the respondent state. Thus coroners are required to make judgment in the light of cases decided about issues in Italy, France, and Turkey or other signatory states that do not have a coroner system.

Section 3 of the HRA provides:

> (1) So far as it is possible to do so, primary legislation and subordinate legislation must be read and given effect in a way which is compatible with the Convention rights.

This means that the interpretation of coroners' law now requires an extra step. After analysis according to ordinary principles, the court will have to ask whether the result produced is compatible with Convention rights. If not, it will be necessary to try to re-interpret it to achieve compatibility. This will apply to the exercise of administrative powers under the Coroners Act and Rules (in decisions such as the requirement for post-mortem examination, etc) just as much as any judgment made in court during an inquest.

Section 6 of the HRA makes it unlawful for a 'public authority' to act in a manner incompatible with a Convention Right. Section 6(3) defines a public authority as including a court or tribunal and any person whose functions are of a public nature. The coroner is therefore a public authority.

Section 7 of the HRA, allows a person who claims that a public authority has acted (or proposes to act) in a manner which is incompatible with a Convention right to bring proceedings to challenge the decision. This would generally be by application for judicial review. Whether this will have any practical impact on existing provision for judicial review of a coroner's decision remains to be seen.

The safeguards contained within the ECHR must be interpreted so that they are 'practical and effective' rather than 'theoretical or illusory'.[120] Consequently there

---

[119] And judgments etc from a number of other sources specified in s 2(1) of the HRA.
[120] Starmer, K, *European Human Rights Law: the Human Rights Act 1998 and the European Convention on Human Rights* (1999, Legal Action Group Books).

are both explicit and implicit rights in the Convention, this has become an important issue in connection with Article 2 deaths.

The following sections briefly examine the relevant individual Articles in the context of a coroner's inquiries.

Article 2: The Right to Life   **4.43**

Article 2 ranks as the most fundamental provision of the Convention from which no derogation is permitted, even in times of national emergency, and the provisions must be strictly construed:

(1) Everyone's right to life shall be protected by law. No one shall be deprived of his life intentionally save in the execution of a sentence of a court following his conviction of a crime for which this penalty is provided by law.
(2) Deprivation of life shall not be regarded as inflicted in contravention of this Article when it results from the use of force which is no more than absolutely necessary:
   (a) in defence of any person from unlawful violence;
   (b) in order to effect a lawful arrest or to prevent the escape of a person lawfully detained;
   (c) in action lawfully taken for the purpose of quelling a riot or insurrection.

Article 2(2) is exhaustive and must be narrowly interpreted.[121] It is not confined to intentional killing, but includes deliberate use of force which has the unintended consequence of causing loss of life.[122] The term 'absolutely necessary' establishes a test which is arguably higher than the reasonable force standard applied in domestic law.[123] The Article also requires the state to take appropriate steps to safeguard life[124] which will include the proper planning and control of the actions in question.[125]

This obligation to protect the right to life also requires that there should be some form of effective official investigation when individuals have been killed as a result of the use of force by, inter alia, agents of the State. Any deprivation of life must be subjected to 'the most careful scrutiny'.[126] This includes inquiry into deaths that occur in custody—when a person dies whilst under the control of police or prison officers, the state is under an obligation to provide a plausible explanation as to the cause of death.[127] It may also include circumstances where the deceased should

---

[121] *Stewart v UK*, 7 EHRR 453, at para 13.
[122] *Stewart* (above) at paras 148–149.
[123] *McCann Savage and Farrell v UK*, 21 EHRR 97 at paras 154–155.
[124] *Association X v UK*, 14 DR 31.
[125] *McCann* (n 123 above) at para 150.
[126] *McCann*, (n 123 above), at paras 147–150.
[127] *Ribitsch v Austria* (1995) 21 EHRR 573 at para 34 and *Aksoy v Turkey* (1996) 23 EHRR 553 para 61. See also *Jordan v UK* 11 BHRC 1 at para 103.

have been protected by the State.[128] In many circumstances the inquest is likely to form a major part of the discharge of this obligation.

A death in hospital arising from negligence may in certain circumstances engage Article 2 although the European Court has held that matters such as errors of judgement or negligent co-ordination will not be sufficient of themselves.[129] Even where the Article is engaged, as the context and scope of the investigation is 'entirely different' from cases such as a death in custody[130] it might be that other steps taken by the State (eg entitlement to bring civil proceedings or an NHS investigation) will suffice to discharge the obligation.[131]

The scope of the inquest where Article 2 is engaged is considered at section 7.06. Article 2 in relation to the verdict is dealt with at section 9.30 *et seq.*

4.44   Article 6: The Right to a Fair Trial

Article 6 states (inter alia) that;

> (1) In the determination of his civil rights or obligations or of any criminal charge against him, everyone is entitled to a fair and public hearing within a reasonable time by an independent and impartial tribunal established by law.

Article 6(3) provides certain further minimum rights for those charged with a criminal offence.

The inquest is not a determination of civil rights or obligations, the findings of a coroner's court are not even admissible as evidence in the civil or criminal courts where rights are determined. Article 6 will not therefore generally apply to inquests. However, on the rare occasions that a coroner needs to take action for contempt or a failure to attend court etc, the provisions of Article 6 would be engaged.

4.45   Article 8: The Right to Private and Family Life

Article 8 provides that:

> (1) Everyone has the right to respect for his private and family life, his home and his correspondence.
> (2) There shall be no interference by a public authority with the exercise of this right except such as is in accordance with the law and is necessary in a democratic society in the interests of national security, public safety or the economic well-being of the country, for the prevention of disorder or crime, for the

---

[128] *Hurst v HM Coroner for Northern District of London* [2003] EWHC 1721 Admin. But see also *R (application of Southall Black Sisters) v HM Coroner for West Yorkshire* [2002] EWHC 1914 Admin.

[129] *Powell v UK,* 12 EHRR 355 at para 17.

[130] *Ibid.*

[131] *R v Secretary of State for Health ex p Khan* [2003] EWHC 1414.

protection of health or morals, or for the protection of the rights and freedoms of others.

The concept of private life is broadly defined. It includes not only personal information, but also an individual's relationships with others, including (in certain circumstances) business relationships. Experience of grief is an intimate part of private life, thus there must be particularly serious reasons before interference with this right could be justified under Article 8(2).[132]

Family life extends beyond the formal relationships created by marriage, and includes relationships between siblings;[133] uncle and nephew;[134] grandparents and grandchildren;[135] an unmarried couple in a stable relationship who are not living together;[136] an engaged couple;[137] children and foster parents or adopters.[138]

Correspondence includes both written communications and telephone calls.[139] It will also extend to electronic communication provided the person concerned can reasonably expect that his communications will be private.[140]

The impact of Article 8 on the coroner is difficult to discern. The list of persons entitled to participate in the inquest under rule 20 will almost certainly be considered as having been extended. However, issues such as the nature and detail of evidence at inquests have yet to be challenged under the Article.

Article 9: Freedom of Thought, Conscience, and Religion 4.46

Article 9 provides that:

(1) Everyone has the right to freedom of thought, conscience and religion; this right includes freedom to change his religion or belief and freedom, either alone or in community with others and in public or private, to manifest his religion or belief, in worship, teaching, practice and observance.

(2) Freedom to manifest one's religion or beliefs shall be subject only to such limitations as are prescribed by law and are necessary in a democratic society in the interests of public safety, for the protection of public order, health or morals, or for the protection of the rights and freedoms of others.

The private practice of a person's religion or beliefs is absolutely protected under Article 9. Further, s 13 of the HRA requires a court to have particular regard to the

---

[132] *Dudgeon v UK*, 4 EHRR 149, at para 52.
[133] *Moustaquim v Belgium*, 13 EHRR 802. Contrast this with rule 20 (section 7.09) which does not specifically accord brothers or sisters the right to examine witnesses at an inquest.
[134] *Boyle v UK*, 19 EHRR 179.
[135] *Marckx v Belgium*, 2 EHRR 330, at para 45.
[136] *Kroon v Netherlands*, 19 EHRR 263.
[137] *Wakefield v UK*, 66 DR 251.
[138] *Gaskin v UK*, 12 EHRR 36; *X v France*, 31 DR 241.
[139] *Klass v Germany*, 2 EHRR 214; *Malone v UK*, 7 EHRR 14.
[140] Although this might obviously apply to 'suicide notes' it is not common practice for these to be placed in the public domain at an inquest, see section 7.44.

Convention right of freedom of thought, conscience, and religion (of a religious organization or its members collectively) when determining a question arising under that Act.

The permissible grounds for limitation under Article 9(2) apply only to the freedom to 'manifest' (display) one's religion or belief. This term refers to public 'worship, teaching, practice and observance'.[141]

Article 9 may raise issues surrounding post-mortems and death rites of religious groups, or retention of the body etc. However, many of the coroner's powers in these regards might be said to be 'in the interests of public health'.

Summary

- The 'fail-safe' system of death registration in this country means that neither disposal nor registration can take place unless proper inquiries have been made.
- Approximately 87 per cent of cases reported to coroners do not result in an inquest, the decisions taken upon these being an administrative matter.
- If a reported death is shown, where necessary by post-mortem examination, to be of an identifiable natural cause (with no issues of neglect etc) then an inquest will not be held.
- If a death is violent, unnatural or remains of unknown cause after post-mortem examination, an inquest must be held.
- Where a person will be dealt with before the Crown Court for causing the death, the coroner must adjourn the inquest until the conclusion of such proceedings.

---

[141] *Arrowsmith v UK*, 19 DR 5. The applicant, a pacifist, had been convicted of incitement to disaffection for distributing leaflets urging soldiers to refuse to serve. There had been no interference with the applicant's right under Article 9 since the distribution of the leaflets did not constitute the practice of her belief.

5

THE CORONER'S POST-MORTEM

Also all wounds ought to be viewed, the length, breadth and deepness, and with what weapons and in what part of the body the wound or hurt is; and how many be culpable, and how many wounds there be, who gave the wound.
De Officio Coronatoris 1275[1]

---

[1] De Officio Coronatoris (4 Edward I) 1275–1276.

This chapter introduces the reader to the concept of the post-mortem examination[2] ordered by the coroner including:

- the power to order an autopsy;[3]
- the purpose of the examination;
- necessary liaison with families;
- a brief understanding of the techniques and specialties involved;
- special examinations.

5.01 Introduction

The post-mortem is an independent judicially authorized medical examination to ascertain the cause of death. In many cases it is the most significant part of the coroner's obligation to inquire into the death. Although the coroner's officer will have made inquiries at the scene to ascertain the circumstances, it is often only the pathologist who can advise whether the death is entirely natural and how, in medical terms, it has occurred.

Despite its importance, the logistics and methodology of the autopsy examination are frequently misunderstood. The legislation is complex, often confusing and occasionally contradictory. To simplify these issues it is necessary to look at the post-mortem process on a stage by stage basis from the time that a body is discovered.

The Power to Order an Examination

5.02 Possession and Removal of the Body

It is established law that there is no property in a corpse, ie it cannot belong to anyone. In 1996 the Court of Appeal held that the same applied to parts of a body removed for examination at autopsy and that relatives of the deceased had no

---

[2] The phrases 'post-mortem examination' and 'autopsy' are used interchangeably in this text.
[3] From the Greek *autopsia*—the act of seeing with one's own eyes (from *aut* meaning self and *opsis* meaning sight).

particular right to possession 'except perhaps for interment'.[4] Whether the same decision would now be made in the era of human rights legislation is yet undecided.

However, if a coroner needs to take possession of the body for a post-mortem examination there is a right to do so.[5] The coroner may also exercise physical control over the body until the inquest is concluded—although it would normally be released much earlier.

Section 22 of the Act gives the coroner power to order the removal of a body from where it lies to a mortuary, whether within the district or in an adjoining district of another coroner, for the purpose of a post-mortem examination.[6]

Necessity for Examination   5.03

Once a death has been referred to the coroner it must first be decided whether the cause of death can be established without an autopsy. There are many practical difficulties for the coroner in reaching this decision.[7] Apart from anything else, it is quite common for a doctor to be reporting a death to the coroner in circumstances where:

- the cause of death is clearly natural; *but*
- the precise cause of death can only be a matter of supposition to a greater or lesser degree.

There is not always a clear-cut decision apparent and a number of factors will be taken into account, such as age[8] and medical history.[9]

A recent study of more than 550 deaths[10] showed that by taking:

- the known medical history;

---

[4] *Dobson v N Tyneside Health Authority* [1996] 4 All ER 474: a brain had been removed at autopsy but subsequently lost prior to examination. The relatives were unable to pursue a compensation claim in relation to the death because of the loss of this evidence. The court held that the relatives had no right to sue over the error.

[5] *R v Bristol Coroner ex p Kerr* [1974] 2 All ER 719; see also section 4.23.

[6] Subject to the consent of the person providing the mortuary facility there. The restriction of movement to 'an adjoining district' is rather cumbersome, if read literally, in view of the modern trend towards centralization of specialist mortuary facilities. It might be better argued that 'adjoining' could be read in the sense of 'very near' or 'adjacent (near to)' which is the definition in several dictionaries. There is no case law on this point.

[7] See section 5.04 for discussion of the modern trend to reduce the number of post-mortem examinations.

[8] The contrary view is that it is 'ageist' to accord the elderly a less rigorous inquiry as to the cause of death than a younger person. The point could also be made that many of Dr Shipman's patients were quite elderly.

[9] The coroner will also need to take into account any relevant information available from the relatives of the deceased.

[10] Rutty et al, *J Clinical Pathol* (2001) 54, 279.

- information as to the circumstances of the death;
- an external examination of the body,

the cause of death could only be predicted accurately prior to post-mortem in 40–45 per cent of cases. A generalization as to the cause of death could be given in up to 75 per cent of cases. This also suggests that the Scottish 'view and grant' system, whereby a pathologist can issue a medical certificate as to cause of death upon a study of records and a visual examination of the body externally, is not as robust as commonly claimed.

However, on many occasions proper discussions between the reporting doctor and the coroner's officer will lead to a sensible cause of death being identified and certified, even if occasionally in comparatively vague terms such as 'old age'.[11] In the alternative, if a cause cannot be genuinely identified, a post-mortem examination will be necessary.

Where the cause of death is obvious but has arisen from trauma the coroner will almost inevitably order a post-mortem examination to gather evidence for the necessary inquest.[12]

Delegation of decision making by coroners to their officers is dealt with at section 1.32.

5.04   The Modern Trend—Questioning the Need?

Whilst there may be a variety of factors involved, statistics show a steady reduction in the number of autopsies over the last two decades:

- There were 117,700 post-mortem examinations ordered by coroners in 2002. This is a drop of 3,400 on the previous year, despite the number of reported deaths increasing by a small margin.
- In the longer term, since 1995 there has been an 8 per cent increase in the number of reported deaths but a 7 per cent reduction in the number of autopsies. Table 5.1 shows the growing gap in these figures since 1988.
- Post-mortem examinations were only ordered on 58 per cent of reported deaths[13] in 2001, the figure was as high as 88 per cent in the 1970s.

---

[11] See section 3.17 and also n 19 of this chapter.

[12] Approximately 95 per cent of inquest cases are subject to an autopsy but see section 5.04 on the continuing reduction in this figure.

[13] Home Office Statistical Bulletin 06/03. The situation is somewhat different in Scotland; in 1994 there were post-mortems carried out on 41 per cent of deaths reported to the Procurator Fiscal against then 67 per cent of deaths reported to coroners. But this reduced figure arises mainly from the 'view and grant' system which is not without critics—see section 5.03.

Table 5.1. Reported deaths and post-mortem examinations 1988–2001

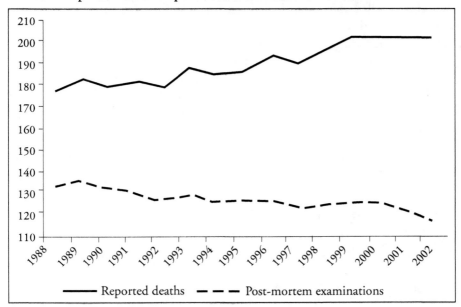

- Significantly, whilst a post-mortem will still be ordered in most inquest cases, the number of inquests where no autopsy took place tripled in the four year period to 2001.[14]

These figures probably reflect the genuine desire of most coroners to reduce the number of unnecessary post-mortem examinations.[15] Nonetheless, the number of autopsies is higher in England and Wales than in most comparable jurisdictions[16] and public dissatisfaction remains:

> No-one we have so far consulted objects to the coroner's power to order a post-mortem to help decide if there has been foul play or something significantly unto-ward about a death. There are however doubts and objections about what seems to some a routine and unfocussed resort to the post-mortem, especially where the likely result is to discover which natural disease or condition caused the death, rather than to help in the assessment of whether there has been foul play.[17]

---

[14] The figures involved are small but in the author's view significant, a leap from 400 to 1,200 cases out of 25,000 inquests. Home Office Statistical Bulletin 06/03.

[15] See also section 5.25 for discussion on the extent of the examination and section 5.26 on non-invasive examinations.

[16] In England and Wales 22.8 per cent of all deaths were subject to autopsy in 2001. The comparable figure for Scotland is 12.2 per cent, in Canada, Australia, and New Zealand it is about 10 per cent. Death Certification and Investigation in England, Wales and N Ireland: the Report of a Fundamental Review 2003 (the 'Coroner Review') at page 19. See also section 1.08.

[17] Coroner Review Consultative Document (2002) at para 55 (see section 1.08).

How far the blame for any 'routine and unfocussed resort to the post-mortem' should be levelled at coroners is perhaps arguable, for they remain caught in an unenviable position. Failure to order an examination in a case that later turns out to be suspicious will result in the most stringent criticism. At the other end of the scale, if a doctor refuses to issue a certificate despite being properly advised as to the law on death certification, there is little option but to order a post-mortem because the coroner has no equivalent to the Scottish 'view and grant' system.[18] At the same time, seeking to minimize autopsies by the use of less precise (but still realistic) causes of death such as 'old age' is subject to increasing caution.[19]

Professional guidance[20] now also requires a pathologist to inform the coroner if a preliminary study of the available information[21] suggests that an autopsy is unnecessary because:

- the death does not truly fall within the coroner's jurisdiction, or
- an examination will add nothing of significance to the coroner's inquiries.

The remainder of this chapter assumes that an examination must be ordered.

5.05 Section 19—Post-mortem Without Inquest

The coroner's power to order a post-mortem examination is most commonly exercised under s 19 of the Act (see Table 5.2 below) which authorizes an examination where:

- there is reasonable cause to suspect that the person has died a sudden death of unknown cause; *and*
- the coroner is of the opinion that an examination may prove an inquest unnecessary.

If the examination [...] 8 of the Act (effectively violent, unnatural, or still or [...] inquest is unnecessary[22] and a certificate will be sent to the registrar of deaths confirming this (as to which see section 4.20).

---

[18] Although this sy[...]
[19] See the Shipma[...] and 174, where it is suggested that 'old age' is an a[...]ve diagnosis, and is not merely put forward in the [...] shows. [...] t 80 was a more suitable starting age than the current 70. See section 3.17.
[20] Royal College of Pathologists, *Guidelines on Autopsy Practice* (2002) at para 3.9 *et seq.* www.rcpath.org.
[21] In some cases, particularly those involving a death in hospital, the pathologist may have more information available at the time of the examination than the coroner had at the time of the decision to order an autopsy.
[22] Although an apparently natural death can become unnatural through an intervening event or failure—see section 2.19.

Table 5.2. Section 19: Post-mortem examination without inquest

(1) Where a coroner is informed that the body of a person is lying within his district and there is reasonable cause to suspect that the person has died a sudden death of which the cause is unknown, the coroner may, if he is of opinion that a post-mortem examination may prove an inquest to be unnecessary :

    (a) direct any legally qualified medical practitioner whom, if an inquest were held, he would be entitled to summon as a medical witness under section 21 below; or

    (b) request any other legally qualified medical practitioner, to make a post-mortem examination of the body and to report the result of the examination to the coroner in writing.

(2) For the purposes of a post-mortem examination under this section, the coroner and any person directed or requested by him to make the examination shall have the like powers, authorities and immunities as if the examination were a post-mortem examination directed by the coroner at an inquest into the death of the deceased.

(3) Where a post-mortem examination is made under this section and the coroner is satisfied as a result of it that an inquest is unnecessary, he shall send to the registrar of deaths a certificate under his hand stating the cause of death as disclosed by the report of the person making the examination.

(4) Nothing in this section shall be construed as authorising the coroner to dispense with an inquest in any case where there is reasonable cause to suspect that the deceased:

    (a) has died a violent or an unnatural death; or

    (b) has died in prison or in such a place or in such circumstances as to require an inquest under any other Act.

Thus it may be argued that the power under s 19 is not so much to establish whether the death was due to natural causes but rather to ascertain whether an inquest might be unnecessary in a case that, prima facie, fell within s 8.

Rather strangely, the wording of s 19 (1)(a) gives the coroner authority to demand that the deceased's GP, or even the pre-registration house officer who cared for the deceased in hospital, perform a post-mortem examination. Plainly this is a nonsense and normally the coroner will rely upon the powers under s 19(1)(b) to instruct 'any other legally qualified medical practitioner',[23] ie the chosen pathologist.[24]

Section 19 does *not* include a power for the coroner to direct a special examination,[25] but the issue of histology in s 19 autopsies is dealt with further at section 5.31 below.

---

[23] A 'legally qualified medical practitioner' simply means a person appropriately registered with the General Medical Council, it does not mean a doctor who also has a qualification in law.

[24] See section 5.22 as to who should perform the examination.

[25] See sections 5.07 and 5.35 *et seq* below.

5.06 **Section 20—Post-mortem With Inquest**

Where it is already clear that an inquest will be required, (eg the death has arisen from an unnatural event) the coroner will use the power to order examinations contained in s 20 of the Act (see Table 5.3 below) to ascertain the precise cause of death and gather any evidence required for the inquest. Section 20 also allows a coroner to request any person (ie not necessarily a doctor) whom he considers to possess appropriate qualifications to make a special examination.[26]

Table 5.3. Section 20: Request to specially qualified person to make post-mortem and special examinations

(1) Without prejudice to the power of a coroner holding an inquest to direct a medical witness whom he may summon under section 21 below to make a post-mortem examination of the body of the deceased, the coroner may, at any time after he has decided to hold an inquest:
   (a) request any legally qualified medical practitioner to make a post-mortem examination of the body or a special examination of the body or both such examinations; or
   (b) request any person whom he considers to possess special qualifications for conducting a special examination of the body to make such an examination.

(2) If any person who has made a post-mortem or special examination in pursuance of such a request is summoned by the coroner as a witness, he may be asked to give evidence as to his opinion upon any matter arising out of the examination, and as to how, in his opinion, the deceased came by his death.

(3) Where a person states upon oath before the coroner that in his belief the death of the deceased was caused partly or entirely by the improper or negligent treatment of a medical practitioner or other person, that medical practitioner or other person:
   (a) shall not be allowed to perform or assist at any post-mortem or special examination made for the purposes of the inquest into the death; but
   (b) shall have the right, if he so desires, to be represented at any such post-mortem examination.

(4) In this section 'special examination', in relation to a body, means a special examination by way of analysis, test, or otherwise of such parts or contents of the body or such other substances or things as ought in the opinion of the coroner to be submitted to analyses, tests, or other examination with a view to ascertaining how the deceased came by his death.

In many situations the cause of death in inquest cases will appear obvious, eg an elderly lady hit by a bus whilst crossing the road, or a young boy impaled on railings after a fall from a tree. However, it is almost invariable practice for the coroner to order a post-mortem examination in such cases so that all circumstances relating to the body are properly explored and recorded. This may on occasion

---

[26] See section 5.07.

produce surprises. It might be found that the elderly lady hit whilst crossing the road was having a stroke.[27] Examination of the boy who fell from the tree might show some small damage to the underlying tissues of the neck where he was hit by an air gun pellet fired by his friend—not sufficient to cause death but certainly enough to explain the fall. Nonetheless, the number of inquests where no autopsy took place tripled in the four-year period to 2001.[28]

Section 20—Special Examinations 5.07

By s 20(1)(b) the coroner may, at any time after he has decided to hold an inquest, request a special examination of the body. This is defined as an analysis or test of such parts or contents of the body as the coroner thinks ought to be submitted to analysis, test or other examinations with a view to ascertaining how the deceased came by his death. The decision on this might commonly take into account advice from the pathologist conducting the post-mortem examination.

In practice the authority to conduct a special examination given by s 20(1)(b) allows such matters as toxicological examinations of the brain in by a neuropathologist, or the examination of lung tissue by a pathologist specializing in respiratory diseases. Whether microscopic examination by the pathologist undertaking the post-mortem examination would constitute a 'special examination' is presumably a question of scale, see section 5.31 below.

Special examinations are further considered at section 5.35 *et seq.* Issues arising from the retention of organs are dealt with under section 5.10 and 5.17 *et seq.*

Section 21—The Power to Summon Medical Witnesses 5.08

This section provides that the coroner may summon as a witness at an inquest:

- a doctor who attended the death or during the last illness; or
- a doctor in practice near the place where the death occurred.

The medical witness may be asked to give evidence as to how in his opinion the deceased came by his death. Further, the coroner may direct such a medical witness to make a post-mortem examination of the body of the deceased.

The author has some difficulty with this section which is said to have been taken, almost word for word, from the Coroners Act 1836.[29] In modern times, how is a doctor 'in practice nearby' going to be able to assist? Secondly, how does the power to direct a medical witness to make a post-mortem examination add anything to

---

[27] For example, a case where detailed medical examination eventually showed it likely that the deceased had had a heart attack and fallen off the kerb into the path of a car, rather than stepping out whilst attempting to cross the road as originally appeared.

[28] See n 14 above.

[29] Current Law Statutes Annotated 13-2.

s 20? Finally, what does any of s 21 add to s 11(2), which requires the coroner to examine on oath all who have knowledge of the facts of death—seemingly a clear power to summon any witness (medical or otherwise) who can give relevant evidence?

5.09   Power of a Jury under Section 21

Section 21(4) provides that if the inquest is held before a jury who feel that the cause of death has not been satisfactorily explained by the evidence, they may require the coroner to (a) summon another doctor named by them and (b) direct him to undertake a further post-mortem examination. If the coroner fails to comply with such a direction he would be liable on conviction on indictment[30] to two years imprisonment and/or a fine.

This power might have been practical in times when a jury inquest was literally held over the body. In virtually every case now the inquest will have been opened and the body released a long time before a jury inquest could be held. It might be argued that if the coroner releases the body for funeral and the jury later decide to exercise their powers under s 21(4) the coroner will be unable to comply and thus liable to imprisonment. However, *Jervis*[31] suggests that if the body has been released and cremated then there is no body upon which the jury may exercise their power. The reader may form the view that an anachronism such as this simply underlines the necessity for the current review of the law (see section 1.08).

5.10   Retention of Tissue—Rules 9 and 12

In many cases, the coroner's pathologist will need to take small samples of internal organs for histological examination (ie under a microscope). Very occasionally, whole organs have to be retained for examination or as evidence.[32]

Examination of these tissues will not usually be completed until after the body has been released and the funeral taken place. For example, proper examination of a brain requires that it be allowed to 'fix' in special fluids for at least two weeks so that it can be dissected without loss of form.

The power to retain these tissues arises from rule 9 of the Coroners Rules 1984, which requires the pathologist to make provision 'for the preservation of material which in his opinion[33] bears upon the cause of death for such period as the

---

[30] Meaning the case can only be dealt with at Crown Court.
[31] *Jervis on Coroners* (12th edition), para 6-21.
[32] See sections 5.31 and 5.36 for a more detailed discussion of histology.
[33] The Royal College of Pathologists guidelines for retention of tissues and organs at post-mortem make clear that a coroner's autopsy must not be used as a pretext to obtain tissue for research and that to do so without proper authorization contravenes the Human Tissue Act.

coroner thinks fit'. Rule 12 makes an identical requirement in respect of a special examination.

Whilst the phrase 'for such period as the coroner thinks fit' is not further defined, the coroner's powers in this regard[34] will generally cease once the cause of death has been ascertained or, where appropriate, the inquest has been concluded. Whilst it might properly be argued that retention is in order for a short time thereafter, in case of queries or judicial review, this would normally be only a matter of weeks.[35]

The coroner's powers to retain tissue arise only in connection with investigation of that particular death and there is no power to retain or use tissue for research or teaching, no matter how small the samples are, nor how vital the research may be to society. Donation of tissue for teaching or research is a matter for the next of kin—see section 5.17 below.

Any retention of material should be recorded on the post-mortem report.

Issues of liaison with the family in relation to tissue retention are dealt with at section 5.17 *et seq.*

Second Examinations—Request by the Family   5.11

The coroner's power to order a post-mortem examination is not exclusive. If the next of kin are dissatisfied with the result of the coroner's post-mortem there is no bar to them instructing another pathologist to carry out a further examination. Whilst the consent of the coroner is required, as the person in lawful possession[36] of the body, case law makes it clear that such permission should only be refused on good grounds.[37]

Alternatively, there is nothing to stop the family having a further examination carried out once the coroner has released the body to them. However, if some previously unobserved mark or damage were then found there could be allegations that the body has been interfered with after leaving the coroner's possession.

Such a request from the family is unusual and only likely to occur in situations where the pathologist chosen by the coroner forms the view that the death was natural whilst the family suspect foul play or some other unnatural event.

Section 5.15 below deals with the right of a family (or others) to be represented by a doctor at the coroner's autopsy.

---

[34] There may be a different argument as to when the coroner's overall powers to investigate the death cease (see section 2.25) but here the issue relates only to the *need* to retain tissues.

[35] But see also section 5.19. The situation would be different if the coroner or pathologist became aware that some civil litigation concerning the death was likely, retention for a rather longer period might be wise.

[36] See section 5.02.

[37] *R v HM Coroner for Greater London ex p Ridley* (1986) 1 All ER 34.

5.12   Second Examinations—Homicides

Rather more commonly, solicitors representing those accused of a murder or manslaughter wish to have their own chosen pathologist examine the body.[38] There is no statutory power for the coroner to order or permit such an examination but it is accepted practice that they do take place.[39]

It is a most distressing prospect for the family of the deceased if the body is to be further disturbed by those representing the person(s) accused of causing their loss in the first place. However, for the coroner to deny such an examination would now undoubtedly be regarded as a breach of the prospective defendant's rights. Thus it may have to be explained to the family that refusal by a coroner to allow such an examination could ultimately end in the acquittal of the person charged, not an outcome that they would wish to envisage.

Unfortunately second post-mortems can cause delay in release of the body. In a simple case, where a person is charged shortly after the death, it may be possible for a second examination to be arranged within approximately 14–21 days. Problems occur when the police have no suspect or one whom they cannot immediately charge.

A 'memorandum of good practice' agreed in 1999 by the Home Office[40] with representatives of other interested groups (eg ACPO and the Law Society) has gone some way to remedying at least part of this problem. Where no-one has been charged with a suspected homicide within 28 days of the death the coroner will commission a second autopsy by another pathologist. This will be available to any subsequent defendant and would normally be disclosed to the police. In the event that the first and second examinations differ in their conclusion, the coroner will order a third.

The memorandum deals with a range of issues, including problems arising from the existence of multiple defendants. Unfortunately, in seeking to avoid delay in circumstances where a person *has* been charged, the memorandum relies on the ideal that the initial forensic pathology report will be available to all parties within 14 days of the examination, a time limit which can rarely be met.

There is some confusion as to whether second autopsies should be allowed (or the memorandum followed) where the death arises from an allegation of death by dangerous driving. The author's view that this will not always be justified seems

---

[38] See section 4.32 *et seq* concerning suspicious deaths generally.

[39] *R v Bristol Coroner ex p Kerr* [1974] 1QB 652 and *R v HM Coroner for Greater London ex p Ridley* [1985] 1 WLR 1347. See also Home Office Circular 30/1999.

[40] Home Office Circular 30/1999; Memorandum of good practice re: early release of bodies in cases of suspicious death.

supported by the terms of the Home Office Circular accompanying the memo-randum.[41]

Testing for Other Purposes   **5.13**

On occasions coroners are asked by the police or relatives to arrange for DNA testing to be performed on the body.

The police interest might arise from a wish to determine whether the deceased had been involved in a serious crime. The Home Office view is that the police do not have authority to make such a request, nor does the coroner have power to under-take such a test other than for the statutory purposes of identification of cause of death. The police have accepted that they have no power to undertake the random removal of blood or other tissues with a view to speculative checks against the DNA database.

Very occasionally the police may seek the removal[42] of a hand or finger from a body that has already been identified to match a finger or palm print against one found at the scene—eg to place the victim as having been in the defendant's house or car. Again this is outside the coroner's authority and the Home Office have con-firmed in a circular letter to Chief Constables (18 June 2001) that the only way to proceed would be with the written consent of the next of kin, and even then only where essential.

Family members might seek DNA investigation for paternity testing. However, the taking of a sample of blood to ascertain the paternity of a child requires a direc-tion from the courts under Part III of the Family Law Reform Act 1969[43] and the Home Office have advised coroners not to agree to such requests in the absence of a court order.

Questions also arise about the propriety of testing bodies for serious communica-ble diseases[44] prior to an autopsy. Generally this should not be necessary, reason-able universal precautions should be used in any mortuary and thus there is no justification in testing to 'protect' staff under the pretence of seeking diagnostic information.

Appropriate tests may of course be necessary where it is thought that such an infection may be related to the cause of death, especially if no life-time diagnosis was made.[45]

---

[41] The memorandum itself only refers to 'some cases under s 1 and s 3(a) Road Traffic Act'.

[42] This arises when decomposition changes to the body make it necessary to deal with the tissues in a laboratory.

[43] Part III of the Family Law Reform Act 1969 as amended by s 89 of the Children Act 1989 and Schedule 16 (paragraph 3) of the Courts and Legal Services Act 1990.

[44] Most commonly HIV and the Hepatitis B or Hepatitis C virus.

[45] The question is sometimes asked whether it is permissible to avoid recording a serious communicable disease on the cause of death, whether at autopsy or otherwise. This would be a very

However, difficulties arise from time to time when either a healthcare worker or rescuer has come into some contact with the deceased that might put them at risk if there were an infection. Current guidance from the GMC[46] to doctors and, more specifically, to pathologists from the Royal College[47] makes it clear that testing may be undertaken in this situation if there is 'good reason' to suspect the existence of an infection. It is perhaps an arguable point whether such a test is being done on behalf of the coroner (who has no statutory power to order this) but in any event it seems clear that the pathologist has ethical and professional justification if a query is raised.

The coroner should ensure that next of kin who might have been at risk are informed of a positive diagnosis, whether the test was done in relation to the cause of death or because of injury.

Families and the Post-mortem Examination

5.14 Introduction

Society's attitudes to death and to care of the body after death have evolved significantly in recent years. Publication of the Redfern Report[48] in January 2001 proved a watershed in the recognition of the family's right to information about autopsies and tissue retention. At the same time the Chief Medical Officer issued advice on the removal and retention of human tissue.[49] In response the Health Secretary announced a number of measures, including the review of the coroner service (see section 1.08).

The issues were then variously considered and in April 2003 the Department of Health issued a Code of Practice[50] giving guidance for those communicating with families at the time of an autopsy.

---

dangerous practice legally, apart from any question of distorting important health statistics, as insurers may be misled into making a payment that they would otherwise refuse. To assist in this knowingly might amount to conspiracy to defraud. From the medical point of view, the *Guidelines on Autopsy Practice* (2002) from the Royal College of Pathologists (paragraph 6.9.4) make it clear that the public health information outweighs the private concerns of relatives.

[46] *Serious Communicable Diseases*: General Medical Council. Rather curiously the advice in this booklet (paragraph 11) is that 'you should *usually* seek the agreement of a relative before testing' without saying either what the criteria for this decision are or what is to happen if the relative refuses.

[47] Royal College of Pathologists, *Guidelines on Autopsy Practice* (2002) (at para 6.9)—www.rcpath.org.

[48] *Report of the Inquiry into the Royal Liverpool Children's Hospital NHS Trust*, sometimes known as the Alder Hey Report: www.rlcinquiry.org.uk.

[49] *The Removal, Retention and Use of Human Organs and tissue from Post-mortem examination, Advice from the Chief Medical Officer* (January 2001); Published by the Department of Health and available at www.doh.gov.uk/tissue. Responses and an update on progress are on the same site.

[50] *Families and post mortems; a Code of Practice*. Published by the Department of Health and available at: www.doh.gov/tissue/familiesandpostmortemscode.pdf.

This is a complex subject and is summarized below in sections relating to:

- information about autopsies given to families;
- dealing with objections to the post-mortem;
- information about tissue retention given to families;
- whether retained tissues will be returned;
- particular difficulties with potential criminal cases.

Information about the Autopsy to Families   5.15

The Coroners Rules (rule 7) only require that the coroner gives information about the time and place of the examination to any relative of the deceased 'who has given notice of their desire to attend or be represented'.[51] Even this may be dispensed with if it is impracticable to do so or it would cause undue delay.

Most families do not, of course, give any such notice to the coroner. Taking rule 7 at face value, this generally leaves the coroner with no specific duty to advise families even that a post-mortem examination is to take place. Understandably, this is no longer considered acceptable.

The Coroners' Model Charter[52] suggested by the Home Office indicates that when a post-mortem examination is considered necessary the immediate next of kin will be given:

- an explanation of why a post-mortem examination is necessary[53] and what is involved, if requested;
- a notice of the arrangements, so that they may be represented by a doctor if they wish;[54]
- a copy of the post-mortem report if requested.[55]

The Code of Practice[56] reinforces this and goes on to point out that the purpose of a post-mortem examination ordered by the coroner is only to identify the medical causes leading to death.[57] It should therefore be made clear to the family that the results may necessarily be limited in scope. If the family wish for fuller

---

[51] Rule 7(3) indicates that the right to be notified carries an entitlement to be represented by a doctor at the examination. Thus the reference to a relative 'who has given notice of their desire to attend' is not to be taken as meaning that the relative can actually demand to attend.

[52] See section 1.13.

[53] This gives the coroner an opportunity to take into account any previously unknown information which the family can provide that might avoid the need for an autopsy in the first place—see section 5.16.

[54] However the Charter also points out that notice may not always be possible because a post-mortem examination must be conducted as soon as possible after discovery of the death.

[55] The Code of Practice (see n 50 above) recommends that the family should be told before the examination as to when the results are likely to be available.

[56] See n 50 above.

[57] See sections 5.05 and 5.06.

information about the death than a coroner's post-mortem could provide, this might be agreed and the necessary consents recorded in advance.

The Code of Practice[58] also indicates that all NHS hospital trusts should have a designated individual available to provide support and information to families where an autopsy may be required, whether a coroner's case or not. This follows a specific recommendation in the Redfern Report[59] but unfortunately few Trusts have such personnel in place at the time of this text going to press. Many pathologists are willing to talk with families to discuss the autopsy findings after the examination, a practice that is to be commended, but it is scarcely practical to expect the pathologist to carry the load of providing support and information before the post-mortem.

The Home Office have recommended to coroners that a record should be kept of the steps taken to notify relevant persons about any proposed post-mortem examinations. It would seem logical that this be extended to provide an audit trail of all information that the family should be given, both about the autopsy and any tissue retention. However, this might prove difficult in some jurisdictions on present staffing levels.

See section 5.24 concerning notification of the post-mortem examination to those involved other than the family.

5.16 Objections to Post-mortem Examination

On occasions families raise strong objections to a post-mortem examination. This may arise on religious grounds or on the basis of distress at perceived violation of the body.

Coroners are likely to appreciate the distress of the relatives, particularly if a child is involved. Nonetheless, the decision must be made on objective grounds; if an autopsy is needed then the law requires that it is carried out.[60] It would also be grossly unfair to those bereaved who suffer in silence if special exemption were given to others simply because they complain or threaten judicial review.[61]

It might be argued that in exercising the powers under s 19 or s 20 against the wishes of family members, the coroner would need to be satisfied that the autopsy was a proportionate interference with their rights under Article 8 ECHR[62] and

---

[58] See n 50 above.

[59] *Report of the Inquiry into the Royal Liverpool Children's Hospital NHS Trust,* sometimes also known as the Alder Hey Report: www.rlcinquiry.org.uk.

[60] See *R v HM Coroner for Northumberland ex p Jacobs* (2000) 53 BMLR 21.

[61] There will also be isolated cases where an objection is based on a desire to prevent the true cause of death becoming known.

[62] Article 8 (right to respect for private and family life) of the European Convention on Human Rights, given effect in UK domestic law by the Human Rights Act 1998. See section 4.45.

was justified in order to protect public health or to investigate potential crime. It is generally recognized that ascertaining a proper cause of death is necessary for registration and public health purposes, for the reality is that if no doctor is prepared to sign a medical certificate as to cause of death there is no prospect of a funeral without an autopsy.

The author would submit that the proper course of action when such objections become apparent is:

- to establish the basis of the objection[63] and reconsider, in the light of any fresh information, whether the cause of death may be obtained by alternative means;[64]
- to ensure that the person objecting realizes the true nature of the coroner's responsibilities, that the decision to order an examination is necessary, has been carefully considered, and may even be to the ultimate benefit of the family;[65]
- if the objection continues, to agree to postpone the actual examination for a short period where possible (say 24 hours) to allow the objector to take legal advice.[66]

In the author's experience many relatives, if handled sensitively, given a proper explanation, and afforded the opportunity to ask questions, will appreciate the necessity for an examination, however unfortunate. Objections continuing to the point of judicial review are almost unknown.[67]

Information about Tissue Retention   5.17

There were considerable repercussions through 2001/02 following earlier tissue retention[68] at post-mortem examination without notification to families.

There is now clear advice to coroners that the process of any necessary tissue retention[69] must be transparent, ie that families must be told at the time of the examination:

- the reason for retention;

---

[63] Probably through the coroner's officer.
[64] Eg further inquiry of the deceased's doctors.
[65] Eg may reveal evidence of inherited disorders or provide vital evidence in a future civil action.
[66] This would normally be sufficient time to allow the objector to commence judicial review proceedings if he felt the coroner was acting unlawfully—obviously the examination would be further postponed if the coroner then received proper confirmation that an application was actually being made.
[67] *R v Greater Manchester Coroner ex p Worch* [1987] 3 All ER 661 in which the coroner's decision to order an examination was upheld.
[68] In this text the description 'tissue' is taken to mean organs, tissues, or body fluids etc of any kind.
[69] The power of the coroner to retain tissues is dealt with in section 5.10 above.

- the material to be retained, whether it be blood, small samples of tissue, or whole organs;
- the duration of the retention for tissues or organs that can be returned;
- that some material such as blocks and slides will be retained indefinitely as part of the medical record;
- the options for disposal of returnable tissues.

Whilst the coroner does not need the consent of the relatives for an autopsy or retention of tissues that bear upon the cause of death,[70] the examination also provides an opportunity for relatives to donate tissues for medical research or teaching purposes. These might be the same tissues required by the coroner, once the tests are finished, or different tissues altogether. The coroner's autopsy carries absolutely no right for the pathologist or coroner to permit use of tissues for teaching or research and such retention could only take place on the basis of informed consent from the next of kin.

Thus the Code of Practice[71] introduced in April 2003 indicates that whenever possible the family should be asked *before* a coroner's post-mortem takes place whether they might agree to the subsequent retention of tissue and organs and their use for certain specified medical purposes (eg research) once the cause of death has been established and the coroner's duties are complete.

To support implementation of this code, the Department of Health and the Welsh Assembly Government have produced model consent forms and information leaflets, for both coroners' and hospital autopsies. Whilst few coroners' jurisdictions will presently have staff available to seek consent to donation with the rigour anticipated, the Department of Health indicates that NHS Trusts may also wish to agree protocols with coroners locally.[72] This seems likely to tie in eventually with the provision of Bereavement Advisors by NHS Trusts recommended both by the Redfern Report[73] and the Chief Medical Officer as described in the Code of Practice.

5.18 Tissues Retained Indefinitely

In general, whole organs can be returned to the body or separately disposed of within a few weeks—see section 5.19 below. Nonetheless, the wax blocks (from

---

[70] Special examinations necessitating retention of tissue are also dealt with at sections 5.07, 5.10 and 5.35 *et seq.*

[71] See n 50 above.

[72] A view endorsed by the Home Office in a letter to coroners dated 1 May 2003. But some feel there are difficulties with the coroner's own staff asking about tissue donation for the NHS. It has been claimed that the independence of the coroner may appear to be compromised or (worse) that some relatives might feel the autopsy is only being ordered to obtain tissue donation. All of this underlines the need for careful handling of this issue.

[73] *Report of the Inquiry into the Royal Liverpool Children's Hospital NHS Trust*, sometimes also known as the Alder Hey Report: www.rlcinquiry.org.uk.

which slides are prepared for microscope examination) and the slides themselves will be retained long term.[74] These contain very small amounts of tissue embedded within them. There was some argument as to whether these should be retained as part of the deceased's medical record (like x-rays or scan results) or whether they should be made available for return.[75] However, the Code of Practice has now clarified the position:

> This code assumes . . . that . . . an integral part of most post-mortem examinations is the removal of tissue samples and indefinite retention of tissue blocks and slides for use in diagnosis, audit and review. This must be explained to the family. Specific consent must be obtained for organs or tissue to be used for research.

The Royal College of Pathologists recommends[76] that clear protocols should be agreed with the coroner about the retention of tissue. In any event, retention of material (permanent or otherwise) should be recorded on the post-mortem report.

Return of Tissues   5.19

Once retained tissues are no longer required for the coroner's purposes there are a number of options for disposal. This will usually only apply to whole organs, as tissue blocks and slides are likely to be retained indefinitely—see section 5.18 above.

The options for the family are:

- if the funeral has been delayed until the organ or tissues can be released, they may be placed with the body[77] before the burial/cremation;
- the tissues are returned[78] for the family to make separate funeral arrangements;
- the hospital are asked to dispose of the tissues;[79]

---

[74] The microscope glass slides are not a permanent record, the dyes can fade leaving the histological features hard to identify and the slides are fragile and can get broken. Retaining the tissue blocks from which further slides can be made gives a more permanent record, allowing the prospect of second opinions and further review if new investigative methods are developed. See section 5.36 for a description of the process involved.

[75] See *R v HM Coroner for Northumberland ex p Jacobs* (2000) 53 BMLR 21 where the court refused to order the return of 'microscopic pieces of tissue, processed and prepared for laboratory purposes' saying (inter alia) that the release of the deceased's remains had already taken place.

[76] Royal College of Pathologists, *Guidelines on Autopsy Practice* (2002): www.rcpath.org.uk.

[77] It is not possible to replace tissues and organs in their original precise location and the brain (especially if fixed) cannot usually be returned to the cranial cavity, so in a few cases an organ might need to be placed *with* the body rather than *within* it.

[78] Generally through an undertaker.

[79] The phrase 'respectful disposal' is often used but this has been criticized as a value judgement term that might mean different things to different people. Appropriate methods might include disposal separate from other clinical waste or marked by some form of non-denominational ceremonial process—the key point is that the family ought to be able to make an informed choice about their options.

- agreeing to donate the tissue for education, training, audit, or research.

If the intention is to cremate the remains, a new procedure allowing this has been introduced by the Cremation (Amendment) Regulations 2000, but it may be appropriate to advise the family that the cremation of small amounts of material may not result in any ashes remaining.

5.20 Criminal Cases

Different questions arise where tissues need to be retained in connection with the investigation of homicide, a situation which may cause families some distress.

In such cases, the retention of relevant tissues may be of extreme importance. Firstly, it will be necessary in order to ascertain the cause and circumstances of the death to a high degree of confidence. Secondly, in the interests of fairness to any prospective defendant, it is essential that experts instructed by the defence lawyers can conduct their own scientific examination of the tissues if they wish.

In some cases the question of returning or disposing of the tissues will still arise when these examinations are complete. However the Code of Practice issued under the Criminal Procedure and Investigation Act 1996 provides for the following minimum retention periods for material considered relevant to a prosecution:

- three years in respect of a conviction after a not guilty plea at a trial on indictment;
- if an appeal is lodged, until after the appeal is determined,

although many would now argue that longer periods are appropriate.

See also section 5.13 in relation to requests from the police to examine materials other than in relation to the cause of death.

Before the Post-mortem Examination

5.21 Necessity for a Full History

Although a pathologist[80] will usually visit the scene of a suspicious death, in the vast majority of cases the pathologist will see the body of the deceased for the first time as it lies in the mortuary. The pathologist is entirely reliant on information gathered by those who have attended the scene, usually the coroner's officer or the police, but should also be given access to hospital records in appropriate cases. In

---

[80] If the circumstances required a scene visit it would normally be a forensic pathologist who was instructed.

cases of trauma the issues may be particularly complex, needing a more detailed history.

It is also important that the family of the deceased be given reasonable opportunity to add any relevant information that might help the pathologist.[81]

A post-mortem examination performed with insufficient background inquiry can be unhelpful and misleading. Those providing the coroner (and thus the pathologist) with a history will need to ensure that the following matters are covered where known:

- details of the identification;[82]
- date and approximate time of death;
- the circumstances in which the deceased collapsed or, if more appropriate, when he was last seen and how he was found;
- any relevant occupational history, eg retired miner;
- any relevant past medical history (the word 'relevant' is important; minor operations or illnesses many years ago will be unlikely to interest the pathologist but a major event such as a heart attack, even some years before, will be of significance);
- recent hospital admissions with the name of the responsible clinician;
- known or suspected use of alcohol or recreational drugs;
- a list of medications currently prescribed to the deceased (which will provide a number of valuable pointers for the pathologist);
- details of the deceased's GP, including a contact number;
- where the death has occurred in hospital, especially if some procedure or treatment may be involved in the causation, the pathologist must be given full access to the medical notes together with a contact number for the relevant clinician;
- in peri-operative deaths, it is often useful if the clinician attends the post-mortem examination. Indeed, where the care of the deceased may be criticized, the hospital has a right to attend;[83]
- in cases where there are factors known about the deceased's lifestyle which suggest the body might pose a health risk, the fact of a known risk[84] should

---

[81] Which in some cases can even remove the need for an autopsy altogether, eg news of a previously unknown recent hospital admission where the discharge letter has not yet reached the GP or gone astray.

[82] See section 5.28.

[83] Rule 7(3), see section 5.24 below.

[84] Exactly what is communicated will differ according to who is involved. Undertakers might need to be informed only that there is a hazard of infection but the pathologist should have the fullest information.

be clearly communicated to those dealing with the body such as undertakers and mortuary technicians.[85]

5.22   Choosing the Pathologist

There are a number of factors to be considered by the coroner in choosing the pathologist. Some issues are not entirely straightforward, others may seem clear-cut but can lead to difficulties in practice. Further there is a considerable shortage of pathologists at present even in major centres, rural areas can present a very limited choice for the coroner.

5.22.1   *General principles*

Rule 6(1)(a) requires the coroner to instruct, whenever practicable, a pathologist with suitable qualifications and experience who has access to laboratory facilities.[86] However, the person undertaking a special examination under s 20 may often be a scientist without necessarily being medically qualified.

The choice of pathologist is a matter almost completely in the discretion of the coroner.[87] Rule 6 prohibits certain people from undertaking the autopsy and also requires the coroner to liaise with the Chief Officer of Police in cases of suspicious death, but beyond this the choice is unrestricted.

Wherever possible the coroner will wish to engage a specialist paediatric pathologist for baby and child deaths (see also section 5.22.4). In a suspicious death the coroner will almost inevitably instruct a forensic pathologist, ie an experienced pathologist specializing in criminal cases.

So far as routine cases are concerned, inevitably the coroner will get to know the local pathologists and will favour those who provide a sensible report without undue delay and are prepared to make themselves available when required at court. A competent manner in the witness box, with the ability to explain technicalities in terms that the family will understand, is also likely to win the coroner's approval.

However, if the coroner restricts himself to a chosen few he will, in the end, do a disservice. If the younger generation of pathologists are not given an opportunity

---

[85] Some have argued that this is a breach of patient confidentiality. The author would strongly suggest that this is a fundamental misunderstanding of the doctor's duty of confidentiality which must surely take account of protection of the living.

[86] Surprisingly, it has been suggested to the author that, in a few areas, coroners continue to instruct doctors without a formal qualification in pathology.

[87] A survey carried out in the summer of 1995 showed that 72 per cent of coroner's autopsies were then carried out by general histopathologists, 17 per cent by forensic pathologists (primarily in Greater London), 2 per cent each by paediatric and neuropathologists, and 7 per cent by other identified doctors including trainees and others working under supervision. *Coroner's Post-mortems in England & Wales; Report for the Department of Health*, June 1997.

to learn the nuances of the coroner's post-mortem, and how to give evidence at court, then they will never become the next generation of competent experts. Royal College of Pathologists guidelines[88] indicate that whilst all coronial autopsies should be performed by or under the supervision of histopathologists on the GMC specialist register, trainees[89] need to have some experience of performing coroner's post-mortem examinations. Whilst in no way binding upon coroners, this guidance puts senior pathologists under an obligation to involve their junior colleagues.

Rule 6—matters to be taken into account   **5.22.2**

Rule 6 sets out the matters to be taken into account by the coroner when deciding who should be requested to make the post-mortem examination. Rule 6(i)(a) states what is perhaps obvious in modern times, that the examination should be made by a pathologist with suitable qualifications and experience.

Rule 6(i)(b) requires the coroner to consult with the Chief Officer of Police as to the identity of the pathologist if the death is suspicious (ie someone may be charged with murder, manslaughter, or infanticide). The coroner is not obliged to follow the wishes of the police in this matter, although frequently will. It is virtually inevitable that the pathologist chosen would be from the Home Office list of accredited forensic pathologists.[90] Indeed the police are likely to have a contract with one or more of the pathologists on the Home Office register and will obviously hope that one of these will be used.

However, the main thrust of rule 6 lies in paragraph 6(i)(c) which directs the coroner not to instruct a pathologist on the staff of a hospital if the death has occurred there *and* the conduct of any member of the hospital staff is likely to be called into question. Whilst there is a saving clause concerning 'undue delay', in many areas there are sufficient alternative sources of pathology to render the provisions of rule 6 valid and meaningful. Rule 6(i)(c) is occasionally inconvenient but does provide an important measure of overt independence.

Which specialty?   **5.22.3**

The coroner will also have in mind that there are many sub-specialties within pathology and one pathologist may be much better equipped to deal with a particular death than another.

Most District General Hospital pathologists are likely to have a broad range of skills, although there may be particular expertise in locally prevalent industrial

---

[88] Royal College of Pathologists, *Guidelines on Autopsy Practice* (2002): www.rcpath.org.
[89] Generally those approaching the Part I examinations (ie after about three years training in the speciality). The coroner's consent would be required and the supervising pathologist is responsible for the conclusions drawn from the autopsy (para 4.2).
[90] Home Office Circular 9/93.

diseases such as pneumoconiosis. However, in a teaching hospital or a busy metropolitan area with specialist cardiac, neurosurgery, or infectious diseases units etc, individual pathologists will have become recognized for their expertise in very specific fields. The coroner may wish to take advantage of this, although it can occasionally work against rule 6(i)(c) (above)—whilst it may be easy to find another histopathologist locally, it is less likely that an alternative neuropathologist or paediatric specialist can be found promptly.

Recent guidelines[91] on autopsy practice recognize that pathologists need to acknowledge their own limitations of expertise and seek assistance from specialist colleagues in difficult and unusual cases. The guidelines further require pathologists to decline any autopsy for which they do not possess the necessary skills.

5.22.4 *Paediatric or forensic pathologist?*

In a case involving the suspicious death of an infant or child[92] it may be queried whether the expertise of a forensic pathologist (used to interpreting injuries) or a paediatric pathologist (an expert in the causes of childhood death) is best involved.[93]

Whilst a joint examination by the two specialists may appear an attractive option this is not universally acceptable to forensic pathologists, or indeed many paediatric pathologists. Criminal court work is a very particular specialty and difficulties might ensue for a prosecution if a witness has little experience of the rigours of the witness box in this setting.

Guidance to coroners in a Home Office Newsletter[94] following the Clothier Report into the deaths caused by Beverley Allitt at Grantham suggested that at the very least the opinion of a paediatric pathologist should be sought as assistance. Guidelines from the Royal College of Pathologists[95] suggest that where child abuse may be involved, or the death is suspicious, a pathologist with forensic training *and* experience in paediatric autopsies should perform the examination. Unfortunately this clear advice is somewhat compromised, as the guidelines then go on to say that ideally a forensic and paediatric pathologist should perform the autopsy together to provide a combined report.

---

[91] Royal College of Pathologists, *Guidelines on Autopsy Practice* (2002) at para 4.2: www.rcpath.org.

[92] The largest single group of homicides relates to children under the age of one: Criminal Statistics England and Wales 1999: www.official-documents.co.uk.

[93] In a survey carried out in the summer of 1995 it was found that 51 per cent of all child post-mortems were carried out by general histopathologists, 21 per cent each by forensic and paediatric pathologists, and 1 per cent by neuropathologists. *Coroner's Post-mortems in England and Wales; Report for the Department of Health* (June 1997).

[94] Home Office Newsletter No 22, December 1996.

[95] Royal College of Pathologists, *Guidelines on Autopsy Practice* (2002) at para 10.2: www.rcpath.org.

The Foundation for the Study of Infant Death has suggested a protocol for the multi-disciplinary investigation of such deaths that has been adopted in a number of coroners' jurisdictions after various local modifications.[96]

Suitable Premises 5.23

Although rule 11 contains restrictions and requirements for the premises in which the post-mortem takes place, they are of little value today. Rule 11(1) forbids a post-mortem examination to be made in a dwelling house or in licensed premises, a prohibition more rooted in history rather than in present day reality. By rules 11(2) and 11(4) the post-mortem examination must be made in adequately equipped premises, that is to say 'supplied with running water, proper heating and lighting facilities and containers for the storage and preservation of material'.

In effect, the only part of this rule of any relevance is 11(3) requiring that if a person has died in a hospital 'so equipped', any post-mortem examination shall be made in those premises but even this is *unless the coroner otherwise decides.* In many circumstances the coroner will feel it entirely appropriate for the post-mortem examination to take place at the hospital. However, if an independent pathologist is being instructed under the provisions of rule 6(1)(c) it may sometimes be necessary to move the body to the pathologist rather than the other way round.

It is also worthy of note that the discretion given to the coroner to use any 'adequately equipped' premises leaves a relatively free hand in the choice of a temporary mortuary in the event of a major disaster.[97]

Notification of Post-mortem 5.24

Section 5.15 above details current guidelines on notification of post-mortem examinations to families. However there are also obligations under rule 7 to give notice to the list of persons set out within rule 7(2).

By rule 7(3) the right to be notified of the post-mortem examination includes the right to have a doctor present but, with the exception of the police, does not include the presence of the person so notified. A person allowed to attend a post-mortem is prohibited (by rule 8) from interfering in any way with the performance of the examination.[98]

---

[96] The Foundation also produces a helpful 'Suggested approach for police and coroner's officers'. See www.sids.org.uk/fsid/pubsdownload.htm.

[97] For a detailed discussion on the requirements of a temporary mortuary see section 11.15 *et seq.*

[98] This subject is further considered in the context of suspicious deaths at section 4.36.

5.25 Considering Alternatives—The Limited Autopsy

In line with the more questioning approach to post-mortem examinations generally, there is now a body of opinion amongst both coroners and pathologists[99]
favouring a limited approach to the examination in some cases. For example, if a
grossly obvious cause of death is found on examination of the thoracic cavity (eg
ruptured aortic aneurysm) is there justification to continue and remove the brain
from the skull?

The Royal College of Pathologists Guidelines on Autopsy Practice[100] state:

> As best practice the College stands for as full examination as possible within the . . .
> coronial authorisation. Where an autopsy is considered necessary after proper inves-
> tigation of the circumstances of the death, that autopsy should be a high quality
> examination, which addresses all the questions that may be raised by the death.

Undoubtedly there are dangers in the pathologist stopping at the first apparent
abnormality, it might sometimes be easy to find *a* cause of death rather than showing what was clearly *the* cause of death. The question will always need to be asked
whether the approach under consideration provides the means to answer the
question(s) raised by the death, yet the author suspects that the limited autopsy
may become increasingly common practice over the next decade.

As a separate issue, it may be appropriate for the coroner and pathologist to agree
that the examination take a limited form where there is a known or suspected
Category 3 (eg tuberculosis) or Category 4 (eg Lassa fever) pathogen.

5.26 Considering Alternatives—The Non-invasive Autopsy

Recent improvements in technology and the increasing disinclination of the public to accept the necessity for a complete autopsy have led to greater thought on
the prospect of a 'non-invasive' or 'minimally invasive' examination.[101]

Whilst much of the discussion focuses on the prospects of magnetic resonance
imaging[102] (MRI scanning) there are also future possibilities for other techniques[103] including:

- percutaneous needle biopsies of specific organs;
- laparascopic (keyhole) investigations to sample organs or tissues;

---

[99] See para 7.6 of the Royal College of Pathologists *Guidelines* (n 95 above).
[100] See n 95 above, para 7.6.2.
[101] Bisset R et al, 'Post-mortem examinations using magnetic resonance imaging: four year
review of a working service', *BMJ* (2002) 324, 1423–4.
[102] A recent paper reports on the first study to assess the MRI in the investigation of sudden adult
death; Roberts et al, 'Accuracy of magnetic resonance imaging in determining cause of sudden death
in adults: comparison with conventional autopsy', *Histopathology* (2003) 42, 424–430.
[103] For a useful study of the various alternatives to a full autopsy see Benbow and Roberts, 'The
autopsy: complete or not complete?', *Histopathology* (2003) 42, 417–423.

- organ removal or examination through a limited incision.

Again, the question will always need to be asked whether the technique under consideration provides the means to answer the question(s) raised by the death.

MR Imaging is expensive under present arrangements and, even for the living, is not yet as universally available as might be desired.[104] Imaging is of value in the diagnosis of those diseases that show structural changes within the body and is particularly good in the central nervous system.[105] This may give a specific advantage on studies of brain tissue where conventional techniques require the brain to be fixed in formalin for a period before study. The current generation of research scanners (which might be in more general use in another five or so years) have a resolution which would allow individual coronary arteries to be studied but as yet even severe coronary artery atheroma is not generally detectable by MRI.[106]

Scans cannot show metabolic disease or poisons. MR Imaging is also unlikely to be of assistance in the study of post-operative deaths, multi-organ failure or intestinal infarction. However, imaging has proved successful in the case of foetal deaths[107] which looks promising (on the basis of as yet unpublished research work) for the study of neonatal deaths.

Although imaging may never replace the invasive autopsy for accuracy it seems possible, in the fullness of time, that MRI may be commonly used in non-suspicious deaths with an option to proceed to the invasive autopsy if a diagnosis cannot be made. In particular, the MRI may be targeted to situations where there are specific clinical questions that prevent certification of death, eg a suspicion of an intracranial event or a malignancy. Imaging also has the advantage of providing an instant audit record that can be used for a second opinion or even recalled years later for further interpretation. Conventional examinations on the other hand may be a somewhat subjective opinion, difficult to audit in a meaningful manner.

This will be a welcome development for many of the public at large but most particularly those communities who have religious and cultural objections to the complete autopsy. Much work remains to be done before this becomes a viable and practical alternative although there may be an increasingly strong wish in Government to see progress made.[108]

---

[104] Roberts et al correctly identify a very real question as to the public acceptability of MRI scanning at short notice to diagnose a cause of death when many living patients in the UK wait several months for diagnostic scans—see n 102 above.

[105] Especially with typical intracranial events such as haemorrhage, stroke, and tumour: Roberts et al—see n 102 above.

[106] Roberts et al; see n 102 above.

[107] Griffiths et al, 'Post-mortem Magnetic Resonance Imaging of the fetal and stillborn central nervous system', *American Journal of Neuro-radiology* (2003) 24, 22–27.

[108] The Department of Health has indicated that a scoping study of the available national and international literature and current practice on less-invasive approaches to post-mortem

There would certainly seem to be no *legal* bar to MRI scanning in place of the invasive autopsy when appropriate. Statute does not restrict the coroner to the traditional autopsy and indeed there is no specific definition of 'post-mortem examination' in the Act. Section 19 only requires a 'legally qualified medical practitioner' to make a post-mortem examination of the body and report the result. MRI scans are performed at the direction of, and interpreted by, radiologists who are inevitably legally qualified medical practitioners. The phrase 'post-mortem examination' means no more than an examination after death for the purpose of ascertaining cause.

Further, there would be ample justification for regarding a MRI scan as a special examination although the circumstances in which these can be undertaken are restricted by s 20.[109]

The Post-mortem Examination

5.27 Nature of the Examination

Under rule 5, any post-mortem examination is to be made as soon after the death as reasonably practicable. There is therefore a specific requirement for expediency.[110]

There is no statutory requirement as to the actual nature of the work undertaken in the examination. The nearest to legislative guidance is contained in rule 10(1) which requires the pathologist to report to the coroner in a form similar to that set out in Schedule II of the Rules. The schedule contains a detailed list of all the major organs of the body, which at the very least implies that these should be examined.

5.28 Identification

It is essential that the body is correctly identified to the pathologist. In many hospital cases this will be by a patient wristband. If such a marker is missing, the pathologist may need to call for someone from the ward to identify the body.

Identification of a body following a sudden death in the community requires great care. The police or coroner's officer should obtain a satisfactory identification at the scene or in the mortuary and the body should then be adequately marked with

---

examinations has been completed and that further research is planned: www.doh.gov.uk/cmo/progress/organretention/recomm17.htm.

[109] See section 5.07.

[110] Expediency is one thing—a post-mortem performed with insufficient information is another, for this can be unhelpful, misleading, and potentially disastrous. See section 5.21.

no possibility for confusion. This should be checked by the pathologist against the name given on the papers provided.

Proper identification can be a considerable nuisance but the chances of error are high, particularly considering the number of bodies passing through a busy mortuary in any one day. The system must be such as to ensure that each is correctly marked, for getting it wrong just once will result in anguish for the bereaved and merciless publicity.

Who should Eviscerate the Body?   5.29

The pathologist will be assisted in the post-mortem suite by one or more technicians. There is no formal qualification required for this post although it is becoming increasingly common for technicians to hold the Certificate or Diploma in Anatomical Pathology.[111] The Department of Health has announced that it intends to make mortuary technicians subject to statutory regulation by 2005 as part of the healthcare scientist workforce. The regulations will include standards of proficiency, conduct, performance, and ethics.

A competent and experienced technician can do much to assist the pathologist but this should be within defined limits. It is suggested that whilst it is perfectly proper for the technician to prepare the body for the post-mortem examination, this must take place in the presence of the pathologist. In the vast majority of routine cases such caution may not be necessary, but once a body is stripped it is too late to decide that the clothing may have provided vital evidence about particular aspects.

The pathologist may be prepared to allow an experienced technician to eviscerate the body organs (ie remove them in one or more blocks) for individual dissection and examination by the pathologist, although this should only be done under the *direct* supervision of the pathologist. The technician must have sufficient knowledge to know when to stop the evisceration if there is something unusual. However, even this is inappropriate within post-operative deaths, maternal deaths, traumatic deaths, asphyxial deaths, young adult deaths, and deaths likely to lead to litigation. In these cases the pathologist should carry out all of the work, except perhaps opening the cranial cavity.

The Royal College of Pathologists Guidelines set out clear advice on the work that should be delegated to technicians.[112]

---

[111] Royal Institute of Public Health and Hygiene.
[112] See n 95 above.

5.30 Process of the Examination

The pathologist will firstly carry out an external examination of the body (not forgetting the back). The height and weight of the body should be measured. An incision will then be made from the neck to the lower abdomen enabling the organs to be removed. These are then carefully dissected and examined. The weight of individual organs will be compared with the norm.

The cap of the skull will be removed to enable the brain to be taken from the cranial cavity and similarly examined. A technique is used allowing the scalp and hair to be pushed forward temporarily so that the appearance of the body is restored (at least facially) once the cap of the skull can be replaced.

In some instances (although comparatively few) it may be necessary for further dissection to take place. For example, the pathologist may investigate an operative site (perhaps in the leg) if it is thought this might have some bearing on the death. In other instances it may be appropriate to examine the veins within the leg to find the source of a pulmonary thrombo-embolism.[113] In some cases a detailed examination of the spinal cord may be required, the technique for removal of which requires a particular degree of expertise.

In most situations the vast majority of the tissues/organs removed for examination can be returned to the body immediately. In some instances it is necessary to retain all or part of an organ for a further, more detailed, examination. See also sections 5.07, 5.10, and 5.17.

5.31 Taking Histology and Toxicology Specimens

Histology. More commonly the pathologist will retain only small amounts of tissue which will then be processed and sectioned onto glass slides suitable for microscopy. Samples are commonly taken from the heart, lungs, liver, and kidneys and would usually consist of a 20 × 20 × 3 mm slice (about the size of a postage stamp). More detailed consideration of this process is given in section 5.36 below.

How far histology should actually be considered part of a standard autopsy (as opposed to being a special examination) can be a vexed question. Royal College of Pathologist guidelines[114] state that sampling of all major organs for histology is best practice in any autopsy, whether under s 19 or s 20, and it seems unarguable that if the pathologist limits investigation just to those tissues that *look* abnormal

---

[113] A clot of blood which commonly forms in the deep veins of the leg but then partially breaks away flowing through the vascular system until causing an occlusion, commonly in the pulmonary arteries, ie the rapidly narrowing branch of arteries within the lungs.

[114] See n 95 above.

on initial inspection then lesions elsewhere might be missed. But whether histology may properly be regarded as part of a s 19 autopsy (by the same pathologist undertaking the post-mortem examination) is presumably a question of scale. This difficulty is a further anachronism of the legislation that underlines the need for change.

Toxicology. Samples of blood and urine or other body fluids, for example stomach contents or vitreous humour (the fluid to be found in the eye), will be collected in appropriate cases and retained for examination by a toxicologist. Even the choice of a site for the sample to be taken can require expertise and experience on the part of the pathologist. There is also a good deal of sophisticated chemistry involved in the choice of preservative methods for the storage of body fluids pending such an examination.

In any appropriate case, blood samples should be obtained by the pathologist *before* evisceration.

Because of the complex and technical nature of toxicological investigations, the cost of these is comparatively high and the necessity must be carefully considered. However, whilst coroners might be entirely guided by a pathologist as to the necessity for histology or microbiology, they are likely to be more proactive in ordering toxicology, having a wider view of the circumstances surrounding the case than the pathologist.

Toxicology is considered further in section 5.35 *et seq* (special examinations).

Interpreting the Post-mortem   5.32

In most cases of traumatic or suspicious death the actual physical cause may be clear. A gunshot wound to the heart or massive head injuries caused in a road traffic accident will leave little doubt as to cause,[115] although exact interpretation of the manner in which the injuries were sustained may require further comment by a pathologist with special expertise.

However in many routine cases the situation is not quite so straightforward. Approximately 60 per cent of sudden or unexpected deaths arise from a problem within the cardiovascular system but only about one third of these will show an acute visible change. Thus in a large number of examinations (usually of the elderly) the death may be attributed to heart disease on the basis of minor changes and exclusion of other causes rather than a specific identifying factor.

For example, a pathologist examining a body with no specific and obvious cause of death finds that one of the three main coronary arteries has a degree of

---

[115] But there will be exceptions, see section 5.06 on what may still be revealed by post-mortem examination where there is an 'obvious' cause of death.

stenosis[116] in excess of 75 per cent. It may be said that the death was caused by ischaemic heart disease,[117] even though there are only chronic changes within the organ itself rather than anything marked such as evidence of a recent myocardial infarction.[118]

Such issues make it all the more important that those taking a history for the coroner identify apparent links of disease within a family.

5.33 Difficulties of Interpretation

Even in some cases with clear evidence of an acute abnormality, it may be difficult to ascertain whether the process was natural. Again this is an area where the pathologist's experience may be of greater value than pure academic knowledge.

For example, pathologists are quite commonly asked to examine decomposed bodies. The priority of the autopsy is to confirm that the cause of death was non-suspicious, ie that there are no injuries to the body which might have been caused by another. Hopefully the pathologist would be able to refine this further by distinguishing whether the cause of death appears to be natural or may have resulted from trauma accidentally suffered by the deceased (such as a fall or hypothermia).

If possible, the pathologist will then go on to be more precise about the exact natural cause of death. Despite decomposition, the major organs may still provide clues. Histology and toxicology may help, toxicology being done on any blood still obtainable, or urine remaining within the bladder or tissue samples from the liver.

In a few cases the pathologist will not be able to ascribe a cause of death. In some senses pathology remains a matter of medical judgement rather than a totally objective science. In such instances there is a crucial need for detailed information about the deceased's background and medical history, and for a close examination of the scene. Epilepsy, diabetes, asthma, and chronic alcohol abuse could all lead to a sudden death, leaving little for a pathologist to see.

In all of these cases a realistic approach is usually better than an academic stance requiring a high degree of certainty before the pathologist is prepared to give a cause.

5.34 Release of Bodies

It is clearly desirable that the body be released to the family as soon as possible after the conclusion of the examination. In the majority of cases this presents no

---

[116] Narrowing caused by fatty deposits within the arteries.

[117] Damage to the heart muscle caused by a poor blood supply over a long period.

[118] Thomas et al, 'Community study of the causes of "natural" sudden death', *BMJ* (1988) 297, 1543.

problem, particularly if the pathologist can provide the coroner with an indication of the cause of death on the same day as the examination. If an inquest is unnecessary the body can be released immediately, the coroner providing a Form B[119] and cremation certificate.[120] If an inquest is to be held, the body will be released once the inquest has been opened,[121] usually within 2–3 working days of the examination.

Where the death is suspicious and a criminal inquiry is in progress the inquest will not be opened, nor the body released, until the coroner is satisfied that it is not required for any further examination.[122] The agreed protocol for the release of bodies in potential homicide cases is dealt with at section 5.12 above.

Very occasionally, problems may be caused by the early release of a body, for example a toxicology result reveals a totally unexpected reason for suspicion but the inquest has already been opened and the body released. Other than delay every funeral until every result is known, there is little that can be done to prevent the occasional error; this simply underlines the need for vigilance and individual consideration of each case by both the coroner and pathologist.

Special Examinations

A special examination[123] is the study of material above and beyond the basic post-mortem examination. This may be performed by the pathologist or another with special expertise. Such examinations form an increasingly important part of the investigation into a death.

The power to order a special examination only arises under s 20, ie where the coroner has already decided to hold an inquest.[124]

A special examination should not be confused with a post-mortem examination requiring special skills (commonly a forensic autopsy in a suspicious death), as to which see section 1.25.

Toxicology   5.35

As laboratory methods become more sophisticated, it is increasingly common for toxicology (the study of body fluids and tissues for the detection of drugs) to provide definitive information as to the manner of death. In some cases this may go

---

[119] See section 4.20.
[120] See section 4.29.
[121] See section 7.16.
[122] See section 5.11 *et seq* on the subject of further examinations of the body.
[123] See section 5.07 for the definition contained within the Act.
[124] See section 5.06.

far beyond a simple indication of the cause of death (such as 'heroin overdose') by providing clues on the length of time between taking the drug and the death occurring. Information of this kind may be very useful in deciding the truthfulness of an account by a witness present at the time. Nonetheless, toxicology is expensive and it is inappropriate for public funds to be spent in such a manner unless there is some realistic purpose.[125]

The need will usually be apparent on the basis of the background information to the death:

- If the body is that of a young adult with no obvious cause of death, it will be appropriate to consider a drugs screen.[126] This may be strengthened by evidence found at the scene, such as syringes or burnt tin foil etc.[127]
- In a road traffic case it is usually appropriate to test for alcohol and other common drugs, both prescription and abuse.
- If a suspected suicide might be drugs related again there is an obvious need.
- If death has apparently occurred as a result of the inhalation of exhaust fumes, or as the consequence of a defective boiler/flue causing a build-up of carbon monoxide in a room, it is appropriate to measure carboxyhaemoglobin.
- Finally, in a fire death it would be essential to check blood for the products of combustion such as carbon monoxide and cyanide. At the very least these will indicate whether the victim was capable of inhaling (and thus alive) at the time of the fire.[128]

In general terms the toxicologist must be asked a question before being expected to provide an answer. That is to say, there must be at least some idea of what is to be looked for although it is possible to do a general screen for the more common drugs of abuse. It may be useful to supply a copy of the police report to the toxicologist, and, in difficult cases, the provisional post-mortem report.

---

[125] The author noted with interest the practice in Ontario (since January 2000) which is to 'bank' a blood sample in any medico-legal autopsy, even where toxicology is actually undertaken at the time. Dr Barry McLellan, Deputy Chief Coroner (Forensic Services) comments that this has the obvious advantage of providing for unanticipated questions in the future but also reduces costs by lifting the pressure to undertake toxicology 'now or never'. The practice is provided for in the protocol for autopsy which is enabled by legislation.

[126] A report by the Advisory Council on the Misuse of Drugs in June 2000 recommended that coroners should always order toxicological screening where there is reason to believe that drugs were implicated, including on all deceased aged 15–50 where the cause of death is not evident. (*Reducing drug related deaths*: www.drugs.gov.uk).

[127] Used for inhalation of various drugs but most commonly cocaine and heroin.

[128] The presence of soot particles deep in the lung may also confirm inhalation before death.

Histology   **5.36**

Histology is the examination of tissues under a microscope[129] to either:

- confirm a naked eye diagnosis such as bronchopneumonia[130] or liver cirrhosis;
- reveal conditions not visible to the eye such as myocarditis (an inflammation of the heart which can be caused by infection).

In general, histology samples are commonly taken from the heart, lungs, liver, and kidneys. This may bring a good deal of information to the pathologist beyond that learnt from the macroscopic (ie naked eye) examination. If injection sites are an issue, samples would be taken from those areas in an effort to age the site and to see if there had been previous injections in the same location. In suspicious deaths, particularly in children, histology may play a very important part in the ageing of injuries such as skin bruising and rib fractures.

Samples would commonly consist of a 20 × 20 × 3 mm slice (about the dimensions of a postage stamp) of the tissue or organs involved.[131] These are referred to as 'tissue blocks'. The samples are fixed in formalin and then processed in a laboratory to withdraw water and impregnate with wax, allowing very thin[132] sections to be cut for microscope slides. Special staining techniques are sometimes used to make specimens such as bacteria more visible in the sample.

For a further consideration of this subject see section 5.31. Issues of retained tissues in relation to families are dealt with at section 5.17 above.

Neurological Cases   **5.37**

Bleeding within the linings of the brain[133] or within the brain itself would normally be visible by naked eye examination at the time of the post-mortem. However, for the accurate interpretation of injuries (particularly those caused by shaking), or the effects of hypoxic brain damage, a specialist examination may be required. Brain tissues are comparatively soft and if a detailed examination is required it is essential to firm the whole brain by placing it in formalin for approximately a month. The brain can then be sectioned, usually by a neuropathologist, to provide a detailed interpretation.

Further issues of retained tissues in relation to families are dealt with at section 5.17 above.

---

[129] Usually at a magnification of 20–400 times.

[130] A 1995 study showed that only 69 per cent of the initial diagnoses of bronchopneumonia were confirmed when histology was undertaken: Hunt et al, *J Clin Pathol* (1995) 48, 120.

[131] See section 5.10 for discussion on the power to retain such samples.

[132] About 4 microns thick, no more than the width of a human hair.

[133] Subarachnoid or subdural haemorrhages.

5.38 Industrial Lung Diseases

In some coroners' jurisdictions industrial disease is by far the largest single verdict recorded. Although there are a vast number of recognized industrial diseases, the great majority arise from exposure to asbestos or coal dust. A detailed examination of the lungs will generally provide an accurate assessment of the degree of disease and its distribution.

The most common asbestos-related disease is a malignancy of the lung lining called mesothelioma, rather than asbestosis (scarring of the lungs themselves). Although the cancer or lung damage would be visible to the naked eye at post-mortem, further examination is required to establish the level of asbestos fibres contaminating the lungs and so establish whether the disease is likely to be due to industrial exposure. This fibre count is a specialist technique in which dried lung tissue is chemically digested and the remaining fibres assessed under a microscope. Further techniques will give some indication of whether the fibres are asbestos or of other origin. Surprisingly there are fibres (many of which will be asbestos) within the general population to such an extent that a normal city dweller might have 50,000[134] mineral fibres per gram of dried lung tissue.[135] Industrial exposure might be argued if the count showed in excess of 250,000 fibres per gram.

Pneumoconiosis is the disease in which nodules of dust (eg coal) are formed within the lungs. Although this is usually visible macroscopically[136] at post-mortem, an experienced opinion may be required to evaluate what part the disease has played in the death. Since 1994, fatalities arising from other diseases of the chest, such as chronic obstructive airways disease or emphysema, are also regarded as industrial disease if the deceased had worked underground in a coal mine for 20 years or more.

Industrial diseases are further considered in the context of verdicts at section 9.21.

5.39 Payment

The coroner's power in respect of post-mortems or special examinations (and so the ability to make payment) begins and ends with the question of 'how' the deceased came by his death. The coroner cannot authorize any examination

---

[134] This is only on examination by light microscopy; study by the more sensitive electron microscope might show up to five million fibres: see Corrin, B., *The Lungs* (Churchill Livingstone, 1990) (ISBN 0-443-03094-4).

[135] A normal pair of lungs is the equivalent of about 100 grams of dried tissue so it will be seen that the average city-dweller has a massive number of mineral fibres within the lungs.

[136] Meaning 'to the naked eye'.

beyond that point, whether as a matter of interest, research into an area of public importance, or otherwise.[137]

It must also be stressed that the only power to pay for a special examination is under s 20 of the Act, ie for examinations ordered by the coroner *where it has already been decided* to hold an inquest. But it is quite common for pathologists to take samples for histological examination in cases under s 19—a post-mortem ordered with a view to establishing whether an inquest is necessary.[138] After all, in some cases it is only by microscope examination of histological samples that the pathologist can decide whether the death was due to natural disease, thus allowing the coroner to dispose of the case without inquest.[139] In some instances it is perfectly satisfactory to suggest that such work should be included within the normal post-mortem fee. Yet whilst it is reasonable to expect that there should be some form of swings and roundabouts effect, for one case will be simple and another more difficult, this overlooks the fact that histological samples cost money in terms of laboratory time and effort.

There is no easy answer but in most jurisdictions the system continues to creak along on goodwill and co-operation between pathologist and coroner. This will not inevitably be the case in the future, particularly if hospital accountants seek payment for the materials and staff time involved in processing the tissues.

The situation is far easier for the more complex special examinations ordered under the provisions of s 20 when there is to be an inquest. There is no specific fee set out and it will be a matter between coroner and pathologist (or other person undertaking the special examination) as to what is fair and reasonable. As far as toxicology is concerned, many coroners will have an agreed scale of charges with the hospital or laboratory undertaking this work for them.

The Post-mortem Report

By rule 10(1) the person making the post-mortem examination must report to the coroner either in the format set out within Schedule II of the Rules or in a form to the like effect. Discussion of the medical content of the post-mortem report is outside the remit of this work. However, it is appropriate to comment on several issues.

---

[137] Neither the Coroners Act 1988, the Anatomy Act 1984 nor the Human Tissue Act 1961 permit such research without the permission of the next of kin—see section 5.10 above. See also the Isaacs Report, May 2003: www.doh.gov.uk.

[138] There is sometimes confusion on this point. In the author's view taking a limited amount of histology does *not* amount to a special examination (under s 20) and does *not* require an inquest to be opened—see section 5.31 above.

[139] See section 5.05 above.

5.40 Need for Accuracy

Whilst it may be stating the obvious, accuracy of the report, even on minor detail, is vital. It is increasingly common that relatives of the deceased request a copy of the report from the coroner[140] and some will not hesitate to query or complain about incorrect details such as age or height, etc that the pathologist may regard as minor or typographical errors. In extreme cases this can lead to allegations that the body has been wrongly identified.[141]

5.41 Clinical History

The report should contain a clinical history to make clear the context of the examination, ie a brief synopsis of how any injuries are understood to have been sustained, or the course of the last illness and/or the deceased's treatment in hospital. However, there is some variance as to the level of detail that may be thought appropriate.

The author would suggest that a *short* outline is very useful—particularly in cases involving trauma (eg a road death). The evidence given at the inquest often finishes at the point of the victim being removed to hospital and then resumes with the post-mortem examination which may be a week or more later. Some brief details of what has happened in the meantime will complete the picture.

Whilst individual cases may vary, the pathologist must be cautious about giving too many particulars, otherwise the report will take on the appearance of detailed evidence about the clinical treatment—matters of which the pathologist has no direct knowledge at all.

Some pathologists have adopted the practice of repeating, word for word, the entire history given to them (usually from the police report to the coroner). In the author's view this is quite unnecessary and can lead to problems when any of these details are disputed by the family.[142]

5.42 The Summary and Conclusion

A brief, well-written, summary is often of considerable use to the coroner. In many cases[143] it is unnecessary to call the pathologist to give oral evidence at court

---

[140] Rule 57, see section 5.44.

[141] See section 5.28 for further comment on the routine identification of bodies.

[142] In the author's experience some families do not appreciate that the pathologist is simply referring to details put forward by others and it is not unknown for strong objection to be taken to the report on the basis of some repeated detail that the pathologist would have probably regarded as irrelevant—see also section 7.42 on the admissibility of written evidence at the inquest.

[143] For example, with many traumatic deaths the medical evidence will only need to establish that (say) the victim died of multiple injuries; indeed the relatives are unlikely to thank the coroner for giving a detailed recital of each injury. Obviously there will be occasions where it is appropriate

and a straightforward summary can be read out as the evidence under the provisions of rule 37.[144] On the other hand, a report without a summary—or a summary written in incomprehensible medical terminology—presents the court with a difficulty. Although the legally qualified coroner will have gained some medical knowledge and could often explain the conclusion in simple terms for those in court, this brings (unqualified) interpretation into the report. It is preferable for the pathologist to phrase the summary in such a way that everyone in court, most particularly the relatives of the deceased, can understand the medical cause of death.[145]

The author has heard it suggested that a separate report, written in non-technical language, might be prepared for the family in cases where the deceased was a baby or child. On the face of it this may be admirable but great care would have to be taken to ensure that this 'lay report' accurately reflected the fuller, technical document. It is easy to envisage a situation where allegations of a cover-up could arise if there were any room for claims of discrepancies between the two reports. It may be more helpful to encourage the family to talk through the pathologist's full report with their GP, who could explain the medical terminology and assist with any queries.

The report should make specific mention of any tissues that were retained at the autopsy—see sections 5.10 and 5.17 above.

Delay in Submitting the Report   5.43

Exactly how long the pathologist takes to produce the written report will depend upon the circumstances. If there is no histology or other special examination to be undertaken, it may be that the pathologist can dictate the report immediately after the examination and let the coroner have the completed document a day or so thereafter. On the other hand, if the brain is to be subject to a special examination there may be a delay of approximately a month before that work can be completed.[146] However, it is only in the most exceptional cases that there should be delay beyond this point and there seems little justification for the delays of three or four months that are known to occur from time to time.

Delay can bring very considerable inconvenience, distress, and even suspicion to the bereaved for a number of reasons:

- if the coroner is waiting to set the case down for inquest, little progress can be made until the report is at hand;

---

to go into rather more detail, perhaps the direction from which the injury was sustained, but these cases are relatively few.

[144] See section 7.42.

[145] See section 5.45 *et seq* for further mention of the pathologist's evidence at court.

[146] See section 5.37.

- in many cases (even non-inquest deaths) insurers demand sight of the report from the coroner before making payment to the family;
- even in straightforward cases the deceased's family may want to consult their GP for an explanation of the cause of death.

Guidelines from the Royal College of Pathologists[147] suggest that:

- a provisional report (to include at least: a preliminary cause of death where possible, a summary of the major findings, details of retained tissues and a note of further investigations necessary) should be sent out within five working days of the examination;
- where there are no complex investigations the complete report should be sent out within one week of the examination;
- results of further investigations (eg histological findings, results of toxicology or microbiology) with a commentary or conclusions and the stated cause of death should be sent within one week of availability of those findings.[148]

One significant criticism levelled in the Redfern Report[149] was the lack of any system within the coroner's office to chase up final autopsy reports or realize that histology reports remained outstanding when a preliminary report had been sent. Perhaps the answer to this is as simple as not allowing case files to be archived until all reports are accounted for and making a check on unarchived files every month or so.

5.44 Release of the Report

By rule 57(1) (which is considered more fully at section 6.14) the coroner must, on payment of the appropriate fee, supply to any person who in his opinion is a properly interested person[150] a copy of any report of the post-mortem examination or special examination. It is not made clear whether this entitlement arises at the time the report is received by the coroner (ie before any inquest) or only after proceedings are completed. The exceptions to disclosure would be cases of suspicious death or where release of information may hinder an ongoing police inquiry.

By rule 10(2), unless authorized by the coroner, the pathologist must not supply a copy of the report to any person other than the coroner. Rule 13 makes similar provision in respect of special examinations. These are blanket prohibitions against disclosure and apply in all circumstances. Thus, in theory at least, a

---

[147] See n 95 above, at para 8.6.
[148] Home Office (ie forensic) and peri-natal cases fall outside these guidelines, although with the latter it is expected that the report will be available to discuss with the parents within six weeks.
[149] *Report of the Inquiry into the Royal Liverpool Children's Hospital NHS Trust*, sometimes also known as the Alder Hey Report: www.rlcinquiry.org.uk.
[150] As defined within rule 20—see section 7.09.

forensic pathologist submitting a post-mortem report in a case where someone has been charged with murder must send the report to the coroner rather than to the investigating police officers. A pathologist reporting on a coroner's post-mortem in a hospital may not give the clinicians involved in the case a copy of the report unless and until the coroner agrees.

In the past there has been a division of opinion between coroners as to whether post-mortem reports should be made freely available or not. Most coroners now take a pragmatic view on this matter; indeed a survey for the Department of Health conducted in the summer of 1995 did not support the perception that coroners were unwilling to provide copies of reports. Instead the evidence implied that the reports did not always get to those who needed them and suggested that one solution was to improve internal hospital communications.[151]

Thus it would now be common for the forensic pathologist to send a copy of the report directly to the investigating officer, either at the same time or shortly after supplying the coroner with a copy. A hospital pathologist may be instructed to ensure that the clinicians receive a copy of the report in all deaths occurring within the hospital.

Indeed, Home Office Circular 62/1994 issued following the Clothier Report (into the deaths of children at Grantham Hospital at the hands of Beverley Allitt) recommended that:

> . . . in every case coroners should send copies of post-mortem reports to any consultant who has been involved in the patient's care prior to death, whether or not demanded under rule 57

and the Home Secretary asked that coroners review their procedures to ensure that access to reports was facilitated and dealt with as speedily as possible.

The deceased's GP will also wish to have sight of the report, although in a busy jurisdiction it is more difficult to arrange for the automatic distribution of reports to GPs.

There is provision under the Coroners' Records (Fees for Copies) Rules 2002 for a charge to be made for the supply of such documents,[152] although there is some argument as to whether the wording of the Fees Order only permits a charge to be made where an inquest was held.

The family of the deceased may not realize that they are entitled to a copy of the post-mortem report[153] unless they are told (which should be prior to the

---

[151] *Coroner's Post-mortems in England & Wales; Report for the Department of Health,* June 1997.

[152] The current fee is £1.10 per sheet, ie about £3.30 for an average report: Coroners' Records (Fees for Copies) Rules 2002. However, a costing exercise in 1998 suggested that the then overall cost of sending out a copy post-mortem report was in the order of £16.

[153] Rule 57, which is further discussed at section 10.09 *et seq.*

autopsy—see section 5.15). In the author's jurisdiction families attending to pick up the Form B for the registrar[154] are given a note reiterating their entitlement. This results in a surprisingly high take-up rate. The report, when available, is sent to the next of kin but is contained within another envelope. This has a label stating that the family can either open the envelope and read the report for themselves or, should they wish to avoid any distress, can take the envelope to their GP who may go through the document for them.

The Coroners' Model Charter produced by the Home Office (see section 5.15) also suggests that a copy of the report should be made available to the family.

In releasing a post-mortem report prior to an inquest, it may be appropriate for the coroner to make it clear that the report is on a preliminary basis. The pathologist may wish to alter the conclusions having heard the results of other inquiries or medical investigations and the evidence given at the inquest hearing.[155]

The Pathologist's Evidence at Court

5.45 Documentary Evidence

Very often the pathologist's evidence at the inquest is taken by way of a written report under rule 37.[156] For example, there is little point in calling a pathologist in the average road traffic death simply to state that death was due to multiple injuries—this information could be dealt with adequately by the coroner reading out a short summary contained at the end of the post-mortem report.[157] This underlines the usefulness of a well-written conclusion and summary to the post-mortem report.

However, the rest of this section assumes that the pathologist is required to give oral evidence at court.

5.46 Preparation for Court

The pathologist will wish to prepare fully for the court appearance and much of the advice given at section 6.31 *et seq* might apply.

Obviously the pathologist will make sure to take all the proper documentation, including original notes and any learned articles or even textbooks that may need to be quoted. Some element of familiarization with the papers is necessary, as is a

---

[154] See section 4.20.
[155] See below in relation to the pathologist at the inquest hearing.
[156] See section 7.42.
[157] Contrast this with circumstances where it is unclear whether the deceased might have crashed his car because he was having a heart attack, in which case it would be essential to call the pathologist to give evidence in person.

degree of forethought as to how complex matters can be explained in simple language.

Giving Evidence 5.47

All of the advice contained within section 7.41 applies equally to a pathologist giving evidence. However, because of the nature of the pathologist's task there are additional factors to be considered.

The pathologist is presenting specialist evidence, often of a most complex nature. This evidence is central to the inquest, particularly so in peri-operative or questionable deaths. There may be a temptation for the pathologist to give evidence in terms that the coroner will understand, but forgetting that there are others in court who will not. The pathologist's evidence is in many ways a complete waste of time if the family of the deceased leave court without having understood a word.

The pathologist must therefore be able to give concise and medically accurate answers, yet present the evidence in such a way that the layman finds easily understandable. This is a particular skill which requires a great deal of forethought and practice.

Change of Opinion 5.48

The pathologist will normally give an opinion as to the cause of death when submitting the report. Occasionally, there may be a need to refine the preliminary opinion given in the report, having had the benefit of hearing factual evidence of the circumstances from the other witnesses.

This situation can arise where the police report, given to the pathologist at the time of the examination, has completely missed a point that the witness now considers important. Sometimes even the most thoroughly prepared history will be no substitute for a pathologist actually sitting and hearing the explanations of fact given by the other witnesses.

Providing that proper explanation is made, there is usually no great difficulty with the occasional change of opinion. However, this leads to the problem of when the pathologist should give evidence in the chronological order of the inquest.

When Should the Pathologist Give Evidence? 5.49

It is often tempting for the coroner to call the pathologist as the first witness. In this way, those in court quickly learn the medical cause of death, the issues for the inquest may be considerably narrowed, and the minimum amount of the pathologist's time has been expended. On the other hand, this deprives the pathologist of an opportunity to hear what the other witnesses have said. If the pathologist is called last, there is the benefit of having heard the other witnesses, but the inquest may have had to endure many irrelevancies along the way.

It is of course possible that the pathologist is called as the first witness to give initial evidence but then is recalled at the end to establish whether there is anything to add in view of the factual evidence. The same effect may perhaps be achieved if the coroner takes the view that any person requesting sight of the post-mortem report prior to the inquest is given a copy.[158]

Summary

- The coroner has almost complete discretion in the choice of pathologist and place of post-mortem but must consider a number of issues.
- Liaison with the family is now an important part of preparation for the examination.
- Full disclosure of tissue retention (taken for the purpose of ascertaining the cause of death) must be made to the family at the time of the examination.
- Consent is needed for the use of tissue for education, training, or research.
- The pathologist must be given a detailed history if the autopsy is to have a full value.
- Thorough preparation before a court attendance is as important for the pathologist as for any other witness.

---

[158] See section 5.44.

6

PREPARING FOR THE INQUEST

Their duty is to investigate deaths, fully, fairly and fearlessly, not on behalf of relatives but on behalf of society at large. Coroners must make their way through a maze of conflicting interests and disputed facts, acting fairly and openly and seeking to arrive at the objective truth of the cause and circumstances of the death.[1]

The importance of thorough preparation before an inquest cannot be overemphasized. This chapter deals with various aspects of making ready for the proceedings:

---

[1] Lord Bassam of Brighton, Parliamentary Under Secretary of State at the Home Office during a debate in the House of Lords on 24 January 2001 (Hansard).

- issues of preparation affecting the coroner and officers;
- advising those involved of the hearing;
- securing the attendance of witnesses;
- the release of documentation by the coroner;
- preparing a written report for the court;
- advising the client before the inquest;
- how a witness should prepare for the hearing.

6.01 Introduction

Unfamiliarity with the inquest process may leave those called to attend court uncertain as to what may happen and how best to prepare. Yet the witness or advocate who has given little consideration to the hearing is likely to feel and appear conspicuous for all the wrong reasons. Opportunities to help the court's inquiry, and even the chance to put forward a reasonable explanation for a particular point, may be lost due to lack of preparation.

Further, inquests are often conducted under a media spotlight with consequent opportunity for adverse publicity in a poorly prepared case.

This chapter has special relevance for medical witnesses. Doctors are much more likely to be called to an inquest than any other professional group. They will usually have to prepare their own evidence for the court, whereas other witnesses will have a statement taken by the coroner's investigating officer. Doctors are often required to deal with complex issues in their evidence and may be questioned closely by the coroner or those representing families. Time spent in preparation by the prospective medical witness will rarely be wasted.

The Coroner's Preparation

6.02 The Coroner's Responsibility

The coroner is the sole arbiter as to which evidence will be heard at the inquest which carries a responsibility of ensuring that a fair and balanced account of the death is presented at the hearing. This means that the circumstances must be properly investigated by those acting on the coroner's behalf, and that the relevant witnesses must be called to give evidence to the court and be questioned by properly interested persons.[2]

This responsibility was outlined in the leading case of Jamieson:[3]

---

[2] A properly interested person is defined by rule 20—see section 7.09.
[3] *R v HM Coroner for North Humberside ex p Jamieson* [1995] QB1 and (1994) 3 All ER 972; see also section 9.25 and Appendix 2.

It is the duty of the coroner, as the public official responsible for the conduct of inquests . . . to ensure that the relevant facts are fully, fairly and fearlessly investigated . . . he fails in his duty if his investigation is superficial, slipshod or perfunctory.

The Investigation   6.03

The coroner must become fully conversant with the results of the inquiry into the death. This may involve consultation with, and directions to, the investigating officer during the inquiry. The coroner will examine the papers once they have been submitted, but cannot rely unquestioningly on these and may well decide that further inquiries are appropriate. It may be necessary to instruct an independent expert witness to assist the court on technical issues.

Once all the necessary information is to hand the coroner will decide which witnesses are to be called. Issues of disclosure (see section 6.14 *et seq*) will be considered and instructions given for the witnesses to be warned to attend court. Relatives of the deceased, and any other properly interested persons[4] must also be given sufficient notice.

Choosing the Witnesses   6.04

Deciding which witnesses to call can sometimes be more of an art than a science and is a matter of personal judgement for the coroner, based upon experience. The coroner will be seeking to ensure that a balanced and representative picture of the evidence is available in court, but at the same time will want to keep the evidence as straightforward and easily understood as possible.

The coroner must not discount potential witnesses on the basis of an investigating officer's opinion that they would be unreliable:

> It is the coroner's obligation under the Rules to examine those who may be able to give relevant evidence and he must form his own view as to their credibility and the reliability of their evidence. He may not decline to hear witnesses simply on the basis of a police officer's assessment of their reliability. That would be to abdicate his own responsibility to conduct a proper investigation into the matters referred to in rule 36.[5]

If a number of witnesses are likely to give essentially the same version of a factual event, it might be sufficient to call only one or two of them and take the remainder as documentary evidence under rule 37.[6] If there are two people with different versions of the same incident it is usually appropriate to call them both rather than choose one over the other. Evidence that is unlikely to be challenged in court, perhaps on background information, can be taken as documentary evidence. On the

---

[4] See section 7.09.
[5] *R v Avon Coroner ex p Bentley* (2002) 166 JP 297.
[6] Under rule 37, see section 7.42.

other hand, the coroner is often provided with statements which, once the inquiries are complete, turn out to have no relevance at all, and these will be put aside.

6.05 Plans and Photographs

In some instances photographs of the body at the place of death provide graphic evidence of how the death came about. On other occasions, photographs of the scene, even after the body has been removed, can provide answers to important questions. Plans of an area may also be valuable. The coroner will need to review any such evidence, deciding what is appropriate for the inquest and whether further plans or photographs are needed.

Photographs can raise a number of difficulties at an inquest. Although photographs showing a body *in situ* are comparatively rare, pictures of a scene (perhaps including damaged vehicles) are common. Whilst it might be obvious that a picture of the deceased hanging from a tree will cause upset to relatives, it may not be appreciated that a picture of a damaged car can be nearly as traumatic.

The coroner will need to consider how such complications might be avoided. Where photographs are used it will usually be appropriate to offer sight of the album to the family or others involved, although they will rarely wish to take up the opportunity. Obviously this must be handled with great sensitivity and it is better if there is a chance to view the photographs in private, perhaps some time before the hearing.

6.06 Viewing the Scene

The coroner will rarely need to visit the scene of a death in preparation for an inquest. Photographs and plans are usually quite sufficient to depict the area at the time of the death. Important aspects of the scene may have been altered or removed since the incident, making a visit inappropriate. The geographical features of an area (eg the view at a particular road junction) may already be well known to the coroner.

However, in some circumstances, visiting the location can be of great assistance, and the coroner will have to consider whether it is appropriate to do this before the inquest or whether a formal view should be part of the proceedings.

6.07 Pre-inquest Review

It has become more common in recent years for coroners to hold a pre-inquest review in complex cases. There is no set procedure or even statutory authority for this, but it is plainly good case management that some issues are resolved prior to a date being set for the full inquest.

Generally such a review would be held in open court (and hence open to the public). All properly interested persons should have an opportunity to be present, including those persons whose conduct might be called into question.

Issues that might commonly be determined include:

- who should be considered as properly interested persons;
- the necessity for a jury;
- the list of witnesses to be called in person or to be taken as documentary evidence;
- necessity for any witness summonses;
- any applications on the anonymity of witnesses;
- an estimate as to the time that should be set aside for the case;
- whether a formal view of the scene is necessary and when this might take place;
- disclosure of any internal inquiry reports by organizations involved;
- whether there is a necessity to exclude witnesses from the court before their evidence;
- applications that the inquest hear from a witness put forward by one of the parties.

The coroner may be in a position to make an immediate decision on any applications put forward or may choose to reserve the decision to be announced a short time thereafter.

Notification of Hearing

By rule 17 every inquest must be heard in public.[7] This means that the family and other interested persons must have proper notice of the hearing and that the press must have a reasonable opportunity to attend.

The Family and Other Interested Persons 6.08

By rule 19(a) a spouse, near relative, or personal representative must be informed of the date, time, and place of the inquest, if their name and address are known to the coroner.

In many cases it is sufficient for the coroner's officer to notify the family member who has been dealing with the matter and ask that they inform all other relatives who wish to attend. However, care must be taken if there is an obvious split in the family. It is not uncommon for the deceased's blood relatives to have fallen out

---

[7] See section 7.12, although there is a (seldom used) provision allowing an inquest to be held in camera in the interests of national security.

with the surviving spouse and the officer will need to ensure that both sides of the family are notified.

By rule 19(b), any properly interested person[8] who has requested that the coroner notify him of the inquest, and who has supplied contact details for this purpose, must also be given proper notice of the hearing. The Mental Health Act Commissioners will generally be regarded as interested persons in appropriate cases.[9]

Should the coroner receive a request for notification from a person not 'properly interested' there is, technically, no obligation to comply. However, apart from issues of common courtesy, it might well be that the person does have good reason for wanting to attend although not actually take part. They may also be entitled to a hearing on whether or not they are a properly interested person and a decision simply to ignore their request should not be taken lightly.

The Coroners' Model Charter suggested by the Home Office[10] sets out that those required to attend an inquest will be notified of:

- the date and time of the hearing at least 10 working days in advance;
- details of the location of the court and the facilities available;
- a telephone number and named contact for inquiries.

The Model Charter also refers to a Home Office leaflet (which explains the purpose and procedures of inquests)[11] being made available and that those who express a wish to do so should be told that they may attend an inquest as an observer beforehand.

6.09 Persons whose Conduct may be Called into Question

Rule 24 requires the coroner to give notice of the hearing to any person 'whose conduct is likely to be called into question' at the inquest. Although there is no further definition within the legislation it is suggested that this should be given the same meaning as rule 20(d) (part of the list of persons entitled to examine witnesses):

> any person whose act or omission, or that of his agent or servant, may in the opinion of the Coroner have caused, or contributed to the death of the deceased.

Such individuals will usually be called to the inquest as a witness in any event, possibly with the formality of a witness summons.[12] Depending on the circum-

---

[8] See section 7.09.
[9] See section 7.09.
[10] See section 1.13.
[11] *When sudden death occurs*, see www.homeoffice.gov.uk/justice/legalprocess/coroners. This site also contains versions of the leaflet in Bengali, Chinese, Gujerati, Hindi, Punjabi, Somali, and Urdu.
[12] See section 6.12.

stances, it may also be appropriate for the coroner to write to the person involved with a specific notification in terms of rule 24 to ensure that they understand the gravity of the situation and have ample time to seek legal advice if they wish.[13] This may help to avoid late requests for an adjournment.

An interesting point arises where the witness is an employee being called to give evidence in relation to a death arising (potentially) in connection with his/her work—for example, an electrician visiting a site where someone is later electrocuted. It may be tempting to assume that the employer of the witness is aware of the hearing but rule 24 would appear to require specific notice.

The Press   6.10

The press are entitled to make inquiry of the coroner's staff as to forthcoming inquests and a Home Office Circular[14] encourages co-operation with this practice.

This is not straightforward. Other courts can meet their obligations by the issue of a court list but the very nature of inquest proceedings makes it difficult to publish a list, unless this were to contain no more than the name of the deceased and date of death. Unlike a court list at a criminal court (which contains details of the charge against the accused) this would be of very little use to a reporter deciding whether to attend. Further, inquests are usually opened at very short notice and there is certainly no obligation upon the coroner's staff to telephone each local press office to give notification.

In practice, a reasonable working relationship is likely to develop between local media and the coroner's staff. This can be useful, as there will be occasions when the coroner actively seeks publicity about certain cases in an effort to publicize a particular danger (eg drugs deaths).

Warning the Witnesses   6.11

In a majority of cases the notification of witnesses to attend court is done on an informal basis. It is sufficient for the coroner's officer to telephone the witness, speaking with them personally or perhaps leaving necessary details with a responsible person. However, if the witness fails to attend in these circumstances there is little that the coroner can do other than adjourn the hearing and take more formal steps to secure attendance on a future occasion.

In cases where a large number of witnesses are to be called it may be sensible to ensure that those required are warned by letter or perhaps a personal visit from the

---

[13] Although there is generally no provision for legal aid in the coroner's court—see section 6.28.
[14] Home Office Circular 53/1980.

police. This usually avoids any necessity for an adjournment due to absent witnesses.

6.12 Witness Summonses

On occasions, notably with deaths related to the misuse of drugs, it will be apparent to the coroner that some witnesses will not attend unless under compulsion. In these instances it is entirely appropriate for the coroner to issue a witness summons.

The coroner has power to issue a summons requiring the attendance of a witness[15] and can enforce this by a fine under s 10(2) of the Act.[16] The summons must be served personally upon the witness.[17] If appropriate, conduct money[18] must be given to the witness. The police officer who has served the summons should endorse a certificate of service on a copy and return this to the coroner.

It is sometimes said that a coroner's witness summons is valid only if served within the county in which the coroner has jurisdiction.[19] The author is not clear why such a limitation should be assumed for there seems to be no legislation or case law[20] suggesting this. This interpretation may arise from no more than the fact that a coroner is appointed to a geographical district and has jurisdiction only within the county in which the district lies.[21]

The author would argue that to assume such a limitation is without logic. Firstly, wherever the witness resides, the summons is issued within the coroner's jurisdiction and relates wholly to proceedings which will take place there. Nor would anyone suggest that a coroner's warrant for the arrest of a witness (or juror) who failed to attend on a validly served summons can only be executed within the county.[22]

More importantly, by way of comparison, a magistrate is appointed to a Commission (usually a county) and may sit only within a Petty Session inside that

---

[15] A suitable form of wording is set down in Form 8 of Schedule IV to the Rules.

[16] The current maximum is £1000.

[17] There is no specific requirement for a coroner's witness summons to be served a set number of days prior to the hearing; it will be a matter for the coroner to decide whether reasonable notice was given.

[18] Conduct money is a sum equivalent to the full amount of expenses which the witness is likely to incur in giving evidence, including reasonable loss of earnings. It must be offered to the witness when the summons is served. However, if refused the witness cannot later rely on non-payment as a reason for not attending court. See *HM Coroner for Kent v Terrill & Terrill* [2001] ACD 5.

[19] Although in Wales a coroner has jurisdiction for the whole of the country.

[20] In *Re Dr AS Rayan* (1983) 148 JP 569 the court specifically avoided any decision on this point.

[21] According to Blackstone's Commentaries on the Laws of England (1765) the coroner's power, like that of the Sheriff, only extended to the county to which he is appointed. Nonetheless, it is of interest, if hardly compelling, that mid-19th century textbooks on coroner's law envisaged no geographical restriction on the coroner's power to summon.

[22] A suggested form for such a warrant is shown at para A3-11 of *Jervis on Coroners* (12th edition).

area (usually a specific town) but a summons or witness summons to attend a Magistrates' Court is accepted as valid if served anywhere within England and Wales.

Jervis[23] suggests the restriction is valid and that 'logically it must still be [good law], there being no statutory provision or regulation which covers this point'. But this assumes that there was such a limitation in the first place, for failing that the lack of regulation could be better argued in reverse. In any event, if such a limitation is correct, it is anachronistic and should be addressed in future legislation.

The alternative procedure open to coroners would be to request a witness summons be issued in a county court (or less likely, the High Court) under Part 34.4 of the Civil Procedure Rules 1998. This authorizes a witness summons (no longer referred to as a subpoena) to be issued in aid of a court or tribunal which does not have the power to issue such a summons in relation to the proceedings before it. The witness may ask the issuing county court to set the summons aside giving two days' notice of the hearing to the coroner. Any enforcement action on failure to attend following such a summons would be for the issuing court rather than the coroner.

For discussion of the coroner's powers when witnesses fail to appear see section 7.45.

Compelling Production of Documents   6.13

In the 1983 case of *Hicks*[24] it was said that the coroner has no power to order the production of documents although may apply to the High Court for a *subpoena duces tecum* compelling production. No reason was given for this view. The modern equivalent would be a witness summons requiring the witness to attend the inquest and produce a specified list of documents, issued by a county court under Part 34.4 of the Civil Procedure Rules 1998.

Nonetheless, production of documents rarely causes a difficulty. Any witness asked to bring relevant papers to court would generally do so, especially knowing that refusal would simply cause the case to be adjourned whilst a summons was obtained. A medical witness is under a professional obligation to assist the inquest (see section 3.05) and would normally be expected to produce documents such as medical notes without hindrance.

---

[23] *Jervis on Coroners* (12th edition) at para 3-31.
[24] *R v Southwark Coroner ex p Hicks* (1987) 2 All ER 140.

Releasing Documentation before the Inquest

There are no legal provisions for advance disclosure[25] in the coroner's court. In strict terms it can be argued that there is no requirement for such, the inquest is the coroner's inquiry on behalf of the Crown—the interested persons are only there to assist with this, although they are granted the right to question witnesses. However, the reality is that there is an increasing expectation that coroners will release details of the evidence that they intend to call at the inquest.

6.14 The Post-mortem Report

Rule 57 gives a clear right for a properly interested person[26] to obtain a copy of the post-mortem report on payment of the appropriate fee[27] or to inspect the document without charge at the coroner's office. Unfortunately what is not made clear is when the right to inspection or a copy of the report arises. *Jervis*[28] suggests, correctly in the author's view, that the right to sight of the report exists from the point that the coroner receives the document.

In 1994 the Home Secretary supported a recommendation[29] for early disclosure to clinicians involved in a patient's care prior to death (whether or not requested under rule 57). The Coroners' Model Charter[30] suggested by the Home Office in 1999 envisages early disclosure of the report, and a number of reports[31] since that time all support this practice.

In any event, the writer would suggest that there are a number of advantages in open disclosure of the report at an early stage. In this way:

- the issues at the inquest are often considerably narrowed down;
- the witnesses and 'interested persons' have a chance to prepare themselves appropriately;
- it may be pointed out to the coroner that there are other witnesses who could assist the inquiry as regards specific matters.

One clear exception to early disclosure of the post-mortem report is where the police are undertaking a homicide investigation. Although the report still belongs to the coroner in such cases, it would be a serious matter if information were to be

---

[25] A term used in the criminal courts to denote the disclosure by the prosecution before the commencement of proceedings of the evidence upon which it will rely in the case against the accused.

[26] See section 7.09.

[27] See Coroners' Records (Fees for Copies) Rules 2002.

[28] *Jervis on Coroners* (12th edition) para 18-34.

[29] Home Office Circular 62 of 1994.

[30] See section 1.13.

[31] Most recently the Code of Practice on post-mortems (see section 5.14) and the Report of the Fundamental Review (see section 1.08 and n 73 of this chapter).

disclosed which hampered the police efforts to catch the killer. For that reason a request for a report in such a case, even from the deceased's doctor, is likely to be met with a refusal until such time as the criminal proceedings have progressed sufficiently.

Statements of Witnesses who will give Oral Evidence   6.15

Whilst it may now be common for post-mortem reports to be made available prior to the inquest, the same cannot necessarily be said for other documentation. Often such statements are supplied to the coroner by agencies (eg NHS Trusts,[32] Health and Safety Executive[33]) who retain ownership of the documents and might object to their release to others. Even statements taken by the police will often have been obtained for their own investigative purposes rather than to support the coroner's inquest. If such statements are then supplied to the coroner to assist in the identification of witnesses for the inquest, in the absence of any current power to disclose, the coroner is in a difficult position.

The questions of ownership of witness statements and the entitlement to see copies of statements taken by the police (given to the coroner to assist the inquest) were dealt with in the cases of *Peach*[34] and *Hicks*.[35] In short, the courts have made it clear that an interested person has no power to require the coroner to produce documents disclosed to him in confidence. This view was endorsed by Home Office Circular 20/99 and was held still to be good law in the 1999 *Hay* case.[36]

The High Court has more recently expressed the view that the coroner has a *discretion* to provide disclosure of relevant documents, which must be exercised fairly in the circumstances of the case and by modern day standards. However, this was said in the context of the provision of documents to be taken as documentary evidence under rule 37 (see section 6.17 below) rather than 'ownership' of statements.[37]

There are also very real practical difficulties for coroners working with limited administrative support to review and prepare disclosure in even moderately sized files. Nonetheless, with the increasing tendency towards transparency, it is becoming more common (although certainly not universal) that some form of disclosure is made voluntarily. This may be by the provision of statements or by details of

---

[32] See section 6.20 below.
[33] The Health and Safety Executive will sometimes require the coroner to agree that statements will *not* be disclosed before they are supplied, a difficulty that arises in part through the HSE's statutory powers to *make* a witness give a statement under s 20(2)(j) Health and Safety at Work Act 1974.
[34] *R v Hammersmith ex p Peach* [1980] QB 211; [1980] 2 WLR 496.
[35] *R v Southwark Coroner ex p Hicks* (1987) 2 All ER 140.
[36] *R v HM Coroner for Lincolnshire ex p Hay* (1999) 163 JP 666.
[37] *R v Avon Coroner ex p Bentley* (2002) JP 166 297.

witnesses to be called, including a brief summary of the anticipated evidence (see section 6.16 below).

Whilst there has not yet been a decision of the High Court with regard to the effects of the ECHR[38] on this point, it is not difficult to imagine that a court in the future will regard the ability of the family (or others) to play a full part in the proceedings as falling within either Article 8 or (less likely) Article 6.[39] However, whether this would ever amount to an automatic right of full disclosure in every case is an entirely different question.

Cases that may fall within Article 2 ECHR, where the deceased either died at the hands of agents of the State (eg a police shooting) or more commonly was in the care of the State at the time of death (eg in prison or in hospital) bring other issues of disclosure which are dealt with at sections 6.18 and 6.19 below.

There would seem to be nothing to prevent a witness requesting a copy of his/her own statement, unless the coroner felt that this was for an improper purpose such as collusion. The situation is less clear when an employer seeks copies of statements made by workers.

6.16 Disclosure of Witness List

It may be unrealistic to expect advocates for various parties to come to court with no more than a blank sheet of paper. Indeed the advocates will, hopefully, be anxious to ensure that the coroner is aware of all the relevant evidence and may wish to suggest further witnesses if the court is not intending to call them. For this purpose it may often be helpful for the coroner to disclose a list of the witnesses with a brief summary of their place in the chain of evidence. In a particularly complex case the coroner may hold a preliminary hearing to deal with issues of this nature.

The 1999 case of *Hay*[40] held that there was no general rule requiring a coroner to provide interested parties with such a witness list prior to the inquest but commented that it would be good practice to do so in complex cases. This was reinforced in the 2003 *Bentley* case.[41]

---

[38] European Convention on Human Rights, given effect in UK law by the Human Rights Act 1998—see section 4.41 *et seq.*

[39] Article 8: Everyone has the right to respect for his private and family life. Article 6 relates to 'a fair and public hearing' in the determination of civil rights and obligations. However, it seems clear at present that an inquest is not a determination of such rights—see section 4.44.

[40] *R v HM Coroner for Lincolnshire ex p Hay* (1999) 163 JP 666.

[41] *R v Avon Coroner ex p Bentley* (2002) 166 JP 297.

Release of Documentary Evidence   **6.17**

Rule 37 requires only that interested persons be told of statements intended to be taken as documentary evidence at the commencement of the inquest.[42] If followed literally, without any form of prior disclosure, many complex inquests would come to a halt at that point. Interested persons, learning for the first time in court that anticipated witnesses are not to be called, or that statements with which they may disagree are to be read out, have a clear entitlement to object.

Whilst the exact nature of the evidence to be called remains a matter for the coroner, there is an obvious requirement in natural justice for a full and open inquiry. As a result the coroner might be forced to adjourn and resume the hearing at a later date, having arranged for the additional witnesses to be present.

Consequently it is usually better, particularly in more complicated inquests, if information is also disclosed on those witnesses intended to be taken as documentary evidence, including a copy of their statement. In reality this amounts to little more than the provisions of rule 37(3) being complied with at such a time that any objection is not going to cause difficulties.

The High Court has said that although the requirements of fairness would vary from case to case, generally when straightforward disclosure of potential rule 37 documents was requested in advance by a properly interested person who would in the end be entitled to see it, it should be disclosed.[43]

Deaths in Custody—Disclosure by the Authorities   **6.18**

Formal protocols for voluntary disclosure were issued by both the Prison Service[44] and Home Office (ie in relation to police custody deaths) in 1999. These recognized the difficulties of disclosure for coroners, whilst wanting to promote some element of transparency in custody deaths, following a recommendation by the Stephen Lawrence Inquiry.[45] It should be noted that in both cases it is the appropriate service which makes disclosure rather than the coroner.

Disclosure is of all material supplied to the coroner and would be to all those likely to be considered a properly interested person[46] at the inquest. However, this would not generally include disclosure of the investigating officer's report unless

---

[42] See section 7.42 *et seq* below.

[43] *Bentley* (n 41 above).

[44] The Prison Service has made some element of disclosure on an informal basis since 1994.

[45] The Lawrence Inquiry (www.official-documents.co.uk) had recommended (Rec 42) disclosure in all inquests, but the Home Office only accepted this in relation to custody deaths. This may have been an understandable outcome but nonetheless is a little surprising since the Lawrence case had nothing to do with custody deaths.

[46] See section 7.09.

there was good reason. There is provision for the coroner to be consulted about disclosure—but there is no power for the coroner to prohibit or order disclosure of any particular document.

So far as disclosure by the police is concerned, a death 'in custody' is now very widely defined and will include most deaths arising during contact with the police—see Appendix 4 at page 375.

The Home Office guidance for police on disclosure was updated in June 2002 and is contained in Home Office Circular 31/2002. The Prison Service Protocol was first published on 1 April 1999.

Both protocols envisage that disclosure should be mutual—that is to say that families or other interested persons receiving disclosure should also make clear any relevant information that they possess, whether it supports their view of the matter or not. Whilst it is difficult to see how this can be enforced in any direct sense, solicitors or barristers acting for families in this situation are clearly under a professional obligation to the court.

It may be that some such deaths engage the provisions of Article 2 ECHR which might have an effect on decisions about disclosure—see sections 4.43 and 9.30 *et seq.*

6.19 Reports from NHS Staff

A coroner investigating a death in hospital may seek written reports from medical and/or nursing staff involved. It is common that these are supplied to the coroner in confidence and are not meant for disclosure to other properly interested persons.[47] An exception might be where such a document was suitable to be taken as documentary evidence under rule 37 (see section 7.42), the coroner may reasonably assume that there would be no objection from the maker of the statement. However, in a few cases there will remain issues about the disclosure of information that could affect other people.[48]

Whilst disclosure would remain a matter for the Trust rather than the coroner, with the Government's commitment to transparency and openness it is difficult to see how a refusal to provide such disclosure will continue to be justified in future years. This might particularly be the case with the death of a patient detained under the Mental Health Act where parallels could be drawn with the protocols on disclosure by the police and prison service (see section 6.18).

---

[47] See also section 6.23 below.

[48] For example, a psychiatrist might prepare a report in which it is indicated that the patient, now deceased, claimed to have been abused by a parent whilst they were a child. The doctor might have justifiable concerns if the unedited report were disclosed to other family members without warning.

Following the 2003 case of *Khan*[49] it seems clear that certain hospital deaths can engage the provisions of Article 2 ECHR, although it is less certain how often the inquest will be the appropriate vehicle to discharge the State's obligation to investigate. Where this is the case,[50] calls for disclosure of reports and statements may be more compelling—see sections 4.43 and 9.30 *et seq.*

Health Records

6.20

It may be argued in reply to the above that the Access to Health Records Act 1990 provides a route for some measure of disclosure, albeit not directly for the purposes of the inquest.

This gives a statutory right for a patient's personal representative to obtain a copy of the deceased's medical records from the Trust or Health Authority concerned, where a claim arising out of the death is contemplated. In most instances the request must be met within 40 days. A post-mortem report, or result of any special examination, carried out at the direction of the coroner does not form part of the medical records for this purpose, unless a copy has been forwarded to the clinicians and placed in the notes.

The Health Authority or Trust have no right to refuse discovery of documents in civil proceedings or under the Access to Health Records Act simply because the inquest is not yet complete.[51] Assuming that the request is not made at the last minute, it should be perfectly possible for relatives of a deceased to obtain all relevant records before the inquest in appropriate cases. However this does not of itself carry an entitlement to copies of any reports made to the coroner by the hospital staff.

Privileged Documents

6.21

In some instances the disclosure of documents is not a matter of discretion for the coroner. For example, the coroner would commonly be given a copy of the report by an officer investigating a death on behalf of the Police Complaints Authority. It has been made clear that such a report (as opposed to statements or other documents)[52] is generally subject to public interest immunity and is not for the coroner to disclose.[53] See also section 7.40.4.

---

[49] *R (Khan) v Secretary of State for Health* [2003] EWCA Civ 1129.
[50] Which might be more likely where the patient was detained under the Mental Health Act 1983.
[51] *Stobart v Nottinghamshire Health Authority* [1992] 3 Med LR 284.
[52] *R v Chief Constable of W Midlands ex p Wiley* [1995] 1 AC 274, where it was held that there was no general public interest immunity for other documents.
[53] *Taylor v Anderton* [1995] 1 WLR 447 and *R v HM Coroner for Lincolnshire ex p Hay* (1999) 163 JP 666.

Preparing a Report or Statement

Most witnesses from outside the medical profession will have been asked to give a statement to the police which is then passed to the coroner. However, deaths related to a medical procedure are not usually investigated by the police, being dealt with by the coroner in the light of the medical notes and reports from those involved. Such reports will usually be prompted either by a formal letter of request or telephone call from the coroner's officer. In some cases the request will be made direct to the doctor but many hospitals have an agreement that the coroner's officer will channel all such matters through a named senior administrator.

6.22 The Legal Position

The witness is under no obligation to prepare a statement or report for the coroner. A witness who refuses to do so is not open to any direct sanction, nor is such refusal a common law obstruction of the coroner. However, a number of points must be borne in mind.

If a witness refuses to make a written statement the coroner will have no option but to require that the witness attend court and give oral evidence. The witness *must* attend court when so directed and *must* answer the coroner's proper questions unless these fall within rule 22. This allows a witness to request being excused answering a question which might incriminate, but does not extend to questions which might involve civil liability or disciplinary matters.[54] A medical witness is also under a professional obligation to assist the coroner. GMC guidance[55] now states:

> [32] . . . you must assist the coroner . . . by responding to inquiries and by offering all relevant information to an inquest or inquiry into a patient's death. Only where your evidence may lead to criminal proceedings being taken against you are you entitled to remain silent.[56]

In any event, there is little to be gained by a witness refusing to provide a written statement or report. There is a prospect that the document, if not controversial, might be acceptable as documentary evidence under rule 37[57] and be read out in the absence of the maker. Even if the witness knows that they will be required to attend the inquest there is still much to be gained by providing a well-constructed and carefully thought out statement.

---

[54] See section 7.40.1—in the author's view Article 6 ECHR has not altered this.
[55] General Medical Council, *Good Medical Practice* (September 2001).
[56] See also section 3.07 which refers to guidance from the Chief Medical Officer and n 34 of Chapter 3.
[57] See section 7.42.

In the absence of a statement the coroner will be forced to examine the witness on the basis of a mass of other documentation, possibly including complex medical notes. The witness will be unable to foresee the pattern of questioning and will have great difficulty in preparing for such an examination. On the other hand, the coroner who has a good quality statement in front of him is likely to focus on that and go through the issues in the order they are set out in the statement. The witness can effectively set the agenda of at least the initial part of the examination, although the coroner will inevitably deal with matters not referred to in the statement.

Who May See the Report 6.23

Some coroners take the view that any report or commentary supplied is confidential. For example, a report from a doctor might not currently be released to the relatives of the deceased without the agreement of the maker. Similarly, if the relatives wrote to the coroner with a list of concerns about a death in a hospital, the coroner would not divulge the exact details of the letter.[58]

It should be stressed that there is no legislation or official guidance covering this point and individual coroners may adopt different attitudes. It also seems inevitable to the author that this lack of disclosure will change in the future—see section 6.19 above.

There may also be alternative ways in which a report could find its way into another's possession quite legitimately. If the report were read out in court in the absence of the maker under rule 37, the report becomes public and interested persons are then entitled to a copy under rule 57. However, in circumstances where the report is appropriate to be taken as documentary evidence it seems doubtful that the report becoming public would generally cause any concern.

Whilst it is unlikely that a coroner could be forced to release a statement received by him as part of any litigation process, it might be that the witness's own copy of the document would have to be disclosed as part of civil pleadings[59] depending upon the circumstances.

Contents of the Report 6.24

Wherever possible, the report should only be written when the maker understands the overall circumstances of the death. In particular, the witness should have regard to the post-mortem report. Where appropriate, a report or statement

---

[58] Although in common sense terms it may be necessary to indicate the nature of the concerns when asking for reports from the doctors involved.

[59] The mutual pre-trial exchange of documents in a civil claim—see also section 7.40.2.

should not be written from memory; it is essential to have any medical, nursing, or other contemporaneous notes available for reference.

It may be stating the obvious to say that a report to the coroner should deal with matters relevant to the inquest in chronological order, with a logical structure and in an accurate and professional manner. The report must be factual and written with care, using unambiguous language. It must be accurate, for, once committed to paper, incorrect or misleading details will take a lot of explaining in the witness box.[60]

Unfortunately, in the author's experience, these criteria are not always met. Common faults include failing to mention important issues, making assumptions (sometimes without even making clear what is being assumed) and not giving sufficient thought to the purpose of the report or the needs of the court.

Another common error is the use of a string of complex technical phrases which will be unintelligible to the layperson. Although most coroners are lawyers rather than doctors, they are likely to have acquired a passable understanding of medical phraseology. However, if the report is to be read out in court as documentary evidence, in the absence of its author, the coroner is faced with the task of converting the complex phraseology into readily understandable English. This is undesirable for a number of reasons, not least because it introduces an element of unqualified interpretation. There is rarely any good reason why simple English could not have been used in the first place. If particularly complex terminology is thought essential, a straightforward explanation in brackets should be added.

The rules of evidence in the coroner's court are comparatively relaxed[61] and hearsay evidence is quite regularly admitted.[62] For that reason it would be acceptable for the author of a report to include something relevant said to them by another.

On rare occasions, with issues of a particularly complex nature, an anatomical diagram may be of assistance.

It is important that any report is provided promptly, Home Office figures show that in 28 per cent of inquests taking longer than six months to conclude, the primary reason is delay in provision of medical reports.

It is often appropriate for the document to be concluded with a summary, drawing together the various parts of the report and providing a conclusion, which

---

[60] There is an old lawyer's joke about the witness who asks whether they should be telling the truth, *or* the whole truth, *or* nothing but the truth. The reality is that a partial or misleading answer will often become quietly apparent and, even if not pursued by the court, will have damaged credibility beyond repair.

[61] *R v Manchester Coroner ex p Tal* 1985 QB 67.

[62] Hearsay evidence relates that which was said by another person, see section 7.49.

might include an element of opinion. The coroner may not wish to take this opinion as formal evidence but might find it useful in assessing what questions to ask of the witness or what further evidence should be obtained.

Any temptation to mislead the court in a report (perhaps by an effort to 'smooth over' difficulties) must be carefully resisted for it could lead to dire consequences. A criminal case in 1994[63] made it clear that deliberately misleading an inquest could amount to 'perverting the course of justice':

> An act has such a tendency [ie to pervert the course of public justice] if it gives rise to the possibility that it will mislead a tribunal concerned with public justice and might cause a miscarriage of justice. Public justice is any judicial proceedings which might arise from the death of [the patient] including an inquest, civil or criminal proceedings.

Seeking Legal Advice   6.25

A report may be requested in circumstances where it is clear that only a factual description of background events is required, and that there is no prospect of the witness being called to attend court. For example a short report might be requested from a doctor confirming that a person who has recently been found in circumstances suggestive of suicide has never sought treatment for a depressive illness. It is unlikely that the witness would feel a need for legal advice in such a case.

However, it will often be apparent from the nature of the request that the circumstances are more serious and that the witness should seek informed advice at an early stage. If the report is to be vetted by legal advisers it would be prudent to acknowledge the coroner's request and explain that there may be a short delay.

Leaving it until the last minute to seek legal advice, or realizing part way through a hearing that the situation is serious, may lead to the witness having to ask the coroner to adjourn the hearing. There is no guarantee that such an application would be granted.

Whilst the medical witness will always be able to obtain advice from a defence organization or, where appropriate, solicitors for the Hospital or Trust, the majority of those called to an inquest have no such advantage. Trade unions or insurers may be of assistance in some circumstances but many will be reliant on their own resources.

---

[63] *R v Sinha*, The Times, 13 July 1994, where a doctor was said to have falsified records to make it appear that he was not at fault for a death.

The Advocate

Inquests are almost unique within the English and Welsh legal system; their rules, procedures, and even their purpose match little else that the advocate will have met elsewhere. With the relatively small number of inquests that take place and the almost complete lack of public funding for representation, many experienced advocates will only attend the coroner's court on a few occasions in their career. This inevitably leads to difficulties in preparation for the hearing but it is important that the advocate and the client are ready to take a full role in the inquiry.

6.26 Taking Instructions

The author would respectfully suggest that the first question the newly instructed advocate should ask themselves is whether or not they have appropriate experience to appear for the client at the inquest. Many inquests are unlikely to present even a moderately experienced advocate with difficulty once the inquisitorial nature of the proceedings is fully appreciated. Others will present complex technical points both of fact and law that are best dealt with by those with significant inquest experience.[64]

It is also important to assess whether the client has relevant evidence to offer the inquest. It might be dangerous to assume that the client will automatically be called as a witness, thus if no statement has been provided it may be appropriate to take a proof of evidence and forward this to the coroner. This should be submitted well in advance of the hearing as it is entirely possible the coroner will want to follow up by making further inquiries of other witnesses. It is helpful if an indication is given of whether there is any objection to the statement being shown to others in advance of the hearing.[65]

6.27 Contact with the Court

Even if there is no statement to supply to the court, it is essential that advocates advise the coroner of their instructions at an early stage. This will assist with decisions on timescale and sometimes the venue of the hearing. It is also useful if the advocate specifies exactly who the clients are; there may be other family members who wish to take part in the hearing[66] and the coroner will need to know whether the advocate represents the whole family or just one element.

---

[64] For example, a number of technical issues of fact are likely to arise with custody deaths where lack of familiarity with the normal procedures could be a distinct handicap. Complex medical deaths will also present difficulty for those without relevant experience.

[65] See sections 6.17 and 6.23.

[66] See section 7.09. It is also sometimes confusing as to whether an advocate acts for a person involved or just his/her insurers, who may have a different interest.

The opportunity can also be taken to request any disclosure that the coroner is willing to make. Whatever else may be said on this subject (as to which see sections 6.14 *et seq*) it is usually the case that nothing will be provided unless it is requested, particularly if the coroner is not aware of the advocate's existence.

Where documents disclosed, such as an autopsy report, are of a complex nature the advocate should ensure that they are properly understood, taking expert advice in good time if necessary. If any instructed expert is giving a contrary opinion the court should be informed of this at an early stage so that the issues can be further considered.

In a complex case the advocate may wish to inquire whether a pre-inquest hearing is contemplated, to consider the issues set out in section 6.07. If the advocate thinks that the presence of a jury is warranted (see section 8.03 *et seq*) it is probably better to ensure that the court is working on the same basis than to arrive at the hearing and find out that crucial issues have not been brought to the attention of the coroner.

Any request to an NHS Trust for medical notes under the Access to Health Records Act 1990 (see section 6.20) should also be made in good time.

Applications for Funding   6.28

The circumstances in which funding will be made available for legal representation at an inquest are extremely narrow. The reader is directed to Chapter 11 of *Inquests; a practitioner's guide*[67] for a more detailed account of this topic. However, the following may be useful background.

Although the Legal Aid Acts 1949 and 1974 included provisions for assistance at inquests within their terms, those sections were never brought into effect. This has been criticized on a number of occasions, not least by the 1971 Brodrick Report.[68] It has been argued that in the absence of legal aid, those who have the greatest interest (the family) are effectively denied the right to be represented.[69]

The Stephen Lawrence Inquiry[70] recommended that legal aid be available for families of victims to cover representation at an inquest in appropriate cases. The government response was that this would not be appropriate in the great majority of inquests as the proceedings were inquisitorial (rather than adversarial) with a limited scope. However, it was agreed that help should be made available in

---

[67] Thomas, Friedman and Christian, *Inquests; a practitioner's guide* (2002, LAG Books).

[68] Report of the Committee on Death Certification and Coroners, September 1971, Cmnd 4810.

[69] Grealis and Coles, 'Inquests: redressing the balance' *Solicitors Journal* (April 1994) at 321.

[70] Report of an Inquiry by Sir William MacPherson; CM4262-I; available on www.official-documents.co.uk.

'exceptional cases'. As a result s 6(8) of the Access to Justice Act 1998 permitted the Lord Chancellor to require the Legal Services Commission to fund appropriate applications.

It is now accepted by the Legal Services Commission[71] that funding should be considered if 'the circumstances of the death appear to be such that that funded representation is necessary to assist the coroner investigate the case effectively and establish the facts'. The guidance goes on to say that 'such representation may well be needed for inquests concerning agencies of the State', ie where Article 2 ECHR is engaged.[72] There is a streamlined procedure where the death occurred in custody or during an arrest or pursuit etc. Applications evidently take some time to process and should not be submitted at short notice.

This still means that in the vast majority of cases the family of the deceased are thrown upon their own resources. Despite the (valid) argument that the coroner's proceedings are inquisitorial, few can take comfort at the occasional sight of numerous counsel representing various commercial or authoritarian interests at an inquest, with the family of the deceased standing on their own. The 2003 Coroner Review[73] commented that the number of cases where a *public* authority (eg NHS Trust) is represented whilst the family are not is 'fairly small' at just under 3 per cent of all inquests. Nonetheless, the Review recommended that whilst the current criteria for awarding legal aid are 'broadly satisfactory' there should be a more liberal interpretation of those criteria in cases where a public authority is represented.

In a few cases there may be other routes open to relatives. In certain circumstances insurers of the deceased might agree to meet the costs of legal representation, but their interests are not always identical with those of the bereaved. Very occasionally, when liability is already clear, another party[74] will agree to meet the cost of representation for the bereaved. Finally, there are an increasing number of lawyers willing to represent clients on a *pro bono* basis.

---

[71] Lord Chancellor's revised guidance on applications for exceptional funding: www.legalservices. gov.uk.

[72] *R (Khan) v Secretary of State for Health* [2003] EWCA Civ 1129 which makes it plain that not every medical death will engage Article 2 but in those that do funding should be made available by the Government regardless of means. This will obviously also apply to other (non-medical) Article 2 cases.

[73] Death certification and investigation in England, Wales and Northern Ireland; the report of a fundamental review 2003: CM 5831 (at chapter 12 para 30). Available on www.official-documents.co.uk/document/cm58/cm5831.htm. See also section 1.08.

[74] Such as transport insurers in a mass disaster, or a hospital trust who cannot hope to deny a negligence claim in the particular circumstances of the death.

Briefing the Client   **6.29**

If the inquest is unfamiliar ground to some advocates, it is all the more beyond the experience of the bereaved or witnesses who generally have little clear idea of what to expect or hope for at the proceedings.

Against this background, it is incumbent upon advocates to ensure that their clients understand the true purpose and limited remit of the inquest, in particular that it is not an ill-defined substitute for a civil or criminal trial;[75]

> All too often, it seems to me, the grieving relatives of the deceased are encouraged by their lawyers to attempt to use the inquest to establish criminal or civil liability. That is not the purpose of those proceedings.[76]

It is to no-one's benefit if the clients have false expectations of the inquest, raising hopes that the court can never meet. This will leave the client unhappy with the inquest, with a diminished regard for the law and a loss of faith in their own lawyer, who may be perceived as failing to achieve the intended target.

> It is of critical importance to recognise the true purpose of an inquest. Sadly, the public's perception of such purpose does not always match the reality, and those caught up in the process expect more . . . than it can, or is permitted to, deliver thereby adding to their distress.[77]

It is worth mentioning that those attending an inquest commonly place false emphasis on the 'verdict' recorded[78] and ignore the very real benefits of the information ascertained during the hearing.[79] A prime purpose of the inquest is to provide an opportunity for witnesses to the facts of a death to be questioned in a structured environment where the questions must be answered[80] without evasion or obfuscation. This is an opportunity that other proceedings related to the death are unlikely to offer, making an inquest the optimal chance for the family to understand what happened.

It is particularly ironic that the inquest has often fulfilled it's proper role—and perhaps even revealed an undesirable state of affairs—yet is condemned out of hand because the verdict (in accordance with rule 42)[81] fails to apportion blame.

---

[75] See section 7.02 *et seq.*

[76] *R v HM Coroner for Lincolnshire ex p Hay* (1999) 163 JP 666.

[77] *R v Birmingham Coroner ex p Benton* (1997) 162 JP 807.

[78] The conclusion such as natural causes or accidental death—see section 9.07 *et seq* for an explanation of the various components of the verdict.

[79] Some experienced inquest advocates would make the point that they do give their clients clear advice not to become too focused on the verdict but that it is very difficult for the client to take this on board.

[80] Within certain limitations—see section 7.39 *et seq.*

[81] See section 7.04.

A proper, and knowledgeable, briefing of the client plays an important part in the overall worth of the inquest, as does a thorough debriefing on the information gained after the hearing.[82]

6.30 Final Arrangements

Conference facilities at the coroner's court may not be suitable for any detailed last minute issues and it is probably better to arrange to see the clients the day before. This gives an opportunity to ensure that the meaning and implications of disclosed documents (eg autopsy or toxicology reports) are fully understood.

It may also be useful to check whether all members of the client group want to stay in court during any difficult evidence. It is not uncommon that some relatives prefer to sit outside whilst the pathologist gives details of injuries etc. If there are likely to be plans or photographs that could be distressing, the advocate might ascertain whether the client wishes to see these during the hearing or not.

Where appropriate, it might be useful to warn the family of the potential for a media presence and to decide whether they (or the advocate) will speak with the press.

Finally, arrangements should be made for any necessary debrief after the inquest (see section 10.22). The emotional atmosphere at the conclusion of an inquest generally means that any time spent in the immediate aftermath of the hearing is unlikely to leave a lasting impression with the client, however convenient this might otherwise be.

The Witness

Few of those required to attend an inquest have ever been inside such a court before. The average witness arrives not knowing whether they will be giving their evidence standing or seated, who will be asking the questions, what documents they are allowed to refer to, or even how they should address the coroner.[83] This absence of information may be very unsettling for the witness at a time when they need to be as focused as possible.

6.31 The Dangers

Many inquests, particularly those where it might be suggested that there is some fault on the part of an authority, receive considerable publicity from local newspapers and television. The coroner's court is a very public place to look foolish and

---

[82] See section 10.22 on debriefing following the inquest.
[83] Generally 'sir' or 'madam'—but the author recalls a lorry driver who persistently addressed him as 'Your Grace'.

yet witnesses attend having given little thought to what is involved. Lack of preparation may also prevent the witness from ensuring that the evidence *they* consider to be important is given.

Further, badly prepared witnesses can easily present themselves as unreliable, incompetent, and uncaring, factors hardly likely to influence the coroner's decision for the better.

Two Weeks before Court   6.32

If the witness is relying upon any statistics or professional papers, these should be prepared in advance and copies made for the court with the relevant sections highlighted for ease of reference.

Where a witness has made notes about the deceased during their life (most often the case with medical witnesses) they must ensure that the *originals* of those records are in court. It is insufficient to assume that the coroner will have the documents or that someone else will have brought them. Attending without the original notes shows a lack of forethought and may even be met with a blunt demand that the witness returns immediately to the hospital to obtain them.

If a GP has submitted the deceased's notes to the Family Health Services[84] following the death, the request for them to be sent back to the surgery must be made in good time.[85] There will be little sympathy for the witness who turns up without the notes because there was insufficient time to find them following a request made only the previous day.

X-ray films and similar documents are renowned for going astray within hospitals, which is hardly surprising considering the number of such materials in circulation. But x-rays can often be good evidence to support a particular set of facts and a last minute claim that a film has been lost is likely to be met with scepticism if the evidence suggests that the x-ray would have proved the point one way or another. Whilst such documents are usually genuinely lost, the fact remains that they are also occasionally mislaid with a measure of deliberation. The coroner (or indeed the family of the deceased) has no way of knowing which is the case and may therefore think the worst. Doctors must check that all of the relevant x-rays are in the envelope, together with any associated documents, at least 10–14 days before the inquest. This gives plenty of time for a thorough search if any have gone astray.

The witness who attends court without documentation or some other important item gives the impression of less than proper concern for the circumstances of the death.

---

[84] Following a death, GP notes are submitted to the local Family Health Services office who will retain them for 25 years.

[85] And probably more than the two weeks envisaged by the rest of this section.

If the witness has never attended the coroner's court before, it may be worthwhile investing time in a visit to watch another case. As the court is open to the public, this is easily arranged by a phone call to the coroner's officer. The witness will be able to gauge the pace of the court, the procedures followed, and the physical attributes of the particular courtroom (which often have poor acoustics). For example, many courts provide the witness with a seat and desk upon which papers can be spread, but an equal number have the witness standing with only a narrow ledge for notes and other documents. Dropping papers and scattering them on the floor is likely to be disastrous so it might be sensible to plan ahead and put papers into a rigid binder that will more easily balance on the narrow ledge.

Thought should be given to the questions that might reasonably be expected. The coroner will be very familiar with the case papers and the issues involved, some lawyers representing participants will be extremely well prepared, others rather less so. The prospect of difficult and complex questions should not be under-estimated.

Finally, by this point the witness should be spending some time thinking of the evidence *that they wish to give*. All too often, witnesses leave a court complaining that they have not had the chance to explain their case fully because they were not asked questions relating to an area that they wished to emphasize. However, with some forethought, the intelligent witness can nearly always answer a question in such a way as to encompass the desired point.[86]

6.33 The Day before Court

Preparation on the day before court should consist of ensuring that all the papers are in the right place and in an order familiar to the witness. If complex papers such as medical notes have passed through a number of hands (perhaps the pathologist, the coroner's office and the Trust's solicitor) things may have become misplaced from their normal order.

Witnesses are not expected to memorize the notes, indeed it might be suspicious if a witness went through complicated evidence without having to refer to the notes. Nonetheless, they are generally expected to know where information is to be found without a seemingly endless search, flicking backwards and forwards through the pages. The pressures of the witness box are likely to induce the sort of mental fatigue which allows familiar documents to go unrecognized when they cannot be found at the first attempt. It is sensible to use adhesive notes to mark those sections which are likely be relevant. This should include any test result or x-ray reports that the witness may be relying upon.

---

[86] See also section 7.41 on giving evidence.

If the court is in an unfamiliar place, obtaining a street map may save a last minute disaster.[87] Similarly, noting telephone numbers that could be required (eg of hospital administrators and senior colleagues) can occasionally turn out to be time well spent. If the inquest is being heard in a Magistrates' or Crown Court building there may well be a security search at the door; occasionally mobile phones are confiscated so a telephone credit card is useful.

If the witness is legally represented, it may be wise to have the final consultation on the day prior to court. Coroner's courts do not always have conference rooms for a private discussion on the morning of the inquest. A hurried consultation about important matters on the stairs leading to the courtroom, with witnesses squeezing past, is not conducive to settling nerves or clearing the mind.

On the Day of the Inquest   6.34

Dress   6.34.1

A surprising number of witnesses, even from the medical profession, attend court inappropriately dressed. What is considered suitable for the witness's normal occupation may be quite unsuitable for the formality of a court investigating a death. Wherever possible the witness should attend in business type wear or at least dressed in a manner likely to identify them as a competent professional. Relatives of the deceased are likely to be wearing dark colours and the witness may suddenly feel out of place if insufficient thought has been given to the solemnity of the occasion.

Arriving early   6.34.2

Witnesses are frequently seen running up the steps of the court with only a few moments to spare. Whilst they may have had important business in other places, this allows little chance for composure and establishing who is who before the proceedings start. If the late attender ends up being first into the witness box, they may still be suffering a high degree of stress.

Courts (of any type) are not known for a sense of humour when witnesses are even a few minutes late—those involved should aim to reach the court building at least 15 minutes before the time set for the inquest. On arrival they should make their presence known to a receptionist or a coroner's officer. If the witness would prefer to affirm or take the oath on another Holy Book rather than the Bible this needs to be mentioned before going into court.

It is not generally acceptable for drinks (even small bottles of mineral water) to be consumed in the courtroom so a packet of mints may go a long way in dealing

---

[87] For those working in the South East or West of England, a useful pocket book is available describing where the courts are, how to get to them and the local refreshment facilities: Goodman, A., *The Court Guide* (2002, Blackstone Press, ISBN: 184174171X).

with the inevitable dry mouth. However, the witness box will generally have a carafe of water to one side; if not it is worth asking the coroner's officer or usher if something can be provided.

Although there is no obligation upon the coroner to release statements in advance of the hearing[88] it is generally regarded as permissible for witnesses at court to see any statement that they have made, so that they might refresh their memory before giving evidence.[89] However, this is unlikely to occur unless the witness asks to see the statement. Care must be taken with this, for if a group of witnesses are seen looking through each other's statements this may give an appearance of collusion.

Finally, before going in to the courtroom, any pagers or mobile phones *must* be switched off.

6.34.3 *Avoiding harassment*

Staff at coroner's courts are well aware that relatives of the deceased and the witnesses may no longer be on the best of terms. The family of the deceased may be there in large numbers which can feel intimidating in itself, however courteous their intentions.

Unfortunately, on a few occasions families arrive at an inquest with a firm intention to confront or harass a witness. If a witness thinks that this may happen (to themselves or another) they should inform the coroner's staff in advance so that appropriate steps can be taken. This will usually involve shepherding the family of the deceased into one waiting area and ensuring that witnesses are placed elsewhere until the moment that the inquest is ready to start.

Arriving late may initially seem an attractive proposition in such circumstances but is actually more likely to lead to a last minute confrontation outside the doors of the courtroom. If all else fails, attending early and checking in with the coroner's officer means that the witness can at least have a quiet and thoughtful walk around the surrounding streets for a few minutes.

6.34.4 *Noting prior evidence*

Almost invariably, witnesses are allowed to sit in an inquest hearing before giving their own evidence.[90] The final act of preparation may be to make a note of any relevant issue raised by previous witnesses. This might then either be the subject of a confirmatory comment during the witness's own evidence or perhaps a stated

---

[88] See section 6.14 *et seq.*

[89] The exception would be where the coroner considered that the witness was asking to see the statement for an improper purpose, eg collusion or giving misleading evidence to the court: Home Office Circular 82/1969.

[90] Exceptions to the general rule are discussed at section 7.19.

and reasoned disagreement. Either way, the coroner is likely to appreciate the witness raising the issue without having to cross-reference previous evidence.

Summary

- The coroner has almost complete discretion over which witnesses will be called at an inquest but must present a fair and balanced view of the evidence.
- There is no formal provision for advance disclosure of documents prior to an inquest but coroners will generally release a copy of the post-mortem report if requested.
- If requested, the coroner may also agree to provide a list of the witnesses to be called and copies of any statements that will be taken as documentary evidence.
- Whilst there is no strict legal obligation upon a witness to provide a statement or report for the coroner, there is little to be gained by refusing and a number of advantages in supplying a carefully prepared document.
- The coroner's court is a very public place to suffer embarrassment; thorough preparation is likely to be time well invested.

7

INQUESTS

Idiots, madmen and lunatics during the influence of the frenzy are incompetent to give evidence, but during the lucid intervals lunatics may be examined.[1]

[1] From the second edition of *Jervis on Coroners*, published in 1854.

This chapter deals with the issues arising in the conduct of the inquest which include:

- the legislative purpose of the inquest;
- who may be heard at an inquest;
- the public nature of the hearing;
- the use of documentary evidence;
- the rules of evidence.

7.01 Introduction

The inquest[2] is usually seen as the *raison d'être* of the coroner. Although inquests only form about 13 per cent of the caseload,[3] the hearing is the public facet of the coroner's work and often subject to intense scrutiny and publicity.

Inquest proceedings are virtually unique within the English legal system, being inquisitorial by nature rather than adversarial; ie an inquiry led by the coroner to ascertain the true facts, rather than a trial between two parties each trying to make their own case.

There are no parties to an inquest and no formal allegations or pleadings.[4] The purpose of the hearing is simply to ascertain the truth about a death, not establish whether a particular claim is proved.[5] Even experienced lawyers may be unused to such proceedings. For members of the public, the inquest will be wholly outside the limited experience of courts that they may have gained from television and media.

The High Court has also made it plain on several occasions that the coroner holds considerable discretion and, within the basic statutory framework, may run the proceedings as is thought appropriate:

> . . . the coroner is by law an inquisitor, the witnesses called are those whom he . . . thinks it expedient to examine and he is very much the master of his own procedure.[6]

---

[2] From the Latin 'inquisito' meaning inquiry.

[3] Home Office Statistical Bulletin 06/03.

[4] Pleadings are the formal statements of claim and defence that form the basis of a civil suit.

[5] It may come as a surprise to non-legal readers to find that in most proceedings the court is more concerned with whether the prosecution has proved the charge, or the plaintiff substantiated his claim, than with 'the truth'.

[6] *R v HM Coroner for East Kent ex p Spooner* (1987) 152 JP 15.

The inquisitorial nature of the proceedings places a heavy burden on the coroner, who has sole responsibility for ensuring that the inquest is a forceful and independent inquiry into the circumstances surrounding the death.

The Purpose of the Inquest

The Coroner's Remit   7.02

Section 11(5) and rule 42 limit the purpose of the inquest to ascertaining the identity of the deceased and establishing when, where, and how he came by his death. Rule 36 is a specific provision forbidding an expression of opinion on any other matter. Riders to a verdict are no longer allowed[7] although rule 43 permits the coroner to make a report about the circumstances to an appropriate authority:[8]

The leading case of *Jamieson*[9] summarized the remit of the inquest:

> An inquest is a fact-finding inquiry conducted by a coroner with or without a jury to establish reliable answers to four important but limited factual questions. The first of these relates to the identity of the deceased, the second to the place of his death, the third to the time of death. In most cases these questions are not hard to answer but in a minority of cases the answer may be problematical. The fourth question, and that to which evidence and inquiry are most closely directed, relates to how the deceased came by his death.

The Meaning of 'How'   7.03

The question of 'how' the deceased came by his death goes beyond the narrow sense of the medical cause. It is generally understood as 'by what means' did the death occur, a narrower question than either 'why' or 'in what circumstances'. An authoritative explanation was given in the 1994 case of Homberg:[10]

> Although the word 'how' is to be widely interpreted, it means 'by what means' rather than 'in what broad circumstances'. In short the inquiry must focus on matters directly causative of death and must indeed be confined to these matters alone.
>
> . . . the duty to inquire 'how' does not to my mind properly encompass inquiry also into the underlying responsibility for every circumstance which may be said to have contributed to the death.

Bingham MR considered the same issue in the *Jamieson* case:[11]

---

[7] The ability to add a rider was abolished by the Coroners' Amendment Rules 1980 but see section 9.30 *et seq* in relation to findings of system neglect.

[8] See section 7.07.

[9] *R v HM Coroner for North Humberside ex p Jamieson* [1995] QB 1 and (1994) 3 All ER 972.

[10] *R v HM Coroner for Western District of East Sussex ex p Homberg* (1994) 158 JP 357.

[11] *Ex p Jamieson* (n 9 above).

It is noteworthy that the task is not to ascertain how the deceased died, which might raise general and far reaching issues, but how the deceased came by his death, a more limited question directed to the means by which the deceased came by his death.

However, the same judge went further on this point in the case of *Dallaglio*,[12] heard only shortly afterwards:

The court did not however rule that the investigation into the means by which the deceased came by his death should be limited to the last link in the chain of causation. That would not be consistent with conclusion 14 . . .[13] and it would defeat the purpose of holding an inquest at all if the inquiry were to be circumscribed in [this manner]. It is for the coroner conducting an inquest to decide on the facts of a given case at what point the chain of causation becomes too remote to form a proper part of his investigation.

Nor is other case law entirely restrictive of the coroner's task. In *Homberg*,[14] the court approved a passage from the 11th edition of *Jervis* that it is 'right and proper that the coroner should inquire into acts and omissions which are directly responsible for the death'.

7.04   The Conflict with Rule 42

Thus, despite the fact that rule 42 forbids a verdict imputing civil or criminal liability,[15] it is frequently necessary for the court to examine the circumstances of negligent acts and omissions relevant to the death.[16] On the face of it, this creates a conflict, but it is the duty to inquire which must take priority. In any event rule 42 relates only to the wording used in the verdict and not to the inquiry itself:

. . . in a case of conflict the statutory duty to ascertain how the deceased came to his death must prevail over the prohibition in rule 42. The scope for conflict is small. Rule 42 applies, and applies only, to the verdict. Plainly the coroner and the jury may explore facts bearing on criminal and civil liability.[17]

Even if the culprit will be readily identifiable, although unnamed, the rule 42 prohibition takes second place.[18]

7.05   The Nature of the Inquiry

The nature of the coroner's task was described by the Master of the Rolls in the *Jamieson* case:[19]

---

[12] *R v Inner West London Coroner ex p Dallaglio* (1994) 4 All ER 139.
[13] Referring to conclusion 14 in the *ex p Jamieson* judgment (n 9 above).
[14] *Ex p Homberg* (n 10 above).
[15] But the prohibition on criminal liability only refers to naming an individual; see section 9.12.
[16] See also *R (Scott) v HM Coroner for Inner West London* [2001] EWHC Admin 105.
[17] *Ex p Jamieson* (n 9 above).
[18] *R v HM Coroner for N Humberside ex p Jamieson* (1993) 158 JP 1 (the original judicial review).
[19] *Ex p Jamieson* (n 9 above).

It is the duty of the coroner as the public official responsible for the conduct of inquests, whether he is sitting with a jury or without, to ensure that the relevant facts are fully, fairly and fearlessly investigated. He is bound to recognise the acute public concern rightly aroused where deaths occur in custody. He must ensure that the relevant facts are exposed to public scrutiny particularly if there is evidence of foul play, abuse or inhumanity. He fails in his duty if his investigation is superficial, slipshod or perfunctory. But the responsibility is his. He must set the bounds of the inquiry. He must rule on the procedures to be followed.

The coroner's inquest is inquisitorial, its sole purpose to find the true answer to the questions set out by s 11(5) and rule 36. It is not meant to be a trial;

> It is an inquisitorial process, a process of investigation quite unlike a trial . . . the function of the inquest is to seek out and record as many of the facts concerning the death as [the] public interest requires.[20]

Nonetheless, the following quote from a paper by experienced counsel accurately reflects some of the tensions between the inquisitorial theory and the sometime adversarial reality:

> In reality, the kind of cases in which advocates usually appear do indeed have all the hallmarks of an adversarial forum in which facts are vigorously disputed and issues of liability are hotly contested. Because of the nature of the hearing . . . it is inevitable that there will be times when it has all the appearance of a trial of the issues between opposing parties.

> [Those parties] are almost certain to want to make sure that the evidence comes out in such a way as to establish the position they are contending for.[21]

Increased Scope where Article 2 is Engaged   7.06

Despite these limitations, the current effect of recent case law relating to the Human Rights Act 1998[22] is that there are circumstances in which the inquest must examine issues beyond rule 36, in order to satisfy the obligations arising under Article 2 ECHR.[23] This would involve scrutiny of the operational measures taken by the State to protect an individual's life.[24] Examples might include the training and control of firearms officers involved in a fatal shooting or the adequacy of systems protecting a suicidal prisoner.

---

[20] *R v South London Coroner ex p Thompson* (1982) 126 SJ 625.

[21] Munyard T., *Inquests: law & practice for advocates* (25/11/99): www.2gardenct.law.co.uk.

[22] Most recently: *R (Amin) v Secretary of State for the Home Department* and *R (Middleton) v West Somerset Coroner* [2002] 3 WLR 505. This text refers to 'the current effect' of these cases as the major decision (*Middleton*) is under appeal to the House of Lords at the time of going to press. See also section 9.31.

[23] Article 2 European Convention on Human Rights, given effect in UK law by the Human Rights Act 1998. See section 4.43 on Article 2 generally and section 9.30 on the obligation to investigate.

[24] The issue of a related verdict is dealt with at section 9.30 *et seq.*

The coroner may widen the remit of the inquest where he is satisfied that:

- Article 2 is engaged, ie there is sufficient evidence of a substantive breach[25] of Article 2 that the obligation to investigate is triggered; *and*
- taking into account the nature of the death, the inquest is the only vehicle for the State to fulfil the obligation under the investigative requirement of Article 2.

In considering the latter point, the coroner will have regard to all the measures taken by public authorities to respond to and investigate the death, from central government or otherwise. In other words, has the State done enough to minimize the risk of future like deaths, to give the beginnings of justice to the bereaved, and to assuage the anxieties of the public?[26] These requirements will vary according to the circumstances of the death, being more difficult to meet where the death was at the hands of agents of the State (eg police shooting) than where the deceased was merely in the care of the State (eg prison suicide).

The requirements are applicable in the public health sphere (eg death resulting from system failure in a hospital).[27] However the obligation may be more easily satisfied as the context and scope of the investigation is 'entirely different' from cases such as a death in custody.[28] But a remedy in civil litigation, professional proceedings or another investigation (eg NHS inquiry) is unlikely to suffice where there are cogent allegations of gross negligence made by an independent expert and substantive concerns about a 'medically orchestrated cover-up'.[29]

The effect on verdicts of widening the scope of the inquest is considered at section 9.30 *et seq.*

7.07 Rule 43—Prevention of Similar Fatalities

Although the rider to a verdict has been abolished[30] and the coroner is forbidden from passing an opinion on matters outside the questions of who-when-where-how, the prevention of future fatalities remains one of the most potent rationales for the inquest. Accordingly, the coroner (rather than jury) has power under rule 43 to report the circumstances of the case to an appropriate authority with a view to remedial action being taken.

---

[25] See section 9.33 for the test for such a breach.

[26] *Middleton* (n 22 above).

[27] *Erikson v Italy*, App No 37900/97 (26/10/99). See also *Costello-Roberts v UK* (1993) 19 EHRR 112 which by analogy *might* suggest that the obligation would be no different following a death in a private hospital.

[28] *Powell v UK*, 12 EHRR 355.

[29] *R (Khan) v Secretary of State for Health* [2003] EWCA Civ 1129 where the court commented that the inquest 'furnishes the natural occasion for the effective judicial inquiry into the cause of a death that the Convention requires' (at paras 69 and 70).

[30] Coroners' Amendment Rules 1980 but see section 9.30 *et seq* in relation to system neglect verdicts.

As a result, it might be that witnesses are asked questions bearing on avoidance of such an event in the future even if this, in the narrow sense, is outside the question of how that particular death came about:

> The coroner has to equip himself, by carrying out a sufficient investigation, by investigating the relevant facts 'fully fairly and fearlessly', with material on which he can decide 'whether action should be taken to prevent the recurrence of fatalities similar to that in respect of which the inquest is being held.

According to some authorities,[31] the avoidance of future fatalities is a major purpose of the inquest:

> . . . an inquest can provide the family with the only opportunity they will have of ascertaining what happened. In addition . . . an inquest verdict can have a significant part to play in avoiding the repetition of inappropriate conduct and in encouraging beneficial change.[32]

Overall Purpose of the Inquest   7.08

The essential grounds of public interest served by a coroner's inquiry were identified by the Brodrick Committee[33] in 1971 (a Government inquiry into death certification and coroners):

- to determine the medical cause of death;
- to allay rumours or suspicions;[34]
- to draw attention to the existence of circumstances which, if unremedied, might lead to further deaths;
- to advance medical knowledge;
- to preserve the legal interest of the deceased's family, heirs, or other interested parties.

This was noted with approval more recently in *Homberg*[35] but it is interesting to note that the Brodrick list contains no direct mention of:

- the simple desirability of establishing the true facts of a death in public, so ensuring that there has been no masking of the circumstances;
- the advantages for the family in having a right to ask relevant questions of witnesses in a structured forum where the questions must (within certain limits) be answered without prevarication.

---

[31] Authorities on this point differ, the 1996 case of *In the matter of Captain Christopher John Kelly* commented that whilst rule 43 was a valuable power in the public interest, it was still ancillary to the main purpose of the inquest: 161 JP 417.

[32] *R v Inner South London Coroner ex p Douglas Williams* [1999] 1 All ER 344.

[33] Report of the Committee on Death Certification and Coroners, September 1971, Cmnd 4810.

[34] For example, in the face of media allegations that a child bled to death because it took 40 minutes for an ambulance to arrive, evidence at an inquest showed conclusively that the ambulance had only taken eight minutes. This resolved an important matter of public concern.

[35] *R v HM Coroner for W District of East Sussex ex p Homberg* (1994) 158 JP 357.

The long-term value of the public inquest was described in 1980:

> It is worth remembering that if the public arena for discussion (albeit in limited terms) of sudden deaths at the inquest is allowed to wither away, the alternative is likely to be secret administrative decisions about deaths.[36]

It is sometimes clear that those involved have been given no clear appreciation of the true purpose and value of the inquest by their legal representatives. Briefing the client[37] plays an important part in the overall worth of the inquest, as does a thorough debriefing on the information gained at the hearing.[38]

A Public Hearing

7.09 Who May Take Part

The list of persons who may take part in the inquest[39] is restricted by rule 20 (see Table 7.1). This sets out specific classes of person who may question witnesses.

In terms of family, whilst spouses, parents and children are amongst those specifically entitled to take part, this class does not automatically extend to other close blood relatives such as brothers and sisters.[40] However, the rule must now be read in the light of Human Rights legislation,[41] and it seems clear that a rather wider interpretation is appropriate.

However, whilst the rule gives the coroner a discretion to allow others not within the set categories to take part if 'properly interested', this would usually only include persons with an interest in that specific death as opposed to a mere witness or a group that had a more general interest.[42] In the 2001 case of *Al-Fayed*[43] the court upheld a decision not to allow the father of a passenger killed in a vehicular incident to take part in the (separate) inquest of another victim. The judgment accepted that the appropriate question was whether the person had any close similarity with any of the other categories.

---

[36] Fenwick, 'Misadventures of the Coroners' Inquest' *New Law Journal*, 11 December 1980.

[37] See section 6.29 on briefing the client.

[38] See section 10.22 on debriefing following the inquest.

[39] Notification of the hearing date for interested persons or witnesses is dealt with at section 6.08 *et seq.*

[40] In *R v HM Coroner for Portsmouth ex p Keane* (1989) 153 JP 658 the court upheld the coroner's decision not to regard the brother of the deceased as a properly interested person but see also *R v South London Coroner ex p Driscoll* [1993] 159 JP 45 where a wider interpretation was necessary.

[41] The European Convention on Human Rights (in this context Article 8 thereof) given effect in UK domestic law by the Human Rights Act 1998.

[42] *Ex p Driscoll* (n 40 above).

[43] *R v Coroner of the Queen's Household ex p Al-Fayed* LTL 24/4/01.

Table 7.1. Rule 20

---

20. Entitlement to examine witnesses

(1) Without prejudice to any enactment with regard to the examination of witnesses at an inquest, any person who satisfies the coroner that he is within paragraph (2) shall be entitled to examine any witness at an inquest either in person or by [an authorized advocate as defined by section 119(1) of the Courts and Legal Services Act 1990]:

Provided that—

    (a) the chief officer of police, unless interested otherwise than in that capacity, shall only be entitled to examine a witness by [such an advocate];

    (b) the coroner shall disallow any question which in his opinion is not relevant or is otherwise not a proper question.

(2) Each of the following persons shall have the rights conferred by paragraph (1):—

    (a) a parent, child, spouse and any personal representative of the deceased;

    (b) any beneficiary under a policy of insurance issued on the life of the deceased;

    (c) the insurer who issued such a policy of insurance;

    (d) any person whose act or omission or that of his agent or servant may in the opinion of the coroner have caused, or contributed to, the death of the deceased;

    (e) any person appointed by a trade union to which the deceased at the time of his death belonged, if the death of the deceased may have been caused by an injury received in the course of his employment or by an industrial disease;

    (f) an inspector appointed by, or a representative of, an enforcing authority, or any person appointed by a government department to attend the inquest;

    (g) the chief officer of police;

    (h) any other person who, in the opinion of the coroner, is a properly interested person.

Following a protocol agreed with the Coroners' Society, the Mental Health Act Commission will generally be regarded as having a proper interest in cases involving the death of a detained patient.[44]

In relation to the Omagh bombing inquest, the House of Lords held that the Northern Ireland Human Rights Commission had a right to take part.[45] The statutory provisions relevant to that case do not affect inquests in England and Wales but the decision was referred to in the 2002 *Southall Black Sisters* case.[46] The High Court said that the House of Lords decision did show that an organization with no direct knowledge of the primary facts may, in appropriate circumstances,

---

[44] The protocol is shown in the Practice Notes for Coroners which can be found on the Coroners' Law Resource website: www.kcl.ac.uk/depsta/law/research/coroners/contents.html.

[45] *R v Greater Belfast Coroner ex p Northern Ireland Human Rights Commission* (2002) ACD 95; Decision appealed TLR 11/5/2001.

[46] *R (application of Southall Black Sisters) v HM Coroner for West Yorkshire* [2002] EWHC 1914 Admin.

be permitted to take part. However, the court refused the Southall Black Sisters application, holding it a relevant consideration that the organization had virtually no connection with the family of the deceased. The fact that they had no direct knowledge of the circumstances was also 'relevant but not conclusive in isolation'.

As the phrase 'properly interested person' is used throughout coronial legislation without any further definition, the importance of rule 20 goes far beyond a simple list of who may take part in the inquest.

7.10 Nature of the Right to Ask Questions

With the exception of a Chief Officer of Police, who must always be legally represented, interested persons may either take part in the inquest themselves or have legal representation.[47] However, this does not carry an absolute right to ask *any* question desired of the witnesses; the coroner is obliged under rule 20(1)(b) to disallow any question that in his opinion is not relevant or is otherwise not a proper question.

It is extremely rare for the police to take part in an inquest unless they have a direct involvement in the death. However, the 2000 case of *Hart*[48] held that as rule 20(2)(g) gives the Chief Officer of Police an entitlement to participate (by counsel or solicitor), this must be to enable him to pursue his functions, including the detection of crime. Whilst witnesses can only be examined within the remit of the inquisitorial process, that itself may elicit evidence which will provide grounds for charges to be brought (or otherwise).

7.11 Representation

Who may represent an interested person at an inquest can be a subject of misunderstanding. Clearly a solicitor or barrister may do so, but it is sometimes believed that legal executives also have an *automatic* right of audience. This is not the case.

In April 1998 an Order in Council designated the Institute of Legal Executives as an authorized body under the Courts and Legal Services Act 1990. This enables properly qualified Fellows[49] of the Institute to be granted rights of audience in certain proceedings, including inquests.[50] The Institute's requirements before granting the right to appear at inquests are quite stringent and it is not thought that anyone has yet taken the necessary course and examination.[51]

---

[47] As to legal aid see section 7.26.

[48] *R v Derby Coroner ex p Hart* (2000) 164 JP 429.

[49] Particularly experienced legal executives who have passed a range of examinations.

[50] An amendment to rule 20(1) was made by the Coroners' Amendment Rules 1999 to provide for representation by any authorized advocate defined by s 119(1) of the Courts and Legal Services Act 1990.

[51] The applicant has to pass the Institute's civil litigation audience requirements before taking a specific course and examination on coroner's law and practice.

By virtue of rule 20(2)(e), a trade union representative may take part at an inquest if the death of a member occurred by reason of industrial injury or disease. Effectively such a person will be acting as an advocate for family members. However, this does not enable the union representative to appear for another person such as a witness whose conduct is called into question.

Section 27 of the Courts and Legal Services Act 1990 retained the power of a court to give a right of audience to whomsoever the court thinks appropriate. By way of an example, the author has often used this power to permit a very experienced lawyer who qualified as a member of the Florida Bar but now practices in this country to take part in inquests.

An 'interested person', if not legally represented, may have a friend or helper with them to quietly assist and support, perhaps suggesting questions that they might ask. However such a person[52] would have no right of audience.

Inquest to be Held in Public   7.12

By rule 17 every inquest must be held in public. The only exception to this under coroner's legislation is where the evidence would reveal matters of national security, examples of which must be exceedingly rare. In such a case the majority of the inquest would still be held in public but the court would sit behind closed doors for the relevant parts of the evidence.

In general, rule 17 means that any member of the press or public has the right to attend an inquest. However the coroner is under no obligation to provide limitless accommodation and once the courtroom is full there is no further entitlement to enter.

There can also be exceptional circumstances where the public are excluded in the interests of justice. In the 1998 case of *Richards*,[53] the judge in a murder trial was held to have correctly applied the principle that the interests of justice must prevail when clearing the public (but not press) gallery because an important witness would not otherwise give evidence.

A court also has power to direct that the public (but not parties to the case or the press) be excluded from court during the evidence of a child or young person but only in 'any proceedings in relation to an offence against, or conduct contrary to, decency or morality'.[54] Whether this might apply by analogy to a coroner's court

---

[52] Known as a 'Mackenzie man' after the name of the case in which this right was established.

[53] *R v Richards* (1998) 163 JP 246. An 18-year-old witness to a stabbing refused to give evidence in front of the public gallery under any circumstances, her explanations varied but might have included fear of the defendant's family.

[54] Section 37 Children and Young Persons Act 1933 as amended by Youth Justice and Criminal Evidence Act 1999.

does not appear to have been tested; it is not impossible to envisage an occasional inquest involving a young witness that could be described as 'proceedings in relation to conduct contrary to decency or morality'.

The coroner may also remove from the court any person who is causing a disturbance or wilfully misbehaving, whether a properly interested person or member of the public. Obviously the decision to remove a close member of the family from an inquest is not to be taken lightly.[55]

7.13   Screening of Witnesses

Applications are occasionally made that the identity of particular witnesses be kept secret, by giving evidence from behind a screen. This usually involves police officers involved in a fatal pursuit or shooting.

The High Court has considered this twice in relation to inquests. In the 1997 *Newcastle Coroner* case[56] it was accepted that there was a risk to the personal security of the officer who fired the fatal shot if his identity was revealed, but disagreement as to how this should be dealt with in view of the provisions of rule 17.

The court held that in exceptional circumstances the mere screening of a witness, who could nonetheless be seen by the coroner, advocates and jury, was not to be taken as an exclusion of the public in breach of rule 17. The court refused to provide general guidance for coroners as the circumstances giving rise to such applications were so varied that this was impracticable. However, it was said that the persons who should have sight of the witness were the coroner, the jury, legal representatives of any properly interested persons, *and any unrepresented parties who were to be allowed to examine witnesses.* Whilst there is obvious logic in including the latter group, the author wonders whether it might often be such persons who could create the risk to the witness.

In the 1999 *Bedfordshire Coroner* case[57] (where the applicant was a newspaper) it was held that the fundamental principle is open justice and any departure from this must be stringently regulated. The mere fact that the witness was a police officer was not sufficient, nor (generally) was an irrational fear by a witness. However, fears for the personal safety of the witness or his family could take into account previous incidents and special needs (eg member of an armed response group). Once the reason for anonymity had been established on an objective basis, it would then be a balancing act as to how far the effect was a secret hearing—which would include the fact that there was less need for the identity of a witness to be known at an inquest than a criminal trial. This balancing test has also been

---

[55] See section 7.45 *et seq* for a discussion of the coroner's powers to deal with disorder in court.
[56] *R v HM Coroner for Newcastle upon Tyne ex p A* (1998) 162 JP 387.
[57] *R v Bedfordshire Coroner ex p Sunday Newspapers Ltd* (2000) 164 JP 283.

described as 'the risk factor against the open justice factor'.[58] However, if a real and immediate risk is established, the court must also have regard to the State's positive duty to protect the life (of the witness) under Article 2 ECHR.[59]

There have been occasions when it was considered appropriate in the interests of justice to clear the court of members of the public (but not press) during the evidence of a particular witness. See the 1998 case of *Richards*[60] referred to at section 7.12 above, but there the identity of the witness was already known to all concerned.

The Press   7.14

In general the press are entitled to report whatever is said in court. Privilege attaches to an accurate report of the proceedings and the press would be able to publish an allegation made by a witness in court, even if that allegation were completely untrue, without fear of libel proceedings.[61]

There is no power for a coroner to prohibit the press from reporting particular aspects of a case, however disturbing or personal such details may be. Whilst local media will usually take a more responsible attitude to grossly intrusive personal details than the national press, in general it is up to the coroner to conduct proceedings in such a way that sordid details are avoided, unless they are an essential part of the evidence.

For this reason it is rare that suicide notes, which commonly contain very personal details, are read out in open court.[62] It is more likely that the writing would be identified by a witness who will then be asked to confirm that the contents of the letter are indicative of the deceased being in a frame of mind to take their own life.[63]

Although not yet tested, it may be that Article 8 ECHR[64] will require some thought as to the level of personal details that should be admitted in evidence except where absolutely necessary. This is considered in relation to documentary evidence at section 7.43.

---

[58] *R v Lord Saville of Newdigate ex p A* [2000] 1 WLR 1885. This case was considering a different set of circumstances but commented that the necessary supervision by the public 'providing the safeguard against arbitrariness or idiosyncrasy' can still be achieved where a witness's identity remains undisclosed.

[59] *R v Lord Saville of Newdigate* (n 58 above).

[60] *R v Richards* (n 53 above).

[61] Although it must actually be in the course of the proceedings.

[62] Despite the provisions of rule 37 on documentary evidence, see section 7.42 *et seq.*

[63] See section 7.44.

[64] Article 8 (the right to private and family life) of the European Convention on Human Rights incorporated into UK domestic law by virtue of the Human Rights Act 1998: see section 4.45.

It is generally regarded as undesirable that the names and addresses of young witnesses be disclosed in the press,[65] although they will be freely heard in open court. Section 39 of the Children and Young Persons Act 1933[66] gives the coroner power[67] to prohibit publication of the name or any other particulars that could lead to the identification of a witness[68] who is a child or young person, ie under the age of 18.[69]

The coroner will need to keep in mind how far such an order would prevent the press from reporting any detail of the death at all. For example, if the deceased and witness are closely related it may be impossible to publish anything substantial without implying the identity of the witness. The importance of this might depend on the circumstances; a case of genuine and significant public concern involving a 17-year-old witness would differ from a less consequential case with a child of 11.

Although the press have a general right to publish whatever is said in court, there may be occasions when a report would prejudice or interfere with the proceedings, and might amount to contempt of court. For example, it would not be proper for the press to report submissions made in the absence of a jury at such a time that the jurors might read them before the conclusion of the proceedings.

Section 4(2) of the Contempt of Court Act 1981 gives the coroner a power to make a postponement order *delaying* reporting if necessary, to avoid a 'substantial risk of prejudice to the administration of justice in those proceedings or any other proceedings pending or imminent'. Typically this might be a prohibition on reporting an adjourned inquest if it might influence a future jury, but such cases where there was a genuine risk of prejudice would be exceedingly rare.

The coroner could not deal with a breach of such an order himself, for a press report is not contempt committed in the face of the court.[70] An infringement would be reported to the Attorney General for the necessary action.

---

[65] In criminal proceedings it has been held that it would only be in rare and exceptional circumstances that such an order would *not* be made: *R v Leicester Crown Court ex p S (a minor)* 94 Cr App R 34. See also *ex p Sunday Newspapers Ltd* (n 57 above) where it was said that there was less need to know the identity of a witness at an inquest than in a criminal trial.

[66] As amended by s 68 Criminal Justice Act 1991.

[67] The coroner should permit those who have an interest in such orders (eg the press) to make representations before any decision is made.

[68] Although there is no clear case law, it seems likely that s 39 would not apply to a child or young person who was not a witness, ie merely named by others at the inquest. It certainly could not apply to the deceased if he/she was under 18.

[69] A *child* is under the age of 15, a *young person* has not yet attained 18.

[70] See section 7.45 *et seq* in respect of contempt of court.

Photographs and Tape Recorders 7.15

By s 41 of the Criminal Justice Act 1925, it is an offence to take a photograph in the coroner's court or make a sketch of any party to the proceedings before the court. This ban extends to the precincts of the court but does not prevent the press from photographing or filming parties as they enter or leave the building. Nor does it prevent an artist entering the court, memorizing details and then leaving to make a sketch.

This prohibition includes the taking of photographs through the windows of the court, such as a shot of the jury in their retiring room taken with a telephoto lens.

It is an offence under s 9 of the Contempt of Court Act 1981 to bring a tape recorder or similar instrument into the court, or to use such an item there, without the consent of the court. In a Home Office Circular of 1981[71] it was recommended that applications for leave to use tape recorders from parties, their legal representatives or bona-fide journalists should be treated sympathetically. However, any such recording is only for the use of the person making it (eg making an accurate note) and there is a specific prohibition in the same section against publishing the recording or playing it to the public.

In general, the author would suggest that there is a considerable difference between allowing a journalist to use a pocket dictating machine in an effort to ensure accuracy, and allowing a full recording system to be set up in competition to the court's own equipment.

Preliminaries

Opening the Inquest 7.16

The inquest will normally be opened within a few days of the death. This allows prompt release of the body, despite the fact that investigations into the circumstances, and the preparation of a file for the coroner, may take some time.

There is considerable variation in practice between coroners on the opening of the inquest. However, in general the coroner will hear *brief* evidence dealing with:

- identification of the deceased;
- the general circumstances of the death;
- the finding of the body;
- the medical cause of death (if known at this stage).

---

[71] Home Office Circular 79/1981.

This evidence may be given in a written statement (see Table 7.2 below) or verbally, either from the coroner's officer or a member of the deceased's family. In some jurisdictions it is routine for relatives of the deceased to attend, in others it is not.[72]

After hearing this evidence, the coroner will adjourn the case (sometimes to a fixed date but mostly *sine die*) and will sign a certificate for burial or cremation.[73] It is also commonplace that the coroner signs several copies of an 'interim certificate' under rule 30 (see Table 7.3 below) confirming the fact of death and that an inquest has been opened and adjourned. This certificate may assist the personal representatives of the deceased to deal with the estate[74] pending completion of the inquest and registration of the death.

7.17 Adjournments under Section 16

Once the inquest has been opened, if the coroner is told that a person has been charged[75] with one of the offences[76] specified within s 16(1)(a) the inquest will be adjourned until the criminal proceedings are concluded.

Similarly, under s 16(1)(b), if someone is charged with 'another offence connected with the death' which is to be heard at Crown Court, and the Crown Prosecution Service *ask* that the inquest is adjourned, the coroner is bound to accede. The situation is less clear if the prosecution is brought by some agency other than the CPS (eg the Health and Safety Executive) but the author would suggest that it is only logical to treat this in identical fashion.

If the coroner adjourns under s 16, he must send the registrar a certificate (Form 120) setting out the particulars established. This allows the death to be registered, notwithstanding that the inquest is yet to be concluded.

If a person faces only a summary offence in connection with the death, the inquest will not be adjourned to await those proceedings. Indeed it is important that the

---

[72] Although it must always be open for them to attend if they wish.

[73] See section 4.27 *et seq* on disposal of the body.

[74] Some banks, insurance companies, and other organizations will accept the coroner's interim certificate in lieu of a death certificate, particularly for smaller claims, but others will not.

[75] The coroner's power to adjourn is when informed by the clerk of the Magistrates' Court (under requirements in s 17) that a person has been charged before a Magistrates' Court with one of the specified offences. Thus charging by the police and bailing to court is insufficient. However, s 51 of the Crime and Disorder Act 1998 abolished committal from the lower court for indictable only offences, so no one will now be 'charged before a Magistrates' Court' with relevant matters. An amendment to the Criminal Justice Bill at the House of Lords Committee stage is promised for late 2003 to rectify the anomaly.

[76] The specified offences are: murder, manslaughter, infanticide, causing death by dangerous driving or by careless driving whilst under the influence of drink/drugs, aiding and abetting suicide. In theory the inquest could still proceed despite such a charge if the CPS agree, but this is a most unlikely scenario.

Table 7.2. Example of a typical opening statement

THE INFORMATION OF WITNESSES taken orally or admitted as documentary evidence as indicated thereon on behalf of Our Sovereign Lady the Queen touching the death of **THOMAS HENRY SMITH**
at the Coroner's Court in Sheffield on 19th August 2003
before me **Christopher Peter Dorries** Her Majesty's Coroner for the County of South Yorkshire (West District) on an Inquisition into the death of the afore mentioned.

Graham Marsden Coroner's Officer states as follows:

In respect of the body which is the subject of this Inquest enquiries have been made of: JAMES SMITH, 1 High Street, Sheffield, son of the deceased, and the following information ascertained.

The deceased was **THOMAS HENRY SMITH**. He was 75 years of age, having been born on the 27th December 1927. He was a retired grocer and a married man. He lived with his wife at 4 The Common, Sheffield. He enjoyed health in keeping with his age and was not subject to dizzy spells or blackouts. His eyesight and hearing were good.

On 18th August 2003, he was crossing London Road, Sheffield, near to its junction with Hill Street, on foot, when he collided with a motorcycle. He received head injuries and was taken to the Royal Hallamshire Hospital, Sheffield, but was found to be dead on arrival there. The body was conveyed to the Medico-Legal Centre, Sheffield. Later that same date Mr. JAMES SMITH attended and identified the body to PC 5678 JONES of the South Yorkshire Police as that of his father, **THOMAS HENRY SMITH**. PC JONES has today identified the same body to Dr. PLUMB, who has performed a post-mortem examination.

The body is to be cremated.

inquest is heard first[77] to preserve the coroner's right to refer the matter further to the CPS under rule 28 (see section 7.38). The importance of this was underlined in the 2003 case of *Stanley*[78] where it was said that any decision by the CPS *not* to proceed with an indictable offence 'must be regarded as provisional' pending the

---

[77] *Re Beresford* [1952] 36 Cr App R 1; *Smith v DPP & anor* (2000) 164 JP 96.
[78] *R v HM Coroner for Inner North London ex p Stanley* [2003] EWHC 1180 Admin.

Table 7.3. Example of an interim certificate

CORONER'S INTERIM CERTIFICATE OF THE FACT OF DEATH
Pursuant to the Coroners Act 1988 and Rule 30 of the Coroners Rules 1984

DEATH	Ref No. **09562-2003**

Date and Place of Death
Eighteenth August 2003
Royal Hallamshire Hospital, Sheffield

Name and Surname	Sex	**Male**
Thomas Henry SMITH	Maiden Name	

Date and Place of Birth
27th December 1927   Sheffield

Occupation and Usual Address
Retired Grocer
4 The Common, Sheffield, South Yorkshire

Date Inquest Opened
19th August 2003

The precise medical cause of death was as follows:
(Subject to confirmation at inquest)

1a   **Head injuries**

b

c

II

I certify that in accordance with my statutory duty, I have opened an inquest into the death of the above named, and taken evidence of the facts set out, which stands adjourned for the completion of my enquiries.

Signed   Date   **19th August 2003**

Christopher P. Dorries
HM Coroner for South Yorkshire (West)

The Registrar of Deaths cannot issue a Death Certificate until the Inquest has been completed.

conclusion of the inquest.[79] This recognizes that the inquest may reveal facts justifying an indictable charge, but if summary proceedings have already been concluded it may be impossible for the prosecution to take the matter further.

Issues arising in the decision whether or not to resume an inquest adjourned under s 16 are considered at section 4.40.

The Order of Witnesses   7.18

In general the coroner will call witnesses in chronological order. Inevitably there will be exceptions and cases where it is difficult to separate the evidence in such a manner.

However, it is common that the pathologist's evidence is heard first. Once the medical cause of death is known by all concerned, it is easier to direct the remaining evidence as to how the death came about. This issue, and the reasons why a contrary course of action may sometimes be appropriate, are considered in greater detail at section 5.49.

In some cases the coroner may be prepared to give disclosure of witness statements, or at the minimum a list of witnesses, noting the order in which they may be called. Disclosure of evidence is dealt with further at section 6.14 *et seq.*

Presence of Witnesses in Court   7.19

In most circumstances witnesses at an inquest may sit in the court, hearing the evidence being given before they are called themselves. Some might then be required to wait for the end of the proceedings (in case they need to be recalled) but many will be released and can leave if they wish.

Occasionally it may be desirable to order at the start of proceedings that witnesses wait outside the courtroom. In particular, if there is a suspicion that several witnesses might conspire to tell untruths, it is inappropriate to allow them each to sit in court and hear what answers are being given before their own evidence.

This must be balanced against the general rule of natural justice that a person whose conduct may be called into question should be entitled to hear all the evidence before being offered the chance to give their own explanation. Such a witness would normally be asked to give evidence last and there is some unfairness if they are excluded from the court until that point. However, remembering that an inquest is not a trial of any individual, the coroner's statutory duty to ascertain the true facts must hold greater importance than the rights of any individual witness.

---

[79] See *R v DPP ex p Manning & Melbourne* [2001] QB 230 at para 33 where it was said that if a jury returned a verdict of unlawful killing at an inquest implicating an identifiable person 'the ordinary expectation would naturally be that a prosecution would follow'.

7.20   Inquests Heard by Deputy Coroner

If the coroner is unavailable, it may be the deputy coroner or an assistant deputy who sits at the inquest. There is no formal definition of 'unavailable', but it is now commonly interpreted to include the coroner being committed to other matters, even if still in the court building.[80]

Such a deputy has all the powers, rights, and responsibilities of the coroner and will sign the papers relating to the inquest in their own name.

7.21   Coroner Sitting with an Assessor

On rare occasions the coroner may choose to sit with an assessor—an expert in a particular field who can advise and guide the coroner on those matters within their expertise. There is no express provisions for this in the Act but Home Office Circular 61/97 made clear the view that coroners may appoint assessors in cases where they consider it necessary to do so in the interests of justice.

The law on this was reviewed in the 1996 case of *Wright*[81] where it was held entirely permissible for a coroner to sit with an assessor if necessary 'having regard to the technical nature of the evidence which may have to be considered'.

The court further held that:

- there can be no objection to the assessor asking questions of a witness giving technical evidence, provided this is done under the coroner's control and is restricted to matters within the assessor's special experience;
- the role of the assessor should not extend to giving expert evidence—there is a danger that this might appear to attract the special confidence of the coroner and carry greater weight, and it is better that the roles of assessor and expert witness be kept separate;
- at the conclusion of the evidence the coroner should not discuss the circumstances of the death with the assessor (ie the assessor should not retire with the coroner whilst any decision is made).

7.22   Others on the Bench

Occasionally the coroner may invite another person onto the bench during an inquest.[82] It should be made clear to everyone in court from the outset that the person has simply been invited onto the bench as a courtesy and will in no way

---

[80] *Commissioner of Police for the Metropolis v HM Coroner [Inner London South]* (2003) 2 All ER 585.

[81] *R v HM Coroner for Surrey ex p Wright* (1996) 160 JP 581.

[82] For example, a visiting colleague or new deputy. It is also traditional in some areas that the High Sheriff (the sovereign's representative in the county for all matters relating to the judiciary and the maintenance of law and order) will visit the coroner's court.

take any part in the proceedings or decisions about the case. Thus, if the coroner retires to reach a conclusion at the end of the evidence it would be wise for the visitor to remain in open view of the court so that there can be no suspicion that they have taken part in the decision.

Counsel to the Inquest 7.23

Although extremely unusual, there seems nothing to prevent the appointment of 'counsel to the inquest' in a particularly complex case.[83] Other fact-finding tribunals facing a challenging task appoint such a counsel (or solicitor) from time to time.[84]

Counsel to an inquest would have no part in the decision-making process and should carry out the role independently of the coroner. In particular counsel might marshal the evidence that has been obtained for the coroner, setting out chronologies and summaries etc. There would seem to be no reason why the coroner could not direct (in accordance with rule 21) that the principal examination of each witness should be by the counsel rather than from the bench.[85] Submissions on law by the counsel would be to assist the court by ensuring all relevant aspects of an issue have been considered.

Such cases will be exceptional and provision for the (substantial) costs thereof would need to be agreed with the funding local authority.

Joinder of Inquests 7.24

Where more than one death has occurred in the same incident it is common (but not invariable) that the inquests be held together. Each inquest is entirely separate, it is simply a question of the coroner (or jury) reaching the necessary decisions for each individual death from evidence put forward at one time. It is not uncommon for the court to reach different conclusions, for example that a driver died by accident (or misadventure) but that his passengers were unlawfully killed by his dangerous driving.

It would be appropriate to give those involved an opportunity to state any objection but some thought must also be given to possible emotional difficulty or heightened tension where two cases are heard together. For example, it may be legally arguable that evidence of a murder and immediate suicide by the killer could be heard in the same proceedings, but this may make an already difficult

---

[83] See *Jervis on Coroners* (12th edition) at para 12-14.

[84] For example, model rules under consideration by the Council on Tribunals (who supervise the constitution and working of tribunals of many types) allow for the appointment of Treasury Solicitor or Counsel to an Investigatory Tribunal in order to assist the tribunal in seeking and presenting evidence, and to represent the public interest in relation to matters before the Tribunal.

[85] *R v Derby Coroner ex p Hart* (2000) 164 JP 429.

occasion for the various relatives worse. In some circumstances it may be better that such inquests are held in close order but not at the same time.

Further, the 2001 case of *Al-Fayed* [86] made clear that where there is a disagreement between the parties as to which issues are relevant to the inquest, it may be expedient to pursue two separate inquests without the distractions of added controversy and confrontation. If the alternative was an inquest of great difficulty with problems of manageability, the coroner was entitled to deal with this in a way which would avoid tensions between the disparate interests of the relatives.

7.25 Bias

As the inquest proceedings are inquisitorial, and hence largely in the hands of the coroner, it is particularly important that the court is seen to be fair and impartial. [87] A coroner who might be thought to have an interest in the outcome, or some connection with a witness or interested person, should arrange for another to hear the case. Given that a coroner's jurisdiction is essentially local, some knowledge of a participant can be a real prospect.

In particular, the *Law Society Guide to the Professional Conduct of Solicitors* [88] sets out that a solicitor/coroner must make arrangements for another to carry out an inquest where it might be thought that some bias could arise out of a personal or professional connection with the deceased or a near relative.

Where the connection is only tenuous (eg the coroner is distantly acquainted with an uncontroversial witness) it may be sufficient to declare the situation in sufficient time for objection to be taken if desired.

In the 1993 *Stringer* case [89] the High Court found no merit in an allegation of apparent bias because the local authority had involvement in a death and the coroner was appointed and paid by the authority. The court noted that the coroner was wholly independent of the local authority and that, under s 3(4) of the Act, tenure was determinable only by the Lord Chancellor.

In hearing an application that an inquest should be quashed for apparent bias, the High Court will ask whether the circumstances would lead a fair-minded and informed observer to conclude that there was a real possibility or real danger (the two being the same) that the coroner was biased. [90]

---

[86] *R v Coroner of the Queen's Household ex p Al-Fayed* and *R v Surrey Coroner ex p Al-Fayed* 58 BMLR 205 where it was clear that documentary evidence likely to be accepted by one family was unlikely to be accepted by the other.

[87] *R v Inner West London Coroner ex p Dallaglio* [1994] 4 All ER 139.

[88] *Guide to the Professional Conduct of Solicitors*, 8th edition at para 15.06. Law Society Publications: www.guide.lawsociety.org.uk. See also section 1.22.

[89] *R v HM Coroner for South Yorkshire ex p Stringer* (1993) 158 JP 453.

[90] *Re Medicaments and Related Classes of Goods No. 2* [2001] 1 WLR 700. See also *R (on the application of Dawson) v HM Coroner for East Riding and Kingston upon Hull* [2001] ACD 68.

Legal Aid 7.26

There is extremely limited provision for legal aid in the coroner's court. Although the Legal Aid Acts of 1949 and 1974 included such within their terms, those sections were never brought into effect. In the vast majority of cases, the family of the deceased are thrown upon their own resources.

Section 6(8) of the Access to Justice Act 1998 allows the Legal Services Commission to fund appropriate applications but in general this will only apply to those deaths likely to engage Article 2 ECHR (see section 4.43).

This subject is considered in greater detail at section 6.28.

Taking the Evidence

Formalities 7.27

By rule 16 every inquest must be opened and closed formally. Presumably this originates from the time when inquests were held in the upstairs room of a public house and it would have been important for bystanders to distinguish between the legal proceedings and the general business of the day.

In modern inquests the opening of the proceedings is likely to be marked by nothing more formal than the coroner's officer telling interested persons 'all rise' as the coroner enters the courtroom. However, in some jurisdictions it is common at larger inquests for at least part of a formal proclamation to be read whilst the coroner enters court.

Initial Matters 7.28

The coroner will first ascertain who are the interested persons present at the inquest. If there are solicitors or counsel in attendance, their details and the names of the persons that they represent will be recorded.

The coroner may then give a brief indication of the purpose of an inquest. This is likely to take the form of a reminder that inquest proceedings are not designed to attribute blame or guilt upon any person but are intended as a fact-finding exercise to ascertain who the deceased was, where and when he died, and, most importantly, how he came by his death.

The coroner will then announce that the inquest was opened on an earlier date[91] and confirm with the relatives that the evidence of identification given at that

---

[91] See section 7.16.

stage is correct as regards the spelling of the deceased's name, age, and place of birth etc.

The coroner may outline the format of the proceedings, indicating which witnesses will be called in person and which statements are to be taken as documentary evidence. The requirements of rule 37 will be complied with at this point.[92] If the interested persons are not represented, it might be explained that they will have an opportunity to ask questions of the witnesses, relevant to the purpose of the inquest, once the coroner has taken their evidence.

It may be as well for the coroner to check at this stage that any unrepresented interested persons are clear about the procedure to be followed and the way in which they might participate.

7.29 Evidence to be Given on Oath

By s 11(2) of the Act the coroner must 'examine on oath all persons who tender their evidence respecting the facts and all persons having knowledge of the facts whom he thinks it expedient to examine'. See section 7.35 on the effect of this requirement on the evidence of those too young to give sworn evidence.

Any witness wishing to affirm, or swear the oath on a holy book other than a Bible, should advise the coroner's officer or usher of this before the proceedings commence.

7.30 Notes to be Taken of the Evidence

Rule 39 requires the coroner to take notes of the evidence. In most instances this now means that the proceedings will be tape-recorded.[93]

However, the coroner is also likely to take written notes of the evidence for several reasons:

- it is not unknown for tape recording equipment to be faulty without any visible evidence at the time;
- the coroner may need to refer to the exact evidence given by a witness at a later time in the proceedings, either to challenge what was said or to compare two versions;
- if retiring to reach a decision on a case the coroner may also need to refer to the notes on particular details;
- full notes will also assist with summing up in a jury case.

---

[92] Effectively informing those involved that they can see a copy of the statement and may raise objection to it being taken in evidence. For a more detailed explanation of documentary evidence see section 7.42 *et seq.*

[93] Which complies with rule 39: *R v South London Coroner ex p Thompson* (1982) 126 SJ 625.

Relying purely on a tape recording is impracticable in these situations and so, despite modern technology, the witness is likely to find that the salient points of evidence are being taken down in longhand with resultant pauses.

Questioning of Witnesses by the Coroner   7.31

Because the proceedings are inquisitorial (ie it is the coroner's inquiry on behalf of the Crown), it is generally the coroner who will first question the witness. The coroner will usually have a statement or report from the witness and will seek to elicit the relevant parts of the story in a clear fashion, easily understandable to everyone else in court.

Having the benefit of the statements, the coroner will usually know the answers to the questions already, although surprises abound in practice. Nonetheless, it is the inquest's purpose to bring out all the facts in public. In general, leading questions should be avoided[94] unless perhaps on initial matters unlikely to be the subject of dispute.

Many witnesses will be extremely nervous and will be assisted by a courteous reception into the witness box. The coroner can maintain a neutral stance by treating all witnesses in precisely the same manner.

It is not uncommon for a witness, deliberately or otherwise, to answer a question marginally different from that asked. The coroner must keep the witness to the point in issue, repeating the question if necessary. Refusal to answer a proper question is considered at section 7.40 following.

It is the coroner's duty to ensure that all relevant issues are addressed by eliciting and managing the evidence in an orderly and coherent fashion. An inquest 'which leaves too many questions unanswered and too many issues unresolved is not a sufficient inquiry'.[95] It has been made clear that it is the coroner's responsibility to conduct the inquiry no matter who else is in court:

> . . . the coroner is the prime inquisitor. He cannot excuse a failure on his part to ask questions that require to be asked by saying that the family was represented by counsel who could have asked the questions.[96]

It has also been held that it is the coroner's obligation under the Rules to examine persons who may be able to give relevant evidence:

> . . . he must form his own view as to their credibility and the reliability of their evidence. He may not decline to hear witnesses simply on the basis of another's

---

[94] Home Office Circular 68/1955. See also para A.3.1 of the Coroners' Bench Book.
[95] *R v HM Coroner for Coventry ex p O'Reilly* (1996) 160 JP 749.
[96] *R v HM Coroner for Inner North London ex p Cohen* (1994) 158 JP 644.

[eg police] assessment of their reliability. That would be to abdicate his own responsibility to conduct a proper investigation . . .[97]

All evidence that the coroner takes into account must be in the public domain. It is not appropriate for a coroner to have regard to statements read privately or to rely on the results of discussions with the investigating officer.[98]

7.32 Questioning of Witnesses by Advocates

After the coroner has examined the witness, properly interested persons (see section 7.09) will be invited to ask further questions. The witness's own representative[99] (if any) would normally go last. In the nature of inquisitorial proceedings, there is no specific right for advocates to ask leading questions of witnesses that they represent.

Rule 20(1)(b) requires the coroner to disallow any question which is irrelevant or otherwise not a proper question. It is often the case that questions are asked which might be of great interest but are irrelevant to the statutory purpose of an inquest:

> . . . the inquiry must focus on matters directly causative of death and must indeed be confined to these matters alone.[100]

Equally where a question is not clear, or is more in the way of a statement, the coroner should intervene.

Even experienced advocates will have spent the great majority of their time[101] in the normal adversarial proceedings of the criminal and civil courts and will need to remember the distinct nature of a coroner's court:

> Their clients are not . . . parties to adversarial litigation. Their only legitimate interest is one shared by the coroner—to investigate and discover the true circumstances of the death.[102]

Nonetheless, many interested persons at an inquest *will* have an eye upon future litigation, frequently leading to attempts to turn the proceedings into a 'fishing expedition' or a practice run of the civil case. The inquest should not be seen as a specific opportunity to gain an admission or pass the blame. It has been made clear on a number of occasions that an attempt to widen the scope of the hearing is inappropriate:

---

[97] *R v Avon Coroner ex p Bentley* (2002) 166 JP 297.

[98] *Ex p Cohen* (n 96 above) and *R v HM Coroner for Ceredigion ex p Wigley* (1993) COD 364.

[99] As to who may be a representative, see section 7.11.

[100] *R v HM Coroner for W. District of East Sussex ex p Homberg* (1994) 158 JP 357.

[101] A survey for the Coroner Review (see section 1.08) suggested that there is no legal representation for any party at about 79 per cent of inquests.

[102] *Ex p Homberg* (n 100 above).

It is not the function of a coroner's inquest to provide a forum for attempts to gather evidence for pending or future criminal or civil proceedings.[103]

The family's expectation of the inquest will often be greater than the court can fulfil. It is unfortunate if this is exacerbated by a lack of proper advice as to the limits of the inquest and what they might reasonably expect.

Questioning of Witnesses by Unrepresented Persons   7.33

Interested persons do not commonly have legal representation at an inquest.[104] Whilst those unrepresented have exactly the same right to question witnesses, an additional responsibility falls on the coroner in this situation, as the family or others involved may have problems expressing questions for themselves.

In many cases, whatever explanation is given, those involved have difficulty in appreciating that they are only allowed to ask *questions* of the witness at this stage, rather than make a statement of their own experiences and feelings. The art of questioning is unnatural to most people and it may become necessary for the coroner to remain patient and intervene tactfully to remind the questioner of what is expected. Often no progress will be made unless the coroner turns the interested person's statement into a question for the witness. This should be assistance, not advocacy, and must remain neutral.[105]

Nonetheless, such interjections from interested persons can sometimes provide the coroner with a rich source of information. It is not uncommon for the questioner to introduce issues that are highly relevant although not necessarily linked to the witness presently giving evidence. Such information sometimes leads to the inquest going in a totally unforeseen direction and even to a need to send for witnesses whose existence was previously unknown to the coroner.

Evidence Differing from Statement   7.34

In some cases the witness will give evidence which differs from a previous statement. Commonly this will arise through failure of recollection due to the passage of time,[106] but on occasions there are more significant reasons. Where only the coroner has the witness's statement it is unlikely that anyone else will be aware of the discrepancy. It is therefore incumbent on the coroner to make the

---

[103] *R v Poplar Coroner ex p Thomas* [1993] QB 610; sub nom: *R v HM Coroner for Greater London ex p Thomas.*

[104] As to the question of legal aid in the coroner's court, see sections 6.28 and 7.26.

[105] *Simms v Moore* [1970] 2 QB 327.

[106] Witnesses may ask to refresh their memory from a statement prior to the hearing; this would generally be permitted but there are exceptions. See section 6.15 and Home Office Circular 82/1969.

matter public by putting the inconsistency to the witness and seeking an explanation.[107]

The procedure for entering the earlier contradictory statement of a witness, oral or written, is set down under s 4 and s 5 of the Criminal Procedure Act 1865.[108] Effectively the contradiction must be drawn to the attention of the witness so that they might have an opportunity to explain the discrepancy.

7.35 Child Witnesses

All evidence at an inquest must be given on oath. As a result, unlike a criminal court, the coroner can only hear evidence from a child capable of understanding the oath. There is no set age; it is a matter of the coroner questioning the child as to whether they understand what is meant by the truth, what a promise before God means, and that there is a duty to tell the truth, no matter how difficult.

However, as described at section 7.49 below, the inquest can admit hearsay evidence and it may be more appropriate for the coroner to call a witness who has interviewed a young child. There are now good facilities available for the recording of statements from young children and it would be entirely possible for a witness to produce a videotape of such an interview as part of his own evidence.

Section 39 of the Children and Young Persons Act 1933[109] gives the coroner power to prohibit publication of the name or other particulars that could lead to the identification of a witness under the age of 18. Some considerations in making such an order are dealt with at section 7.14.

7.36 Evidence that is Likely to be Distressing

In some cases the facts are likely to be distressing for the family. This may range from details of injuries within the post-mortem report to an eyewitness account of harrowing events. Wherever possible, the coroner will steer clear of causing further anguish but in some cases the needs of the inquest dictate that the facts just cannot be avoided. Forethought by the coroner and officers may enable the family or their advocate to be warned of the situation. Some relatives will choose to leave court and should therefore be given an opportunity to do this at the appropriate time without being made to feel out of place.

Occasionally the court will meet an excitable witness who simply cannot wait to break into a detailed and vivid account of the most gruesome and unnecessary details. Much damage may be done in the few seconds before the coroner can

---

[107] *R v HM Coroner for Inner North London ex p Cohen* (1994) 158 JP 644. This would apply even where others had copies of the statement in question by virtue of disclosure.

[108] The relevant sections of this Act are stated to apply to all courts authorized to hear evidence.

[109] As amended by s 68 Criminal Justice Act 1991. See also section 7.12.

intervene. Where the police or coroner's officer take a statement from someone who shows such tendencies, it is helpful if the coroner is given some advance warning.

Submissions on Law to Coroner   7.37

By rule 40, no person is allowed to address the coroner, or any jury, as to the facts of the case. However, advocates or interested persons may address the coroner with submissions on points of law. Most commonly this would be at the conclusion of the evidence but it may occur during the hearing if the need arises. Submissions might include whether another witness should be called or whether a particular line of questioning should be allowed. If the case is before a jury, they should retire whilst any submission is heard.[110]

The coroner must hear relevant submissions that advocates or others wish to make. Failure to consider submissions has been held as sufficient ground for quashing an inquest. In rejecting a submission, it will usually be appropriate to give brief reasons for the decision.[111]

The 2003 case of *Stanley*[112] held that a coroner should give the opportunity for submissions if considering admitting evidence before a jury of the deceased's convictions, or reference to a decision of the CPS not to prosecute a person involved in the death.

A submission to the coroner as to which verdicts might be left open to the jury (or considered by the coroner) is a matter of law rather than fact:

> The Coroners Rules do not permit submissions as to the facts, but it seems that submissions as to which verdicts should be left to a jury are matters of law, unless it is merely an attempt to persuade the jury of a certain version of the facts. Such submissions can be made in the absence of the jury.[113]

Of course, in most cases there is no jury so the coroner will hear submissions and then decide on the appropriate conclusion. Here the test might also be whether the advocate is trying to persuade the coroner that a particular version of the facts is correct.

Criminal Offences Apparent during Evidence   7.38

Under rule 28, if evidence is given from which it appears that the death is likely to be due to one of the offences specified (murder, manslaughter, death by dangerous driving, etc) *and* that someone might be charged, the coroner must adjourn

---

[110] *R v East Berkshire Coroner ex p Buckley* [1992] 157 JP 425.
[111] *R v Lambeth Council ex p Walters*, The Times, 6 Oct 1993. See also section 7.55 and the case of *Stanley* (below) on giving reasons generally.
[112] *R (application of Stanley) v HM Coroner for Inner North London* [2003] EWHC 1180 Admin.
[113] *Ex p Buckley* (n 110 above).

the inquest and inform the CPS of the circumstances, unless they have already indicated this is unnecessary.

In theory this situation should rarely arise. If the death has been investigated thoroughly in the first place any prospect of a serious offence will have been explored. However, an inquest will occasionally reveal something unexpected or which strengthens existing suspicions, necessitating an adjournment under rule 28.

The provisions of rule 28 are often forgotten by advocates who, at the end of the inquest, ask the coroner to consider an unlawful killing verdict. If there is suffi-cient evidence to justify this, the case should generally be adjourned at that point.

The adjournment is only necessary where 'someone might be charged' which excludes the more common situation of an obvious criminal death with either no culprit identified, or the perpetrator himself dead.

Whilst a letter referring a case to the CPS under rule 28 would not normally be copied to the parties, it may eventually fall to be disclosed by the CPS as unused material under the Criminal Procedure and Investigations Act 1986.[114]

Requirement to Answer Questions

7.39 Competence and Compellability

In general, any witness who is competent to give evidence (ie capable of under-standing the nature of what is required) is compellable as a witness before an inquest.[115] Failure to attend when summoned as a witness is punishable by a fine[116] under s 10(2).[117]

In a criminal court the spouse of the person accused of an offence is generally not compellable. No such protection exists in the coroner's court, but see section 7.40.1.

There are a limited number of general exceptions to the rule of compellability. Certain diplomatic officials hold immunity, as do Members of Parliament during sessions of the House (although this would generally be waived).

---

[114] This will depend to some extent on the content. A simple letter referring to the adjournment and enclosing an appropriate transcript of evidence would not normally be considered 'relevant', although the transcript would be; but a more detailed letter commenting upon the evidence given or the merits of witnesses would normally be disclosed.

[115] See section 7.35 in respect of child witnesses.

[116] The current maximum is £1,000.

[117] See section 6.11 *et seq* on securing the attendance of witnesses.

The General Rule—Witnesses Must Answer Questions   **7.40**

In general, a duly summoned witness must answer any question put by the coroner or which an interested person is allowed to ask. Failure to do so constitutes an offence under s 10(2)(b) which carries a fine.[118] In the worst scenario, this could also amount to contempt of court which can be punished with imprisonment.[119]

In particular, it is often believed that a person who may face a criminal charge arising from the death (eg driving without due care and attention) can refuse to give evidence. This is incorrect, the witness cannot refuse to enter the witness box, although once sworn and properly identified the limited protection of rule 22 (see below) may be available.

Some thought should be given as to why the witness is unwilling to answer questions and they should be given every chance to explain. A witness who has been intimidated is a different proposition from one who is merely truculent, although still required to answer.[120] It might be that the cause of the fear can be resolved.[121] In any event, some time for reflection both by witness and court should be allowed before punitive action is taken. The prospects of punishment should be clearly explained and the opportunity of obtaining legal representation must be given.

There are four exceptions to the general rule that a witness must answer questions.

Rule 22—the statutory protection   **7.40.1**

Rule 22 protects a witness from having to answer questions that may tend to incriminate. This is quite different from a right to refuse to give evidence; the rule is not a general immunity from being asked any questions at all,[122] nor does the privilege prevent questions being asked.[123]

It is sometimes believed that the rule 22 protection extends to questions that may have a bearing upon civil proceedings. This is clearly not so; the word 'incriminate' has a limited meaning restricted only to criminal proceedings[124] and does not include civil action or disciplinary hearings etc.[125] However, the

---

[118] The current maximum is £1,000.

[119] For further discussion of the coroner's powers to keep order in court see section 7.45 *et seq.*

[120] See the case of *R v Wicks* (unreported: 31 January 1995) where the Court of Appeal indicated that witnesses who have been threatened are not thereby excused from answering questions. See Murphy, P (ed), *Blackstone's Criminal Practice* (2000, Blackstone Press Ltd) at para 14.76.

[121] *R v Richards* (1998) 163 JP 246 where a public gallery was cleared in order that a young witness would give important evidence.

[122] *R v HM Coroner for Lincolnshire ex p Hay* (1999) 163 JP 666.

[123] *R v Derby Coroner ex p Hart* (2000) 164 JP 429.

[124] Section 14, Civil Evidence Act 1968.

[125] In relation to disciplinary proceedings, see *R v Institute of Chartered Accountants for England and Wales ex p Nawaz* (1997) COD 111. The case did not concern an inquest. For the purpose of

protection does extend to potential criminal proceedings against the witness's spouse.[126]

The witness must hear the specific question and then tell the court on oath that the answer may tend to incriminate. It is up to the coroner to decide whether there are reasonable grounds to believe that the privilege is made out in all the circumstances. The witness must satisfy the court that answering gives rise to a real and appreciable risk of prosecution. Logic suggests that the interpretation should be in favour of the witness where there is doubt.

If the inquest is before a jury it would be appropriate for them to be excluded while any question of privilege is argued.

If the coroner asks questions of a witness which may be incriminating the witness must be advised of rule 22, although this may commonly be done at the outset of the witness's evidence. This should be done in open court, even if the coroner is aware that the witness's legal representative has previously explained the point. If the incriminating question comes from an interested person or their representative the coroner should halt the proceedings momentarily and give the witness the appropriate warning.

There is no specific form of words necessary, the coroner is only required to make the situation clear in terms that the individual understands. It may be appropriate to remind the witness that, if answering, they are still required to be truthful.

Jervis on Coroners (at para 12-124) infers that the full warning must be given each time a potentially incriminating question is asked, a passage quoted with approval in the 1999 case of *Hay*.[127] In some instances this may become an unduly cumbersome procedure and the author queries whether it might not be sufficient for the coroner to be satisfied that the witness understands his rights. Much will depend upon the circumstances of the case.

Having accepted that a question may tend to incriminate the witness, the coroner must then decide whether the privilege has been waived by reason of answers given by the witness in earlier testimony. In *Hay*[128] the court criticized the fact that two witnesses had been given the protection of rule 22 when questioned by counsel representing another party, having given an account of their involvement in the factual circumstances preceding the death in answer to the coroner's questions:

---

the appeal the court was content to assume (without deciding) that the common law privilege against self-incrimination applied *within* accountant's disciplinary investigations. This is distinct from suggesting that 'incrimination' would include the risk of disciplinary proceedings.

[126] Section 14, Civil Evidence Act 1968.
[127] *R v Lincolnshire Coroner ex p Hay* (1999) 163 JP 666.
[128] *Ibid.*

In giving evidence as [they] did, each of the witnesses waived privilege in respect of the factual matters about which [they] gave evidence, to the extent that any answer to a further relevant and appropriate question about such a fact might tend to incriminate. In our opinion it is beyond sensible argument that [counsel] was entitled and should have been allowed to ask further relevant questions about the earlier testimony of each witness.

The protection of rule 22 is sometimes criticized but it must be remembered that in a trial the defendant does not have to give evidence, at an inquest the witness is required to do so.

Legal professional privilege   **7.40.2**

Legal professional privilege extends to communications (oral or written) made between a solicitor or barrister and client if the dominant purpose of such communication was litigation. Whilst the client may waive the privilege the lawyer may not.

On very rare occasions, a solicitor may be called as a witness because it is apparent that they can assist the purpose of the inquest by virtue of their own client's affairs. The circumstances in which a client's confidences can be overridden are more fully set out in paragraph 16.02 of the *Guide to the Professional Conduct of Solicitors*.[129]

Protection of a journalist's source   **7.40.3**

Under the Contempt of Court Act 1981, a journalist is protected from revealing the source of information unless it is established that disclosure is necessary in the interests of justice, national security, or for the prevention of disorder or crime.

It is unlikely that this would have any relevance to the coroner's court, although it is clear that proceedings at an inquest do come within the meaning of the phraseology 'interests of justice'.[130]

Public interest immunity   **7.40.4**

A witness may seek to be excused answering questions, or supplying documents, on grounds of public interest immunity, ie it is to the greater benefit of the public that the witness is not compelled to disclose the information. This concept was described in the 1968 case of *Conway v Rimmer*:[131]

> . . . courts have a duty to hold a balance between the public interest (as expressed by a Minister) to withhold certain documents or other evidence and the public interest in ensuring the proper administration of justice.

---

[129] *Guide to the Professional Conduct of Solicitors* (8th edition) Law Society Publications: www.guide.lawsociety.org.uk.
[130] *R v Dr Arun Sinha*, Times Law Reports, 13 July 1994, see section 3.06.
[131] *Conway v Rimmer* (1968) AC 910, 952.

In general terms a document will need to have a clear relationship to national security or governmental matters at the highest level before such privilege might exist. Obviously it is also a matter of public interest that the identity of a person who might be placed at serious risk, such as a police informer, is not gratuitously disclosed in documentation or oral evidence.[132]

There may be a temptation for public bodies to seek immunity for matters that are merely embarrassing rather than those which risk substantial harm to the public interest, but this is clearly outside the scope of any such protection.

A claim for immunity will usually be made in a certificate from a Government Minister setting out why the immunity is necessary. The court has discretion whether or not to accept the claim and where appropriate may inspect any related documents before deciding.

Although claims for immunity are rare in the coroner's court, the issue can arise in connection with reports from an investigating officer[133] to the Police Complaints Authority (PCA), perhaps following a police shooting or similar death. It was held in the 1995 case of *Taylor v Anderton*[134] that such a report would attract public interest immunity.

Nonetheless, the PCA would normally give the coroner a copy of the investigating officer's report to assist with interpretation of other material and identifying further lines of inquiry. The police may (exceptionally) disclose the investigating officer's report if they wish, but without the recommendations or conclusions. The 1997 case of *Devon Coroner ex p Hay*[135] made it clear that an application to the coroner from interested persons for disclosure of the report should be rejected.

7.41 Giving Evidence

The key to giving evidence usefully and successfully is preparation, a subject considered in detail at section 6.31 *et seq*.

Once at court, the witness should inform the usher or coroner's officer if not wanting to take the oath on the Bible. It is possible to affirm or swear on the Old Testament or another holy book. All those attending an inquest must ensure that mobile phones or pagers are turned off before entering the courtroom. A ringing

---

[132] In *Goodwin & another v Chief Constable of Lancashire*, The Times, 3 November 1992, an officer injured in training sought disclosure of relevant sections of the police training manual on public disorder. The Court of Appeal held that it was in the wider public interest for the manual to remain confidential because of the danger of criminals obtaining details of police tactics.

[133] This refers only to the report of the investigating officer as opposed to statements or other documents arising from the inquiry. In *R v Chief Constable of W Midlands ex p Wiley* [1995] 1 AC 274 it was held that there was no general public interest immunity for such documents.

[134] *Taylor v Anderton* [1995] 1 WLR 447.

[135] *R v HM Coroner for County of Devon ex p Hay & Hay* (1998) 162 JP 96.

mobile phone is likely to earn a very sharp rebuke, no matter how switched off it was thought to be.

So far as conduct in the witness box is concerned, the prospective witness may wish to bear the following in mind:

- Answer questions loudly and clearly—there is little more annoying than having to ask a witness to speak up for the third or fourth time.
- If answers are being written down (often the case), watch the coroner's pen and only proceed to a subsequent part of the answer when appropriate.
- Keep answers short, sharp, and to the point—but don't speak too quickly.
- Be precise and factual.
- Use simple language as far as possible—if describing technical concepts, do not answer in terms that only those with a special knowledge will understand; everyone in the court, particularly the family, must comprehend the evidence.
- Do not refer to a written report submitted to the coroner, eg 'as I said in my report' for the case is being decided only on the evidence actually heard.[136]
- Do not stray outside your field of knowledge—if you don't know the answer to a question, say so.
- Do not rely on memory to give an answer if there is a written record available.
- It is generally better to direct an answer to the coroner rather than an advocate or other person asking questions; this is less adversarial and helps to diffuse the situation when tensions are mounting.
- Keep your eye on the evidence, not on your personal feelings.
- The witness who slouches in the witness box gives a very poor impression—'stand at ease, not easy'.

Any answer given *must* be right. Having to backtrack later, however caused,[137] is embarrassing, does incalculable harm to credit, and leaves the rest of the evidence given in doubt.

The questioning at an inquest must often deal with acts or omissions responsible for a death. This can lead to a very difficult and uncomfortable time for a witness. But many inquests remain straightforward and undramatic, if a little nerve-wracking for those unaccustomed to courts. Families are often genuinely appreciative of the explanations they are given by witnesses.

---

[136] Reports are generally only to assist the coroner to decide which witnesses to call and which questions to ask, see section 6.23.

[137] See section 6.24.

Documentary Evidence

7.42 Documentary Evidence—Rule 37

Rule 37 (see Table 7.4 below) allows written evidence to be admitted in the absence of the person who made the statement[138] if it is relevant to the inquest and, in the coroner's opinion, is unlikely to be disputed. This usually relates to the statements of witnesses whose evidence is comparatively peripheral to the matter or who are merely confirming facts given by others called in person.

Table 7.4. Rule 37

37. Documentary evidence

(1) Subject to the provisions of paragraphs (2) to (4), the coroner may admit at an inquest documentary evidence relevant to the purposes of the inquest from any living person which in his opinion is unlikely to be disputed, unless a person who in the opinion of the coroner is within Rule 20(2) objects to the documentary evidence being admitted.

(2) Documentary evidence so objected to may be admitted if in the opinion of the coroner the maker of the document is unable to give oral evidence within a reasonable period.

(3) Subject to paragraph (4), before admitting such documentary evidence the coroner shall at the beginning of the inquest announce publicly—
    (a) that the documentary evidence may be admitted, and
    (b) (i) the full name of the maker of the document to be admitted in evidence, and
        (ii) a brief account of such document, and
    (c) that any person who in the opinion of the coroner is within Rule 20(2) may object to the admission of any such documentary evidence, and
    (d) that any person who in the opinion of the coroner is within Rule 20(2) is entitled to see a copy of any such documentary evidence if he so wishes.

(4) If during the course of an inquest it appears that there is available at the inquest documentary evidence which in the opinion of the coroner is relevant to the purposes of the inquest but the maker of the document is not present and in the opinion of the coroner the content of the documentary evidence is unlikely to be disputed, the coroner shall at the earliest opportunity during the course of the inquest comply with the provisions of paragraph (3).

(5) A coroner may admit as evidence at an inquest any document made by a deceased person if he is of the opinion that the contents of the document are relevant to the purposes of the inquest.

(6) Any documentary evidence admitted under this Rule shall, unless the coroner otherwise directs, be read aloud at the inquest.

---

[138] Some readers may be more familiar with the broadly similar provisions of s 9 Criminal Justice Act 1967 which applies to the introduction of written evidence in criminal proceedings.

However, a properly interested person is entitled to object and thus prevent the evidence being used. In general terms this objection would be based upon a disagreement with the evidence and a resultant wish to question the witness in person.

Although without statutory provision, the author would suggest it logical that the coroner may disallow such an objection if insufficient reason is given. For example, if the objection were based on the fact that a material part of the statement were untrue or that the witness could add significant relevant information if called, the coroner would be bound to take account of the objection. However, if the dispute centred on an irrelevancy or matters more appropriate to civil proceedings, there might be grounds for the coroner to exercise discretion and proceed.[139]

Even if there is an objection about the use of a particular statement as documentary evidence, by rule 37(2) the coroner may still use the statement if the maker of the document is unable to give oral evidence within a reasonable period. This must be carefully interpreted; it is not open to a coroner merely to take documentary evidence simply on the grounds of expediency (eg to avoid an adjournment for the witness to be brought), or that it would not be convenient to call the witness.[140] Natural justice demands that such a provision be used sparingly, probably only in circumstances where the witness is ill and likely to remain so for some time, or is genuinely unable to be traced.

Some documents (such as the transcript of a police interview) are exhibits produced by a witness, rather than a document that falls within rule 37, and thus cannot be objected to on that basis.[141]

Requirements for Using Documentary Evidence 7.43

Rule 37(3) sets out the procedural requirements for using documentary evidence. The coroner is required to announce at the commencement of the inquest that documentary evidence is to be used, giving the name of the person who made the statement, a brief account of the document, and that any properly interested person may object and/or ask for a copy of the statement. Offering to provide a copy of a document only after it has been admitted in evidence does not amount to compliance with rule 37(3).[142]

---

[139] There would also seem to be no reason that the coroner could not take an 'edited' version of the statement into account. See also reference to Article 8 ECHR in section 7.43 following.

[140] *R v Avon Coroner ex p Bentley* (2002) 166 JP 297.

[141] *R v HM Coroner for Lincoln ex p Hay* (1999) 163 JP 666.

[142] *Ex p Bentley* (n 140 above).

Rule 37(4) contains a saving provision for evidence which only becomes available during the inquest; the provisions of rule 37(3) must then be complied with at the earliest opportunity.

As an objection on the day of the inquest would cause obvious difficulties, it may be more appropriate, particularly in complex inquests, that the coroner disclose in advance which witnesses are to be called in person, those witnesses to be taken as documentary evidence, and (at the very least) a brief account of such statements. In many cases it may be appropriate to disclose a full copy of the potential rule 37 statements.[143] In reality this amounts to little more than complying with the provisions of rule 37(3) at such a time that any objection is not going to cause an adjournment.[144]

By rule 37(6) documentary evidence must be read aloud 'unless the coroner otherwise directs'. This exemption may have increased importance in view of Article 8 ECHR[145] (the right to private and family life) as the coroner should consider the level of personal detail necessary to be given in open court. This may be a fine balancing act between respect for family life and the necessity for open justice, but the main principle of rule 37 is that the evidence is not in contention and that a copy of the document is available to properly interested persons.

7.44 Suicide Notes

Under rule 37(5) a coroner may admit a document made by a deceased person if the contents are relevant to the purpose of the inquest. There is no provision for objection. The rule refers to 'a deceased person' rather than 'the deceased' and so could include a statement made during the investigation into the death in issue by another who has since died, but the provision might most commonly apply to 'suicide notes'. The author wonders if it might be more convincingly argued that such a note is not a document within rule 37 at all but simply an exhibit to be produced by the investigating officer.

It is uncommon for a coroner to read the contents of a suicide note out publicly. It is usually better to refer to the document in general terms and have one of the witnesses (often the investigating officer) confirm that the note is written in such terms that it was clear the deceased was in a frame of mind to take their own life.

In general, whether rule 37 document or exhibit, suicide notes are private documents belonging to the person to whom they are addressed, but when taken as evidence at an inquest the contents must generally be disclosed, in so far as relevant, to those involved.

---

[143] *Ex p Bentley* (n 140 above).
[144] See also section 6.14 *et seq* on disclosure generally.
[145] Article 8 of the European Convention on Human Rights given effect in UK law by the Human Rights Act 1998. See section 4.45.

A difficulty sometimes arises with such notes where, for whatever reason, the family or others involved have not been shown the contents before the inquest. Great trauma can be caused if family members are asked to look at the note for the first time in a public setting and it may be better that the coroner adjourn for a few minutes so that this can take place in private.

Keeping Order in Court

Failure of Witness to Attend   7.45

By s 10(1) of the Act, a witness or juror who fails to attend court having been duly summoned is liable to a fine by the coroner.[146] Duly summoned means that the witness has received written notice of the obligation to attend together with any necessary conduct money.[147] Section 20(5) contains similar provisions in respect of medical witnesses.

The coroner must be satisfied that the witness has received the summons, which will require sworn evidence of personal service. It must be established that the witness had been 'duly summoned', taking into account the notice given and the likely ability of the witness to get to the court, including any question of conduct money. It is also necessary to confirm that the witness had been 'openly called three times'.

Thereafter the coroner may issue a warrant to have the absentee arrested and brought before the court.[148] This would allow any police officer to detain the witness (whether inside the coroner's district or not) and produce them in custody at the next available opportunity. There is no provision for such a warrant to be backed by bail.[149]

Failure to attend on a witness summons issued in the county court or High Court (under Part 34.4 of the Civil Procedure Rules 1998—see section 6.12) must be dealt with by that court rather than by the coroner.

Once the witness has been produced, they should be given every chance to explain the omission, calling witnesses if necessary. The prospect of punishment should be clearly explained and they must have the opportunity of obtaining legal

---

[146] This may also amount to contempt of court, which carries imprisonment, but the witness must be dealt with under one provision or the other, not both.

[147] The summoning of witnesses to attend court, including conduct money, is dealt with in detail at section 6.12.

[148] A suggested form is set out at para A3-11 of *Jervis on Coroners* (12th edition).

[149] A warrant 'backed by bail' allows the arresting police officer to bail the witness to attend before the coroner at a set time.

representation.[150] The coroner may deal with the defaulter either under the provisions of s 10 of the Act or as contempt of court but not both.

It is clear that a failure to attend when duly summoned does constitute 'contempt in the face of the court' carrying imprisonment, although mere late appearance at court where there is some excuse and no intention to delay the proceedings might not generally be so regarded. However, bearing in mind that the witness is exactly that, a *witness* to a death rather than facing a criminal allegation over the matter, it may seem unduly harsh to consider any penalty other than a fine[151] for a first non-attendance. In imposing any fine the coroner should have proper regard to the means of the defaulter.[152] If the witness's failure has already resulted in several hours in custody, this may also be taken into account.

If the inquest was adjourned for lack of the witness, it is extremely unlikely that the case will be able to proceed at short notice on the arrest. Thus, having dealt with the witness for the original non-attendance, the coroner will need to ensure that the same situation does not arise again. The witness summons should be re-dated and further served upon the witness before he leaves the precincts of the court, with conduct money if necessary. A firm and clear warning might be given in open court about the consequence of a further non-attendance.

It occasionally happens that the witness also fails to attend the adjourned hearing, necessitating yet another adjournment. Such a failure would be difficult to regard as anything other than the most blatant contempt in the face of the court, probably justifying the use of a short term of imprisonment.[153]

7.46 Failure of Witness to Answer Questions

By s 10(2) of the Act, a duly summoned witness who refuses to answer a question put to him without lawful excuse may be fined by the coroner. Lawful excuse would generally mean the provision against self-incrimination contained in rule 22 or the other matters referred to in section 7.40 where this topic is dealt with in greater detail.

Many difficult witnesses are being difficult about irrelevancies, but in some instances (perhaps a repeated refusal to co-operate in any way) the failure to answer may be taken as contempt in the face of the court.

---

[150] This might be the only circumstance where the provisions of Article 6 ECHR could be said to apply to a coroner's court—see section 4.44.

[151] The current maximum is £1,000. Fines are notified to, and collected by, the local Clerk to the Justices.

[152] The coroner may also have in mind any conduct money that was originally given to the witness.

[153] See *HM Coroner for Kent v Terrill & Terrill* [2001] ACD 5 where the High Court felt that a fixed term of four days' imprisonment was lenient for a deliberate non-attendance. See also *R v Yusuf* (The Times) 12 May 2003 where the court held it was a serious matter when witnesses defied a summons to attend court. If witnesses failed to attend court 'there would be anarchy'.

Disorder in the Courtroom   7.47

Inquests can be emotionally charged occasions and from time to time there may be some form of minor disorder in court. In the great majority of cases, this will amount to little more than an isolated irate outburst needing only a few polite words from the coroner. Often the offender will freely apologize at the end of the hearing.

Where the problem is likely to continue, it might pay to mark clearly the first sign of real disturbance in order to prevent the trouble escalating. If necessary, after a suitable warning, the troublemaker can be removed from court—but this has obvious difficulties if they are a close relative of the deceased.

If the disturbance seems intended to intimidate a witness it may be necessary to act immediately. The witness has been required to attend by the coroner and it would be quite unfair to allow any element of harassment. Where such a problem is suspected in advance, care must be taken that a vulnerable witness is not made to wait in the same area as the others. It may be necessary to enlist the help of the police at an early stage, both to get the witness into the court without intimidation outside and to prevent disorder in the courtroom.[154]

In a few instances the disorder will be of a serious nature. The coroner has power to punish summarily any contempt committed in the face of the court.[155] A contempt is 'any act inconsistent with the proper dignity of the court' and may range from shouting out during the proceedings to throwing something at the bench. Such contempt may be dealt with by way of a fine[156] or imprisonment of up to 28 days.[157]

In dealing with the contempt, the coroner must exercise proper judicial principles, giving ample opportunity for representation and explanation.[158] It would also be proper to allow the defaulter an opportunity to apologize, which might commonly suffice. Certainly the coroner must adjourn for a short period if becoming angry at the situation.

Despite the powers to punish for contempt, disorder presents the coroner with a problem. The offender may be a close relative of the deceased and unless the disorder is of the utmost gravity the coroner will be reluctant to take serious punitive

---

[154] See section 6.34.3 on preparing for a hearing where such a problem is likely.

[155] *R v West Yorkshire Coroner ex p Smith* (1985) 1QB 1096.

[156] The current maximum is £2,500 under s 14(2) of the Contempt of Court Act 1981 (as amended by s 17 of the Criminal Justice Act 1991).

[157] The coroner's powers of imprisonment are limited to 28 days but this is a power to order the witness to be detained until a date 28 days hence—meaning that the witness will serve exactly that long in custody. If the coroner sentences the witness to 28 days imprisonment in the normal fashion then the witness will receive remission and be released after 14 days.

[158] See also section 4.44 in relation to Article 6 ECHR.

action against such a person. Not only must there be some understanding given to the emotional pressures facing the bereaved, but the headline 'GRIEVING WIDOW JAILED BY CORONER' is unattractive to say the least.

The coroner has no power to deal with contempt committed out of court, such as a newspaper report of submissions to the court in the absence of the jury. These matters would be reported to the Attorney General for action.

Evidential Matters

7.48 Introduction

Both civil and criminal courts are restricted in the types of evidence that might properly be heard. Many protections have been developed to ensure that an accused is only convicted on the basis of the best evidence available. Although the rules for a civil court are less rigorous than those in a criminal court, they still exist, for the claimant has to *prove* his allegations against the defendant.

The general rule is that to be heard before a court, evidence must be both relevant and admissible. The facts should also be proven by the best evidence available.

7.49 The Coroner's Discretion

The inquest is designed to find out the truth of a situation (rather than whether allegations are proven or not), and the coroner has a good deal of discretion as to how that end is achieved. Consequently a less restrictive view of the rules of evidence may be taken.[159] As an example, it is common for hearsay evidence[160] to be admitted at an inquest.

Nonetheless, the coroner must always act in a fair and proper manner, with due regard for the requirements of natural justice. There will be a limit to any relaxation of the rules of evidence, varying from case to case. For example in a cell death, where the conduct of prison staff is under close scrutiny, it might be appropriate to follow the rules of evidence more closely than in a straightforward suicide, where the only question was whether the deceased took an overdose deliberately or accidentally.

---

[159] *R v Manchester Coroner ex p Tal* (1985) QB 67; *R v HM Coroner for Lincoln ex p Hay* (1999) 163 JP 666.

[160] Hearsay evidence is that which is said by somebody else. For example A sees a man fall out of a window and tells B what he saw. On the strict rules, B cannot give evidence of what A said as proof that the man fell out of the window.

Relevance of Evidence 7.50

Evidence must have a direct bearing on those matters that are to be dealt with at the inquest; the identity of the deceased, when and where he died and by what means the death came about.[161] Evidence of other facts may be of considerable interest but is not relevant to the purpose of the inquest and by rule 20(1)(b) must therefore be excluded.[162]

Admissible Evidence 7.51

Evidence must also be provable in one of the methods acceptable to the court. For example evidence given in the witness box on oath by a witness is admissible. However, if a member of the deceased's family introduced the same account whilst asking questions of a witness, this is not of itself admissible evidence and would need to be repeated in the witness box, under oath, and subject to examination by others.

Admissibility also covers such issues as the acceptance of admissions made in dubious circumstances, for example through fear or in hope of some advantage. This will not commonly be relevant at an inquest.

Opinion Evidence 7.52

An expert witness, that is to say somebody of recognized skill and experience in a particular field, is generally allowed to give an opinion on matters falling within that special expertise. For example a forensic pathologist may give evidence of an opinion that a knife wound was inflicted whilst the deceased was seated, even though not present to witness the assault. However a clear line needs to be drawn between opinion evidence, which marries together a number of known facts with experience, and speculative evidence—merely asking an expert to postulate as to how a particular incident might have come about on the basis of no more than supposition.

Evidence of Character 7.53

On rare occasions it may be appropriate for an inquest to hear some evidence of the character of a witness so that it can decide upon the accuracy of his evidence about the facts in issue. For example, a witness at an inquest into a drugs death might need to be asked about their own drug taking, not for any purpose of criticism but rather to establish physical or mental state at the time of the incident.

---

[161] See section 7.02.
[162] In *R (application of Stanley) v HM Coroner for Inner North London* [2003] EWHC 1180 Admin it was held that evidence of a decision by the CPS not to prosecute an officer involved in the death was not relevant, the jury had to make a determination in the light of the evidence before it and not in the light of the view of the CPS. See also section 7.53 on evidence of character.

On rare occasions it might be necessary for the coroner to consider whether evidence of the deceased's character is relevant, perhaps by way of previous convictions. For example, if a man was shot by police officers who claimed that they thought he was armed and feared for their lives, it may be relevant that the officers knew he had convictions for using firearms. But if such convictions were unknown to the police at the time of the shooting, they can hardly have had an effect upon the officer's decisions and thus are irrelevant to the inquest. Worse, to introduce evidence of the convictions before a jury would be 'prejudicial rather than probative'.[163]

The 1998 case of *Fields*[164] dealt with the opposite side of this equation. The deceased was struck with a police baton when officers were trying to arrest him, it being claimed this was necessary due to his violence. The veracity of the officer's account was seriously challenged by the deceased's family. The High Court held the coroner was correct to allow evidence of previous convictions of the deceased showing a propensity to violence.

If admission of such evidence is contemplated it is appropriate to give an opportunity for submissions before a decision is reached.[165]

7.54 Documents

In general an original document must be submitted in evidence rather than a copy. However, the court has discretion to accept a copy if the original is no longer available.

Some documents, such as Acts of Parliament, are regarded as originals in their own right even though they may only be a print of the original Act. Equally, there is statutory provision for the acceptance of copies of particular documents such as bankers' records.

Inquests are often less particular about copies than other court proceedings, provided there is no suggestion of fraud. However, witnesses must still make every effort to produce original records unless specifically told that a copy will suffice.

---

[163] *Application of Stanley* (n 162 above).
[164] *R v Southwark Coroner ex p Fields* (1998) 162 JP 411.
[165] Application of Stanley (n 162 above).

Concluding the Inquest

Delivering the Verdict   7.55

When sitting without a jury the coroner will normally conclude the case[166] by giving the decision together with reasons and, where appropriate, a summary of the facts found.

Whilst there is no statutory provision, the 2003 case of *Stanley*[167] confirmed that coroners should give reasons (albeit briefly) for decisions of fundamental importance. Although this duty does not apply to every aspect of an inquiry,[168] clearly some form of explanation as to the choice of verdict must be given, rather than a bald statement of the matters to be addressed under rule 36. Without reasons, those involved will not know whether the court has misdirected itself. It has also been said that reasons are required if decisions are to be acceptable to the parties and members of the public.[169]

The coroner should set out what happened and explain succinctly why the decision was reached.[170] This need not involve a lengthy judgment,[171] even a few sentences may suffice to give an appropriate explanation in some situations.[172] But it does require the identification of those matters critical to the decision and where appropriate, a brief explanation of why the evidence of one witness was preferred to another.[173] It may be unnecessary to detail or even summarize the evidence in question. If submissions of law were heard, it should be made clear which were accepted and which were rejected.

Such a summary is not an opportunity for the coroner to express any substantive personal opinion, and rules 36 and 42 still apply. However, in the event that the coroner is going to take action under rule 43 (reporting the matter in writing to a person or authority who has power to take action for the prevention of similar fatalities, see section 7.07) this may be announced immediately following the verdict.

---

[166] Home Office statistics for 2001 show that approximately 12 per cent of inquests were concluded within one month of first notification of the death, 44 per cent within three months and 78 per cent within six months.

[167] *Application of Stanley* (n 162 above). The decision in issue was which verdicts should be left to the jury. See also *Flannery v Halifax* [2000] 1 WLR 377 in relation to the necessity for an explanation of decisions generally.

[168] *R v Higher Education Funding Council ex p Institute of Dental Surgery* [1994] 1 WLR 242.

[169] *English v Emery Reimbold* [2002] 3 All ER 385. It was also said that reasons render practicable the exercise of rights of appeal, although in the case of an inquest this would more correctly be the right of judicial review.

[170] *Westzucker v Bunge* [1981] 2 Ll Rep 130.

[171] *English v Emery* (n 169 above).

[172] *Stefan v GMC* [1999] 1 WLR 1293.

[173] *English v Emery* (n 169 above).

It is customary for the coroner to conclude by offering condolences to the family.

Summary

- The purpose of an inquest is to establish who the deceased was, when and where he died, and, most importantly, how he died (meaning 'how did the death come about').
- The court is forbidden from a finding which appears to indicate guilt or blame but the remit of the inquest may be widened where Article 2 ECHR is engaged.
- Properly interested persons are entitled to question witnesses on matters relevant to the inquest.
- The rules of evidence will generally be applied less strictly at an inquest than other court proceedings.
- The coroner has power to punish non-attendance at court, refusal to answer questions, or contempt in the face of the court.

8

JURIES

If a builder constructs a house for a man with the result that the house which he builds collapses and so causes the death of the owner of the house . . . the builder shall be put to death.[1]

---

[1] Hammurabi, Emperor of Babylon in 170 BC. This is said to be the first effective example of health and safety legislation.

This chapter sets out the issues to be considered when an inquest is held before a jury, including:

- which cases must be heard before a jury;
- how a jury is called;
- how the jury are dealt with in court;
- summing up to the jury.

8.01 The Problems

Jury service in the coroner's court is a difficult task. The atmosphere at inquests can be extremely tense as bereaved relatives come face to face, probably for the first time, with those they hold responsible for the death. Occasionally jurors will find the detailed descriptions of traumatic death to be upsetting. It is sometimes necessary for jurors to view distressing and distasteful photographs, however much the coroner may wish to avoid this.

Moreover, the legal complexities of a verdict in the coroner's court can be immense. The jury may be asked to deal with two different standards of proof, the potential for an open verdict, and a choice of several conclusions. Perhaps most complicated of all, they must set out their findings as to the circumstances in a brief statement of the event.[2]

The jury will need careful guidance through this minefield. In conducting the inquest and in summing up, the coroner must leave the jurors in no doubt as to the task expected of them and the manner in which they should go about this. The coroner must be clear and concise in the directions that are given. At the same time, dealing with a jury is the exception rather than the rule for the coroner, with only 3 per cent of inquests[3] each year being held in this manner.

8.02 Historical Perspective

The coroner's jury has origins in the Grand Jury of medieval times and does not share a modern history with the institution with which we are so familiar in the criminal courts.

Juries have been an integral part of inquest proceedings since the office of coroner was created in 1194.[4] Initially the jury would include every male over the age of 12 from four or more neighbouring townships. It was common for jury members to give evidence about the death. However in 1259 it was regarded as sufficient 'that there come enough for the making of those inquests fully'.[5] The Coroners

---

[2] As to which see section 9.09.
[3] Amounting to 690 jury inquests between about 125 coroners: Home Office Statistical Bulletin 06/03.
[4] See section 1.02.
[5] 43 Henry III c24.

Act of 1887 required a coroner to summon a jury of between 12 and 23 (although only 12 would give a verdict) but in 1926 this was reduced to the present composition of between seven and eleven.

Until the Coroners' Amendment Act 1926, *every* inquest was heard before a jury. This Act limited the requirement to that applicable today[6] plus homicides and road traffic deaths, the two latter circumstances being removed in 1977 and 1980 respectively. This leaves only a small proportion[7] of the coroner's caseload which necessitates summoning a jury.[8]

In medieval times (and later) the inquest was held in the presence of the body, but a more civilized procedure gradually developed of only requiring the coroner and jury to view the corpse, normally at the first sitting of the inquest. Whilst it was argued that this practice brought 'a sense of reality and responsibility' to the jurors it was also noted that they 'merely filed past, often with averted faces'.[9] This torment of jurors was ended by the 1926 Act, although coroners faced the necessity to view the body for a further 54 years.

Prior to the Coroners' Juries Act 1983, jurors had been picked in a haphazard manner, sometimes leading to a full-time, virtually professional jury. The 1983 Act introduced the present requirement for coroners to select jurors in a manner similar to the Crown Court.

The Requirement to Call a Jury

The vast majority of inquests are now heard by the coroner sitting alone. However, s 8(3) of the Act sets out a number of instances where a jury must be called.

Deaths in Prison   8.03

> Section 8(3)(a)—the death occurred in prison or in such a place or in such circumstances as to require an inquest under any other Act.

A death within a prison gives a clear requirement for an inquest before a jury, even if the cause of death is entirely natural. Unfortunately, there are also a number of anomalies raised by the wording of the sub-section.

---

[6] Under s 8 of the Coroners Act 1988, see section 8.03 *et seq* below.

[7] The number of jury inquests is dropping, the 2002 figure (690) is the lowest number recorded: Home Office Statistical Bulletin 06/03.

[8] The Brodrick Committee in 1971 recommended the virtual abolition of the coroner's jury, retaining only a power for the coroner to summon a jury where it was considered that there were special reasons for doing so.

[9] Chalmers Committee 1910—Report of the Departmental Committee appointed to inquire into the law relating to coroner's and coroner's inquests and into the practice in coroner's courts (Cmnd 5004).

If taken literally, s 8(3)(a) would not apply to a person removed from the prison to die in hospital. Clearly, Parliament's concern was to require an inquest before a jury where the *cause* of death arose behind the closed doors of a prison but that is not actually stated. However, the 1989 case of *Linnane*[10] and various Home Office Circulars[11] made it clear that the phrase 'in prison' should be interpreted in the widest sense and would include someone taken ill in a prison but later dying in hospital.

Secondly, the sub-section refers to a death occurring *in a prison* rather than the death of a prisoner. Thus the death of a prison officer or civilian administrator within the prison, or even of a visitor who had just stepped through the gate, would require an inquest before a jury.

The word 'prison' is not further defined and, strictly interpreted, might not include other places of detention such as a Young Offenders Institution. The phrase immediately following; 'or in such a place' brings an apparent answer but is ambiguous and should perhaps be more properly taken to be part of the requirement 'or in such a place or in such circumstances as to require an inquest under any other Act'. Whatever the interpretation intended, it is widely accepted practice that 'prison' is taken to mean any such institution.

The cause of death is immaterial; even if the death is wholly due to natural causes the requirement for a jury inquest applies.

The reference to 'in such a place or in such circumstances as to require an inquest under any other Act' does not currently have any validity.

8.04   Police Deaths

> Section 8(3)(b)—the death occurred whilst the deceased was in police custody, or resulted from an injury caused by a police officer in the purported execution of his duty.

This is a further anomaly in that whilst s 8(1)(c) requires the holding of an inquest for a death in prison, whatever the cause, it makes no mention of deaths in police custody. Section 8(3)(b) only demands that if an inquest *is* held into a death in police custody that it must be before a jury.

If taken literally this could be interpreted as meaning that a death from natural causes in a police cell did not require an inquest. This is quite at odds with the spirit of the legislation and the public interest which surely necessitates an inquest into the death of any person held in detention, whatever the cause.

---

[10]   The deceased was serving a prison sentence but because of his illness was in hospital without any guard when he died. It was held that he was 'in prison' for the purpose of the Act. *R v Inner North London Coroner ex p Linnane* [1989] 1 WLR 395.

[11]   Home Office Circulars 35/1969, 23/1981, and 109/1982.

Similar comments to those made at section 8.03 might apply to the actual place of death. Parliament would surely have intended a prisoner who suffers an injury in police cells to be the subject of a jury inquest even if the death followed several days later in hospital.

Home Office Circular 109/1982 indicated the Secretary of State's view that it was desirable for an inquest to be held, with a jury, on all deaths occurring in *any* form of legal custody, even though the death may have occurred in hospital or elsewhere and even though it may have been due to natural causes.[12] The author would submit that 'police custody' must be interpreted in broad terms to include a person arrested or detained in virtually any circumstances.[13]

In similar fashion, 'an injury caused by a police officer in the purported execution of his duty' must be widely defined.[14] It could be argued that there should be a jury inquest into the death of someone killed driving their car into a wall whilst being chased by the police, even if there was no evidence of a collision between the police car and the deceased's vehicle. The requirement is certainly to be taken as including deaths in road traffic accidents involving police cars.[15] Although there is no statutory definition, some assistance may be found in the criteria for 'death of a member of the public during or following police contact' which police forces must report to the Home Office. This extended definition (revised in April 2002) was contained within Home Office Circular 31/2002 and is shown at Appendix 4 on page 375.

Finally, use of the phrase 'police officer' is itself interesting; most other legislation refers to a 'constable' which has a slightly wider meaning including those who may have similar powers but are not police officers, such as the UK Atomic Energy Authority Constabulary, some of whom carry firearms.

Deaths Reportable to a Government Department   8.05

Section 8(3)(c)—death caused by an accident, poisoning or disease notice of which must be given to a government department or inspector.

This generally relates to deaths reportable by employers or a person in control of premises to the Health and Safety Executive (or in some cases the local authority) under the Reporting of Injuries, Diseases and Dangerous Occurrences Regulations 1995 (RIDDOR).

---

[12] Which is at odds with the lack of discretion on whether to hold an inquest referred to at section 4.14 but the Circular was cited with apparent approval in the *Linnane* case (n 10 above).

[13] Although there must be a query as to whether this should include someone detained by such as store detectives—the author would think not.

[14] According to Home Office statistics, 52 people died in police custody or otherwise following contact with the police between April 2000 and March 2001. The definition here is very widely drawn but does not include those involved in a fatal traffic accident with a police car.

[15] Home Office Circular 109/1982.

Regulation 3 makes a death (or injury) reportable if it occurs as a result of an accident or disease arising 'out of or in connection with work'. Accident is widely defined and includes an assault upon a person at work, or a suicide which occurs on or in the course of operation of a railway or tram system.[16]

The deceased does not have to be at work, it is sufficient if the death results from an accident 'arising out of or in connection with work'. For example, the death of a shop customer crushed by a falling pallet of goods, or a pedestrian falling down a manhole cover in the street left open by workmen would be reportable and require a jury inquest.

Some areas of common relevance to coroners may include the following:

Hospitals and nursing homes. Regulation 10 excludes some medical deaths, ie those arising directly from the conduct of an operation, examination, or other medical treatment carried out or supervised by a doctor or dentist.[17] However, many deaths in the healthcare sector will still be reportable. HSE guidance[18] specifically includes as reportable the examples of a confused patient falling from a window, or a patient scalded by hot water in a bath. The same guidance gives examples of deaths that would not be reportable, such as a patient committing suicide, or a frail resident falling (unless caused by an obstruction or defect in the premises).

Road deaths. Regulation 10 also excludes incidents arising out of or in connection with the movement of a vehicle on a road unless the death was related to;

- exposure to a substance being carried by the vehicle;
- loading or unloading of the vehicle, or the activities of another who at the time was engaged in work connected with loading or unloading;[19]
- work being carried out on or alongside a public road (including structures adjacent to the road);
- the movement of a train on a road—as the definition of a train under regulation 2 includes a tram this will have significance for those cities where trams move with traffic on the roadway.

---

[16] Regulation 2(1)(b), RIDDOR 1995.

[17] This raises the question of deaths during therapeutic or diagnostic procedures carried out by other healthcare workers not under the supervision of a doctor or dentist, eg midwives or chiropractors. The issue of when a healthcare worker is 'supervised' by a doctor was considered in a different context in *Royal Colleges of Nursing of the UK v DHSS* [1981] 1 All ER 545.

[18] HSE Health Services Information Sheet No. 1 gives a number of useful examples of healthcare sector injuries, diseases, and dangerous occurrences that are reportable or otherwise: www.hse.gov.uk/pubns/hsis1.pdf. See also A Guide to the Reporting of Injuries, Diseases and Dangerous Occurrences Regulations 1995; ISBN 0-7176-2431-5.

[19] See *R (on the application of Aineto) v HM Coroner for Brighton & Hove* [2003] EWHC 1896 Admin, where the court held that the death of a pedestrian crushed beneath a refuse lorry moving 32 metres between bins was reportable as it arose from the activities of a person (the driver) engaged in work connected with loading and unloading.

Further, certain incidents involving a road tanker (including overturning or fire involving the load) are classed as 'dangerous occurrences' and thus reportable.

Gas supply deaths: Regulation 6 requires the reporting of a death or injury arising out of or in connection with the supply or distribution of flammable gas whether through a fixed distribution system or refillable[20] containers such as LPG. Similarly, regulation 6(2) requires the reporting of an incident where a gas fitting, flue, or ventilation system has led to injury or death in specified circumstances.[21]

Rail deaths: Deaths of railway workers arising out of their work clearly fall within the category of reportable deaths. Schedule 2 of the regulations also sets out a considerable number of incidents[22] regarded as 'dangerous occurrences' *where they arise out of or in connection with work* and which are reportable even where no death or injury results. However, trespassers on a railway line (sometimes but certainly not always with suicidal intent) have long been a conundrum for coroners. The death of a trespasser—or even of a passenger falling from a train—is not set out as a dangerous occurrence within Schedule 2.

As noted above, the definition of 'accident' includes a suicide on a railway but the regulations still require that the death arises 'out of or in connection with work' to become reportable.[23] On the one hand it is difficult to see how the death of a railway trespasser can be said to be 'arising out of or in connection with work', but the opposing argument is that it is even more difficult to see why the regulations specifically extend to include suicide (and restrict this to a relevant transport system) unless such were intended to be reportable.

Jervis[24] suggests that such cases do not fall within RIDDOR and do not require a jury, criticizing the Home Office view that whilst the victim was not at work, the train driver was. *Jervis* argues that this would extend the definition too far and include many other cases where one of those involved or even just present was 'at work'. Perhaps the more recent case of *Aineto*[25] does not support this contention.

In any event, whilst the analysis put forward in *Jervis* is inviting, it does not claim to be entirely compelling. The pragmatic view is that such deaths *are* inevitably reported by the railway operator[26] and are subject to at least an initial investigation

---

[20] Curiously, this does not extend to a *disposable* gas container.

[21] The regulations can be obtained in full from the HMSO website at www.hmso.gov.uk following the link for 1995 statutory instruments (SI 1995/3163).

[22] For example, failure of a lift, or a train striking a vehicle at a level crossing.

[23] By reg 2(2) 'arising out of or in connection with work' includes an accident attributable to the plant used for the purposes of an undertaking—which presumably includes a train.

[24] *Jervis on Coroners* (12th edition) at para 15-10.

[25] *R (on the application of Aineto) v HM Coroner for Brighton & Hove* (n 19 above) where the driver of a refuse lorry was at work when a pedestrian was killed so the death was reportable under RIDDOR and a jury required.

[26] Form F2508 is provided for this purpose—confirmation that all such deaths *are* reported to the Railway Inspectorate has been given to the author in personal communication.

by HM Railway Inspectorate (HMRI). Only if there are no continuing matters of public safety revealed (which will usually be the case) does HMRI cease to take a further active interest.[27]

Industrial diseases: An interesting situation arises in respect of industrial disease deaths. If, at the time of death, the deceased still worked for the employer where it is alleged the disease was contracted, then the matter is reportable and there should be a jury inquest. However, as will most often be the case, if the employee has retired or moved occupations before death there is no such requirement. Given the number of industrial disease inquests that some coroner's jurisdictions attract, this is a distinction of considerable importance.

8.06 Deaths Concerning Public Safety

> Section 8(3)(d)—the death occurred in circumstances the continuance or possible recurrence of which is prejudicial to the health or safety of the public or any section of the public.

Again there is some anomaly in the choice of words even though the issue may be clear enough. If taken literally this sub-section would mean that if a death occurred in circumstances which might cause another fatality, should they re-occur, then there must be a jury. Such a description could be given to virtually any death that a coroner ever dealt with—if somebody else takes an overdose of the same tablets, or sits in another car with a hose pipe attached to the exhaust, then there will be a further death.

Plainly the section must be read to encompass circumstances which are a (preventable) risk for the public at large. This point was considered in the 1980 case of *Peach*:[28]

> . . . circumstances of such a kind that their continuance or recurrence may reasonably and ought properly to be avoided by the taking of appropriate steps which it is in the power of some responsible body to take.

The court then went on to consider the public interest aspect:

> . . . what is envisaged must, I think, be something which might be prevented or safeguarded by a public authority or some other person or body which activities can be said to affect a substantial section of the public.

In *Ferrante*[29] the court made the important distinction between a systemic failure and a simple isolated incident. A systemic failure might reoccur but may also be

---

[27] The Railway Inspectorate Inspection Manual states that cases of *adult* trespass leading to death, or apparent suicide, will always be investigated by the police initially after which HMRI is advised if railway operational matters are at issue. Fatal trespass by a child is treated differently.

[28] *R v Hammersmith Coroner ex p Peach* [1980] QB 211. See also *R v HM Coroner for Surrey ex p Wright* [1997] QB 786 which approves this.

[29] *R v HM Attorney General ex p Ferrante* [1995] COD 18.

prevented in the future (presumably 'by a public authority or some other body whose activities can be said to affect a substantial section of the public'). Such a failure will fall within s 8(3)(d). An isolated or individual incident of which no repetition might reasonably be expected is unlikely to qualify.

Consequently, if it appears on the information initially available that there is reasonable cause to suspect that the death was contributed to by 'system neglect' within the meaning of Article 2 of the ECHR case law dealt with in section 9.30, the coroner must summon a jury.

Persons Detained under the Mental Health Act   8.07

Although sub-sections 8(3)(a) and (b) are obviously aimed at persons who are compulsorily detained, the Act makes no reference to a patient detained under the provisions of the Mental Health Act in a local psychiatric hospital.

A small proportion of compulsorily detained patients in a mental hospital are held under ss 35–48 of the Mental Health Act 1983, that is to say by order of a criminal court. Most coroners would consider such people as falling within s 8(3)(a) but a patient detained under other sections of the Act[30] does not have to be similarly regarded.[31]

This creates an anomaly. The inmate (or even staff member) of an open prison dying of a heart attack requires a jury inquest, but a mental patient detained compulsorily on a locked ward and subject to enforced treatment does not. For the future, the Report of the Fundamental Review[32] recommends (at page 80) that a public inquest should be mandatory on the death of a person detained under mental health legislation unless the Statutory Medical Assessor certifies beyond reasonable doubt that the death was caused by natural disease. The Report further suggests (at page 109) that a jury should be empanelled in cases where someone compulsorily in the care of the State has died in unclear circumstances.

Reason for Summoning Jury becoming Apparent   8.08

In a small number of cases it may become apparent during the evidence that the circumstances fall within s 8(3) of the Act and that a jury should have been summoned:

> 8(4): if it appears to the coroner either [before] or during an inquest begun without a jury that there is any reason for summoning a jury then he may proceed to summon a jury in the manner required by sub-section (2).

---

[30] Sections 2–5 of this legislation give power to detain a person for assessment, diagnosis, or treatment in closely prescribed circumstances.

[31] *R v Northants Coroner ex p Wilson* (unreported: 24/7/02) where the coroner's refusal to empanel a jury in such a case was upheld. Whether there might be Article 2 ECHR implications (see section 4.43) in a particular instance would depend upon the circumstances.

[32] Death Certification and Investigation in England, Wales and Northern Ireland; The Report of a Fundamental Review 2003: CM 5831 (at chapter 12 para 30). See section 1.08.

The use of the word 'may' is curious as it suggests that the coroner has a discretion about adjourning to restart the case before a jury.

The equally curious wording of s 8(5) suggests that a s 8(3) case heard without a jury would be perfectly lawful:

> 8(5) In the case of an inquest or any part of an inquest held without a jury, anything done by or before the coroner alone shall be as validly done as if it had been done by or before the coroner and a jury.

In reality the law can only properly be interpreted as meaning that a case requiring a jury *must* be held before a jury and that if this requirement only becomes apparent during the evidence then the case *must* be halted and restarted before a jury. However, see section 8.10 for comment on opening the inquest without a jury.

8.09 Coroner's Discretionary Power

Under s 8(4) the coroner has a clear discretion to summon a jury, even on cases falling outside s 8(3):

> if it appears to a coroner that . . . there is any reason for summoning a jury, he may proceed to summon a jury in the manner required by sub-section (2) above.

8.10 Opening an Inquest without a Jury

The legislation may be interpreted as meaning that an inquest requiring a jury must be *opened* before a jury as well as ultimately *resumed* before a jury.[33] In fact this is never the case and would be wholly impracticable. It generally takes at least six weeks to summon a jury whereas the coroner will be looking to open the inquest within four or five days of the death. Presumably it is precisely this situation which gives some meaning to s 8(5) referred to above.

8.11 Deaths Abroad

The coroner must still have regard to the requirement for a jury where the death occurs abroad, assuming that the body of the deceased has been returned to this country for burial or cremation.[34]

The 1995 case of *In re Neal*[35] made plain that the provisions of s 8(3)(d)[36] applied to deaths abroad but queried whether this might be so for the other sub-sections.

---

[33] For a discussion on the opening of an inquest see section 7.16.

[34] See section 2.14 for the obligation upon the coroner to inquire and, where appropriate, hold an inquest into a body returned from abroad.

[35] *Re Neal* (1997) 37 BMLR 164: the deceased was on holiday in Spain and died from carbon monoxide poisoning due to a faulty water heater. The court held that it was just as important that those who travelled to Spain were protected from the dangers of gas heaters as those who stayed at home.

[36] Circumstances prejudicial to the health or safety of the public—see section 8.06.

The author would suggest that, on the present interpretation of the law, there is no justification for treating a death in custody abroad any differently to such a death in this country. Section 8(3)(c)[37] brings different considerations, for deaths abroad do not generally need reporting to a Government Inspector etc in this country.

Administrative Matters

Warrant to Summon a Jury   8.12

Once the coroner is ready to proceed with one or more cases which are to be heard before a jury, s 8(2) requires that a warrant[38] is issued to the jury officer, commonly one of the coroner's officers. This directs that between seven and eleven persons are summoned to attend as jurors and inquire into the death. Failure to issue such a warrant has been taken as sufficient irregularity to render the inquest a nullity.[39]

Summoning a Jury   8.13

The jury in the coroner's court is summoned in a manner identical to the procedure of the Crown Court. The jury officer[40] will obtain a list of randomly selected prospective jurors from the Jury Central Summoning Bureau (JCSB).[41] A summons will be sent out to the juror[42] in the form specified within the Rules (which is identical to that used at Crown Court) and the juror must answer the summons within three days stating whether or not he/she is eligible for jury service.

Jurors must:

- be not less than 18 nor more than 70 on the date required for service;
- be registered as an elector;
- have lived in the United Kingdom[43] for at least five years since the age of 13.

---

[37] Deaths from accident disease or poisoning that require reporting to a Government Inspector or Department—see section 8.05.

[38] Form 3 in Schedule IV of the Coroners Rules 1984.

[39] *R v Merseyside Coroner ex p Carr* [1994] 1 WLR 578. The coroner had listed a case without a jury but following submissions agreed to call a jury. To save delay, he arranged for spare jurors from the Crown Court to attend the same day but in doing so omitted to give a written warrant to his officer.

[40] The coroner should not personally interfere with the selection or summoning of the jury: *re Mitcheldown Inquisition* (1888) 22 LR Ir 279.

[41] The JCSB was created in 2002 as a single source of randomly selected local jurors for the Court Service across England and Wales.

[42] The summons must be served at least six days before the juror is required.

[43] Including the Channel Islands and the Isle of Man.

Certain persons are wholly ineligible for jury service in any court (eg the mentally disordered; those who have ever been sentenced to more than five years imprisonment; those sentenced to any term of imprisonment or a community order in the last ten years). Although certain occupations were previously ineligible (eg solicitors and prison officers) or entitled to be excused if they so wished (eg doctors or nurses) many of these exemptions are expected to be removed by the Criminal Justice Act 2003.

However, by s 8(6) of the Act, there is a specific disqualification for service in the coroner's court—if the inquest concerns the death of a prisoner then 'neither a prisoner in the prison nor any person engaged in any sort of trade or dealing with the prison shall serve as a juror . . .'.

The Home Office now produce a leaflet for jurors giving information about the coroner's court and what will be expected of them in general terms. Coroners are encouraged to send this out with the jury summons.

8.14   Composition of the Jury

Section 8(2) requires that between seven and eleven jurors be assembled and that they be sworn in a proper manner to inquire into the death.[44] However, it is occasionally necessary for the coroner to discharge a juror[45] during an inquest, more commonly for illness or because it becomes clear they know a witness than for misbehaviour, so it is wise for the jury to start with a minimum of eight or nine, rather than just seven.

8.15   Insufficient Number of Jurors Present

By rule 48 the coroner is empowered to require any person in the vicinity of the court to act as a juror without written notice if it seems likely that the jury would otherwise be incomplete. In practice, coroners sitting in towns or cities with a Crown Court would probably attempt to 'borrow' a juror from any surplus there.

It is perhaps stating the obvious to note that additional jurors can only be brought in before the jury is sworn.

8.16   Failure of Juror to Answer Summons

Any person duly served with a summons for jury service who fails to appear at the proper time without reasonable excuse may be dealt with by the coroner under s 10(1) of the Act and fined. This would entail a warrant being issued for the arrest of the juror who would then be brought before the coroner to give an explanation

---

[44] Form 7 of Schedule IV of the Coroners Rules 1984—see section 8.18.
[45] See section 8.21.

and show cause why he/she should not be fined. However, this would need clear evidence of service which may be difficult when a jury summons is usually sent out by ordinary post.

The Jury in Court

The Role of the Jury
8.17

Most inquests are heard by a coroner sitting alone who must examine the witnesses to elicit their evidence, consider the necessary law and then reach the decisions necessary to complete the inquisition.[46] However, where the coroner is sitting with the jury there is a marked division of labour:

- The coroner (and any advocates or interested parties) will have elicited the evidence for the jury by asking questions of the witnesses. The coroner will control the proceedings, sum up the evidence for the jury, and direct them as to the relevant law.
- The jury will listen to the evidence, ask appropriate questions if they wish, and then reach a factual verdict based upon the evidence.

Preliminary Matters
8.18

Once the coroner has identified the properly interested persons[47] present in court the jury will be called in by the officer. There is no strict requirement for the jury to be called by name,[48] although this is generally the practice in the Crown Court.[49]

The jury will take an oath or affirm, usually collectively:

I swear by Almighty God that I will diligently inquire on behalf of Our Sovereign Lady the Queen into the death of C.D. and give a true verdict according to the evidence.[50]

Objection to a Particular Juror
8.19

Although there is no specific power for an interested person to object to a particular juror[51] the coroner may discharge any juror who might be thought to be less than impartial for some good reason (eg known to a relative of the deceased or a

---

[46] As to which see section 9.07 *et seq.*
[47] See section 7.09.
[48] *R v Comerford* [1998] 1 WLR 191.
[49] It may be better practice to do so, other than in the rare event of fears for the safety of the jury should they be identified by name.
[50] Form 7 in Schedule IV of the Coroners Rules 1984.
[51] In the Crown Court there is a right for either side to challenge a limited number of jurors 'as of right' and an unlimited number for good cause.

witness), or who appears to be incapable of taking part in the proceedings (eg through deafness).[52] Properly interested persons would have the right to ask the coroner to discharge a juror but this would rest entirely in the coroner's discretion.

When considering whether a juror should be excluded or discharged for apparent bias the question to be asked is whether the circumstances[53] would lead a fair-minded and informed observer to conclude that there was a real possibility or real danger (the two being the same) that the juror was biased.[54]

8.20 Introducing the Case before a Jury

The coroner will usually address the jury in open court before calling any evidence. The length at which this will be done may depend upon whether this is the first case in the jury session or not.

The coroner would briefly explain the purpose of an inquest to the jury, will outline their role in the proceedings[55] and give them an idea of the sort of matters they will have to decide. They will be advised how they might go about asking questions of a witness, should they wish,[56] and will be warned that they should not discuss the case during adjournments until sent out to consider their verdict.

8.21 Power to Discharge a Juror

Rule 52 allows the coroner to discharge the summons of a juror brought before the court *prior* to the inquest where there is doubt as to effective capacity on account of physical disability or insufficient understanding of English. In practice this would probably become clear, and be dealt with, well before the inquest without any need for attendance of the juror.

It sometimes occurs that a member of the jury has to be discharged *during* an inquest, perhaps because of illness, apparent bias, or some other reason causing an inability to pay proper attention to the case.[57] Although there is no statutory power, it is well recognized in common law that the coroner may discharge an individual member of the jury, provided always that seven or more jurors

---

[52] See section 8.21 below.

[53] Including where appropriate the result of any investigation into those circumstances.

[54] *R (on the application of Dawson) v HM Coroner for East Riding and Kingston upon Hull* [2001] ACD 68; sometimes referred to as *R v HM Coroner for Hull ex p Dawson*. See also section 7.25.

[55] This is particularly important, for without a clear explanation of the purpose of the jury at an inquest a degree of bewilderment may follow—see also section 8.30 *et seq* below.

[56] It is usually better if jury members write down their question and pass it to the foreman of the jury to read out.

[57] A juror who refuses to discharge his/her obligations in accordance with the jury oath may be in contempt of court (as to which see section 7.47). *R v Schot* [1997] 2 Cr App R 383.

remain.[58] For this reason a coroner will nearly always summon more than seven jurors to start the case.

Length of Sitting   8.22

It must be remembered that the jury may not have experience of concentrating on the spoken word for long periods and they should be given a break at regular intervals, probably sitting no more than 90 minutes at a time. They should have a proper facility for refreshments and an opportunity for lunch at an appropriate time. In general they should not be expected to sit beyond normal business hours.

In several cases inquisitions have been quashed because juries have been required to sit for too long at one session or were allowed to carry on hearing a case into the evening to reach a decision, even though they had expressed a preference for this rather than returning the next day.[59] Anything which has an appearance of rushing the jury towards a verdict must be avoided.

Allowing the Jury to Ask Questions   8.23

The jury should be given an opportunity to ask questions of a witness once the coroner and any interested parties have done so. Whilst it is appropriate for the coroner to allow the jury to ask questions, it is equally important that close control is kept on this situation to ensure that only relevant and proper questions are raised. Nor should the jury be allowed to ask questions in such a way that they are seen to be 'entering into the arena' by cross-examining a witness.

Viewing the Scene   8.24

It is uncommon for a jury to be taken to the scene of the death for a 'viewing'. Photographs or plans of the relevant location will generally be a sufficient and more lasting record for the jury. However, there are occasions when nothing other than a visit will convey the necessary information to the jury. If so, it may be that the coroner would wish to visit the locus prior to the case starting; apart from anything else care must be taken that no important feature has changed since the death occurred.

The coroner should view with the jury but must not discuss the issues with them at the scene. It is a matter of discretion for the coroner whether interested parties

---

[58] *R v Merseyside Coroner ex p Carr* [1994] 1 WLR 578. See also *R (on the application of Dawson) v HM Coroner for East Riding and Kingston upon Hull* [2001] ACD 68 where the discharge of a juror (for apparent bias following alleged racist remarks in the jury room) was accepted without demur by the High Court. Bias of a juror is further dealt with at section 8.19 above.

[59] *R v City of London Coroner ex p Calvi*, The Times, 2 April 1983; *R v Southwark Coroner ex p Hicks* [1987] 1 WLR 1624.

also attend at the same time. There would generally seem to be no reason why not and this should assuage any fears of the jury being improperly influenced at the scene.

The other persons attending must have different transport from the jury. There should be no opportunity for discussion with them and no attempts to influence them by gestures such as shaking of heads whilst looking at a particular feature. If the family have not previously visited the scene, this would no doubt be an emotional occasion for them and it may be better that they view separately to the jury.

8.25 No Person to Address the Jury

By rule 40, no person is allowed to address the coroner or the jury as to the facts of a case. This is a clear prohibition on anyone other than the coroner addressing the jury. Advocates representing interested persons will not be given an opportunity to make a closing statement putting forward a particular case, as would happen in a criminal court. Should any person wish to address the coroner on a point of law (before the summing-up) this must be done in the absence of the jury.[60]

8.26 Seclusion of the Jury

The jury are generally free to go about as they wish until they retire to consider their verdict, although they should be warned whenever they are given a break that they must not discuss the case with each other during the adjournment.

Once the evidence has been heard and the coroner has summed up to the jury,[61] the jury officer will take an oath before the court:

> I swear by Almighty God that I shall well and truly keep the jury upon this inquiry, that I shall not suffer any person to speak to them nor shall I speak to them myself unless it be to ask if they have agreed upon their verdicts, until they shall be so agreed.

The jury will go to their retiring room and will stay in seclusion until such time as they have reached a verdict. Until recent times, if a jury were unable to reach a verdict on the same day that they had retired, it was necessary for them to be kept together overnight at a hotel.[62] However, by virtue of the Criminal Justice and Public Order Act 1994[63] it is now possible for the jury to go to their homes overnight, although they must be clearly warned that:[64]

---

[60] See section 7.37 on the coroner giving an opportunity for such submissions to interested persons.

[61] See section 8.29 *et seq.*

[62] Although there was some argument as to whether this requirement applied to a coroner's jury.

[63] Section 43.

[64] *R v Oliver* [1996] 2 Cr App Rep 514.

- it is the nature of the jury system that they reach their verdict only when together in the jury room and that the verdict be based only on the evidence heard in the court;
- they should not further discuss this case amongst themselves until told to do so, nor attempt to contact one another about any aspect of the case;
- having left the court they should not discuss the case with anyone else nor allow anyone to speak with them about any aspect of the case;
- they should not seek to find any further evidence or information about the case;[65]
- when they return for the next sitting they should go straight to the jury room to wait but not discuss the case until brought back into court and told to continue with their deliberations.

Unanimous and Majority Verdicts   8.27

It should be explained in the summing up that a unanimous verdict is required. Nonetheless, by s 12, a majority verdict can be accepted once a reasonable time (which must depend on the particular circumstances) has gone by. Interestingly, the coroner's court has had this power since 1926 whilst it was only introduced in the criminal courts in 1976.

Although the question of when to accept a majority verdict is solely a matter for the coroner, it is unlikely to be in less than the two hours ten minutes allowed in a criminal court.[66] It may be felt appropriate to resume the court in the absence of the jury and give the lawyers for interested persons a chance to comment on the intended course of action.

The jury will then be recalled, asked if they have reached a verdict and (assuming they have not) given directions about a majority verdict. No more than two (irrespective of the total number of the jury) can dissent.[67] If the jury remain deadlocked after a further period has passed they will be discharged and the whole inquest re-heard before another jury.[68]

In taking the eventual verdict the coroner should ask if the verdict is unanimous and then ascertain the number of dissenters as appropriate. The jury *excluding the dissenters* should sign the inquisition form[69] after the hearing (rather than identifying the dissenting jurors in open court).

---

[65] The case of *Oliver* involved a complex fraud; after the jury had been home for the night one juror came to court with two textbooks on accounting which he wanted to take into the jury room.

[66] *Practice Direction (Crime: Majority Verdict)* [1970] 1 WLR 916.

[67] Section 12(2) Coroners Act 1988.

[68] Section 12(3) Coroners Act 1988. However, *Jervis on Coroners* (12th edition) at para 13-08 rightly comments that in a complex case lasting several weeks it may be appropriate to allow the jury two or three days for their deliberations before considering discharging them under s 12 (3).

[69] See section 9.07 *et seq.*

8.28 Recording the Verdict

In recording the jury's conclusions the coroner must be careful not to lead them, although the jury may be questioned where necessary 'for the purpose of removing ambiguity and uncertainty'.[70] If there has been confusion, it may be better to read back the completed inquisition to the jury for confirmation. Where the jury are unclear on a point the coroner should give further directions and ask them to retire so that they may consider the particular issue again.

It is improper for any part of the inquisition form to be pre-typed with answers that the coroner anticipates, except insofar as matters are not in dispute.[71]

Finally, the jury will be required to sign the inquisition as a record of their decision.[72] If the jury returned their verdict by a majority, only those agreeing should sign the inquisition.

Summing Up

8.29 Introduction

By rule 41 the coroner, when sitting with a jury, is required to sum up the evidence and direct them as to the law before they are sent to consider a verdict. Their attention must also be drawn to rules 36(2) and 42, (see section 8.31).

The 1998 Court of Appeal case of *Douglas-Williams*[73] noted that as there were no opening or closing speeches to the jury by counsel at an inquest, the need for clarity by the coroner when summing up on the law was of particular importance.

The same case suggested that it was sensible for the jury to be encouraged to take notes during the summing up. It was also said that it may be wise to prepare a written statement of the matters which the law requires in relation to each possible verdict, which could be considered by any lawyers attending the inquest (and be the subject of submissions) before being handed to the jurors. This was supported in the 1999 case of *Hay*[74] where it was said that the availability and use of standard directions might eliminate a lot of needless difficulties in the future.

---

[70] *R v West Yorkshire Coroner ex p Clements* (1993) 158 JP 17.

[71] *R v East Berkshire Coroner ex p Clara Buckley* (1992) 157 JP 425; eg the name of the deceased or particulars required for the Registration Acts are rarely in dispute but it is unwise for the medical cause of death or the circumstances of the injury to be entered in advance, however straightforward the case may appear.

[72] Section 11(5).

[73] *R v Inner London Coroner (South District) ex p Douglas-Williams* [1999] 1 All ER 344.

[74] *R v Lincolnshire Coroner ex p Hay* (1999) 163 JP 666. The Coroners' Society subsequently prepared a Bench Book for coroners incorporating specimen written directions for juries.

There is no specific definition of 'summing up' contained within coronial legislation but this is obviously a well-defined judicial responsibility. The summing-up is likely to include:

- a reminder of the purpose of the inquest;
- a specific explanation of rules 36(2) and 42;
- an explanation of the questions to be answered on the inquisition sheet;
- an explanation of the conclusions which they are to consider and any relevant law;
- an explanation of the necessary standard of proof;
- a summary of the important points of evidence;
- instruction on how the jury might go about assessing the evidence;
- a full and careful direction on any issues of causation;
- a direction that the verdict must be unanimous (initially);
- brief advice as to how the task should be approached.

Some of these issues are considered in detail in Chapter 9 in relation to verdicts but a brief explanation may assist at this point.

The Purpose of the Proceedings   8.30

The coroner will probably have explained the purpose of an inquest to the jury at the outset.[75] A reminder at this stage is likely to be well placed and the coroner may perhaps quote one of the several cases which underline the inquisitorial nature of the hearing:

> It should not be forgotten that an inquest is a fact finding investigation to find out how a person died. It is not a method of apportioning blame. There are no parties as such, seeking [the coroner's] ear. There is no indictment, no prosecution, no defence, no trial, simply an attempt to establish facts. It is an inquisitorial process, a process of investigation quite unlike a trial . . .[76]

Rules 36 and 42   8.31

Rule 41 requires that rules 36 and 42, which are discussed more fully at sections 7.02 and 9.12 *et seq*, are specifically brought to the attention of the jury. It is perhaps only necessary to set out here that these rules dictate the remit of the inquest, ie:

- that the evidence must be directed to ascertaining who the deceased was, how, when and where he died;
- that neither coroner nor jury must express an opinion on any other matter;
- that the verdict must not be framed in such a way as to appear to indicate criminal liability of a named person or civil liability.

---

[75] See section 8.20.
[76] *R v South London Coroner ex p Thompson* (1982) 126 SJ 625.

8.32 Questions to be Answered on the Inquisition Sheet

The coroner will first have to explain to the jury exactly what is required of them in terms of their verdict, outlining the meaning of each of the questions within the inquisition form which together form the verdict (this is more fully discussed in Chapter 9).

In particular the jury will need careful advice on the manner in which they should complete box 3, stating the time, place, and circumstances at or in which the injury was sustained (see section 9.09). The coroner may explain here that the jury are asked to summarize the facts of the death whilst still remembering the limitations placed upon them by rules 36 and 42.

8.33 Verdicts to Consider

Having heard submissions on the relevant law from advocates, the coroner will only set down for the jury those verdicts considered appropriate as a matter of law and as justified by the evidence. The question to be asked (known as 'the Galbraith principle') is whether, taking the evidence at its highest, a reasonable jury, properly directed, *could* reach that particular verdict to the required standard of proof.[77]

In the 1997 case of *Palmer*[78] the court held that it was the coroner's duty to act as a filter to avoid injustice by only leaving to a jury those verdicts which it would be safe to return. If the evidence was 'so inherently weak, vague or inconsistent with other evidence' that it would not be safe for a jury to come to the verdict, the coroner must withdraw the issue from them. But the court also recognized that there will always be borderline situations where it is necessary for the coroner to exercise a discretion.

In 1998 the Court of Appeal[79] confirmed that coroners should use the 'Galbraith principle' but could take other factors into account:

> . . . the coroner's role is more inquisitorial, even when sitting with a jury, than that of a judge . . . a coroner must decide the scope of inquiry which is appropriate and the witnesses to be summoned. He therefore must, at least indirectly, have a greater say as to what verdict the jury should consider than a judge at an adversarial trial.

> . . . so far as the evidence called before the jury is concerned, a coroner should adopt the Galbraith approach in deciding whether to leave a verdict. [But] the strength of the evidence is not the only consideration and in relation to wider circumstances the coroner has a discretion. If it appears there are circumstances which in a particular situation mean in the judgement of the coroner, acting reasonably and fairly, it is

---

[77] *R v Galbraith* [1981] 1 WLR 1039.
[78] *R v HM Coroner for Exeter and East Devon ex p Palmer* [1997] EWCA Civ 978.
[79] *R v Inner London Coroner (South District) ex p Douglas-Williams* [1999] 1 All ER 344.

not in the interest of justice that a particular verdict should be left to the jury he need not leave that verdict.

This might be best summarized as the coroner has a discretion to leave for the jury only those verdicts which sensibly reflect the thrust of the evidence as a whole and is not slavishly bound to place every possible verdict before them. Indeed, with a very complex case it may be inappropriate to do so.[80]

Some particular assistance was given on when neglect verdicts might be left to a jury in *Commissioner of Police for the Metropolis* (2003). It was said that, provided all the other elements of neglect are present, the word 'gross' imports a value judgement and so whether a failure amounts to 'a gross failure' would normally be a jury issue.[81] This is similar to the guidance on gross negligence in *R v Adomako*.[82]

Within reason, the jury should be given an option of conclusions although this may commonly be a choice between a substantive verdict and the open verdict.

If submissions on law have been made by advocates, the coroner should give brief reasons (in the absence of the jury) as to why particular verdicts have been included or excluded:

> It will be exceptional for a coroner not to explain, albeit briefly, why he is not pre-pared to allow the jury to consider a verdict sought by the deceased's family and in relation to which there has been some relevant evidence.[83]

The issue of giving reasons for decisions is dealt with in more detail at section 7.55.

Issues for the Jury   8.34

Questions of the credibility of the evidence are matters for the jury to determine and the coroner must be careful not to usurp the function of the jury.[84] It should also be made clear to the jury, where appropriate, that they are not necessarily bound by the narrow opinion of experts (important as they may be) but must consider the evidence as a whole.

The High Court considered these points in the 1993 case of *Diesa Koto*.[85] The deceased was a prisoner who died in a struggle with prison officers. The pathologist could only say that there was 'a strong possibility' of death from acute cardiac failure during a prolonged struggle. There were only minor internal injuries although a prisoner gave evidence that officers had jumped up and down on the

---

[80] *R v HM Coroner for Hull ex p Dawson* [2001] ACD 68.

[81] *R (application of Commissioner of Police for the Metropolis) v HM Coroner for Southern District of Greater London* [2003] EWHC 1829 Admin.

[82] *R v Adomako* [1995] 1 AC 171. See section 9.36.2.

[83] *R v HM Coroner for Inner North London ex p Stanley* [2003] EWHC 1180 Admin.

[84] *R v HM Coroner for Exeter and East Devon ex p Palmer* [1997] EWCA Civ 978.

[85] *R v Inner North London Coroner ex p Diesa Koto* (1993) 157 JP 857 (some references have this case as *R v Coroner for Greater London ex p Diesa Koto*).

deceased. Jumping on the prisoner would clearly have been an unlawful act and, if it had led to acute heart failure, would have amounted to unlawful killing. However, the coroner removed unlawful killing from the jury on the basis that there was no *certainty* as to the cause of death.

The High Court held this was an error, effectively on two grounds:

- Even though the prisoner's evidence largely conflicted with the pathology it was still capable of belief, and should have been left for the jury to assess.[86] The court said that a verdict should be left to the jury where there was evidence, that could not be rejected as incredible or worthless on which the jury *could* return such a verdict.
- The coroner had taken too narrow a view of the medical evidence as to cause of death. Although scientists seldom speak in terms of certainty, the scientific evidence, *together with all the other circumstances of the case*, may be enough to satisfy the jury so as to make *them* feel sure.

The same point was considered more recently in the case of *Dawson*[87] where the court held:

> It is quite true that in many places the doctors qualify their views with appropriate notes of caution. However, scientific certainty is not required, even when a matter must be proved to the criminal standard. The jury have regard to all the evidence, including the expert opinions, when reaching their decisions.

Some distinction must still be made with the situation where there is *no* evidence upon which a properly directed, reasonable jury could reach a verdict, whether on the balance of probabilities or otherwise. There is also a considerable difference between leaving a jury to decide whether they believe unlikely evidence that a particular thing happened and allowing them to *guess* which of two possible situations occurred where there is nothing to indicate which actually took place.

8.35   Standard of Proof

The coroner will need to direct the jury as to the standard of proof, that is to say the level to which particular facts have to be proven in order to reach one verdict or another. This is often no easy task, for the jury may have to appreciate the difference between 'beyond reasonable doubt' (ie the criminal standard of proof which applies to suicide or unlawful killing) and 'on the balance of probabilities' (ie a lesser test which applies to all other verdicts).[88]

---

[86] See section 4.13 on the issue of concentrating on the medical cause of death to the exclusion of other evidence.
[87] *R v HM Coroner for Hull ex p Dawson* [2001] ACD 68.
[88] See section 9.05 *et seq.*

The jury will also have to understand the proper meaning of the open verdict and in particular that it is not a fallback position if they cannot agree between themselves.[89]

The jury will be told that they must first seek to agree a unanimous verdict, as to which see section 8.27 above.

In appropriate cases, any temptation on the part of the jury to succumb to emotion or sympathy should be countered by a clear warning and direction on the standard of proof required.[90]

Summary of the Important Points of Evidence   8.36

It is obviously desirable that the coroner reminds the jury of salient points of the evidence, quoting the phraseology used by witnesses where the importance of the point merits this. The detail with which this will be done will vary according to the length of the case. It may be helpful to take the jury through a chronology of events, connecting the evidence of the various witnesses and contrasting disparities where necessary.

The summing up must reflect the evidence both accurately and fairly, both for and against the particular verdicts left for the jury to consider. In the 2000 case of *Hart*[91] it was said that the correct approach was to put both sides of the evidence carefully, point by point as 'a balance sheet'. It is improper for the coroner to suggest the jury's verdict for them but it may be appropriate to say that if they find a particular set of facts to be true that this would likely lead them towards a certain verdict.

Whilst the coroner is entitled to raise queries on the plausibility and credibility of the witnesses, there should be no indication of a personal disbelief of particular evidence. It might also be made clear that the jury are in no way bound by any view of the coroner's that has been inadvertently expressed about the evidence (as opposed to questions of law where the jury must follow the coroner's directions). The Judicial Studies Board[92] specimen direction for judges summing up to a jury suggests the following warning at the start of the summing-up:

> If I mention or emphasise evidence that you regard as unimportant, disregard that evidence. If I do not mention evidence that you regard as important, follow your own view and take that evidence into account.

---

[89] See section 9.19.

[90] It may also be appropriate in some cases to remind the jury that their verdict has no bearing on future civil litigation.

[91] *R v Derby Coroner ex p Hart* (2000) 164 JP 429.

[92] The body providing training for judges.

The coroner must avoid any temptation to explain expert evidence (whether medical or technical) to the jury either during the summing-up or during the evidence itself. To do so would not only be giving evidence but also introducing an element of unqualified interpretation. It is more appropriate to ensure that a clear explanation in simple terms is given by the witness during their evidence and then repeat this during the summing-up.

8.37 Assessing the Evidence

In appropriate cases, particularly where there are conflicting versions of how the death came about, the jury may be told that:

- they should reach their verdict only upon the evidence heard at the inquest, not upon speculation or supposition;
- they should view the evidence as a whole and their conclusion must be reached having regard to all the evidence;[93]
- nonetheless, having considered the whole of the evidence they may choose to qualify or even reject certain parts of it as incorrect or untruthful;[94]
- even if the medical or scientific evidence apparently fails to come to a definite conclusion they can be reminded that their task is not to judge with scientific certainty but so that as sensible people they are satisfied to the required standard of proof.[95] The medical evidence is not in a special category but is simply part of the overall evidence to be reviewed and decided upon by the jury.[96]

8.38 Issues of Causation

Where appropriate, and especially with verdicts incorporating neglect or unlawful killing, the jury must have a full and careful direction on the question of causation. In particular they must be told that they should not return a verdict including neglect unless there is a clear and direct causal connection between the conduct in issue and the death.[97] It will usually be appropriate for the coroner to elaborate this point by reference to the evidence actually given.

Any case involving a potential 'unlawful killing' verdict[98] will also need clear advice to the jury on the necessary relationship between the various elements which must be proven, particularly the act in question and the cause of death.

---

[93] *Ex p Hart* (n 91 above).
[94] *R v Galbraith* [1981] 1 WLR 1039.
[95] *R v HM Coroner for Inner North London ex p Diesa Koto* (1993) 157 JP 857.
[96] *R v Bracewell* [1979] 68 Cr App R 44—see also section 8.34.
[97] See section 9.27.
[98] See section 9.34 *et seq.*

Advice as to the Jury's Task 8.39

In general it is a matter for the jury as to how they approach the decisions which must be made. However, some advice from the coroner on particular points may be appropriate:

- It is better for the jury to discuss the evidence in it's entirety and agree between themselves what they find to be the true facts before they turn to the issue of verdicts. In particular, the jury should identify at an early stage whether there are any conflicts in the evidence and carefully consider which version (if any) they believe to be accurate.
- In considering verdicts the jury should first examine any which require the higher standard of proof (ie suicide or unlawful killing) and only if that is not made out should they consider the verdicts involving 'balance of probabilities'.[99]

Although written directions on law can be given to a jury, this must only be done with great care; interested persons or their advocates should see the directions and have a chance to address the coroner.[100]

The Right to Ask for Further Advice 8.40

Finally, the jury should be reminded that it is open to them to return to court in order to ask questions if they find that they are unclear upon any matter on which they have received directions. However it is not open to the coroner to call further evidence.

It is improper for the coroner to deal with any question from the jury in private. If the jury seek clarification of a particular point or send out a question to the coroner this should be dealt with in open court.

Documentation in the Jury Room 8.41

The jury are entitled to take with them any exhibits such as plans or photographs. If there are larger exhibits, there should be a facility for the jury to further examine these if they wish. Similarly, if video or tape-recorded evidence has been given the jury may wish to see/hear these again but this would normally be done in open court. Statements read to the court as documentary evidence should also be made available for the jury to read again if they wish.

---

[99] *R v Wolverhampton Coroner ex p McCurbin* [1990] 2 All ER 759.
[100] *R v West London Coroner ex p Gray* [1988] QB 567. See also section 8.29.

It is improper for the jury to be given any item which has not previously been introduced in evidence save perhaps a *blank* copy of an inquisition sheet so that this can act as an aide-memoir of the questions that they will have to consider and answer. Even then it may be better for the coroner to give any lawyers present an opportunity to object to this course of action.

Summary

- The criteria for holding an inquest before a jury are set out in s 8(3) of the Coroners Act 1988—only about 3 per cent of inquests require a jury.
- An inquest before a jury will be required for any death in prison custody, whatever the cause.
- The coroner's jury is chosen at random from the electoral list in the same manner as at the Crown Court.
- The coroner's jury consists of between seven and eleven persons rather than twelve.
- At the conclusion of the evidence the coroner is required to sum up for the jury and direct them upon the law, drawing their attention to rules 36(2) and 42.

9

THE VERDICT

It shall not be lawful for any coroner to issue a warrant, directing the interment of the remains of persons, against whom a finding of felo de se shall be made, in any public highway or with a stake driven through the body of such a person.
Interments (felo de se) Act 1882[1]

---

[1] An Act prohibiting the former practice of requiring that burial of a person who had committed suicide should take place at the junction of four highways, at night and with a stake driven through the body—see n 53 below for further explanation of 'felo de se'. Forfeiture of goods from those who committed suicide was abolished in 1870.

This chapter introduces the reader to:

- requirements of the inquisition;
- standard of proof required;
- limitations upon the verdict;
- the verdicts that may be recorded by the coroner or jury.

The verdict of 'neglect' is fully discussed, together with the implications of recent Human Rights case law. Manslaughter by gross neglect (recorded as 'unlawfully killed'), which is an increasingly important issue, is also dealt with in outline.

9.01 Introduction—The Problem with Verdicts

The conclusion, such as suicide or accidental death, is usually referred to as the 'verdict' although in reality the verdict incorporates a number of findings by the coroner or jury.

Considerable significance is inevitably placed on the recorded[2] verdict, but the word 'verdict' is of itself misleading and suggestive of an adversarial trial, inferring that the finding of the inquest can be contained within a one or two word label. It is this latter difficulty which has led to the increasing use of so-called 'narrative verdicts'[3] by coroners.

Admittedly the verdict is the formal conclusion in a Court of Record. If the court has to consider verdicts of suicide or unlawful killing, or is dealing with a potential 'neglect' verdict, there may be considerable emotional and public interest in the chosen conclusion.[4] Sometimes the conclusion also shows which of two competing versions of events the court finds to be true.

Yet the inquest is primarily a fact-finding exercise and the actual discovery of those facts by the examination of witnesses is fundamental. The inquest may have spent several hours (sometimes days) discovering the precise details of how the death came about. Interested persons are offered their first chance to question witnesses in a structured environment where answers must (generally) be given. Consequently it is unfortunate if the proceedings are to be judged on the basis of a one or two word label that has no legal significance elsewhere.

The Brodrick Report[5] summarized the problem succinctly in saying that there is a difference between a form of proceedings which affords others the opportunity

---

[2] Strictly speaking, a coroner sitting alone 'records' a verdict whilst a jury 'returns' a verdict.
[3] See section 9.23.
[4] See *R v Inner London Coroner (South District) ex p Douglas-Williams* [1999] 1 All ER 344 where the Court recognized that an inquest verdict can have a significant part in avoiding repetition and encouraging beneficial change.
[5] Report of the Committee on Death Certification and Coroners, September 1971, Cmnd 4810.

to judge an issue, and one which appears to judge the issue itself. The inquest was never designed to be the latter but is increasingly seen to fulfil this role.

Differences of Approach   9.02

Such is the historical independence of the office that, whilst there is a basic statutory and case-law framework dealing with matters such as the standard of proof, much has been left to the development of individual practice and discretion in different jurisdictions.

For example, there is no definition in law for the verdict of misadventure. It was suggested in one judicial review some years ago that the verdict was no longer appropriate but this 'advice' has been almost universally ignored.[6] Many coroners continue to use the verdict, but each following their own definition of misadventure, sometimes marginally different from that applied in the next county.

Greater consistency is one priority identified by the Coroner Review (see section 1.08) but for the moment the prospect of diversity remains. The reader is therefore advised to take this chapter as background and inquire as to any local practices or variations.

No Definitive List of Verdicts   9.03

Whilst there is a list of suggested verdicts it is important to understand that this is not definitive. The list is only contained in the notes to the suggested form of inquisition set down under the Coroners Rules 1984.[7] The notes do not form part of the Rules and are not binding.[8] Whilst coroners are encouraged to stay within the suggested list (and usually do) there is nothing to prevent a verdict using words of the individual's choice. All that is necessary is that the conclusion is expressed in 'concise and ordinary language so as to indicate how the deceased came by his death'.[9]

Thus some coroners might use accidental death or misadventure in suitable instances of a hospital death, a few have a preference for using the conclusion 'medical misadventure' in essentially the same circumstances, whilst others have used phrases such as 'complication of [necessary] medical treatment'.

Although there are increasing exceptions, coroners mostly restrict themselves to the suggested list. Using the time-honoured phraseology is less open to misinter-

---

[6] Only a year or so later the High Court itself seemed to approve the use of misadventure in the case of *McCurbin*—see section 9.17.

[7] Schedule 4.

[8] *R v HM Coroner for Greater London ex p Thomas* (1993) 2 WLR 547.

[9] *R v Southwark Coroner ex p Kendall* (1988) 1 WLR 1186, quoted with approval in *R v HM Coroner for Birmingham ex p Secretary of State for the Home Dept* (1990) 155 JP 107.

pretation, at least in one sense. Nonetheless there are occasions when the suggested list does not meet a particular case and some variance is worthwhile.

9.04   The Future

Verdicts are undoubtedly one of the most controversial areas of coronial legislation at present and a subject desperately in need of reform. This has been recognized by the Coroner Review (see section 1.08) which recommends abolition of the present 'short-form verdicts' which are described as 'outcome labels'. The Review recommends putting 'a greater emphasis on what the coroner's inquest can achieve but civil and criminal processes cannot'. This amounts to an outcome which is a factual account of the cause and circumstances of the death, analysing systemic failings and any steps that should have been taken by authorities to prevent the death.

However, some classification of deaths is likely to be necessary for statistical purposes and the Review suggests a list of 'types of death'. This is virtually the same scenario in which the present suggested list of short-form verdicts was created and great care will need to be taken by those in the reform process that one problem is not replaced with another.

The Standard of Proof

Before reaching a particular verdict, the coroner or jury must be satisfied on the necessary facts to the required standard of proof.[10] For a verdict of suicide[11] or unlawful killing the standard is at the same level set in a criminal court, that is to say 'beyond reasonable doubt'.[12] For all other verdicts the lesser (civil) standard applies, ie 'on the balance of probabilities'.

9.05   The Standard of Proof—Conclusion as to the Death

'Beyond reasonable doubt' has been well defined in the criminal courts. In modern terms it means that the facts have been proven to such a level that the coroner or jury are 'sure' of what has happened. In terms of suicide verdicts, this has also been defined as 'other possible explanations being totally ruled out'.[13]

It is well established that 'beyond reasonable doubt' does not mean beyond *any* doubt at all. A reasonable doubt has been defined as 'a doubt to which you can give a reason as opposed to a mere fanciful sort of speculation'.[14]

---

[10] Often wrongly referred to as 'the burden of proof', a phrase that really relates to the duty on the prosecution or plaintiff to prove their case.
[11] *R v West London Coroner ex p Gray and others* [1987] 2 All ER 129.
[12] *R v Wolverhampton Coroner ex p McCurbin* (1990) 1 WLR 719.
[13] *R v Essex Coroner ex p Hopper* ILR 23.5.88. See also section 9.18.1.
[14] *R v Yap Chuan Ching* (1976) 63 Cr App Rep 7.

'On the balance of probabilities' is a significantly lower standard of proof. It means that the coroner or jury conclude that it is more likely than not that particular events occurred. However, this must amount to more than mere speculation; there should be some specific evidence upon which the decision can be based.

> It must carry a reasonable degree of probability, but not so high as is required in a criminal case. If the evidence is such that the tribunal can say 'we think it more probable than not', the burden is discharged, but if the probabilities are equal it is not.[15]

If the coroner or jury are faced with events which could give rise to a verdict from either standard, eg suicide or accidental death, the verdict at the higher standard of proof must be considered first.[16] If that is not made out, then the verdict with the lesser standard of proof should be considered.

The open verdict is discussed in detail below at section 9.19. It might be argued that this does not carry a standard of proof as it is a decision of the coroner or jury that the evidence does not meet the requirements for any other verdict.

It is essential that any jury are directed as to the required standard of proof. In the absence of this the inquisition may be quashed, particularly where verdicts of suicide or unlawful killing are involved. Where there is no jury, it is important that the coroner refers to the necessary standard when giving reasons for the decision[17] to show that this has been taken into account.

The standard of proof in the context of assessing expert medical evidence is dealt with at sections 8.34 and 8.35.

The Standard of Proof—Other Matters   9.06

The inquisition records more than the conclusion of the coroner or jury as to the death (see section 9.07 *et seq*) and it is interesting to consider what standard of proof applies to details such as the identity of the deceased and the medical cause of death. This point does not seem to have been decided by the High Court but the common sense solution seems for all such matters to be 'on the balance of probabilities', no matter what standard is required on the 'conclusion as to the death'.

It is also possible that the court will be completely satisfied as to the identity of the deceased and the medical cause of death (eg an overdose of a particular medication) but is unable to determine whether the overdose was accidental or suicidal. The facts that *are* known should be recorded on the inquisition even though an open verdict is returned.

---

[15] *Miller v Minister of Pensions* [1947] 2 All ER 372.
[16] See section 8.39.
[17] See section 7.55.

Requirements of the Inquisition

Section 11 of the Act requires that the verdict of the inquest be certified by an inquisition, signed by the coroner and/or jury. This must set out who the deceased was and how, when and where he came by his death, together with particulars required under the Registration Act 1953. The Act requires the inquisition to be in such form as the Lord Chancellor may prescribe by rules, but there is currently only a suggested rather than prescribed form.[18]

However, the suggested form (see Table 9.1 below) is commonly used and this sets out:

- the name of the deceased;
- the injury or disease causing the death;
- the time, place, and circumstances at or in which injury was sustained;
- the conclusion of the coroner or jury as to the death;
- particulars required by the Registration Act.

9.07 **Name of the Deceased**

The identity of the deceased is rarely in issue but can occasionally lead to confusion. For example, some people use several different names, or adopt a first name that is not on their birth certificate. The proper course of action is for the name to be recorded as the deceased was known, together with any alias.

There are occasions when the identity of the body remains unknown, indeed some go to great lengths to ensure that their identity remains a mystery. In such instances the name may be recorded as 'an unknown male/female' or 'unascertained'.

9.08 **Cause of Death**

The injury or disease causing the death is generally taken to mean the medical cause of death in the World Health Organisation approved format.[19] The coroner is not obliged to adhere exactly to the medical cause of death given by the pathologist, although logically there would have to be good reason to disregard such evidence. However, the inquest does have the advantage of considering the pathology report in the light of all other evidence, which may show the original stated cause of death in a new context.[20] There are also occasions when the

---

[18] Whilst there is a form (form 22 of schedule 4) contained within the Rules, rule 60 only states that the forms *may* be used, and with such modifications as circumstances may require.

[19] See section 4.04 and n 14 thereto for a discussion of the WHO format.

[20] Which raises issues of when the pathologist should be called in the chain of witnesses, see section 5.49.

Table 9.1. Inquisition

INQUISITION

An inquisition taken for our Sovereign Lady the Queen

At	in the	of	
On the	day of	19	

[And by adjournment

On the	day of	19	]

[Before and by] [1] me

One of Her Majesty's coroners for the said

[and the undermentioned jurors] touching on the death of
[a person unknown] [concerning a stillbirth]

The following matters are found

1 Name of deceased

2 Injury or disease causing death: [2]

3 Time, place and circumstances at or in which injury was sustained: [3]

4 Conclusion of the jury/coroner as to the death: [4]

5 Particulars for the time being required by the Registration Acts to be registered concerning the death

a Date and place of birth   e Date and place of death

b Name and surname of deceased   f Occupation and usual address

c Sex

d Maiden surname of a woman who has married

Signature of coroner:

Signature of jurors:

Please turn over

263

coroner is asked to hear the evidence of a second pathologist or expert medical witness which may give an alternative explanation for the death.

9.09 Statement of Circumstances

This section should be read in conjunction with section 9.23 on narrative verdicts.

The third question of the inquisition (often referred to as 'box 3') allows the coroner or jury to set out concisely the 'time, place and circumstances at or in which injury was sustained'. In one sense it may be easiest to understand this as the s 11(5)(b)(ii) requirement to state 'when and where and how' the deceased came by his death.[21] The word injury is widely interpreted as 'that which caused the death' and is not restricted to matters of trauma, but it is generally inappropriate to complete this section where the death arises from a natural cause or an industrial disease.

The limitations of rules 36 and 42[22] apply and the phraseology of the statement of facts should remain neutral. In *Jamieson*[23] the court accepted that the inquisition could properly contain a brief, neutral, factual account of the death but said that this must express no judgement or opinion and that it is not the court's function to prepare detailed factual statements.

At the same time the phraseology should not be so bland as to deprive the statement of any meaning, and should amount to a brief encapsulation of the essential facts[24] upon which the court bases the conclusion.[25]

In *Stringer*[26] (the judicial review of the Hillsborough Disaster inquest) the court explicitly approved of an invitation in the coroner's summing-up for the jury to expand on the most basic elements in box 3 in the following terms:

> You could say 'died on 15th April 1989 as a result of crush injuries sustained . . .' and you could add if that is what you thought the evidence said, '. . . following over-crowding and/or crowd movement and/or following the opening of concertina

---

[21] In *R v HM Coroner for South Yorkshire ex p Stringer* (1993) 158 JP 453 the court said that the purpose of the inquisition asking for the 'circumstances' in box 3 must be to seek an answer to the question of 'how the deceased came by his death'.

[22] See section 7.02 on rule 36 and section 9.12 *et seq* on rule 42.

[23] *R v HM Coroner for North Humberside ex p Jamieson* [1995] QB 1.

[24] See *In re Bradley and Larkins Application* (unreported 7/4/95: QBD Northern Ireland) referred to in Leckey and Greer, *Coroner's Law and Practice in Northern Ireland* (1998, SLS Legal Publications NI).

[25] As a simplistic example, merely to say that the deceased 'was hit by a train' does not explain very much unless it is a reflection that the circumstances are unknown (thus open verdict). To say 'stepped in front of a train' shows how the court comes by a verdict of suicide, to say 'fell in front of a train whilst crossing the line' explains an accidental death conclusion.

[26] See n 21 above.

gates' or anything else that relates to the circumstances which you feel ought to be found in relation to that death and which you think ought to be included.[27]

Conclusion as to the Death   9.10

Whilst all the facts recorded on the inquisition form part of the coroner's verdict, it is the 'conclusion as to the death' which is consistently given the greatest significance, both by those involved in the inquest and the media.[28]

The notes to the suggested form of inquisition in Schedule IV of the Rules contains a list of verdicts but these notes are not a part of the Rules and not mandatory. Coroners are not bound to the suggested verdicts and may use any concise and ordinary language which they consider adequate.[29]

Common verdicts, and the possibility of a narrative verdict, are considered from section 9.15 following.

Particulars under the Registration Act   9.11

The coroner or jury must also record certain personal details of the deceased for the purpose of registration of the death under the Registration Act 1953. These are straightforward matters such as the date and place of birth, or the maiden name of a woman who has married. Provided that the identity of the deceased is known, these will rarely present a problem. If details remain unknown they would simply be marked as such.

Limitations of the Verdict—Rule 42

Prior to 1977 it was a function of the inquest, in cases of murder, manslaughter, or infanticide, to name the alleged perpetrator which had the effect of committing that person for trial at the Crown Court. This was abolished by the Criminal Law Act 1977[30] and rule 42 of the Coroners Rules 1984 now sets out that:

42. No verdict shall be framed in such a way to appear to determine any question of—
  (a) criminal liability on the part of a named person, or
  (b) civil liability.

This restriction is one of the principal tenets (and contentions) of modern coronial law.

---

[27] This was described in the judgment as giving the jury an opportunity to bring in a narrative verdict (see section 9.23) which perhaps underlines the close relationship between the statement of circumstances and a so-called narrative verdict.
[28] See section 9.01 for further commentary on this point.
[29] See section 9.03.
[30] See section 1.07.

9.12 Criminal Liability

Despite the requirement to adjourn[31] under s 16, the coroner will sometimes deal with a case where it is clear that murder or manslaughter, etc has been committed. This might arise in a number of ways: the killer may have committed suicide after the act or might even have died naturally; the perpetrator might never have been traced despite a prolonged police inquiry; or the Crown Prosecution Service might consider the evidence insufficient to lay charges.

In such cases it is almost inevitable that the evidence given during the inquest will refer to the killer (assuming the identity is known) and in all probability no one will be in the slightest doubt as to who was responsible. Even so, the verdict must simply be that the deceased was 'unlawfully killed' without naming the perpetrator.

9.13 Civil Liability

So far as civil liability is concerned, a conclusion from the suggested list, used on its own, will not be in breach of rule 42. The greater danger is that the brief summary set out under 'time, place and circumstances at or in which the injury was sustained', or a narrative verdict, will contain some indication of civil liability. Care must be taken to use neutral phraseology, whilst at the same time not being so bland as to rob the account of any meaning. This is considered further at section 9.09.

Narrative verdicts, as to which see section 9.23, pose a greater difficulty.

9.14 The Duty to Inquire—A Conflict with Rule 42?

Despite the clear difference[32] between the concepts of neglect and negligence, it may be questioned whether rule 42 is contravened when the coroner or jury return a verdict incorporating the words 'contributed to by neglect'[33] or, more recently, 'system neglect'. However, the High Court has made it plain on several occasions that the duty of the coroner to inquire and record the appropriate verdict outweighs rule 42:

> It is clear . . . that the coroner's over-riding duty is to inquire 'how' the deceased came by his death and that duty prevails over any inhibition against appearing to determine questions of criminal or civil liability. Any apparent conflict between section 11 and rule 42 must be resolved in favour of the statutory duty to inquire whatever the consequences of this may be.[34]

---

[31] See section 7.17.
[32] See section 9.24.
[33] See section 9.25.
[34] *R v HM Coroner for East Sussex ex p Homberg* (1994) 158 JP 453, citing an earlier comment from *R v Surrey Coroner ex p Campbell* [1982] 2 All ER 545.

This point was clarified further in *Jamieson*[35] which held that rule 42 applies only to the verdict and that during the proceedings the court may explore facts bearing on criminal and civil liability.

Common Verdicts

Verdicts of neglect, system neglect, and unlawful killing are dealt with in separate sections starting at sections 9.24, 9.30, and 9.34 respectively.

Natural Causes   9.15

Definition   9.15.1

As with most of the conclusions used by coroners, there is no statutory definition of 'natural causes' but it may be suggested that this is the normal progression of a natural illness, without any significant element of human intervention. The Coroners' Bench Book offers a definition of 'the result of a naturally occurring disease running its [full] course'.

If there is no formal definition of 'natural', it may be useful to look at the converse. Unnatural death was defined in 1967 as 'wholly or partly caused, or accelerated, by any act, intervention or omission, other than a properly executed measure intended to prolong life'.[36] On this reasoning, whilst a heart attack is an obvious example of a natural death, if it was caused by the victim having been left bound and gagged by a burglar for many hours, the death would not be regarded as natural.

More recently, the case of *Touche*[37] held that a 'wholly unexpected death from natural causes which would not have occurred but for some culpable human failure' was to be regarded as unnatural for the purpose of assuming jurisdiction under s 8 of the Act. The court said that 'deaths by natural causes, though undoubtedly they are, they should plainly never have happened and in that sense are unnatural'.

A rare cause of death is not of itself unnatural despite an apparent reference to this effect in the case of *Thomas*.[38]

The standard of proof applying to a conclusion of natural causes is the balance of probabilities.

---

[35] *R v HM Coroner for North Humberside ex p Jamieson* [1995] QB 1.

[36] Pilling, Herbert H., 'Natural and unnatural deaths', *Medicine, Science and the Law* (April 1967).

[37] *R v Inner North London Coroner ex p Touche* [2001] QB 1206.

[38] *R v Poplar Coroner ex p Thomas* [1993] QB 610, sub nom: *R v HM Coroner for Greater London ex p Thomas*. The court corrected this misunderstanding in *Touche*—see section 2.22.

9.15.2 *Medical deaths*

Although natural causes are mostly self-evident and easily recognized, in some deaths under medical care the dividing line between a natural cause and a death arising from some element of treatment (or lack of it) is very difficult to establish. The 1997 case of *Benton*[39] gave some guidance on this area:

- where the patient was suffering from a potentially fatal condition, and the medical intervention (even if wrongly given) merely failed to prevent the death, the proper verdict was 'natural causes' as it was the underlying condition which had caused the death;
- if there was a failure to give medical treatment to such a patient, even negligently, this would still amount to a death from natural causes (but see section 9.24 *et seq* on neglect);
- if the patient was suffering from a condition which was not life-threatening, but the treatment (for whatever reason) caused death, the proper verdict was accident or misadventure, unless there was a question of unlawful killing.

The court stressed that a verdict of death by natural causes was not in any way a finding of no fault on the part of the doctors, just as the recording of death by accident/misadventure would not imply that there was fault.

It is certainly not impossible to reconcile *Benton* with the later (Court of Appeal) decision in *Touche*[40] particularly with the 'wholly unexpected death' criteria that effectively arises in both. Nonetheless, *Benton* must now be read with *Touche* in mind—even though the latter case was concerning jurisdiction rather than verdicts.

9.15.3 *Osteoporosis*

A common complication in deciding whether a death is due to natural causes arises from osteoporosis.[41] This disease affects a good proportion of the elderly population (predominantly females) and can render bone so weak that it will fracture with almost no physical trauma. Indeed it can be argued that the break preceded the fall. The most common area for a problem is the neck of the femur, ie where the thigh and pelvis join in a ball and socket. Although the injury itself may not necessarily be life-threatening, the immobility and general insult to the patient can often result in death due to bronchopneumonia.

---

[39] *R v Birmingham Coroner ex p Benton* (1997) 162 JP 807. Some would argue that this case was decided very much on its facts and that the same principles would not necessarily be followed today; nonetheless, the judgment rests moderately comfortably with *Touche*. Cf. *R v Avon Coroner ex p Smith* (1998) 162 JP 403.

[40] *Ex p Touche* (n 37 above).

[41] See also section 3.18.

On the face of it this is potentially an unnatural cause of death as the chain of events often starts with some form of trauma. However, if the trauma is comparatively minor and unlikely to have damaged a normal bone, it is generally accepted that it is the disease which is the real cause rather than the trauma. Most coroners will treat this as a natural cause for the decision on jurisdiction, but where an inquest is held (perhaps because the circumstances were initially unclear), the verdict is more likely to be dependent on the individual facts.

Accidental Death   9.16

There is a great deal of confusion and genuine difference of opinion as to the distinction (if any) that should be drawn between accidental death and misadventure. This section should therefore be read in conjunction with the paragraphs on misadventure following. As accidental deaths are commonly the antithesis of natural, reference should also be made to section 9.15.

Most cases falling into the category of accidental death are self-evident, the cause of death arising from some unnatural event[42] which was neither unlawful nor intended by the deceased to result in death.

Where difficulties arise, there are several definitions for consideration. The Coroners' Bench Book offers a global definition that the death arose not from a natural cause but from either an event over which there was no human control; an unintended act or omission; or a deliberate act that unintentionally leads to death. Accident is usually defined in road traffic law as 'an unintended occurrence with an adverse physical effect'.[43]

Accident has also been described as a word 'having its ordinary meaning within the English language' but in recent times the prevalent view has changed. Whilst there is a great deal of difference between 'accidental' and 'unavoidable' it is common for relatives, hearing the death being referred to as 'accidental', to feel that this verdict is trivializing the death. It is assumed that the coroner is finding the death to have been without blame and that no civil liability should lie against another. This is far from the court's intention and it is important for it to be stressed to relatives that the phrase:

- is completely neutral in terms of liability and does not deprive anyone of their civil remedy; *and*
- encompasses a wide scale of scenarios ranging from genuine mischance to deaths which are wholly the result of another's carelessness.

---

[42] See section 9.15.1.
[43] *R v Morris* (1972) RTR 201.

Use of the phrase 'accidental death' is particularly difficult in road traffic cases, sometimes meeting considerable resistance from relatives who rarely see anything 'accidental' in the manner of their loss.[44] Whilst there is probably no legal reason[45] why an alternative phrase, such as 'motor vehicle death' or 'road traffic death' could not be used in some instances, it might be considered that some insurance policies make payment on the basis of an accidental death.

The standard of proof required for an accidental death verdict is the balance of probabilities.

9.17 Misadventure

There is a close connection between misadventure and accidental death and this topic should be read in conjunction with the section above.

In *Anderson*[46] the Divisional Court voiced the opinion[47] that the distinction between accident and misadventure was 'without purpose or effect', that misadventure had had its day as a verdict and should now be laid to rest. In fact it is still commonly used by coroners and the 1990 case of *McCurbin*[48] plainly envisaged that it would continue to be applied. In the 1997 case of *Benton*,[49] the Divisional Court, whilst noting the comment in *Anderson*, referred to the possibility of a verdict of 'death by accident/misadventure'.

There remains uncertainty on a definition of misadventure. The writer would argue that if any logical distinction does exist, misadventure might be applied when someone (not necessarily the deceased) deliberately undertakes a task which then goes wrong, causing the death.[50]

Thurston[51] gave a clear example of this approach—when an adverse drug reaction causes death, 'accident' might imply that the wrong drug or dose was given, whilst 'misadventure' suggests the drug was given intentionally but that misfortune supervened. Similarly, Burton et al suggested that where a boxer hits an opponent intentionally with fatal results, the blow could not be described as accidental but the outcome was not intended.[52]

---

[44] Road fatalities have decreased markedly over the last 35 years (from 7,300 in 1967 down to 3,400 in 2001) whilst at the same time the attitude of the public to such deaths has, perhaps correctly, become rather less forgiving.

[45] See sections 9.03 and 9.23.

[46] *R v Portsmouth Coroner's Court ex p Anderson* [1987] 1 WLR 1640.

[47] This was a comment by the judge ('obiter') rather than a fundamental issue being decided by the court.

[48] *R v Wolverhampton Coroner ex p McCurbin* [1990] 1 WLR 719.

[49] *R v Birmingham Coroner ex p Benton* (1997) 162 JP 807.

[50] The Coroners' Bench Book offers a very similar definition, if misadventure and accident are to be distinguished.

[51] Thurston, Gavin, *Coronership* (1980, Barry Rose Publishers).

[52] Burton, Chambers, and Gill, *Coroner's Inquiries* (1985, Kluwer Law).

The author would argue that there remains a logical distinction between accident and misadventure and that it is right to differentiate a small number of cases as misadventure, even if only to preserve integrity in the phrase 'accidental death'.

Nonetheless, conclusions of accidental death and misadventure are now treated as one for statistical purposes.

Misadventure is, of course, decided upon on the balance of probabilities.

Suicide   9.18

Definition and standard of proof   9.18.1

The verdict generally referred to as suicide is more often recorded by using phrases such as 'the deceased took his own life' or 'the deceased killed himself'. It is no longer common for the words 'whilst the balance of his mind was disturbed' to be added, the author would suggest that this is only appropriate when some calamity of mind overtakes the deceased.[53]

Suicide has been clearly defined as requiring a specific intent:

> Suicide is voluntarily doing an act for the purpose of destroying one's life while one is conscious of what one is doing, in order to arrive at a verdict of suicide there must be evidence that the deceased intended the consequence of the act.[54]

In practical terms this means that the verdict can only be returned where it is shown beyond reasonable doubt[55] that:

- the death occurred as a result of a deliberate act by the deceased; *and*
- that in doing so (and at all material times) he intended that the consequence would be his own death

Suicide can never be presumed[56] but can only be based upon unambiguous evidence that the deceased intended to take his life.[57] The test has also been described as 'have all other possible explanations been totally ruled out'.[58]

It is no longer necessary that the death take place within a year and a day of the act.[59]

---

[53] The phrase 'whilst the balance of the mind was disturbed' seems to have arisen in the Middle Ages when Christian burial was forbidden to those who took their own life—at one time a stake had to be driven through the body of those who were guilty of 'felo de se' or self-murder. Acknowledging that the deceased had killed themselves due to mental disturbance removed such difficulties.

[54] *R v Cardiff Coroner ex p Thomas* (1970) 3 All ER 469.

[55] *R v West London Coroner ex p Gray and others* [1987] 2 All ER 129. See section 9.05.

[56] *Re Davis deceased* [1967] 1 All ER 688.

[57] *R v City of London Coroner ex p Barber* [1975] 1 WLR 1310 and *R v Northamptonshire Coroner ex p Walker* (1988) 151 JP 773.

[58] *R v Essex Coroner ex p Hopper* ILR 23.5.88.

[59] Section 1, Law Reform (Year and a Day Rule) Act 1996.

9.18.2 *Difficulties of proof*

If reliance is placed on a note to show intent, care must be taken to ensure that it is the deceased's handwriting and is of recent origin. Many elderly people leave written instructions on what is to happen after their death which can be misconstrued as a suicide note.

Assessing intent can be difficult in the absence of a note. Commonly the deceased actively misled those about them by appearing to make positive short-term plans. Nor is it unusual for those in a depressed state to appear more cheerful immediately prior to the death.

The facts of such deaths need to be carefully examined. Consideration will be given to whether the deceased might have been expecting to be found by others who were close by, or who were due to arrive shortly. The act might have been intended merely to put the patient in hospital rather than in the mortuary.

9.19 Open Verdict

An open verdict is a decision by the coroner or jury that the evidence 'does not fully or further disclose the means whereby the cause of death arose'.[60] It is a verdict in its own right, indicating that the evidence is insufficient to satisfy any of the other conclusions. This may arise because, despite the best efforts of an investigation, it is impossible to determine whether a death was intended as suicide or came about by accident. In other cases there may be a suspicion that foul play is involved but no proof to the required level.

Whilst an open verdict may be unsatisfactory and leave 'unanswered questions', it is only logical that any inquisitorial procedure has a means of declaring that the exact circumstances remain unknown.

If the inquest is held before a jury, it may be wise to indicate that an open verdict is not to be taken as a failure:

> I would impress upon [coroners or juries] that if they find themselves compelled to return an open verdict, that is not in any sense a reflection upon them. It does not suggest that they are not doing their job properly or are insufficiently perceptive. There are many, many cases where there is real doubt as to the cause of death, where an open verdict is right and anything else is unjust to the family of the deceased.[61]

This is not a verdict to be used by a jury simply because they cannot agree between themselves. Before returning an open verdict it is still necessary for each member

---

[60] The definition contained within the list of suggested verdicts in the notes to the standard (but not mandatory) form of inquisition; Form 22 in Schedule IV of the Coroners Rules 1984.
[61] *R v City of London Coroner ex p Barber* (1975) 1 WLR 1310.

of the jury to agree that the evidence does not reach the standard of proof required for any of the substantive verdicts being considered.[62]

It is widely, but mistakenly, believed that a coroner may reopen a case at sometime in the future when an open verdict has been recorded, for example if further evidence comes to light. In fact there is no such provision. Of course, a coroner or other interested party always has the right to apply to the Attorney General or High Court where new evidence becomes apparent which might merit a different verdict, but this applies in every case and not just to the open verdict.[63]

If there is a clear view by the coroner or jury as to how the death came about (eg accidental) but some of the other particulars required (eg time and place of death etc) remain unclear, this does not justify an open verdict being returned. The proper conclusion should be stated with the other relevant facts either marked as 'unknown' or 'between xx date and yy date'.

Drugs Deaths   9.20

Many drugs deaths, whether from illicit or therapeutic substances, could rightly be classed as accident or misadventure. However, since 1984 the suggested list of verdicts[64] has contained reference to 'dependence on drugs' or 'non-dependent abuse of drugs'. Again there is no statutory or recognized definition of these conclusions.

It might be argued that 'dependence on drugs' means that the substantive cause of death was not so much an overdose on one particular occasion as the general pattern of abuse by the deceased over a period of time.

Non-dependent abuse of drugs presumably refers to the type of case where the deceased takes one dose as an experiment and dies, the issue being more one of risk-taking than addiction.

It was accepted by a Government Minister[65] in the House of Commons in March 2003 that the 1984 verdicts were not entirely satisfactory and that accident or other verdicts may more closely reflect the circumstances of many such deaths. It was said that guidance on a new suggested verdict (whose title was not revealed) was to be issued shortly with the definition:

> Death where the underlying cause is poisoning, drug abuse or drug dependence and where any of the substances listed under the Misuse of Drugs Act 1971 as amended were involved.

---

[62] See section 8.27 on majority verdicts.
[63] See section 10.06 *et seq.*
[64] See section 9.03.
[65] Mr Hilary Benn, Parliamentary Under-Secretary of State for the Home Office: 5 March 2003.

Finally, it should be noted that in 1988 the High Court held that abuse of solvents by inhalation is *not* abuse of a drug.[66] There is plainly some logic in this decision in that a solvent is not normally to be regarded as a drug. However, if it is deliberately inhaled with a view to some form of mind-altering experience it might seem more appropriate to class the use at that moment as a drug rather than as a solvent.

Such cases are again dealt with on the balance of probabilities.

9.21   Industrial Disease

Statute is of limited assistance in determining the meaning of this conclusion. The list of recognized industrial diseases[67] and prescribed occupations for the purpose of compensation and pension under the Social Security Regulations is an attractive starting point. Thus it might be presumed that the verdict would apply if:

- the occupation was prescribed; *and*
- the disease was prescribed; *and*
- the disease was due to exposure at work; *and*
- the disease caused the death.[68]

However, the first two elements are not strictly required. In the 1987 *BP Chemicals case* it was held that for inquest purposes the list in the Social Security Regulations is not exclusive. The court commented that as 'industrial disease' is one of a list of *suggested* verdicts it would be surprising if it had a refined meaning. The death of an office worker (not a prescribed occupation) qualified as 'industrial disease' when arising from a prescribed disease caused by exposure at work.[69] Following this case the converse might also be argued, ie that a non-prescribed disease which has its causation in the deceased's employment (prescribed or otherwise) should also suffice.

This leads to the interesting question of a death from exposure to asbestos through washing overalls of someone who worked with the substance. These cases are becoming more common. Whilst there is clearly an industrial connection, whether that is in relation to the victim's employment is perhaps a social rather than legal question. It has been argued, correctly in the author's view, that it is better to record these cases as industrial disease (rather than accident/misadventure) to ensure that society has an accurate tally of such deaths.

---

[66] *R v Southwark Coroner ex p Kendall* [1988] 1 WLR 1186.

[67] Schedule I of the Social Security Regulations 1985.

[68] See *Terry v Craze (HM Coroner for East Sussex)* [2002] QB 312 where the Court of Appeal confirmed an earlier Divisional Court decision that the fact a diagnosis of asbestosis 'could not be completely ruled out' did not amount to reasonable cause to suspect that the death was unnatural and thus grounds to require an inquest.

[69] *R v South Glamorgan Coroner ex p BP Chemicals Ltd* (1987) 151 JP 799.

An amendment to the Social Security Regulations in 1993[70] added to the list (for social security purposes) the diseases of chronic bronchitis, emphysema, chronic obstructive airways disease, and chronic obstructive pulmonary disease for any person who had spent at least 20 years working underground at the coal face.[71]

In many instances the death of an underground worker occurs primarily from heart disease but one of the nominated respiratory diseases is included under Part II of the cause of death in the pathologist's report.[72] The author takes the view that if a disease is sufficiently well established to be regarded by the pathologist as a *significant*[73] contributory factor justifying inclusion in Part II, then it will have accelerated the demise, and it is appropriate to regard death as due to an industrial disease.[74]

The appropriate standard of proof is 'balance of probabilities'.

Less Common Verdicts 9.22

Stillbirth 9.22.1

This is a very uncommon finding at an inquest, with approximately six such verdicts each year.[75] Stillbirths are not a matter for the coroner unless an inquiry is necessary to establish whether a particular child was stillborn or lived briefly.

By s 41 of the Births and Deaths Registration Act 1953 (as amended in 1992)[76] the definition of a stillborn child is:

> ... one which has issued forth from its mother after the twenty-fourth week of pregnancy and which did not at any time after being completely expelled from its mother breathe or show any other signs of life.

Want of attention at birth 9.22.2

This section should be read in conjunction with 'neglect' below. This is a very old verdict that may have been common in times of poor maternity care but is now likely to relate only to a baby abandoned or ignored by its mother immediately after birth. However, such circumstances will usually amount to infanticide or manslaughter, necessitating different considerations.

---

[70] Social Security (Industrial Injuries) (Prescribed Diseases) Amendment No 2 Regs 1993.

[71] See section 5.38 for a discussion on industrial diseases in the context of the post-mortem examination.

[72] Part II is 'other significant conditions contributing to the death but not related to the disease or condition actually causing it'.

[73] 'Significant' meaning a contribution which is more than negligible: *R v Cato* 62 Cr App R 41. See also Richardson, J. and Thomas, D. (eds), *Archbold: Criminal Pleading, Evidence and Practice* (2002, Sweet and Maxwell) at paras 19-06 and 19-13.

[74] For an explanation of the format of death certification see section 4.04.

[75] Home Office Statistical Bulletin 06/03.

[76] Still-Birth Definition Act 1992.

There are approximately three such verdicts each year. Perhaps strangely, the standard of proof for 'want of attention at birth' is only the balance of probabilities.

9.22.3 *Lawful killing*

Lawful killing means that the death was the result of an action justified in law, such as self-defence. In the present day it will most commonly relate to the shooting of an armed person by the police during a robbery or siege to protect the life of another. Article 2 ECHR considerations are likely to arise, as to which see section 9.30 *et seq*.

There have been an average of three such verdicts annually over the last five years.[77] This verdict is dealt with on the balance of probabilities.

9.23 Narrative Verdicts

Some of the difficulties inherent in the present 'verdict' system are discussed at section 9.01. As a result of these, it has become more common for coroners to avoid the use of the traditional short-form verdict (accidental death etc) in favour of a so-called narrative verdict, where this seems appropriate. Although practice differs, in general terms this is a short factual account of how the death came about, more akin to 'findings' than a 'label'. Obviously the restrictions of rules 36 and 42 must still be borne in mind.

As an example, one widely reported inquest concluded that the deceased had died from a previously undetected aneurysm and went on to say 'the rupture occurred within one hour of [the deceased] being subjected to an assault by two strangers, one of whom spat at her'.[78] One can argue that this is factual and neutral, it is not in breach of rule 42. Such circumstances could not amount to an unlawful killing but it is easy to see that the family of the deceased would not have readily accepted a short-form verdict of 'natural causes' as a true and full reflection of the circumstances.

The author is aware that others have used words such as 'undiagnosed' or 'untreated' as part of a narrative verdict to reflect particular medical circumstances.[79] In another example it was recorded that the deceased died from the effects of pressure sores which developed between May and September whilst the deceased was resident in a care home.

---

[77] Home Office Statistical Bulletin 06/03.
[78] *Re Roberta Hawes deceased*: 16 May 2001. HM Coroner for City of Brighton and Hove.
[79] As opposed to use of the words 'failure to diagnose' or 'failure to treat' which may be seen as more judgemental.

In the 1997 review case of *Benton*[80] the court refused a new inquest but quashed the inquest conclusion in box 4, making no substitute entry, and recorded the following in box 3, without actually calling it a narrative verdict:

> Robert died on [date] at [time] as a result of bilateral tension pneumothorax resulting from artificial ventilation during a bronchoscopy operation at [hospital] carried out at a time when he was suffering from acute tracheobronchitis and bronchiolitis.

Some would contend that the earlier examples may seem to carry inferences and are close to infringing rule 42. Others would argue that they are factual accounts of the circumstances, without any apparent determination of liability. There is a very fine line between the two which should be treated with caution.

The question then arises whether there truly is a legal basis for narrative verdicts. It is clear that the coroner is not bound by the list of suggested verdicts (see section 9.03) and may form a conclusion in 'concise and ordinary language so as to indicate how the deceased came by his death'.[81] Equally, it is apparent that there is no statutory or common law requirement for verdicts to be in any particular form.[82] Even the form of inquisition in Schedule 4 to the 1988 Rules is merely suggested and not prescribed.[83] There would therefore seem to be no reason why the court cannot use a so-called narrative verdict, in whatever form desired, where the situation merits.

Unfortunately there are few clear guidelines as to how it should be done. Apart from *Benton* (above), reference to the decisions in *Stringer*,[84] *Jamieson*,[85] and *Homberg*[86] only suggests that the courts have approved the use of a more detailed account given in box 3, with a normal short-form conclusion in box 4. This was referred to as a narrative verdict in *Stringer* but the author suspects that few coroners would now regard it as such.[87]

The clear disapproval of any judgemental statement apparent in these decisions still has unambiguous force and logic. In *Stringer* (the judicial review of the

---

[80] *R v Birmingham Coroner ex p Benton* (1997) 162 JP 807. The circumstances were that the treatment (correct or otherwise) of a child with a life-threatening condition allegedly brought about the cause of death.

[81] *R v South Glamorgan Coroner ex p BP Chemicals Ltd* (1987) 151 JP 799; *R v Southwark Coroner ex p Kendall* (1988) 1 WLR 1186. *R v HM Coroner for Birmingham ex p Secretary of State for the Home Dept* (1990) 155 JP 107.

[82] *Ex p BP Chemicals Ltd* (n 81 above).

[83] It was accepted in *Kendall* (n 81 above) that whilst s 11(5) requires an inquisition to be in such form as the Lord Chancellor may prescribe by rules, there is no form prescribed. Rule 60 only states that the forms set out in Schedule 4 *may* be used, and with such modifications as circumstances may require.

[84] *R v HM Coroner for South Yorkshire ex p Stringer* (1993) 158 JP 453.

[85] *R v HM Coroner for North Humberside ex p Jamieson* [1995] QB 1.

[86] *R v HM Coroner for West District of East Sussex ex p Homberg* (1994) 158 JP 357.

[87] It should perhaps be remembered that these three cases were all decided a decade ago when the narrative verdict as we now see it used was uncommon or unheard of.

Hillsborough Disaster inquest) the court rejected a suggested verdict of 'accidental death caused by a failure of the police to divert supporters away from the tunnel'. In *Homberg* and *Jamieson* it remains clear that any narrative must be phrased in carefully neutral terms, but the experience of coroners now seems to suggest that this does not rob the exercise of its validity.

The question then arises of where a narrative verdict should be placed, ie in box 3 or box 4. In some ways it seems logical to use box 3 following *Benton,* although this is certainly not the universal practice of those coroners who use narrative verdicts. In *Stringer* the court felt unable to accept a submission that the correct place for any narrative verdict (as then defined) was in box 4. If box 3 is used, what then should happen to box 4? Despite *Benton,* it might be unwise to leave it blank lest it be seen as an 'open verdict'. It has been suggested to the author that to avoid any confusion box 4 could say 'Narrative Verdict (as above)'.

Neglect

These pages should be read in conjunction with those immediately following on 'system neglect'. The author has deliberately kept the two areas separate, however much there may be an overlap in practice because:

- there are still many neglect cases where considerations of system neglect will not arise;
- the complications of system neglect would render a joint discussion of the topics unwieldy;
- more pragmatically, the concept of system neglect may be eradicated or dramatically altered after publication of this text by the House of Lords decision in *Middleton*[88] leaving neglect to be read in this section alone.

9.24 Introduction

Neglect is one of the most important and difficult issues in modern coronial law. A verdict incorporating neglect will have far-reaching consequences for all involved, even if only adverse publicity in the unremitting public arena of the coroner's court. Whatever the strictures of rule 42,[89] such a conclusion inevitably implies some element of censure, usually of an organization or person in authority, and will almost certainly provide powerful ammunition for those seeking civil redress.

As a result, an understanding of the basic principles of neglect is essential for anyone dealing with any but the most straightforward inquest.

---

[88] See section 9.31.
[89] See section 9.12 *et seq.*

Firstly, it is important to distinguish neglect from civil negligence, the much wider concept of failure to accord proper care for another to whom a legal duty of care was owed. For example, a motorist owes a duty of care to other road users and may be adjudged negligent if a careless act injures someone. Neglect is a much narrower concept than this. Originally described as 'lack of care', it was at first taken to mean that the death had occurred because of a failure to look after the deceased properly, causing starvation or exposure etc.

In the 1980s and early 1990s the number of 'lack of care' cases increased, with the distinction from negligence becoming blurred. In some instances the coroner's decision was taken to judicial review with the result that by mid-1994 'lack of care' had been defined a number of times in the Divisional Court, but the inevitable slightly differing decisions led to confusion. A definitive judgment came from the Court of Appeal in the 1994 case of *R v North Humberside Coroner ex p Jamieson*.[90]

The *Jamieson* Case   9.25

The decision in *Jamieson* was a major clarification of coronial law and is likely to remain a definitive judgment for the foreseeable future.[91] The deceased hanged himself in prison, having displayed worrying behaviour for some days. The inquest recorded a verdict of suicide. The family argued that the coroner should have left 'lack of care' open to the jury on the basis that adequate measures had not been taken by the authorities to prevent the suicide. At judicial review the Divisional Court rejected the application but the family appealed.

After setting out the purpose of an inquest, the Court of Appeal dismissed the apparent conflict between rule 42 and a verdict incorporating matters of censure.[92] It was suggested that the words 'lack of care' had themselves been part of the problem in the past, being too similar to the civil claim of negligence, and should be replaced by the concept of a death 'contributed to by neglect'.

The court went on to discourage neglect (described as the opposite side of the coin to self-neglect) from being regarded as a primary cause of death or so called 'freestanding verdict'.[93] The court then defined neglect:

> Neglect in this context means a gross failure to provide adequate nourishment or liquid, or provide or procure basic medical attention or shelter or warmth for someone in a dependent position (because of youth, age, illness or incarceration) who cannot provide it for himself. Failure to provide medical attention for a dependent person whose physical condition is such as to show that he obviously needs it may amount

---

[90] *R v HM Coroner for North Humberside ex p Jamieson* [1995] QB 1.
[91] The 'general conclusions' of the judgment are set out in full at Appendix 2 on page 361.
[92] See section 9.14.
[93] Meaning a verdict of 'neglect' on its own rather than (say) 'natural causes contributed to by neglect'.

to neglect. So it may be if it is the dependent person's mental condition which obviously called for medical attention.

The court went on to emphasize that the proper test is what the person's condition appeared to be, not what it actually was:

> In both cases the crucial consideration will be what the dependent person's condition, whether physical or mental, appeared to be.

The 14 points of principle set out in the judgment are shown in full at Appendix 2 on page 361.

9.26   The Meaning of 'Gross Failure'

The prime features of this definition are the words 'gross' and 'basic', together with the emphasis on the apparent condition. A gross failure is 'total and complete'[94] and is plainly more than a simple error, however catastrophic the consequences. It might be suggested that this reflects a desire from earlier cases for the conduct to have continued over a period of time (even if only a limited period) rather than being an isolated mistake. This requirement was reaffirmed in the 1996 decision of *Wright*.[95]

In a case before a jury, where all the other elements are present, the word 'gross' imports a value judgement and would normally be a jury issue.[96]

The word 'basic' suggested that relevant failures are restricted to a narrow range. Subsequent decisions[97] have followed this line, referring to issues that were 'not complex or sophisticated medical procedures'. It might also be argued that this phraseology reaffirmed a 1992 case[98] which had held that lack of care only arose where there was an act or omission in the events immediately surrounding the death. It was said that in the environment of a prison or special hospital, this could not embrace any criticism of the regime in general, or of the way in which the deceased was generally looked after.[99]

The emphasis on 'what the dependent person's condition appeared to be' apparently left open the question of whether this is a subjective or objective test. In

---

[94] Oxford English Dictionary.

[95] *R v Surrey Coroner ex p Wright* [1997] 2 WLR 16. Much of this case has been overtaken by later decisions but not, seemingly, the need for neglect to be 'non-transient'.

[96] *R (application of Commissioner of Police for the Metropolis) v HM Coroner for Southern District of Greater London* [2003] EWHC 1829 Admin. This follows *R v Adomako* in relation to gross negligence manslaughter; see section 9.36.2.

[97] In particular the case of *R (application of Nicholls) v HM Coroner for City of Liverpool* [2001] EWHC Admin 922. This case is discussed, with other post-*Jamieson* decisions at Appendix 3 on page 365.

[98] *R v HM Coroner for East Berkshire ex p Buckley* (1992) 157 JP Rep 425.

[99] But now see section 9.30 *et seq* on system neglect.

other words, is the test what the carer *actually* thought, however unreasonably, or what *should* have been realized in all the circumstances.

This has been clarified in a number of recent cases defining the circumstances which might amount to a gross failure. In these it is clear that the courts have moved firmly towards the stance taken in *Clegg*[100] rather than the stricter interpretation in the earlier cases of *Cotton* and *Wright*.[101] The author would suggest that the test is now unequivocally objective.

As a result of the developed case law it is now clear that:

- gross failure is not limited to those incidents where a carer has failed to take any action at all. It may be found even where medical or nursing staff have exercised judgement and made a clinical decision or diagnosis;[102]
- the fact that a view was formed by medical staff that the deceased was not at risk was relevant but did not of itself rule out neglect;[103]
- omissions on the part of medical practitioners are capable of forming part of the total picture which amounts to neglect;[104]
- a failure to procure any *effective* medical treatment could amount to a gross failure;[105]
- failure to follow proper and routine procedures such as absolutely standard monitoring[106] or basic search requirements might amount to neglect, dependent upon the circumstances;[107]
- neglect may arise from a serious underestimation of the dependent person's condition;[108]
- it can be argued that the question to be asked is if the carer *should* have realized the need for action in all the circumstances;[109]
- however, this does not extend to saying that every incorrect clinical judgement amounts to neglect. It has been suggested that if doctors consider all the issues and ask themselves the right question(s), an erroneous decision would not amount to neglect;[110]

---

[100] *R v HM Coroner for Wiltshire ex p Clegg* (1996) 161 JP 521.

[101] *R v Birmingham Coroner ex p Cotton* (1995) 160 JP 123; *R v Surrey Coroner ex p Wright* [1997] 2 WLR 16. For a brief summary and discussion of all of these cases see Appendix 3 at page 365.

[102] *R (Application of Christine Davies) v HM Deputy Coroner for Birmingham* [2003] EWHC 618 Admin.

[103] *R (application of Scott) v HM Coroner for Inner West London* [2001] EWHC Admin 105.

[104] *Ibid.*

[105] *R v HM Coroner for Wiltshire ex p Clegg* (1996) 161 JP 521. *R v HM Coroner for Swansea and Gower ex p Tristram* (2000) 164 JP 191, sub nom *ex p Chief Constable of Wales.*

[106] *R v HM Coroner for Inner London North ex p Touche* [2001] All ER 752.

[107] *Tristram* n 105 above.

[108] *R (application of Marshall) v HM Coroner for Coventry* [2001] EWHC Admin 804.

[109] *Tristram* (n 105 above).

[110] *R (application of Mumford) v HM Coroner for Reading* [2002] EWHC Admin 2184.

- there is no precise dividing line between 'a *gross* failure to provide *basic* medical attention' and 'a failure to provide medical attention'; the difference is bound to be one of degree, highly dependent upon the facts of the particular case;[111]
- but it is still not the role of the inquest to criticize every twist and turn of a patient's medical treatment—neglect is not concerned with the correctness of complex and sophisticated medical procedures but rather with the consequences of (for example) failing to make simple checks.[112]

9.27 Causation

Jamieson reaffirmed the need for a clear connection between the neglect and the cause of death:

> Neither neglect nor self-neglect should ever form any part of any verdict unless a clear and direct causal connection is established between the conduct so described and the cause of death.

It was always clear that a conclusion of neglect was to be reached on the balance of probabilities but subsequent case law has clarified the issues:

- It must be shown on the balance of probabilities that, but for the failure to take action, the deceased would have survived or that his life would have been prolonged.[113]
- If the neglect contributed significantly[114] to the death, it need not be the sole or principal cause thereof.[115]

This latter point follows the definition of causation used in the general law of homicide:

> It is not the function of the jury to evaluate competing causes or to choose which is the dominant provided they are satisfied that the accused's act can fairly be said to have made a contribution to the victim's death, 'significant' meaning a contribution which is more than negligible.[116]

This is also consistent with the Court of Appeal decision in *Palmer*[117] on causation in relation to an inquest verdict of unlawful killing:

---

[111] *R (application of Nicholls) v HM Coroner for City of Liverpool* [2001] EWHC Admin 922.

[112] *Ibid.*

[113] *R (application of Khan) v HM Coroner for West Hertfordshire* [2002] EWHC 302 Admin.

[114] Otherwise described as 'making a material contribution'. See the summaries of the *Scott, Dawson, Khan* and *Metropolitan Police Commissioner* cases in Appendix 3 at page 365.

[115] *R v Cato* 62 Cr App R 41 at 46. See also Archbold at paras 19-06 and 19-13.

[116] *R v Smith* (1959) 43 Cr App Rep 121.

[117] *R v HM Coroner for Exeter and East Devon ex p Palmer*, Court of Appeal, 10 December 1997 (unreported).

The . . . act caused the death in the sense that it more than minimally, negligibly or trivially contributed to the death.

Recent Developments

9.28

The important post-*Jamieson* cases to June 2003 are summarized and reviewed briefly at Appendix 3 on page 365.

The law on neglect has also developed in consequence of Article 2 of the ECHR, given effect in domestic law by the Human Rights Act 1998. This complex subject, still very much in the process of formation, is separately discussed at section 9.30 *et seq.*

Summary

9.29

Neglect, as a conclusion within the coroner's court, is now more clearly but also more widely defined. Although the words in *Jamieson* are not to be read as if contained in an enactment, nor applied over-literally[118] the principles[119] remain essentially intact, in that there must be a basis for finding that:[120]

- the deceased's condition was known, or should have been known, to be such that action was necessary;
- the fact that action was not taken amounts to a gross failure;
- the failure to take action had a clear and direct causal connection with the death.

In the author's submission, the recent case law still does not mean that every failure of treatment or misdiagnosis (however well-intentioned) must amount to neglect. Nor should neglect arise simply because, with hindsight, there were a number of things that should have been done differently. The key is still to be found in the words of *Jamieson* 'the crucial consideration will be what the dependent person's condition appeared to be'. Nonetheless, this test has widened and the question might now be asked if the carer *should* have realized the need for action in all the circumstances.

Neglect will often arise from a breakdown in communications rather than being the result of some deliberate act, and will sometimes flow from the combination of a series of small errors by different individuals. It need not be deliberate.

---

[118] *Nicholls* (n 111 above).
[119] The 14 principles of the judgment are set out in full at Appendix 2 on page 361.
[120] *Commissioner of Police for the Metropolis* (n 96 above).

System Neglect

This is a confusing, and arguably confused, area of law that is still very much in the formative stages. The case of *Middleton*[121] is to go before the House of Lords shortly after this text is published; the judgment will hopefully clarify the situation and may even remove the concept of system neglect altogether. The reader is therefore cautioned that much of this section may literally be out of date almost before it is published.

9.30 Background

Article 2 of the ECHR[122] provides that the right to life should be protected by law. In *McCann*[123] the European Court held that this carries with it a requirement to investigate deaths where there has been an arguable breach of this substantive obligation. This requirement is sometimes referred to as the 'adjectival' or 'procedural obligation'. The reader may feel that this is more simply described as an 'investigative obligation'.

Coroners are public authorities for the purposes of the Human Rights Act 1998, and as such the inquest may form part (but not all) of the investigative process of the State. In appropriate cases it is thus necessary for the coroner to decide if the inquest remit should be widened on the basis of the investigative obligation. This is further discussed at section 7.06.

Where Article 2 is engaged, the inquest will need to have in mind the prospect of a verdict that is not otherwise available: 'system neglect'. This has been born of the *Amin* and *Middleton* cases heard together in the Court of Appeal (more particularly the latter case).

9.31 The *Amin* and *Middleton* Judgment

This decision has been heavily criticized in some quarters, not least for appearing to create a verdict without laying down clear criteria for its use. Nonetheless, there are some principles that can be followed pending clarification.

In *Amin* the deceased was murdered in his prison cell. After the murder trial the coroner did not resume the inquest. At review, the court ordered a public inquiry to satisfy the Article 2 investigative obligation. The Court of Appeal considered the case (alongside *Middleton*) but found that the steps taken had already satisfied the obligation and that it was unnecessary for there to be a distinct public inquiry.

---

[121] *R v Secretary of State for the Home Department ex p Amin and Middleton* [2002] 4 All ER 336.
[122] See section 4.43.
[123] *McCann v United Kingdom* (1996) 21 EHRR 97 which concerned the shooting of alleged IRA members by the armed forces in Gibraltar.

The case was subject to further appeal and went before the House of Lords in August 2003. The House of Lords disagreed and ordered such an inquiry. There was no application before the court that the coroner be ordered to resume the inquest although it was commented that many of the issues still to be investigated would be beyond the scope of an inquest. The judgment did not clarify any of the outstanding queries on system neglect.

In *Middleton* the deceased had hanged himself in prison. He had been identified as at risk but the proper safeguards were never put in place. An inquest found that he had killed himself whilst the balance of his mind was disturbed. Neglect was not left for the jury. Nonetheless the jury made clear in a note to the coroner that the Prison Service had failed the deceased.

The matter eventually came before the Court of Appeal, where the arguments bore more directly upon the role of the inquest. The court was asked to decide whether the restrictions on the inquest remit of rules 36 and 42, together with the limitations on a neglect verdict in *Jamieson*, were too restrictive where the obligation to investigate was to be satisfied by the inquest.

The court noted that there were good reasons for the restriction on verdicts of neglect, which should not be lightly discarded, but went on to say:

> On the other hand the inhibition of a coroner's jury bringing in a verdict of neglect can impede the ability of an inquest to fulfil the requirements of Article 2. Despite this inquests still make an important contribution, in the majority of cases, to meeting the implicit obligations of the UK under Article 2.

> This is because usually the Coroner's Rules achieve a sensible reconciliation between conflicting interests, namely:
>   - the interests of the victims and the public in being able to investigate the circumstances surrounding a death, particularly death in prison; and
>   - the interests of those who might be held responsible for the death of the deceased; and
>   - the need to restrict the scope of the inquest in the interests of expedition, affordability and proportionality.

> In general [the Rules] enable coroners to conduct inquests in a way which satisfactorily reconciles those conflicting interests.

However, noting that *Jamieson* predated the Human Rights Act, the court said it had to be decided whether the procedural obligation might require the inquest to return a verdict of neglect in a broader range of circumstances than that contemplated by *Jamieson*.

The court held that a verdict of neglect could perform different functions. For example it might identify a failure in the system adopted by the Prison Service to reduce the incidence of suicide by inmates, perhaps in allowing a prisoner who was a known suicide risk to occupy a cell alone or not requiring that he be kept under observation. Alternatively it may do no more than identify the failure of an individual to perform his duty properly, such as where a prison officer responsible for keeping observation on a known suicidal prisoner fell asleep. To fulfil Article 2 it was more important to identify defects in the system than individual negligence, for this could result in changes to avoid future deaths.

Thus preventing a jury returning a verdict of neglect in relation to a defect in the system could detract substantially from the salutary effect of the verdict and (in some cases) from the capacity of the investigation to meet the obligations arising under Article 2:

> a finding of neglect can bring home to the relevant authority the need for action to be taken to change the system and thus contribute to the avoidance of suicides in the future.

The court heard submissions from counsel on behalf of the coroner that it was wrong to expect the inquest to bear the residual onus for the State's obligations under Article 2. The point was also made that neglect had never been equated with the civil concept of negligence which incorporates the concept of fault. Thus any finding of 'responsibility' would change the fundamental purpose of the inquest, necessitating a wholesale redrafting of the law (as opposed to merely interpreting the law in a manner consistent with the ECHR).

Whilst accepting much of this the court went on to hold that:

> In a situation where a coroner knows that it is the inquest which is in practice the way the state is fulfilling the adjectival obligation under Article 2 . . . rule 42 can and should, contrary to *Jamieson*, when necessary be construed (in relation to both criminal and civil proceedings) only as preventing an individual being named, with the result that a finding of system neglect of the type we have indicated will not contravene that rule.

Importantly, the court went on to say that this was not to overrule *Jamieson* by the back door:

> In general the decision continues to apply to inquests, but when it is necessary so as to vindicate Article 2 to give in effect a verdict of neglect, it is permissible to do so.

The requirements are in fact specific to the specific inquest being conducted and will only apply where in the judgement of the coroner a finding of the jury on neglect could serve to reduce the risk of repetition of the circumstances giving rise to the death being enquired into at the inquest. Subject to the coroner, in the appropriate cases, directing the jury when they can return what would in effect be a rider identifying the nature of the neglect they have found, the rules will continue to apply as at present. The proceedings should not be allowed to become adversarial. We appreciate there is no provision of such a rider in the model inquisition[124] but this technicality should not be allowed to interfere with the need to comply with section 6 of the HRA.

---

[124] See section 9.07 *et seq.*

Post-*Middleton*

Since the *Middleton* decision, a small number of cases have reached the higher courts, of which the following bear mention:

Sacker:[125] The Court of Appeal were dealing with an inquest that had been concluded just prior to the *Middleton* judgment. The coroner had not left *Jamieson* neglect to the jury but subsequently wrote a rule 43 letter raising his grave concerns about a locum Medical Officer who had no working knowledge of procedures related to the self-harm form. In the light of *Middleton* this was held potentially a system failure, the court noted that 'measures may well have been taken, had the procedure in the form been followed, which arguably would have prevented the death'.[126]

The Court of Appeal ordered a fresh inquest but expressed clear reservations on promotion of the 'neglect rider' as the means of vindicating Article 2. It was said that the rule 43 letter appeared a stronger affirmation of the right to life and that juries are ill-equipped to identify and particularize the neglect. This case has now been joined with *Middleton* before the House of Lords.

Hurst:[127] This was primarily a case on resumption of an inquest following criminal proceedings but is a useful reminder that Article 2 does not only apply to those in custody or a hospital etc. The deceased was killed by a man known to be violent and potentially mentally ill, against whom he had given evidence in eviction proceedings. It was argued that the incident was foreseeable and preventable. Resumption of the inquest was ordered.

The test for a breach of Article 2 arose from the *Osman*[128] case, ie had the authorities done all that could reasonably be expected of them to avoid a real and immediate threat to the life of an individual of which they had, or ought to have had knowledge. The court noted that 'the degree of risk described as "real and immediate" in *Osman* . . . was a very high degree of risk calling for positive action from the authorities to protect life . . . from the criminal acts of a third party'.

Commissioner of Police for the Metropolis (Scott Robbins deceased) [see n 96: this case is summarised in Appendix 3 at page 372]. The High Court quashed a jury's rider of 'system neglect' as it was impossible to see how it should have been known that there was a real and immediate risk of the deceased taking his own life. The court doubted that system neglect was really a different issue to *Jamieson* neglect and was plainly working on the basis that any alleged failing must be 'gross' for such verdicts to be returned.

---

[125] *Sacker v HM Coroner for West Yorkshire* [2003] EWCA Civ 217.
[126] Which appears to be a very wide approach to causation.
[127] *Hurst v HM Coroner for Northern District of London* [2003] EWHC 1721 Admin.
[128] *Osman v UK* (1998) 29 EHRR 245.

9.33 Summary

Unless and until the present understanding (imperfect as it may be) is overruled by the House of Lords, it seems that where Article 2 is engaged the court can consider two distinct types of neglect verdict; *Jamieson* neglect and system neglect. *Jamieson* is still good law of itself, requiring a gross failure and clear and direct causal connection between the act or omission and the death.

System neglect will only apply where, in the judgement of the coroner, a finding on neglect could serve to reduce the repetition of the circumstances giving rise to the death. It is less clear whether such neglect would require a 'gross' failure and the test might arguably be described as:

- was there a defect in a system operated by a body of state, such as a lack of proper procedures (as opposed to a person not following procedures properly);
- if so, did that failure cause or materially contribute to the death.

If finding system neglect, the jury should be invited to identify in writing the nature of the neglect found, without naming any individual.

It is possible to argue that the test of whether there was a defect in the system should be: did the authorities do all that could reasonably be expected[129] to avoid a real and immediate threat[130] to the life of a particular individual of which they had knowledge, or ought to have had knowledge. This originates from the assessment for a breach of Article 2 from *Osman* (see above), but was also used by the court in *Middleton*:

> In addition the State has a positive duty to take steps . . . to protect life in cases where its servants are or ought reasonably to be aware that a particular individual who is in the State's care—being a prisoner is the plainest instance—is at immediate risk of death or serious injury.

There may also be similarities to be drawn with the test on necessity for a jury in s 8(3)(d) of the Coroners Act[131] which also has to consider issues of a systemic fault. For this purpose the case of *Ferrante*[132] distinguished a systemic failure as one that might reoccur but could also be prevented in the future by an appropriate authority.

---

[129] *Osman v UK* (n 128 above). The case went on to say that the positive obligation to protect life under Article 2 'must be interpreted in a way which does not impose an impossible or disproportionate burden on the authorities'.

[130] *Middleton* (n 121 above) para 30.

[131] The death occurred in circumstances the continuance or recurrence of which is prejudicial to the health and safety of the public etc. See section 8.06.

[132] *R v HM Attorney General ex p Ferrante* [1995] COD 18.

Unlawful Killing

Whilst unlawful killing is a rare conclusion in the coroner's court, when it does occur the consequences are both startling and potentially serious for those involved. Inevitably this is a complex subject and the writer has set out below only a skeleton of the relevant law. The reader facing entanglement in such a matter is advised to refer to one of the specialist criminal textbooks such as Archbold or Blackstone.

Scope of the Verdict   9.34

Although the coroner is prohibited from using a verdict which accuses a named person of criminal liability,[133] it is acceptable to conclude that the deceased was unlawfully killed without naming the culprit. This verdict would apply where the death was due to murder, manslaughter, infanticide, aiding and abetting suicide, or certain serious driving offences.[134] In theory, such a situation should rarely occur. If a relevant charge is laid the inquest will be adjourned under s 16(1) and is unlikely to be resumed.[135] If the inquest itself reveals evidence for such a charge the coroner is required to adjourn and refer the file to the Crown Prosecution Service.[136]

However, where there is no reasonable prospect of criminal proceedings[137] the inquest will eventually proceed, leaving the coroner to decide whether the death came about because of an offence that justifies a conclusion of unlawful killing.

Unlawful killing can only be recorded if the coroner or jury find the necessary facts proven beyond reasonable doubt.[138]

Road Traffic Offences   9.35

By s 1 of the Road Traffic Act 1988 it is unlawful to cause the death of another person by driving a vehicle dangerously on a road or other public place. Dangerous driving is defined by s 2A as:

- that falling far below what would be expected of a competent and careful driver;

---

[133] Rule 42—see section 9.12 *et seq.*

[134] As to which see below.

[135] However, if the inquest is resumed, the verdict must not be inconsistent with the verdict of the Crown Court: s 16(7). See also section 4.40 re: cases of *Hurst* and *Southall Black Sisters.*

[136] Rule 28, see section 7.38.

[137] For example, the CPS might consider that there is insufficient evidence to proceed with criminal charges; or there might be several people who could have caused the death, without proof of exactly which one; it might be that the 'killer' took their own life at the time of the incident or subsequently; or a dangerous driver might have perished in the collision that took other lives.

[138] *R v Wolverhampton Coroner ex p McCurbin* (1990) 1 WLR 719.

- in circumstances where it would be obvious to a competent and careful driver that driving in such a way would be dangerous.

Both these elements must be shown.[139] The offence also encompasses situations where it would be obvious to a competent and careful driver that driving the vehicle in its current state would be dangerous.

What is obvious to, or expected of, a competent and careful driver, will include circumstances of which the driver *should* have been aware. The dangerous driving does not have to be 'a principal or substantial cause of the death as long as [the court] is sure that it was a cause and there was something more than a slight or trifling link'.[140]

Further, by s 3A of the Road Traffic Act 1988 it is unlawful to cause the death of another by driving a vehicle on a road without due care and attention when:

(a) unfit to drive through drink or drugs (defined as 'when his ability to drive properly is impaired'); or

(b) having consumed so much alcohol that the proportion of it in breath, blood, or urine exceeds the permitted limit; or

(c) within 18 hours from the time of driving was required to provide a specimen of breath etc, but without reasonable excuse failed to do so.

Driving without due care and attention was defined in *DPP v Cox*[141] as 'not exercising the degree of care and attention that a reasonable and prudent driver would exercise in the circumstances'. It was also held that 'the standard is an objective one, impersonal and universal, fixed in relation to the safety of other users of the highway'. In *DPP v Tipton*[142] it was said that on occasions, for example where a driver veered off in the course of overtaking and collided with an oncoming vehicle, the only correct inference that could be drawn was that the vehicle was driven carelessly. There is no requirement that the driving without due care and attention be done deliberately, indeed by its very nature this part of the offence is usually unintentional.

9.36 Involuntary Manslaughter

The criminal law recognizes two basic forms of manslaughter. Voluntary manslaughter is conduct that would be categorized as murder but for one of the recognized defences under the Homicide Act 1957 (provocation or diminished responsibility etc). This would rarely be relevant in a coroner's court.

---

[139] *Aitkin v Lees* (1993) JC 228.
[140] *R v Kimsey* [1996] Crim LR 35.
[141] *DPP v Cox* (1993) 157 JP 1044.
[142] *DPP v Tipton* (1992) 156 JP 172.

Involuntary manslaughter arises where the death (or serious injury) was not intended but has nonetheless been caused by either an unlawful act or gross negligence.

Unlawful act manslaughter   **9.36.1**

This offence will commonly arise in circumstances of an assault where the intent falls short of that required for murder, ie an intention to kill or cause serious bodily harm. Sometimes the death will have occurred as a result of a simple blow when the deceased has fallen badly and suffered a fatal head injury.

The ingredients of unlawful act manslaughter are:[143]

- an unlawful act (eg an assault);
- the act must be dangerous in the sense that any reasonable and sober person would recognize that the assault exposed the victim to risk of some harm, albeit not necessarily serious harm;
- the unlawful act caused the death in the sense that it more than minimally, negligibly, or trivially contributed to the death.

Although it is clear that an individual cannot be named as responsible for the unlawful killing, such a verdict can only be justified if there is (at least) one individual who, either on his own or acting jointly with others, was responsible for an unlawful act which significantly[144] contributed to the death.[145] In other words the court cannot aggregate the conduct of a number of individuals to make one unlawful act.

In relation to drugs deaths, the Court of Appeal case of *R v Rodgers*[146] widened the accepted scope of an unlawful act from direct action (such as injecting the deceased at his own request) to participation, in that instance by applying and holding a tourniquet whilst the deceased injected himself with heroin. The accused was said to be playing a part in the mechanics of the injection which caused death.

Manslaughter by gross neglect   **9.36.2**

This offence arises when death occurs through an error by a person who has a legal duty of care, which is so bad that it amounts to 'gross negligence'. Again there

---

[143] *R v HM Coroner for Exeter and East Devon ex p Palmer*, Court of Appeal 10 December 1997 (unreported). See also *R v HM Coroner for Southwark ex p Douglas-Williams* [1999] 1 All ER 344.

[144] Meaning a contribution which is 'more than negligible'. *R v Smith* (1959) 43 Cr App Rep 121.

[145] *Douglas-Williams* (n 143 above) which reaffirmed the essential elements of the judgment in *Palmer* (n 143 above).

[146] *R v Stephen Rodgers* [2003] EWCA Crim 945 which disapproved of the earlier case of *R v Kennedy* (1999) Crim LR 65 in which the mere handing over of a loaded syringe was regarded as sufficient.

must be at least one individual who is identifiable (although remaining un-named) as responsible for the act or omission amounting to gross negligence, rather than the aggregation of conduct by a number of people. However, it is possible to regard as gross negligence the combined effect of a number of acts by the one person, which separately might not have amounted to such.

In general terms, the leading decision remains the 1993 criminal case of *Adomako*[147] where the Court of Appeal held that the ingredients of 'involuntary manslaughter by breach of duty' were:

- the existence of the duty of care;
- a breach of the duty causing death;
- gross negligence which the jury consider justifies a criminal conviction.

The circumstances were considered with specific reference to inquests by the Court of Appeal in *Douglas-Williams*.[148] It was said that for gross negligence manslaughter there must be:

- negligence consisting of an act or failure to act;[149]
- the negligence caused the death in the sense that it more than minimally, negligibly, or trivially contributed to the death; and
- the degree of negligence was such that it can be characterized as gross, in the sense that it was of an order that merits criminal sanctions rather than a duty merely to compensate the victim.

It is important to distinguish between ordinary negligence and the more serious 'gross' negligence. To some extent, the definition is circular; negligence is gross when a coroner or jury thinks it so bad that it should be described as such, but there are a number of pointers available.

In *Adomako*, the Court of Appeal went on to say that a jury might properly find gross negligence on proof of any one of four states of mind:

- indifference to an obvious risk of injury to health;
- actual foresight of the risk but a determination nonetheless to run it;
- an appreciation of the risk and intent to avoid it but coupled with such a high degree of negligence in the attempted avoidance that the jury feels justifies a criminal conviction;

---

[147] *R v Prentice, Sulman, Adomako and Holloway* [1993] 4 All ER 877 (the Court of Appeal decision).

[148] See n 143 above, which reaffirmed the essential elements of the judgment in *Palmer*.

[149] In this sense negligence would be described as subdivided into two parts; was there a duty of care and was it breached?

- failure to advert to a serious risk, going beyond mere inadvertence, in respect of an obvious and important matter which the defendant's duty demanded he should address.

In respect of the fourth category, it has been said that the person owing the duty of care must *know* of the risk and pay no attention to it.[150] The court must be careful to consider only the degree of negligence rather than the consequence of it.

When the *Adomako*[151] decision was upheld by the House of Lords in 1994, gross negligence was further defined as negligence that the jury consider 'showed such disregard for the life and safety of others as to amount to a crime against the state and conduct deserving punishment'. The court should have regard to 'the seriousness of the breach of duty in all the circumstances in which the defendant was placed when it occurred'. It was also held that, provided the other elements are present, the issue of whether negligence is gross is 'supremely a jury question'.

Effect of an Unlawful Killing Verdict
9.37

An inquest verdict of unlawful killing is not determinative[152] of a prosecution. Indeed the question may not arise, as an inquest can return such a verdict where the identity of the culprit has never been established, or where the act has been committed by one of several people with no clear proof of which.

In the 2000 case of *Manning and Melbourne*[153] the court held that where an inquest has recorded a verdict of unlawful killing implicating an unnamed but identifiable person whose whereabouts are known, the ordinary expectation would be that a prosecution would follow. Where the DPP refuses to prosecute, reasons should be given in the absence of compelling grounds to the contrary.

Involuntary Manslaughter—The Future
9.38

Proposals to reform the law on involuntary manslaughter, including an offence of corporate killing, were published in 2000. In May 2003 the Home Secretary confirmed the Government's intention to proceed. At the time of this text going to press it remains unclear exactly what form the new legislation will take but it is likely to have a significant impact on the coroner's work. This will particularly be the case if the original proposal to include all 'undertakings' (eg NHS Trusts and local authorities) within the remit of corporate killing is carried forward.

---

[150] *R v HM Coroner for Inner N London ex p Keogh* (unreported) Divisional Court, 19 May 1995.
[151] *R v Adomako* [1994] 3 All ER 79 (the House of Lords decision).
[152] *R v DPP ex p Jennifer Jones* LTL 11/6/96.
[153] *R v DPP ex p Manning and Melbourne* (2000) 3 WLR 463.

Summary

- Verdicts of 'unlawfully killed' and 'suicide' must be proven beyond reasonable doubt. All other verdicts are dealt with 'on the balance of probabilities'.
- Suicide requires a specific intent by the deceased that the consequence of the actions taken will be fatal.
- The verdict of 'accidental death' does not mean that no one was to blame for the death, the phrase is completely neutral in terms of liability.
- Neglect is a much narrower concept than negligence and relates to a gross failure to provide the basics of life such as food, warmth, or medical attention.
- An inquest verdict cannot be framed in such a way as to determine either criminal blame on the part of a named person or civil liability.

10

AFTER THE INQUEST

Dying is a very dull dreary affair. My advice to you is to have nothing whatever to do with it.[1]

The legalities of investigating death do not conclude with the verdict. This chapter deals with the matters that follow the inquest, including:

- reports and returns made by the coroner;
- access to documents from the inquest;
- a brief outline of judicial review;
- the aftermath of the inquest.

---

[1] Somerset Maugham 1965; *The Pan Dictionary of Contemporary Quotations* (1989).

10.01 Introduction

Following the inquest the coroner is required to issue papers so that the death can be registered, and may be involved in submitting other returns or reports. The 'properly interested parties'[2] are entitled to inspect or have copies of various documents. The files of papers must be kept securely for a number of years. On occasions, one of those involved at the inquest may seek judicial review.

Administrative Matters

10.02 Form 99—Certificate after Inquest and Registration

By s 11(7) the coroner must supply the Registrar of Deaths with a certificate in Form 99 setting out the date of hearing, the verdict, and particulars of the deceased within five days of the inquest. From the details on this form the registrar will register the death, the presence of an informant (see section 3.05) is not necessary.

If the verdict was 'accidental death' or 'misadventure' the coroner will also supply brief details of the circumstances for statistical purposes by completing the second page of Form 99.

The coroner's officer may check through the completed certificate with the relatives after the inquest to ensure that there are no errors, such as an address spelt incorrectly. In some cases the officer will then hand the form to the relatives so that they may go and register the death themselves. However as the legal obligation to deliver the form within five days falls upon the coroner, it may be better practice to check the form with the relatives and then send it by post to the registrar.

The Home Office Coroners' Model Charter (see section 1.13) suggests that on conclusion of the inquest the next of kin will be provided with a written explanation of how, where, and when a copy of the death certificate may be obtained.

10.03 Notification to Inspectors and Government Departments

In certain circumstances, such as the death occurring on a railway,[3] the coroner is obliged to send a return to the appropriate Inspector or Government department. In other cases, whilst there is no statutory obligation, the coroner is asked to co-operate in statistical collection by submitting basic details of the case to an agency or body. The range of such cases is wide, involving drugs deaths, fatal accidents to horse riders, road traffic accidents and drowning.

---

[2] As defined by rule 20, see section 7.09.
[3] Section 11(8) of the Coroners Act 1988.

Payment of Fees and Expenses 10.04

Following the inquest the coroner must make payment of fees or expenses incurred by witnesses or jurors.[4] This is dealt with in more detail at section 1.25 *et seq* and it may suffice here to list the types of payment that can be involved:

- travel expenses or loss of earnings by witnesses;
- fees payable to doctors for attending court;
- fees payable to independent expert witnesses for reports or attending court;
- expenses and loss of earnings for jurors;
- pathologist's fees for post-mortem examinations and attending court;
- fees payable for special examinations.

By s 24(1), the Secretary of State sets down prescribed fees for payments to witnesses, jurors, and pathologists. These are updated from time to time.

In theory, by s 26 the coroner will initially make payment of the expenses from an 'imprest account'. In most jurisdictions such payments are now made direct from the local authority after the coroner has signed an appropriate authorization. This can take some weeks which may be difficult for a witness (or more particularly a juror) who has immediate deductions made by an employer for absence at court.

Upkeep of Register and Annual Return 10.05

By rule 54 the coroner must keep an indexed register[5] of cases reported, setting out:

- the date upon which the death is reported;
- the name and address of the deceased;
- the age and sex of the deceased;
- the medical cause of death;
- how the case was disposed of;
- what verdict was recorded at any inquest.

The coroner must also, by s 28, send an annual return to the Home Office. This gives details of the number of deaths reported, with the number of cases subject to post-mortem and inquest (in each case divided by sex). The number of verdicts in each category (eg accidental death or suicide) is required, as is the number of cases adjourned under s 16 of the Act.[6]

In recent years coroners have also been required to give details of cases which have taken more than a specified time to deal with. This is set out as:

---

[4] Dealt with in ss 24–27 of the Act.
[5] Access to this register is dealt with at section 10.12.
[6] See section 7.17.

- a Form A case taking more than a week;
- a Form B case taking more than a month;
- an inquest taking more than six months to conclude.

Coroners have also been requested to keep a record of the number of cases referred, to them in which no Form A form has been issued, ie cases which have only amounted to advice to a doctor as to whether or not the death should be referred or as to the wording that should be used on the death certificate.[7]

Judicial Review

10.06 Introduction

Whilst there is no right of appeal against the verdict of a coroner's court, the recognized manner of further consideration is by judicial review[8] either by:

- the statutory remedy under s 13 of the Act (see section 10.07); or
- an application to the Administrative Court under the more general route (see section 10.08).

Judicial review is entirely different from an appeal. Appeal generally means a complete re-hearing of the matter by a superior court which has the power to confirm or alter the original verdict. There is no such procedure for inquests. In a judicial review there is no re-hearing of the facts, for the court is not seeking to establish whether the original verdict of the coroner was correct. Instead, review hears a specific application that the court's decision was unlawful, unjust or that the verdict reached was irrational.[9] In simple terms the procedure might be described as a review of the decision-making process rather than of the decision itself, although there are exceptions.

Since 1887 coroners' legislation has contained a specific but limited remedy allowing review by the High Court with the consent of the Attorney General. Prior to the late 1970s this was the only route that could be followed. However, since then there has been a substantial increase in the number of cases in which tribunals and official bodies of all kinds have had their decisions examined by the High Court following an allegation of error, improper procedure, or unreasonableness. This route provides a more general remedy.

---

[7] Whilst there is no definition as to what constitutes a 'reported case', the author maintains a strong view that it is necessary for *all* cases in which any form of contact is received to be recorded for the reasons set out in detail at section 4.08.

[8] It should only be in the most exceptional circumstances that application for review is made during the proceedings: *R v HM Coroner for Western District of East Sussex ex p Homberg* (1994) 158 JP Repts 357.

[9] *Terry v Craze (HM Coroner for East Sussex)* [2002] QB 312.

Whilst there is very limited provision for legal aid at the inquest itself, application can be made in respect of the High Court proceedings. In some cases this will be the first opportunity for the applicant to obtain detailed legal advice in respect of their concerns.

Judicial review is a highly complex subject outside the scope of this text. What follows is no more than a brief overview of the basic principles. A more detailed explanation, including some guidance on procedure, is to be found in *Jervis* at Chapter 19.[10]

The Statutory Remedy under the Coroners Act 10.07

Introduction 10.07.1

Section 13 of the Coroners Act 1988 grants the High Court a power to act if the coroner:

- refuses to hold an inquest;
- has held an inquest which was unsatisfactory by reason of fraud, rejection of evidence, irregularity of proceedings, or insufficiency of inquiry;
- has held an inquest but new facts or evidence have subsequently come to light.

The application to the High Court can only be made with the authority of the Attorney General. There is no time limit for the submission nor is there specific limitation on who can apply, provided they have a sufficient interest. It may be that even the coroner would wish to apply in circumstances where new evidence has come to light since the original inquest was completed.[11]

What must be established 10.07.2

The applicant must establish:

(a) if no inquest has been held that one ought to be so held; *or*

(b) (i) one of the specific grounds of complaint set out within s 13(1)(b), *and*

(ii) that it is necessary or desirable in the interests of justice that another inquest should be held.

This latter point gives the court a good measure of discretion, even where it is shown there has been irregularity of proceedings or insufficiency of inquiry etc. The court must be satisfied that it is *likely* that there would be a different result if the inquest was re-heard in a proper manner.

Alternatively, if the court accepts that there are new facts or evidence, not available at the time of the original hearing, the applicant may only need to show that there

---

[10] *Jervis on Coroners* (12th edition).
[11] As happened with: *In the matter of Captain Christopher John Kelly*, 161 JP 427.

is a *possibility* that this will bring about a different result, although the court will take the overall circumstances into account.

10.07.3 *The remedies*

The remedies of the court under s 13 are strictly limited:

- the court may order that an inquest be held;
- if an inquest has been held, the court may order that the inquisition[12] be quashed and that a new hearing take place;
- the court may order the applicant or respondent to pay the costs.

It is not open to the court to make an order merely quashing part of the inquisition or substituting another verdict, etc.

10.08 The General Provisions under the Supreme Court Act

10.08.1 *Introduction*

Section 31 of the Supreme Court Act 1981 grants the High Court a power to make certain orders where it considers it 'just and convenient' to do so.

Unlike the s 13 remedy, beside reviewing the inquisition the court has a power to review individual 'interlocutory decisions' such as those made in advance of the hearing (eg whether a jury should be empanelled) and those on the actual conduct of the proceedings (eg whether a specific witness should be called).

There is a strict time limit of three months for submitting the application. The applicant must have some *locus standi* but this may amount to a wider range of persons than under s 13 of the Coroners Act. The intention of the court is to exclude the mere busybody or vexatious applicant; anyone with a genuine interest in the matter is likely to be heard.

10.08.2 *What must be established*

The applicant must show that it would be just and convenient for the relief to be granted having regard to:

- the nature of the matters in respect of which relief may be granted;
- the nature of the persons or bodies against whom relief may be granted;
- all the circumstances of the case.

In effect the goalposts are wider under the general provisions of s 31 than the statutory remedy. The court has significant discretion as to whether or not any remedy ought to be granted.

In relation to inquests, the applicant will normally be seeking to persuade the court that either:

---

[12] The formal record of the inquest upon which the decision of the court is noted.

- the decision was ultra vires, ie a decision that the coroner did not have the power to make; *or*
- the way in which the decision was made was flawed or was in breach of the rules of natural justice (for example a refusal to hear relevant evidence or misdirection to a jury).

The remedies

10.08.3

The remedies of the court under s 31 are wider than those available under the Coroners Act. The court may:

- grant an injunction in respect of the remedy sought (eg prohibiting a coroner from releasing a body);
- order the coroner to hold an inquest if no inquest has been held;
- quash the inquisition and order a new one if an inquest has been held;
- quash the decision made at an inquest and remit the matter to the coroner (ie for a fresh decision rather than a fresh hearing);
- amend the inquisition without recourse to a fresh decision or fresh hearing;
- order costs to be paid by the coroner or any other party to the application.

Rule 57—Supply of Documents

Introduction

10.09

The coroner must keep a record of cases reported and retain the case papers for a set period. A 'properly interested person'[13] may have copies of some (but not all) of these documents.

This section does not deal with any rights of interested parties to view documents *before* an inquest; this will be found at section 6.14 *et seq.*

Register of Deaths

10.10

By rule 54 the coroner must keep an indexed register of the deaths reported, setting out:

- the date on which the death is reported;
- full name and address of the deceased;
- age and sex of the deceased;
- cause of death;
- whether case disposed of by Form A, Form B, or inquest;
- verdict at any inquest.

---

[13] See section 7.09.

There is no provision in the Rules for this register to be inspected by the public but the details given (at least for inquest cases) are mainly those recorded in a public court. The best view might be that they should not generally be considered confidential and that the coroner could normally exercise discretion to allow the register to be viewed if there was proper reason, even if the applicant were not a 'properly interested person'.

The index and register must be retained indefinitely rather than be discarded after 15 years—see section 10.12.

10.11 Retention of Exhibits

By rule 55, an exhibit at an inquest is to be retained until the coroner is satisfied that the item is unlikely to be required in any other legal proceedings. Thereafter the exhibit may be returned to the person entitled to possession or, if no such request is made, be destroyed.

In practice, most exhibits at an inquest are of a documentary nature and can easily be retained with the case papers for the statutory 15 years. However some exhibits may be more substantial, or even hazardous, and the coroner will seek to dispose of them promptly.

Some exhibits, particularly 'suicide notes', have an emotional value for relatives of the deceased. A note written by the deceased prior to death belongs to the person to whom it is addressed and is only held as an exhibit pending the inquest proceedings. The coroner will usually agree to release these as soon as possible after the inquest (although a photocopy will be retained) unless there is some reason to think that the inquest might be challenged. The original of such a letter should only be released to the addressee, a situation that can occasionally cause practical difficulties.[14]

10.12 Retention of Records

By rule 56, the coroner must retain the papers of certain reported deaths for a minimum of 15 years. A proviso allows the coroner to deliver such a document to 'any person who in the opinion of the coroner is a proper person to have possession of it'. This will undoubtedly include archivists and others concerned with the secure storage of documents.

The rule only applies to documents relating to deaths dealt with by inquest or post-mortem examination. Strangely, there is no similar obligation to retain papers where there was no post-mortem examination, ie Form A cases.[15]

---

[14] Although it will probably be necessary for all properly interested persons to be aware of the contents at the inquest. See section 7.44 as to how such notes are commonly dealt with in court.

[15] See section 4.19.

Records of coroners' courts fall within the provisions of the Public Records Act 1958[16] which effectively means that after the 15-year period the coroner has responsibility for the selection and safe-keeping of any records which ought to be permanently preserved. This duty must be performed under the guidance of the Keeper of Public Records, now the Chief Executive of the National Archives.

In 2003 the National Archives issued an Operational Selection Policy document[17] intended to provide a clear direction in determining which records should be permanently preserved. The policy states that:

6.20 Coroners' registers of reported deaths should be preserved permanently in local record offices.

6.21 All files relating to reported deaths which do not proceed to inquest may be destroyed when they are 15 years old or may be sampled by the local record office.

6.22 Ideally all inquest files should be preserved permanently. Where local record offices cannot readily accommodate the volume of these files, the bulk should be reduced by preserving only the key documents for each case.[18] If further reduction is necessary, archivists may preserve a sample of cases in line with the [Public Records Office] published guidance on sampling.

6.23 When sampling is used, files should be selected in addition to the sample if they are potentially of national interest because they

  • set a precedent in law or practice;
  • relate to an individual, accident or crime subject to prolonged or repeated interest from the national media.[19]

The policy goes on (para 8.5 *et seq*) to say that files should be reviewed as they reach their 15th year but it is acknowledged that 'the work should be carried out as resources permit'.

Records selected for permanent preservation should be transferred to a place appointed by the Lord Chancellor under s 4(1) of the Public Records Act 1958 (generally a local record repository or archive). Such records would then be open

---

[16] As amended by the Public Records Act 1967. The definition of records includes not only written documents but also 'records conveying information by any means whatsoever'.

[17] Records Management Operational Selection Policy 6 (records created by and relating to coroners). This is a moderately substantial document, available on the Public Record Office website www.pro.gov.uk under records management.

[18] Annex B para 6 suggests this should be 'the inquest form and police report' and that it would be preferable for family historians for this 'weeding' to take place (by the coroner's office) than for a sample of entire files to be retained.

[19] Home Office Circular 250/1967 suggested a slightly more detailed list of files to be retained, ie those which: relate to a prominent figure; present some unusual features; have some intrinsic scientific interest; illustrate a significant contemporary coroner's practice; involve death from a novel hazard thus illustrating changes in social life or industrial development. The National Archives have confirmed to the author that they consider this still to be good advice, despite the passage of time.

to public inspection 75 years after their creation.[20] Until that time they are only open to those whom the coroner permits access.

If papers are to be disposed of other than by destruction (eg donated to a museum or library) the approval of the Lord Chancellor would be required.

10.13 Rule 57—The Supply of Documents

Rule 57 requires the coroner to supply a properly interested person[21] with a copy of:

- the report of a post-mortem examination;
- the report of a special examination;[22]
- notes of evidence;
- any document put in evidence at an inquest.

The charges for supplying copies of such documentation are set out in the Coroners' Records (Fees for Copies) Rules 2002[23] which are made under s 24(3) of the Act. Alternatively the properly interested person may inspect the original document without charge.

By what would seem to be an unfortunate error in drafting, s 24(3) refers to fees payable for furnishing copies of documents etc. *relating to an inquest.* Of necessity this phraseology is mirrored in the Fees for Copies Rules. *Jervis*[24] expresses the opinion, correctly in the author's view, that there is therefore no power to charge for copies of autopsy reports prepared under s19 of the Act, ie where there is no inquest.

The Home Office Coroners' Model Charter (see section 1.13) suggests that 'the coroner will supply to an interested person on application a copy of the inquest verdict (although this is reproduced on the death certificate) or any of the documents produced in evidence within ten working days of receipt of the prescribed fee' and that an estimate of the fee will be given if requested.[25]

---

[20] Coroners' records are subject to a 75-year restriction rather than the usual 30 years by virtue of Lord Chancellors Instrument 68 (a PRO directive), see Home Office Circular 62/1971. It remains unclear how this will be affected by the Freedom of Information Act 2000 which will not be fully in force until 2005.

[21] See section 7.09 for definition.

[22] See section 5.07.

[23] There is no provision for fees to be charged other than at the prescribed rate but the Home Office have expressed the view that there appears to be no reason why copies could not be provided without charge where the coroner felt it appropriate; Home Office Circular 54/2002. See also section 10.17.

[24] *Jervis on Coroners* (12th edition) at para 18-34.

[25] The charter does not promise a copy of the *inquisition* but not all of the inquest 'verdict' is shown on the death certificate (eg box 3 as to which see section 9.09). Although there is no entitlement under the legislation for anyone to have a copy of the inquisition, it is difficult to see how the formal result of a public court could be denied to someone with a proper interest.

Rule 57 has provoked some difficulties and particular issues are discussed in the sections following.

Reports of Post-mortem and Special Examinations 10.14

Rule 57 entitles a properly interested person to a copy of such a document. The rule does not require that the properly interested person took part in the inquest, only that they would have been entitled to do so had they made application at the time.

In practice, it is common for post-mortem reports to be requested by the deceased's doctors and insurers. It is also increasingly common for relatives of the deceased to exercise their entitlement.

It may be that relatives do not fully understand the nature of the document requested and might be disturbed to read details in the clinical terms in which such reports are inevitably couched. It is practice in the author's jurisdiction to supply relatives with the report sealed inside a second envelope, accompanied by a letter. This suggests that whilst they may examine the document themselves if they wish, they may prefer to take the second envelope unopened to their own doctor for an explanation.[26]

Transcripts and Notes of Evidence 10.15

Whilst the actual wording of rule 57 relates purely to *notes of evidence*, and as such might refer only to the coroner's handwritten notes taken during the actual inquest, it is now common for this wording to be interpreted as entitlement to a transcript of any tape recording taken during the proceedings.

A charge arises for supplying a copy of the written notes of evidence or for the preparation of such a transcript.[27] The basis for charging is complex but may be simplified as £1.10 per sheet for photocopying and approximately £48 per 5,000 words typed.

There is no provision requiring the coroner to provide a copy of the actual tape recording upon request although there seems to be nothing preventing this should the coroner wish to do so. However, this would not fall within the Fees for Copies Rules (see 10.13 above) and thus there is no ability to recoup the cost of doing so.

Documents put in Evidence at an Inquest 10.16

This terminology is without further definition but it is submitted that it must mean:

---

[26] See also section 5.44.
[27] The Coroners' Records (Fees for Copies) Rules 2002 made under s 24(3) of the Coroners Act 1988.

- any exhibit or other such paper referred to during the inquest;
- any statement which was read out in court in the absence of the maker as documentary evidence under the provisions of rule 37.[28]

It is the author's view that rule 57 does not apply to the written statement of a witness who gives *oral* evidence at an inquest, unless for some reason (such as contradiction of an earlier account) the statement was put to the witness during evidence.

10.17 Other Documents

Rule 57 places an *obligation* upon the coroner to supply copies of the documents mentioned above. The question then arises as to how far the coroner has a *discretion* to supply copies of other documents, most commonly the written statements of witnesses giving oral evidence at the inquest or perhaps witnesses who were not called at all during the inquest.

This is a complex question, much may be said to depend upon the original ownership of such statements. In *Peach*[29] it was made plain that whilst the police have a duty to supply the coroner with all relevant material in their possession for the purpose of an inquest, ownership of those documents may rest with others if they were created for the purpose of a police inquiry or (now) an investigation on behalf of the Police Complaints Authority etc. This view was endorsed by Home Office Circular 20/99 and was held to be still good law in the 1999 *Hay* case.[30]

It might be argued that if a statement is taken solely on behalf of the coroner for the purpose of an inquest it is difficult to see why the coroner does not have discretion to release that document if thought appropriate. However, in making this decision the coroner must obviously bear in mind the rights of the person who agreed to make the statement in the first place, the contents of the statement, and the reason why it is requested.[31]

With increasing use of advance disclosure this point may now often be academic but there are still many cases where disclosure cannot readily be given, eg statements required from witnesses by the HSE under their statutory powers to *make* a witness give a statement (s 20(2)(j) Health and Safety at Work Act 1974).

---

[28] See section 7.42.
[29] *R v Hammersmith Coroner ex p Peach* [1980] 2 WLR 496 see also section 6.14 *et seq.*
[30] *R v HM Coroner for Lincolnshire ex p Hay* (1999) 163 JP 666. See also *R v Southwark Coroner ex p Hicks* (1987) 2 All ER 140.
[31] Refer also to sections 6.15, 6.23, and 7.40.4 on this subject.

The Press   10.18

Although every inquest must be held in public[32] and coroners are encouraged
to notify the press of hearing dates,[33] the media will not usually be 'properly
interested persons' within the meaning of the Coroners Rules.[34] This brings the
curious result that although the press are entitled to attend an inquest they would
not generally be entitled to a transcript of what was said during that hearing, even
if only to clarify the exact wording used.

This is unlikely to present much of an obstacle to a reporter. The most common
reason the press might want a transcript would be research for an article, following an allegation about the circumstances of the death from a relative of the
deceased—there would be nothing to stop the relative seeking a transcript and
then passing it on to the press.

Researchers   10.19

Coroners are frequently approached by organizations or individuals who wish to
conduct research and would value access to the coroner's records. There is no
statutory provision for such access and it would be stretching the point to regard
a researcher as a properly interested person.

However, it is plainly in the public interest that bona fide research is carried out
and the general approach amongst coroners is to assist research by appropriate
organizations (eg NHS Trusts or a university) subject to limitations of time. It is
usually necessary to ensure that the research has the appropriate ethical approval
(where required) and to obtain an undertaking as regards confidentiality and
anonymity in the presentation of statistics.

Data Protection and Tracing Inquiries   10.20

The Data Protection Act 1998 replaces the 1984 Act and gives effect in UK law to
the 1995 EC Data Protection Directive. The primary requirement of the Act is
that data must be processed 'fairly and lawfully'. The legislation does not apply to
information about the dead but coroners regularly process information about the
living including relatives, witnesses, and jurors. If this is done on computer the
coroner should be registered with the Data Protection Commissioner.

From time to time coroners are asked for information about missing persons who
might be dead or about those known to be dead. The request will often seek details
of next of kin etc. The Home Office have advised coroners (Home Office Circular

---

[32] Rule 17—see section 7.12.
[33] See section 6.10.
[34] See section 7.09.

35/2000) that if 'fairness' might be compromised by disclosing these details to a third party, it may be appropriate to seek consent for the disclosure from the individual concerned. One way to achieve this would be to offer to forward a letter from the enquirer with an invitation to respond direct. It was said that this might be a particularly appropriate response to tracing inquiries in respect of relatives of a deceased.

The Act contains various exemptions in respect of information required by court order and that disclosed for the prevention or detection of crime.

The Aftermath of the Inquest

10.21   Introduction

For the bereaved, the end of an inquest is a difficult time. The finality of a verdict can be something of a milestone for the family and may well arouse a renewal of grief.

The end of the proceedings may also produce difficulties for the witness as to how the family should be dealt with and what might be said to the press waiting outside.

10.22   Debriefing the Client

A thorough debrief for those involved at an inquest plays as big a part in the overall exercise as preparation beforehand (as to which see section 6.29).

Accepting that the inquest is a fact-finding exercise, it is incumbent upon those representing parties, whether family or others, to ensure that the salient facts revealed, in what may have been a frightening and confusing experience, are clearly understood by their clients. Equally, for an organization involved in a death the post-inquest debriefing is a valuable tool in planning to avoid similar fatalities.

Too often there is excessive emphasis placed upon the verdict, the full meaning of which may not be properly understood—classically the misapprehension that an accidental death verdict suggests no one was to blame. The advocate may wish to reinforce the true purpose and value of the inquest, ie the information which has been disclosed and the lessons which may have been learnt.

10.23   Dealing with Press or Media

By law the coroner must always sit in public.[35] Death is inevitably good copy for the media, more so where there is some element of professional mishap or incom-

---

[35] Rule 17—see section 7.12.

petence involved. Those attending an inquest should give thought in advance as to how they will deal with approaches from the media at the end of the case.

If the press or media have attended, they will almost always run some form of story about the event so it may be better to try and ensure that this is balanced by one's own version and explanation.

If there is no wish to speak with the press, a polite refusal will often be respected—perhaps together with the co-operation of a picture or a film shot of the witness leaving the court doors. It is most undignified (and rarely successful) to try and hide behind a briefcase or an outstretched hand.

However, for a hospital or similar organization there are a number of considerations and some form of press/media policy ought to be considered. Typically this might involve:

- ensuring that any response is co-ordinated at a central level;
- not allowing individual witnesses (eg doctors and nurses) to comment to the press separately;
- anticipating the potential range of verdicts and preparing a statement(s) which can deal with this;
- not attempting to ignore the media;
- where appropriate, an apology and explanation of actions which will be taken to prevent a recurrence.

Rule 43 Reports   10.24

By rule 43, the coroner has a power to report the circumstances of a case to an appropriate authority. This power lies solely with the coroner and should not be confused with the former power of juries (or coroners) to add a rider to the verdict, which was abolished in 1980.[36] Nor should rule 43 be confused with the requirement upon a jury to identify the failures involved when returning a conclusion of 'system neglect' in a case falling within Article 2 ECHR (see section 9.30 et seq) although the coroner would obviously take the jury findings into account when making such a report.

A rule 43 report can be a genuinely useful measure in ensuring that similar fatalities are avoided[37] and has been said to be a valuable power in the public interest.[38]

Rule 43 is often wrongly described as a power to make recommendations. Strictly speaking, there is no *power* to propose particular remedies for any apparent

---

[36] Rule 11 Coroners' Amendment Rules 1980.

[37] Research for the Coroner Review (see n 40 below) found that on average a rule 43 report is used following one inquest in fifty (ie about 450 annually) and that coroners were informed of some remedial action in about half of these cases.

[38] *In the matter of Captain Christopher John Kelly*, JP 161 427.

danger but, if rule 43 is used at all, the coroner may be well placed to set out the action necessary, and informal recommendations are sometimes made.

The Home Office Coroners' Model Charter (see section 1.13) suggests that the coroner will:

- despatch any rule 43 letter within 10 working days of the inquest outcome;
- send copies of the report to all interested persons;
- send copies of any subsequent reply within five days of receipt.

The recipient authority is under no obligation to act upon the report, indeed there is no requirement even to acknowledge the coroner's letter. However, if the coroner is ignored, a query from the press some months later asking what changes have taken place, or worse a further fatality, may produce a difficult situation.

The author would suggest that such a power must be used sparingly or the currency becomes devalued. Despite the coroner's inability to enforce action, a rule 43 report still carries considerable weight in many quarters[39] and most would agree that this is exactly how it should remain.

The Coroner Review[40] recommends little change to this power save the important requirement that the recipient authority would be obliged to notify the coroner of their decision on the report and that the recipient's regulatory body or inspectorate should describe any such 'recommendations or findings' in their annual report, stating whether they are satisfied with the response.

10.25 Admissibility of Evidence given at the Inquest

The coroner's verdict is not of itself admissible to prove a fact within a civil hearing. For example, if the coroner has returned a verdict incorporating neglect this cannot be pleaded as proof of the fact that there was neglect.

However, a transcript of the proceedings, whilst again not evidence of issues in itself, can be used in civil litigation as proof of what a witness said during the inquest. Thus if the same witness is called in the civil case and gives a different account of events, the earlier evidence can be put in cross-examination. The transcript is therefore an important tool in the armoury of the litigation lawyer.

Summary

- The coroner is obliged to keep a register of reported deaths and to retain case papers for 15 years.

---

[39] The considerable media publicity usually given to such reports is probably a factor.
[40] Death Certification and Investigation in England, Wales and Northern Ireland; The Report of a Fundamental Review 2003: CM 5831 (at chapter 8 para 46). See section 1.08.

- Although there is no right of appeal against a coroner's inquest, relevant actions and decisions are open to judicial review.
- 'Properly interested persons' can obtain copies of some court documentation and a transcript of the inquest.
- The coroner can make a report of the circumstances surrounding the death to an appropriate authority with a view to avoiding similar fatalities.
- The inquest has no direct relevance to civil litigation but can provide useful information. What is said on oath at an inquest may be put to the same witness during evidence in another court hearing.

11

DISASTERS

The care with which our dead are treated is a mark of how civilised a society we are. Much goes on for understandable reasons behind closed doors. For this reason there is a special responsibility placed on those entrusted with this work, and the authorities who supervise it, to ensure that bodies of the dead are treated with the utmost care and respect. This is what bereaved and loved ones are entitled to expect and what society at large demands.[1]

---

[1] Charles Haddon-Cave QC, who represented the Marchioness Action Group at the Marchioness (or Clarke) Inquiry: see also section 11.01. The first sentence is based on Gladstone (1871). In his report Clarke LJ said: 'I entirely agree with those sentiments. Respect for the dead and for the relatives of those who have died, especially where the death has been unexpected, is indeed the mark of a civilised society and should be the touchstone against which each question [that] arises should be determined.'

The coroner has a central, independent role in dealing with the aftermath of disaster and it is essential that those who may also be involved in such a tragedy appreciate fully the tasks that the coroner will face. This chapter sets out:

- the role of the coroner in a major disaster and problems likely to arise;
- issues arising in the preparation for a disaster;
- points most likely to cause disquiet amongst the bereaved;
- the use of temporary mortuaries;
- the identification of badly disfigured bodies.

This chapter is not intended to be a comprehensive guide to dealing with disasters and what follows is necessarily brief, giving the reader no more than an appreciation of the early stages of a major incident from the coroner's perspective.

11.01 Other Reading

The problems surrounding identification of disaster victims have received much public attention in the last five years. Many of the guiding principles on handling disasters, for coroners and others, are now to be found in the report of Lord Justice Clarke following the *Public Inquiry into the Identification of Victims following Major Transport Accidents*[2] (referred to here as the Marchioness Inquiry or Clarke Report), which is quoted heavily in this chapter. Anyone likely to get involved in such a scenario *must* have a detailed knowledge of the report by Clarke LJ and his recommendations.

Those wanting to read more detailed guidance are referred to the following:

- *Dealing with Disaster* (Home Office Guidance) (revised 3rd edition).[3]
- *Deaths in Major Disasters—the Pathologist's Role*[4] (2nd edition); Royal College of Pathologists.
- *Dealing with Fatalities During Disasters*. Report of the National Working Party October 1994 (Civil Emergencies Adviser to Home Secretary).[5]
- *The Identification of the Deceased following Mass Disaster*, Metropolitan Police, T020 Branch.[6]
- *Disasters: Planning for a Caring Response* (1991). Report of working party set up by Department of Health, HMSO ISBN 0 11 3213700.
- *Responding to Disaster—the human aspects*. Emergency Planning Society, Pyramid House, Fourth Way, Wembley HA9 0LG.

---

[2] *Public Inquiry into the Identification of Victims following Major Transport Accidents*, March 2001: CM 5012 HMSO. Variously known as the Clarke Report or Marchioness Report.

[3] Obtainable from the website of the Civil Contingencies Secretariat of the Cabinet Office at www.resilienceuk.info.

[4] On the RCP website at www.rcpath.org.

[5] This is currently under review and a new edition is expected.

[6] Set out in Annex G of the Clarke report (n 2 above).

- *Emergency Procedures Manual 2001*, Association of Chief Police Officers.[7]
- Report of Metropolitan Police Working Group, March 2000.[8]
- *Major Incident Procedure Manual*, London Emergency Services Liaison Panel.[9]
- Ladbroke Grove Rail Inquiry (Part 1) by Rt Hon Lord Cullen.[10]

What Makes a Disaster

Special Demands   11.02

A disaster is usually defined in terms similar to 'any event which, because of the scale of its effects, cannot be dealt with by the emergency services and local authorities as part of their day-to-day activities'.[11] Thus a major flood, which might be a disaster for the local community, will not be regarded as a disaster by the coroner if there is only one fatality—an individual death by drowning is not unusual and can be dealt with in the normal way.

Even a significant influx of bodies is, of itself, not necessarily beyond the means of the coroner's office to deal with in a routine manner. Most large jurisdictions will handle between 30 and 50 deaths on the first working day after a Bank Holiday. Whilst this produces a few hectic and difficult hours it is certainly not to be regarded as a *disaster*, for there remains a considerable difference between dealing with a major disaster and a sudden increase in 'routine' deaths.

Obviously a large scale incident brings media and public pressure but primarily the coroner will face difficulties with issues of identification and mortuary arrangements, matters that with an individual death will almost take care of themselves. A disaster can also result in a significant number of body parts even where there is a relatively small number of bodies. The sheer number of fatalities magnifies the importance of getting every detail absolutely correct. The overall effect is that what would normally be uncomplicated procedures are now far from routine.

The general responsibility of the coroner to investigate the cause and circumstances of a traumatic death remains unchanged whether there is one fatality or a thousand.[12] An investigation will take place and, in due course, an inquest will be

---

[7] Generally only available to police officers.

[8] Set out in Annex F of the Clarke Report (n 2 above); reviewing casualty bureau, family liaison, and identification process arrangements following the Ladbroke Grove rail crash, October 1999.

[9] On the website of the London Emergency Services Liaison Panel at www.leslp.gov.uk.

[10] Downloadable at www.pixunlimited.co.uk/pdf/news/transport/ladbrokegrove.pdf.

[11] *Dealing with Disaster*, n 3 above, para 1.3.

[12] The author had often wondered exactly where the line would have to be drawn, eg if there was an immense flood killing 10,000 it might be completely impracticable to deal with individual deaths. However events following the World Trade Centre disaster suggest that a different view may need to be taken—but it is clear that this would be a decision for the Government rather than any individual coroner.

opened into each death. Assuming that the inquests are to be concluded[13] at all, they will usually be held together but in legal terms each will be an inquest into an individual death. The author will therefore make no more than passing comment on the subject of the inquest in this chapter and refers the reader to Chapter 7 'Inquests' and Chapter 9 'Verdicts'. What now follows explains the responsibilities of the coroner, both in planning for a disaster and in the first hours of the incident.

11.03 The Coroner's Overall Responsibilities

The independence of the coroner is even more important in times of disaster than is normally the case. Modern society[14] fears concealment of the truth in any major disaster and the overt independence of the coroner is the best assurance that the truth will become public.

In a major disaster, as with any reported death, the coroner has responsibility for the body until such time as it is released to the relatives. Arrangements must be made for the body to be recovered from the place of death and kept in a proper manner until any necessary post-mortem and forensic examination can take place. The coroner must ensure that there are suitable facilities for such examinations, that the body is properly identified, and that any evidence of crime is preserved for the police to deal with further. There must be liaison with the relatives. Eventually the body, and connected property, must be released for disposal to those lawfully entitled.

Nonetheless, this responsibility must be exercised in co-ordination with the police, who will not only be performing many of these tasks for the coroner but will also be treating the event as a major crime until the contrary is shown.[15]

It does not take much imagination to realize that these duties are immensely complex when talking about 350 bodies scattered from a blazing 747 aircraft across a shopping precinct and housing.

---

[13] The question of the relationship between an inquest and a public inquiry is discussed at section 11.33, but see also sections 4.39 and 7.17 concerning adjournments under s16 of the Coroners Act 1988 pending a criminal trial.

[14] Although it should be remembered that the coroner's involvement in disasters is nothing new. In 1857 Mr Thomas Badger presided over inquests into the 189 deaths at the Lundhill Colliery explosion in Yorkshire. In 1864 Mr John Webster held inquests into the deaths of more than 240 following the collapse of the Dale Dyke Dam near Sheffield, and in December 1866 a further 361 men and boys died in the Oaks Colliery disaster at Barnsley. Further south, in September 1878 more than 640 died when the pleasure steamer 'Princess Alice' sank within four minutes of colliding with another vessel on the Thames.

[15] This paragraph and that preceding (in the first edition of this text) were quoted by Clarke LJ in the Marchioness Inquiry Report: (n 2 above) para 15.15 at p 64.

Preparing for Disaster

Establishing Key Relationships

It is quite obvious that preparation for disaster cannot be left until the telephone rings with news of the dreadful event. Considerable effort must be put into planning for a disaster which in all likelihood will never befall any individual coroner. But disasters *do* happen, and they often take a most unexpected form. It is thus incumbent upon the coroner to have made ready.

Building sound relationships with the other major players in the disaster scenario (updating these contacts as those personnel change), and educating them as to the coroner's responsibilities and intentions is a vital part of preparing for a major incident.

The Police

The coroner is not alone in having to deal with the aftermath of disaster and will receive an enormous amount of help from the local police force. It is vital from the point of view of both coroner and senior police officers that regular contact is maintained so that all parties are familiar with those with whom they may have to deal. It is not ideal for such relationships to be forged on the edge of a muddy field in the pouring rain at night, after the incident has occurred.

Quite apart from formal planning, it is a good foundation for coroners and the officers with whom they will most closely liaise, to have some mutual trust and a broad agreement on the way problems are likely to be tackled. It will be particularly important that the coroner and the police officer likely to be appointed as Senior Identification Manager (SIM) (see section 11.28), or those required to oversee mortuary operation and documentation, have a close understanding of each other's needs in the early stages of a disaster.[16]

Clarke LJ stressed the importance of this pre-planning and mutual understanding in the Marchioness Inquiry Report:[17]

> The evidence given in part one of this inquiry highlights the importance of pre-planning between the local coroner, police force and local authority emergency planning department. It is vital that each agency knows, not only what its role will be in the event of a disaster producing numerous fatalities, but also the role of each of the other organisations involved. This will involve working out who is responsible for collation of information, recording of information, documenting the procedures, contact with families, making of key decisions at every stage and release of bodies or remains.

---

[16] Not forgetting British Transport Police who will have responsibilities in a rail disaster.
[17] See n 2 above.

11.06   The Other Services

However, whilst the police will be the major agency working with the coroner, those from the ambulance and fire and rescue services, health and social services, the local authority, and voluntary services will all have some dealings with either bodies or the bereaved when disaster strikes. There may also be links to the resilience teams at regional government. Most of these organizations will wish to have an input into decisions that the coroner has to take, whilst still respecting who must make the ultimate decision. However, once disaster has occurred it is far too late for these views to be expressed and discussed in a meaningful fashion—again it is incumbent on both parties to take an opportunity in calmer circumstances, even if this involves much supposition.

The local authority will generally undertake responsibility for providing the coroner with the physical structures of any temporary mortuary (see section 11.13 *et seq*), and the temporary mortuary plan will have been written by, or will have significant input from, the Emergency Planning Unit at county or city level. But the mortuary managers and pathologists likely to be involved[18] must also have an opportunity to agree the protocols that may be used:

> In these circumstances I recommend that . . . protocols be developed in each area between the coroner, the police, the local authority, the mortuary and the pathologists setting out clear procedures for the custody and release of the body and body parts in order to ensure that there is no confusion.[19]

In many instances the temporary mortuary facility will be owned by one of the armed services. Establishment of the mortuary at short notice will require a great deal of help and goodwill from the site owner; it would be good practice for the coroner to ensure that there is some mutual understanding of the difficulties both sides will face in an emergency.

11.07   'The Advocates'

Finally, with suitable preparation, the coroner has an opportunity to enlist several hundred 'advocates' in the cause from a number of agencies likely to have significant contact with relatives of the deceased at an early stage. Professional social workers, clergy or volunteers from organizations such as the British Red Cross are well placed to help the coroner.

Many relatives, amidst their grief, will look to any accompanying helper to give some guidance on whether bodies might be viewed, when a funeral might take place or other technicalities. Whilst the advent of police Family Liaison Officers

---

[18]   See section 11.11 for a description of the role of the supervising pathologist.
[19]   Clarke LJ, Marchioness Inquiry Report (n 2 above).

(FLO)[20] is bound to assist in this regard, there will still be many others in close contact with families. Inaccurate or misleading information from these helpers, however well meant, can make the coroner's task extremely difficult, particularly if expectations are raised which are unlikely to be met in reality. On the other hand, good information, explained from a background of knowledge, will help relatives cope with their trauma and may lay secure foundations for future relationships with the police and the coroner.

It is therefore important that both professionals and volunteers who are likely to mix with the bereaved are educated on the relevant topics.[21] This type of work forms part of preparation just as much as poring over lists of equipment to be taken to a temporary mortuary.

The Concerns of the Relatives   11.08

The relatives of the deceased or missing must be kept fully and correctly informed both as to progress, or lack of it, and exactly why certain procedures are being undertaken.[22] Information is often described as 'a cheap commodity' or as 'costing nothing to give but priceless to receive'. Worse, a failure to give a proper amount of information is likely to be perceived as 'covering up' or hiding dreadful facts.

The information given must also be relevant to the needs of the bereaved:

> What we wanted was information about exactly how and why people died, why we were being dissuaded from viewing the crash site, how the identification process worked and why we were not being allowed to see the bodies.
>
> This would have helped far more than counsellors telling us how we should feel.[23]

In his Marchioness Inquiry Report[24] Clarke LJ identified the following questions as likely to be uppermost in the minds of the bereaved, many of whom will be experiencing sudden death and the associated legal procedures for the first time:

- where a body will be taken once it has been found;
- what happens to a body at the mortuary;
- how the identification process will work and who will be involved in it;
- the role of the coroner and the police;
- what is a post-mortem;
- when a post-mortem takes place and why;
- what rights the families have regarding the body and the post-mortem;
- the right, if any, to view the body;

---

[20] See section 11.29 for a detailed note on the role and functions of the FLO.

[21] There may even be an issue of keeping away willing helpers who have not gone through 'accredited volunteer training' run by the local authority where this scheme exists.

[22] Clarke LJ commented (n 2 above) that even where there is no information to give, families should be told that this is the case and the reasons.

[23] Dr Jim Swire, parent of one of the Lockerbie victims.

[24] See n 2 above.

- when the body will be released;
- what will happen to the body after it has been released;
- what an inquest is and the reasons for it;
- what will happen during the inquest.

Other questions that might be raised can include arrangements for a site visit by the relatives or an apparent gap in time between the incident and confirmation of death by a doctor (usually caused by the site not being safe enough to allow the doctor an earlier opportunity).

Initial queries from relatives may include how they will actually find out whether their relative is amongst the dead, when they will get to know anything, what is being done to help them, and how they can stay informed.

A number of problems arise here. It will often be the case in the early stages of catastrophe that those seeking to establish order amongst the chaos simply do not have reliable information, or cannot have confidence in what does seem apparent.[25] An honest answer is the only course but has dangers of misinterpretation unless *very* carefully explained to those who are understandably desperate for news.

Secondly, a significant dilemma is that some form of system *must* be established in a disaster to make things work for everyone. This effectively means suppressing the immediate interests of individual bereaved into 'the system' at the very time when their need for personal treatment is at its highest.

Thirdly, the very real practical problems of dealing with disaster require unusual measures that are not easily understood by the bereaved and which may of themselves seem callous (eg not removing bodies until a proper and methodical recovery can be organized).

So far as the coroner is involved, the concerns[26] likely to be raised might be forecast with some accuracy:

- Why are bodies (or the remains of the victim's bodies) left *in situ* for some time rather than being afforded decency immediately?
- Why are the bodies taken to a temporary mortuary facility (such as a hangar) rather than being dealt with in a proper mortuary?
- Why are we being discouraged from viewing the bodies—are we being forbidden from doing so?
- How do we know that the body released to us really is that of our loved one if it so badly damaged that we cannot recognize it for ourselves?
- Why is there a delay in releasing the body?

---

[25] In a recent rail crash there were initial reports of 13 deaths but this figure was later reduced to 10 as the situation became clearer.

[26] The answer to each of these questions will be considered in the pages that follow.

All of this underlines the need for clear and honest communication with the bereaved—but by whom?

Clarke LJ put forward an initial answer in his Marchioness Inquiry Report:[27]

> One way in which to break down the barriers is for senior members of the police team such as the SIM, SIO or FLO co-ordinator to meet with the families to explain what is happening, how long they might have to wait for their loved ones to be identified and explain the investigation and identification processes.

This is unarguable but the role of the coroner was then considered:

> Likewise, if the coroner felt able to meet with the families as a group to explain what is happening this would probably help the families in their understanding of the position and lessen their feelings of helplessness.

However, Clarke LJ went further at a later stage of the report, recommending that coroners and coroners' staff should meet with families or family groups to explain the identification and other procedures.[28]

Coroners express divergent opinions on this point but the author takes the view that if the coroner's impartiality and role as a 'judicial officer' are to be taken seriously, great care must be exercised in meeting families to discuss issues connected with what may well become a highly controversial investigation and inquest. The families will not be the only parties[29] to the eventual inquest[30] and the others are entitled to the assurance that the coroner's independence and objectivity have not been lost.[31]

In some cases it may be appropriate for the coroner to speak to all the families together as part of a structured meeting[32] organized by the police, but it might be unwise to go beyond this.[33] Much may depend upon the situation and the coroner's own assessment of personal communication skills under such pressure. Presumably the answer, as ever, lies in sensible compromise and careful thought related to the individual circumstances of the disaster.

---

[27] See n 2 above.

[28] Marchioness Inquiry Report, n 2 above, para 29.19 at p 124.

[29] More correctly 'properly interested persons': see section 7.09.

[30] It seems unlikely that any decision will have been made by the Government on a judicial inquiry at such an early stage, this might otherwise remove the need for a full inquest—see section 11.33 below.

[31] See section 7.25 re allegations of bias.

[32] This was done in one (comparatively small scale) disaster, the coroner addressing the relatives in a formal meeting at an early stage. The meeting was seen as beneficial by many of those involved and certainly appears to have laid good foundations for the relatives understanding the nature (and limitations) of the coroner's role. It might be wise for such a meeting to be recorded if possible to prevent later claims by others of a lack of impartiality.

[33] In light of a further recommendation of Clarke LJ the Government is considering the provision of a 'disaster victim information pack' for bereaved which is based on the 'homicide information pack' widely used by the police.

11.09 Summary

Table 11.1 at page 329 shows the formal responsibilities of the coroner in a disaster as agreed by the Cabinet Office but in summary, the coroner must *prepare* for disaster in such a way as to ensure that: [34]

- there are written procedures in place to initiate a proper response to disaster by the coroner's own office;
- the coroner's responsibilities and needs are properly considered by those preparing disaster plans for the community (eg police and social services);
- the identification, establishment, and staffing of a temporary mortuary (with sufficient facilities to handle a large number of casualties) can take place smoothly at short notice;
- there are proper systems in place, understood by all those involved, to deal with the recovery of bodies;
- procedures can be set in progress which will end with a positive identification of each body;
- the responsibilities of the coroner and of the police are understood by both sides and that there are suitable liaison arrangements in place;
- cross-border events can be accommodated in conjunction with neighbouring jurisdictions;
- upgrade options (whether due to scale or complexity of the incident) have been considered.

Temporary Mortuaries

The phrases 'temporary mortuary' or 'incident mortuary' are often misused.[35] These terms are often wrongly used for what is in fact a body holding area at the disaster site (see section 11.23). The description is also misused for a holding and identification centre[36] (such as the gymnasium at the Hillsborough disaster). However, the proper use of the phraseology refers to premises temporarily converted to a full mortuary facility where bodies are subject to a post-mortem examination and identification procedure. The temporary mortuary forms a major part of the response to a disaster and is also a central point of evidence collection in the inevitable criminal inquiry.

---

[34] This list from the first edition of *Coroners' Courts* was quoted by Clarke LJ in his Marchioness Inquiry Report: pp 64/5.

[35] Whilst the accepted phrase is 'temporary mortuary', the alternative of 'incident mortuary' is becoming more widespread: the reader may think that this gives a clearer description. However, to avoid confusion this text uses 'temporary mortuary' throughout.

[36] Following the Hillsborough Disaster in 1989 the bodies were removed from the terraces to the football club gymnasium. Relatives visited this building to identify the dead and give statements to the police. Later that night the bodies were removed to the Sheffield Medico-Legal Centre where they were subject to post-mortem examination before being released.

Need for a Special Facility   **11.10**

Hospital or public mortuaries often have a capacity to store bodies well above their average 'occupancy'. However, it would be a serious mistake to assume that a mortuary able to hold 90 bodies is in any way capable of dealing with a disaster in which 90 persons have died for the following reasons:

- Many disasters relate to transport incidents. The high-speed impact and possible fire involved cause considerable mutilation. In such cases bodies are almost inevitably disrupted or fragmented; it can be unusual for even one entire body to be recovered. There may be many more body parts than there are bodies—it would not be unusual for a disaster involving 20 fatalities to generate 100 body bags each containing a part of a body or fragment of tissue.
- Procedures for examining and identifying mutilated bodies require a great deal more space than is normally the case.
- There needs to be space for several teams to be working at the one time if inordinate delay is to be avoided.
- There will be intense media interest in the matter and a much higher degree of security will be needed than a hospital mortuary could normally provide.[37]
- The single viewing facility at most mortuaries would create considerable delays for those wanting to view the deceased.[38]
- Normal mortuary business has to continue despite the disaster, in any event it would generally be unwise for a major criminal forensic task to be undertaken in a hospital mortuary alongside normal activities.

For all of these reasons it is much better that a temporary mortuary is used, allowing the necessary space to deal with the various problems expeditiously and accurately.

There is no need for each coroner's jurisdiction to have its own site identified for use as a temporary mortuary,[39] it may be better that one site is identified, with the

---

[37] The possibility of attempted press intrusion into the temporary mortuary cannot be ignored. Apart from the obvious undesirability of this, there may be serious repercussions in evidential terms.

[38] Undoubtedly the next of kin have the right to view should they choose to do so despite advice to the contrary. The coroner has possession of the bodies until they are released for disposal so *could* prevent this, but it is difficult to see what would be gained by denying those wishing to view—see section 11.26 for a further discussion on this point.

[39] Statistically speaking, any individual coroner is likely to have a disaster occur within the jurisdiction about once every 105 years. However, this does not seem to stop lightning striking in the same place, for example the Westminster Coroner dealt with both the Clapham and Marchioness cases as well as the Ladbroke Grove rail crash. The East Kent Coroner has had a similar diet of misfortune with the Zeebrugge disaster, the Deal bombing, the M2 coach crash, and the container lorry deaths of 58 Chinese immigrants.

potential for extra facilities on a modular basis, which could be used by four or five coroners.[40]

11.11 The Supervising Pathologist

Each coroner will have nominated in advance a supervising pathologist (and deputy) to take charge of the medical aspects of the temporary mortuary. The supervising pathologist would normally be a Home Office accredited forensic pathologist.

The supervising pathologist will have a central role in planning for the temporary mortuary, in conjunction with other coroners, the police, and the local authority. He/she will be responsible for providing the coroner with details of equipment considered necessary to run a mortuary in any likely scenario, will be familiar with the health and safety aspects of the matter, and will have been involved in choosing the specified site.

At the time of the incident, the supervising pathologist will:

- help the coroner nominate the pathologists who will carry out the actual work in the mortuary, although it must be emphasized that the coroner has the final approval of those chosen;
- advise the coroner on the most appropriate method of dealing with the bodies, considering the degree of disruption and trauma to which they have been subjected;
- in consultation with the coroner and the police commander,[41] advise on procedures necessary either for identification or evidential purposes. For example in some circumstances it may be appropriate to perform a radiographic skeletal survey (full x-ray) of the body, on other occasions this would be superfluous.

There will also be an element of direction and co-ordination in the role. For example it is said that in one comparatively recent disaster some bodies had to be re-examined as no central records had been kept of what the individual pathologists had done in terms of taking DNA samples.

11.12 The Major Disaster Advisory Team

This team comprises police officers from various forces who have practical experience of a variety of disasters. The team can be called upon to attend at short notice to provide *advice* to the local police commanders and thus to the coroner.

---

[40] The coroner in whose jurisdiction the disaster occurred would retain control, notwithstanding that the bodies now lay in another area—see section 2.13 which deals with s 14 of the Act.

[41] And if appropriate with any specialist inspector appointed, eg from the Air Accident Investigation Branch.

Inter alia, expertise is available on body recovery, mortuary management, identification, the casualty bureau,[42] and family liaison.

Purpose of a Temporary Mortuary   11.13

The temporary mortuary will be a major feature of the response to any disaster. The purpose of the facility might be summarized as:

- establishing the identity of each deceased—by careful examination of the body and associated property, obtaining evidence which can be matched with data obtained by the ante-mortem team and the casualty bureau.[43]
- establishing the precise cause of death—with proper examination of the body by experienced pathologists;
- collecting evidence of crime—not only in the cause of death but by examination of clothing and other exhibits recovered from the body, eg bomb fragments;
- preparing bodies for release to relatives by reconstructive techniques where necessary—embalming will be necessary in some cases, particularly if the release of the body may be delayed or it is to be repatriated overseas.

Procedures   11.14

Remembering that virtually all disasters will be treated as the scene of a crime until the contrary is proven, the mortuary plays a central part in the collection of evidence. The police will provide teams of officers to work within the mortuary for documentation purposes. These officers will be in close liaison with the casualty bureau and the ante-mortem teams. The police role is discussed variously throughout this chapter but it is important to comment here that the supervising pathologist will also be advising the senior investigating officer (SIO)[44] and the officer in charge of the mortuary on any criminal matters that fall more within their remit than the coroner's.

Requirements of the Temporary Mortuary   11.15

Co-ordinating the identification of suitable premises for a temporary mortuary is regarded as a task for the local authority to lead but it is important that this is an inter-agency activity including coroners, police, supervising pathologists and environmental health officers.[45]

---

[42] A police facility that matches ante- and post-mortem information in order to assist with victim identification (as to which see section 11.30.2 below).

[43] ie those making inquiries of the relatives etc, see section 11.30.2.

[44] ie the senior detective responsible for investigating the incident, including any criminal inquiry.

[45] *Dealing with Fatalities during Disaster*, paras 3.2–3.5; see section 11.01.

There are a number of specific requirements for a building that is to be used as a temporary mortuary. It must:

- have a limited window area that is open to public view from the outside as it is difficult to blank windows off successfully for any length of time;
- have good access, possibly sufficient for a lorry, but certainly large enough for an ambulance or van to actually drive in;
- have the working area all on one level so that bodies and equipment are not constantly being carried up and down stairs;
- have arrangements to chill bodies[46] if they are going to be stored for a lengthy time. A corner of an area may be chilled by cool air blowers but the ideal is to use a separate adjoining building;[47]
- have an impervious, solid, and level floor with suitable drainage for noxious substances ranging from blood to formaldehyde. This rules out gymnasia which might otherwise be a favoured possibility. Plastic sheeting, properly heat-sealed, is an option but needs to be carefully chosen and laid if it is not to be slippery under foot;
- be capable of being secured against invasions either by the press or those who, for one reason or another, are desirous of moving a body.[48] A building within a secure outer perimeter is ideal;
- be big enough for rest areas and office accommodation, although these could be formed by portable units outside;
- have an area, well away from the working part of the mortuary, suitable for relatives to view the dead, if they so desire, with appropriate administrative areas for waiting and support etc;
- have sufficient power,[49] water supply, and phone connections or the ability to make suitable additions quickly;
- be available at short notice for a period of two or three weeks, possibly longer.

Finally, it must also be remembered that the building will retain some stigma for years as a place associated with mass death. This may in practice rule out a public building such as an ice rink,[50] however suitable it might otherwise be thought to be.

---

[46] It is a common misconception that bodies should be stored in sub-zero or 'deep freeze' conditions, after all this would make the post-mortem examination impossible. The proper storage temperature is plus 4 degrees Celsius for short-term refrigeration.

[47] If refrigerated lorries are to be used some thought needs to be given to any stigma that may be attached to them after the disaster. Further, such a vehicle is only suitable if it can be run from mains electricity once inside a building, otherwise noise and fumes become intolerable. Electric tail lifts are essential to avoid unnecessary manual handling.

[48] It has been suggested that at one disaster three agents of a foreign intelligence service made entry to the mortuary disguised as religious men in furtherance of their own inquiries into the cause of the crash.

[49] Powerful lighting will probably require a three phase source.

[50] A body placed on a pallet above ice will not freeze and will remain at just about the right temperature if other environmental factors are controlled.

Whilst buildings that fit all the necessary criteria are rare, hangars on an RAF base or large military storage facilities are likely to be the nearest available compromise. The chosen site must be the subject of an exercise by all those likely to be involved at regular intervals.

Facilities for relatives to view the bodies should not be forgotten when planning a temporary mortuary,[51] although this is unlikely to be for the purpose of identification. The question of relatives viewing the remains of the deceased is dealt with at section 11.26.

Temporary Mortuary Plan   11.16

Although many of the details of a temporary mortuary cannot be decided until the exact nature of the disaster is ascertained, certain facets are likely to remain constant and can be the subject of a detailed plan which would include such matters as:

- the location of the chosen mortuary and specified access routes;
- arrangements for activation of the mortuary and notification of personnel;
- transportation of the deceased to the mortuary;
- layout of the mortuary;
- command and control of police personnel and medical/technical staff;
- body reception procedures;
- storage space for both bodies and personal effects;
- required conditions for body storage;
- health and safety criteria;
- general procedures for post-mortem examination, x-ray, and odontology;
- measures for dealing with property removed from the body;
- post-examination storage criteria (including embalming where appropriate);
- procedures for liaison with ante-mortem and post-mortem police teams;[52]
- mortuary security including the issue of identity cards for accredited access to different sections of the site;
- procedures for viewing by relatives (where appropriate) with provision for support from others;
- liaison with outside agencies (eg local authorities and social services);
- procedure for the release of bodies;
- disposal of waste materials;
- the prospect of chemical or biological, radiological, or nuclear contamination of bodies may require an alternative plan.

---

[51] Which will also need thought for the specific requirements of religious communities.

[52] See section 11.30—in simple terms, the ante-mortem team gain information from relatives about those thought to be involved, the post-mortem team collate information from the mortuary about those who *were* involved. The casualty bureau matches the two sets of information together and reports to the Identification Commission through the SIM.

In most areas the plan for setting up the mortuary will be undertaken as a local authority responsibility and will have been written by the Emergency Planning Unit at County or City level. In other districts the plan may have been written by the police. In any event the police will have their own operational plan for procedures within the mortuary. Whichever agency is primarily involved, it is essential that the requirements of the other authorities are fully taken into account and that the plan is not written in isolation. It is also essential that the plan is updated regularly.

11.17   Planning for Radiography at the Temporary Mortuary

Radiography (x-ray) facilities are an essential part of any temporary mortuary provision. The technique will assist with identification, ascertaining the cause of death, and the collection of evidential material.

A range of equipment is needed. Several different machines will be used: an image intensifier for fluoroscopy (real time x-ray 'video'); a normal mobile x-ray machine; and dental x-ray equipment. There must also be a facility for processing the films.[53] Radiation protection screens will be needed and, of course, trained and experienced radiographers.

Many existing temporary mortuary plans rely on the NHS to fulfil their radiography requirements. However, radiographers and equipment are currently in short supply in the NHS and not all radiographers are trained in forensic radiography. It may be that local staff will be required to care for the injured in a disaster and will not be released from their department.

It is essential that those involved in writing temporary mortuary plans do not make assumptions about the ready availability of equipment or personnel.[54]

Dealing with the Disaster

11.18   The Role of the Coroner in the Early Stages

Having learnt of the disaster the coroner will need to marshal necessary resources. An experienced coroner's officer may be dispatched immediately to the scene to provide assistance to the incident commander in the setting up of a body holding

---

[53] But the most modern x-ray equipment is 'filmless', utilizing digital technology which removes the need for darkroom equipment.

[54] In the North of England a group of experienced radiographers have formed a team to assist at disasters with both staff and equipment. Information is available from Jacquie Vallis: J.Vallis@tees.ac.uk. There may be centralized efforts to establish a co-ordinated rapid response radiography service for the whole country in due course.

Table 11.1. The coroner's role in disaster

The following has been accepted by the Civil Contingencies Secretariat of the Cabinet Office as a proper summary of the coroner's role in disaster.*

The coroner in whose district the body is lying will:

- in consultation with the relevant council and police, initiate the establishment of the emergency mortuary;
- authorize the removal of bodies of victims;
- appoint a supervising pathologist and authorize the examination of bodies to find a cause of death;
- chair the Identification Commission and take reasonable steps to identify the deceased;
- organize the collection of data concerning those whose bodies may be irrecoverable but who were believed to be victims of the event;
- liaise and co-operate with other coroners who may also have bodies of victims arising from the same event;
- authorize the disposal of those bodies after appropriate examination and documentation is complete – to those who are lawfully entitled;
- at all times liaise with the relevant emergency services and government departments.

---

* This list was prepared for the Cabinet Office by Michael Burgess, then Hon. Secretary of the Coroners' Society of England and Wales. It was published as part of the CBRN Handbook by the Cabinet Office: www.ukresilience.info.

---

area (see section 11.23). The coroner's officer will have a mobile telephone[55] in order to give a first-hand account to the coroner or ask the coroner's advice when problems arise.

The coroner will ensure that the supervising pathologist has been informed and is in a position to alert necessary staff. A decision will be required at an early stage, in liaison with the supervising pathologist and the police incident commander, as to whether a temporary mortuary is required. The site of the mortuary may have been identified in the major incident plan but, if a choice remains, the exact site will now be confirmed.

If the incident has occurred during normal working hours the coroner must bear in mind that reports of deaths will continue in the usual way and normal work has to operate in at least a restricted fashion. This will mean at least one officer delegated to remain separate from the major incident until the office would normally close. Some thought will also be necessary to prevent all available staff (including the coroner) working to exhaustion in the early stages of what might be a lengthy task.

---

[55] Any mobile phones used by the coroner or coroner's officers should be registered by the police under the ACCOLC (Access Overload Control) procedure which gives priority use of the transmitters in the area. This may be necessary considering the large number of calls that others, including innumerable members of the press, will be making in the same area, but the ever increasing number of transmitters may avoid this problem.

11.19   Site Visit

The coroner will generally wish to visit the site at an early stage—those with experience of disaster often comment that this was time well spent. Exactly when this should happen might be a difficult decision; certainly the coroner will have no wish to obstruct attempts to rescue those still living. Nonetheless the coroner carries a great deal of responsibility for events flowing from the disaster and, if there are the usual communication difficulties at such a time, will wish to be present sooner rather than later.

The coroner may be accompanied by the supervising pathologist and will meet with the police incident commander to gain an idea of the scale of the problem. Checks will be made to ensure that the forward base (ie the body holding area) is working satisfactorily. It may be advantageous for the police Senior Investigating Officer (SIO) and/or Senior Identification Manager (SIM) to be present at this time.

The bodies cannot be removed from the scene of the incident without the coroner's permission. However, once the coroner is satisfied that the proper arrangements are in hand, this decision will no doubt be delegated to the SIM and site incident commander. See section 11.22 for a more detailed discussion of the factors to be considered before removal of bodies.

11.20   Mortuary Arrangements

The coroner will by this time have turned to arrangements for the temporary mortuary. Whatever the degree of planning, it is inevitable that omissions and areas of dispute will now become apparent. The coroner will be the final arbiter for those matters within the proper remit, and may wish to be present at the temporary mortuary until such time as the procedures there are fully established and bodies start arriving.

From this point the coroner will primarily be involved with identification of the deceased and, in particular, liaison with the Identification Commission (see section 11.30). In the strictest of legal terms it is up to the subsequent inquest to decide on the identification of each body, but on a practical level the coroner will have to be satisfied on a case by case basis as information from all the sources available becomes clearer.

11.21   The Decision to Open a Mortuary

The criteria for a temporary mortuary are relatively straightforward. They are set out briefly at section 11.15 although they can be discussed and considered at great length. However, the decision as to whether that mortuary should be brought into use for a particular incident will have to be taken quickly and, to some extent, against a background of partial knowledge.

Plainly, if there are 50 bodies or more there is no prospect whatsoever of normal mortuary facilities being able to deal with the incident and a temporary mortuary is essential. All the bodies or body parts *must* be dealt with at one facility, for it would cause endless problems to split the work. For example, if there are unattached limbs in separate body bags, how does one know that the limb(s) and torso have actually been sent to the same place?

However, the mortuary decision can be difficult if the numbers involved are smaller. On the face of it the 12 casualties from the Dunkeswick air crash in North Yorkshire in 1995 could have been dealt with in normal facilities at Leeds, but in view of the pronounced degree of disruption to the bodies it was quickly decided that a temporary mortuary was required. The same temporary mortuary was put into operation following the 10 deaths in the Selby rail crash of 2001. In both cases this was regarded as a considerable success, none of those involved have any doubt that a temporary mortuary was the correct decision on each occasion. Still, had there been considerably less disruption to the bodies an alternative decision may have been appropriate.

Another factor that may be taken into account is whether the identities of those involved are known in general terms (a so-called 'closed scenario' such as where there is a passenger list in an aircraft incident) or wholly unknown ie an 'open scenario' such as a bomb in a shopping centre.

Overall, it is quite impossible to lay down hard and fast rules. The situation will depend entirely on the normal facilities available in the appropriate area, the amount of disruption to the bodies, the number of body bags involved (as opposed to bodies), whether a criminal offence is suspected, and what procedures are thought necessary to identify the bodies.

Plans should also cover moving those who later die in hospital over to the temporary mortuary (if it is still running), rather than the hospital facility. Much will depend on the individual circumstances, including the time elapsed and whether the casualty has been properly identified. This might cause distress for the relatives who learn that the body is being taken from a hospital to a hangar but in reality it may be the best way of ensuring continuity and consistency.

It may also be difficult to decide how long the temporary mortuary should remain active. The majority of body parts removed from the scene might perhaps be dealt with inside a week, yet it could take two weeks or longer to clear the site with a degree of confidence that nothing substantial remains.

Recovering Bodies 11.22

Once death is established there is nothing to be gained by rushing to recover bodies, indeed a great deal may be lost. The understandable wish to act with decency might actually do considerable harm to evidence relevant to identity or a criminal inquiry. Every reasonable effort must be made to avoid unnecessary delay but expediency should not be at the expense of carrying out a meticulous investigation.

11.22.1 *Problems caused by premature removal*

Whilst it is accepted that some bodies may have to be moved in the initial rescue efforts (see section 11.23 below) or because they present a particular problem where they lie (eg trip hazard that is difficult to avoid) every attempt should be made to leave the remaining bodies, and their associated property, in the initial position. Two examples may serve to illustrate this point.

In one disaster the body of a woman was badly burnt and identification may have proved difficult. However, a burnt corpse tends to assume the 'pugilist' position because of muscle contraction in fire, with the arms clamped tight in against the side of the chest. In some instances this can leave fragments of material from clothing comparatively undamaged within the area tightly enclosed under the armpits. On this occasion the fibres recovered were from a dress that the deceased had made herself. The dress-making remnants had been turned into a cushion at her home and it was thus a simple matter to compare the two pieces of material and achieve an identification carrying a considerable degree of confidence. This fragile evidence would have been lost if the body had been hurriedly picked up and swung casually onto a stretcher.

The second example is theoretical but readily believable. As a body is awaiting removal the officer standing guard on it decides to save time and look through a wallet which lies loose underneath the body. In doing so the only identifiable fingerprint is smudged, thus destroying a link from that body to the identification papers in the wallet.

11.22.2 *Practicalities of removal*

Many disasters relate to transport accidents where the impact will cause considerable disruption to body tissues. In such cases it can be unusual for even one entire body to be recovered. A precise and careful approach at an early stage will go a long way towards providing evidence of identification and, where appropriate, evidence of any criminal act that was involved. Several police forces now have officers who are specially trained in body recovery who would be available to other forces under 'mutual aid' arrangements.

It is usually better to wait for first light if the incident occurs in darkness. Whilst arc lights can provide some help they are also a hindrance because of the extent of shadows that they cast. The hours of darkness are better spent marshalling resources, gathering appropriate personnel together, and ensuring that they are thoroughly briefed. It will also take some time to have the temporary mortuary activated and ready to receive bodies.

There is inevitably a reaction from those at the scene of a disaster to afford decency to a corpse. This will be particularly so if there is a public area involved or the press have a vantage point from which they can film (remembering the immense power of telephoto lenses). However, even rushing to place a sheet[56] over a corpse might be a mistake—transferring vital fragmentary evidence[57] on to the sheet from where it will be lost.

During the actual recovery, the ground will be sectioned off into areas and the location of each body part or item lifted will be marked on a plan.[58] This plan will be needed in the temporary mortuary later on, as well as being a significant part of the investigation evidence. Every item will be photographed before being moved and whenever possible the opportunity should be taken for a detailed video. The method of numbering exhibits now in use provides a large waterproof number which is easily distinguishable on camera.

The bodies may then be moved down to a holding area for a short time to assist with the logistics of movement on to the temporary mortuary.

The Body Holding Area
11.23

The purpose of the body holding area is to provide a continuity link between the recovery operation at the scene of the disaster and transit to the temporary mortuary.

It is common for the term 'body holding area' to be confused with the actual temporary mortuary. In fact there is a considerable difference, for the first phrase refers to a small area at the edge of the disaster scene where bodies are collected together awaiting onward transport to the temporary mortuary. No procedures or examination will take place here. In some cases it might even be that no body holding area is necessary at all. In others it may be appropriate to use a vehicle as the body holding 'area' so that the site moves to the body rather than the other way around.

However, there will often be circumstances in the early stage of rescue where those involved have great difficulty in determining who is alive and who is dead. The

---

[56] Placing anything more than a sheet over the corpse is inviting difficulty, for example putting plywood or cardboard over it may lead to later rescuers walking over the body in the confusion of the site.

[57] For example bomb fragments.

[58] Many police forces now have a computerized mapping system available using a theodolite which allows a 3D image to be built up.

firefighter in breathing apparatus, or worse a chemical protection suit, has immense difficulties and may be left in the position of simply pulling out the first human remains that could have a prospect of survival. It may also be necessary to remove bodies during the rescue of those still living.

If possible, bodies removed in these circumstances should not be taken immediately from the site to a hospital but should be kept together until the temporary mortuary is ready to receive the victims. At the same time, every effort must be made to avoid unnecessary delay.

The body holding area is likely to be a tent at one edge of the scene. Its use must be carefully controlled. It is understandable if rescuers want to rush in, deposit a body and rush out back to the incident but this is likely to cause great difficulty in the long term. The author would suggest that an experienced coroner's officer should be sent to the scene of a disaster immediately the facts have been established, specifically to supervise the reception of bodies in the short term until the proper mortuary team can be operational.

11.24   Post-mortem Procedures

A number of procedures may be necessary in order to identify disrupted bodies. In cases where an explosion is suspected there might first be an x-ray examination[59] of the whole body (with clothing) in an effort to establish the direction of the explosion and to screen for artefacts such as bomb fragments[60] or personal possessions.[61] The body must then be carefully searched and stripped in the presence of the pathologist. Property and clothing removed will be carefully recorded and documented.

A full post-mortem will then take place using forensic pathologists. A forensic odontologist may well be involved in examination of the mouth and jaw structures (including dental x-rays)[62] because comparison with dental records gives a good final confirmation of identity. Photographs will be taken at each of these stages. The body would then need specialist reconstruction in an effort to make it presentable.

---

[59] More correctly 'fluoroscopy' using an image intensifier. This can also be used to chart injuries, reveal non-human remains, or even show that there is co-mingling of body parts in one recovered section.

[60] The primary significance of this is obvious but it is also helpful for the pathologist to be aware of objects imbedded within the body, some of which will be razor sharp, before the examination.

[61] If the body is badly decomposed or burnt it can be difficult to find jewellery etc without the use of radiography.

[62] Which means that there might be two sets of x-rays, the general x-rays (including fluoroscopy) before the autopsy and dental x-rays after. Although the dental equipment is different, in planning the mortuary layout it is important not to assume that all x-rays can be done at the same time although there will probably be only one designated 'controlled area' because of the radiological hazards.

Body parts that are separated from the main torso will each be treated as an individual item. They will be bagged and labelled separately, then subjected, insofar as it is appropriate, to the same procedure as the torso. Obviously location, or fragments of clothing, may give some idea of a match to other body parts[63] so it is essential that the mapping information is available in the mortuary. Photographs will be taken of the individual parts and collected together on a board for the pathologists to review from time to time, to see if they match up to an injury they have dealt with.[64]

At the same time, property taken from the body will need careful examination. Personal effects (particularly jewellery) are a good initial indicator of identity and can easily be taken by post-mortem team officers to the relative for confirmation rather than bringing the relative to the temporary mortuary. Such personal effects would normally be cleaned and reconstituted as far as practicable before eventual return to the family.[65] The same applies to clothing and bank notes (which could be replaced).[66] However, property that might form evidence may need to be held in storage for a considerable time.

Extent of the Examination   11.25

Until recently a full post-mortem examination would have been considered a necessity for any disaster victim. In most cases that will still be so, identification or even the matching of body parts will often require the fullest examination. But modern thinking is beginning to waver on this point, there may be exceptional circumstances in which the cause of death is clear without an invasive examination. For example, if a terrorist poison gas attack killed 40 people in a shopping centre it might be asked whether there was justification in a full post-mortem examination of every victim or whether a more limited scrutiny was appropriate. The same might be said of very large-scale disasters.

The problem with this argument is that assumptions can be dangerous. At an early stage the investigators may not know exactly what they are looking for and there is only one opportunity to get the inquiry right. It is too late to back-track once bodies have been released and relatives, no doubt grateful initially at being spared additional trauma, may have cause for regret if their later questions cannot

---

[63] Although if trying to match by clothing it should be remembered that a lot of people buy their clothes from a very small number of High Street shops.

[64] See also the more detailed section on identification at section 11.27 *et seq.*

[65] But the family should be asked first, it would be disastrous if a battered item were repaired only for it to be discovered that it had been in a (much loved) damaged state prior to the disaster.

[66] Again, care should be taken on any such decision, some relatives would not want these items cleaned but would prefer them in their original state; clothing particularly may retain the personal smell of the deceased, or aftershave, or perfume etc. However, current thinking is that this may raise health and safety issues in some circumstances.

be answered. See section 5.25 *et seq* for further discussion of partial and non-invasive post-mortem examinations.

The extent of toxicology is another source of potential problems. It would be easy to undertake a 'full screen' on every victim but what does the coroner then do with information that wasn't actually wanted? For example, a businessman returning from abroad is killed whilst a passenger in a train. Toxicology is done 'for completeness' but the result shows traces of cocaine, a situation of which the family knew nothing. Once obtained this information cannot be hidden—but was the full toxicology ever really needed in the first place? However, some would argue that this presumes the 'innocent passenger' is not the terrorist (possibly 'high on drugs') who caused the incident in the first place. The reality is perhaps that decisions about the extent of examinations will need to be made a long time before there is any element of clarity as to the full circumstances of the disaster.

11.26 Viewing by Relatives

The question of viewing disrupted remains is difficult if the body is still badly disfigured, despite the best effects of the technicians. In general, visual identification should be considered unlikely, particularly as it is not a reliable method in a disaster scenario.[67] However, viewing for identification purposes should not be confused with the family wishing to see their loved one:

> The terms 'visual identification' and 'viewing the body' are often used interchangeably and thus confused. The distinction between the two expressions is an important one, which should not be trivialised. Visual identification is the process by which a relative establishes the identity of a victim by looking at the body and confirming that it is a particular missing person. Viewing the body is the process whereby a relative, friend or other person is permitted to look at, hold or spend time with the deceased, once the identity has been established and confirmed by other means.[68]

Whether this should happen or not is technically within the coroner's discretion in the sense of having control of the bodies—but the reality is that there is little point in preventing families seeing the body, no matter how badly disfigured it is. After all, the body will eventually be released to the relatives who could then simply order their undertaker to open the coffin.

In his Marchioness Inquiry Report Clarke LJ considered it at least arguable that Article 8 ECHR[69] afforded relatives a right to view the body but he continued:

---

[67] Following the Luxor massacre in 1997 it was claimed that two English victims had been visually identified but odontology later showed these identifications to be wrong. See also section 11.32.

[68] Clarke LJ—see n 2 above.

[69] Article 8 European Convention on Human Rights, given effect in UK law by the Human Rights Act 1998.

The importance of viewing the body for the grieving process should be emphasised to coroners and their staff by appropriate means. While the coroner or the coroner's officers may have reservations about the wisdom of viewing the remains of the deceased where there has been disfigurement by trauma, dismemberment, decomposition or mutilation, [they] should be reminded that the members of the family should never be prevented from viewing the remains. Any such viewing is at the risk of the viewer but coroners and their staff should [remember] the assistance to be gained from counsellors, FLOs and religious leaders in this process.

Nonetheless, those involved—coroner, police, and social services—owe a duty to the relatives to ensure that they understand what they will find if they insist on viewing the remains. In many instances the FLO[70] will be best placed to assist the family amongst those providing support, perhaps having either viewed personally or had sight of photographs.

Clarke LJ went on to warn against situations where those actually dealing with families insert their own interpretation of cautions from 'higher echelons' about viewing. Referring to events following the Marchioness sinking he said:

It is likely that the coroner's officers and police liaison officers, acting from the best of motives, namely to avoid distress to relatives, sought to dissuade from viewing those relatives who expressed a wish to view. It is quite possible that such officers used language which suggested that viewing was prohibited rather than ill-advised to achieve what they thought best, namely that a loving parent would not be distressed by the sight of their child's decomposing body.

Identification

Whether there is a single death in a road incident or many deaths in a disaster, one of the major responsibilities of the coroner is to ensure that the bodies of the deceased are correctly identified, so that they can be returned to the correct relatives. Thus any decision on the criteria to be accepted for identification lies with the coroner in practice, even where there is to be a jury at an inquest.[71]

So far as identification is concerned, the legal position is that when the police are dealing with a suspicious death they work on behalf of the coroner because it is he who has both the responsibility for identification and the right to possession of the body until his coronial functions have been fulfilled.[72]

The Difficulties   11.27

In many instances this task will be far from easy. A body that has been subject to massive deceleration trauma and/or involved in a fierce fire may have been broken

---

[70] See section 11.29.
[71] See the Clarke Report (n 2 above) at para 15.11.
[72] See the Clarke Report (n 2 above) at para 16.7; but issues of a criminal investigation not overlapping with the coroner's jurisdiction are a matter for the police alone.

into a number of pieces and then become so charred as to be difficult to distinguish from the wreckage in which it lies.[73] Identification by visual means is not going to be a practical measure and would in any event be highly unreliable (see section 11.32 below).

Another difficulty may be that the identities and even the numbers of those who could be involved are wholly unknown, referred to as an 'open scenario' (such as a bomb in a shopping centre) in contrast to a 'closed scenario' where there is a passenger list in an aircraft incident—although such lists are notoriously unreliable.

Proper identification procedures depend to a large extent upon a methodical recovery of the body parts. Unnecessary handling of property, or thoughtless association of items simply because they are adjacent to one another, can render identification almost impossible.

A suitably planned and properly equipped temporary mortuary is also essential in aiding identification. As set out at section 11.16, a great deal of thought needs to be given to planning this facility.

A careful approach by the ante-mortem team members[74] will provide a large amount of information about those who are missing. The work in the mortuary will have provided a great deal of information about the bodies. What is now required is for this information to be matched up and any further investigations planned. This work falls upon the Identification Commission. With the Commission's assistance, the coroner will make an initial decision on whether the identification has been established to a sufficient level of proof.

11.28   Senior Identification Manager

One of the major initiatives in disaster management of recent years is the creation of a Senior Identification Manager post (SIM) following a recommendation of the Metropolitan Police team reviewing issues from the October 1999 Ladbroke Grove rail crash. This officer, of at least Detective Superintendent rank, will have overall responsibility for the identification process and provides the link between the police investigators, those concerned with identification, and the coroner. The SIM would also have a very important co-ordinating role in decisions about what steps were necessary to identify each individual deceased.

Clarke LJ[75] fully endorsed this initiative:

> The role of the SIM will be to pull together the information, evaluate it and report to the Identification Commission on the identification status of each of the

---

[73] A significant rail crash might involve as much as 900 megajoules of energy, an air crash several hundred—a car hitting a brick wall at 100 mph is said to amount to about one megajoule.

[74] See section 11.30.2.

[75] See n 2 above, paras 16.31–16.32.

deceased, how far the procedures have progressed and what remains to be done in order to satisfy the identification criteria. The SIM creates a bridge between the coroner and his staff on the one hand and the police on the other and, together with the FLOs, forges a crucial link between the police and the bereaved and survivors.

It is anticipated that most police forces will have a number of senior officers trained in the SIM role by the end of 2003.

Use of Family Liaison Officers   11.29

Probably the most significant advance in the way that police forces have dealt with the bereaved in recent years is the introduction of the Family Liaison Officer (FLO). In turn FLOs have become of great assistance to coroners as an additional link with the family.[76]

In almost every suspicious death and (more recently) in many road deaths the police appoint an FLO to provide the family with support and assistance. The properly trained and experienced FLO plays a key role in the exchange of information with the family and will also be able to recognize and gather facts which assist those carrying out the investigation.

It is now well recognized as essential to appoint FLOs to assist the bereaved and remain the primary contact with the family throughout the identification procedure and immediate aftermath of disaster. This may also help to prevent relatives being asked the same question several times by different officers or officials.

The Identification Commission   11.30

Although information about the deceased is being gathered from a number of sources, there must obviously be one central point at which all identification evidence is examined and the prospects of a match of information suitably graded. Ultimately, the decision on whether identification is sufficient is a matter entirely for the coroner but will be based on advice from a panel of experts.

Composition   11.30.1

The Identification Commission is the name given to this team, from a variety of specialities, who will gather together at frequent intervals once identification matches can start to be made.

Although there had previously been divergent views as to who should chair the Commission, Clarke LJ was clearly in favour of this responsibility resting on the coroner:

---

[76] Care must be taken to distinguish the FLO and the investigating officers who have wholly different responsibilities. There can also be difficulties if the roles of FLO and coroner's officer become blurred resulting in territorial misunderstandings, or (worse) omissions when an action falls between the two. Nonetheless, for the many coroners who do not have their own staff available to go out and see the bereaved about particular issues of difficulty, the introduction of the FLO has been an improvement beyond measure.

... in general the coroner should be Chairman of the Identification Commission, but there may be unusual circumstances in which that would not be appropriate. In such a case, as I see it, it must be for the coroner, no doubt in consultation with the overall incident commander, to decide who should take the chair.

Other members of the Commission are likely to include:

- the SIM who will make the arrangements to convene the Identification Commission;[77]
- the Senior Investigating Officer (SIO) who has responsibility for the inevitable criminal inquiry and will also be inquiring into the cause and circumstances of the deaths for the coroner;
- the supervising pathologist who has management of the medical aspects of the mortuary on behalf of the coroner and will provide appropriate medical advice for the Commission;
- the mortuary documentation officer;
- a senior representative of the ante-mortem team;
- a senior representative of the post-mortem team;
- the senior odontologist and fingerprint experts where appropriate;
- the senior scientific support officer from the police who will give advice on technical and scientific matters;
- other experts required from time to time (eg jewellery).

11.30.2 *The Casualty Bureau*

The Identification Commission will receive information (via the SIM) from the Casualty Bureau. This is a police facility[78] collating data from a variety of points with a view to matching details and completing a positive identification. Sources will include:

- members of the public who telephone to say that a relative is missing and may be involved in the incident;[79]

---

[77] The officer in overall operational command of the police response will be termed the 'gold commander', probably working from the Police HQ. The officer in charge at the site will be termed a 'silver commander' as will the SIM and the SIO. The officers in charge at various facilities (eg the temporary mortuary) will generally be bronze commanders. However, there may well be local variations on this theme.

[78] The police major incident computer system HOLMES II has a casualty bureau function which allows one or more of the 43 forces in the country to establish a satellite bureau to assist the force dealing with the disaster. Public calls are answered by any participating force in rota, all with access to the same computer. Additional modules allow update by remote access and information matching, even amongst vast levels of data. Further details are shown on www.holmes2.com.

[79] At the Marchioness disaster where there were 51 fatalities, more than 2,000 were reported missing. The Ladbroke Grove rail crash involved 38 dead but there were more than 8,600 calls. At Hillsborough there were more than a million attempts to access the information line with just 14,000 getting through.

Table 11.2. Sources and routes of information

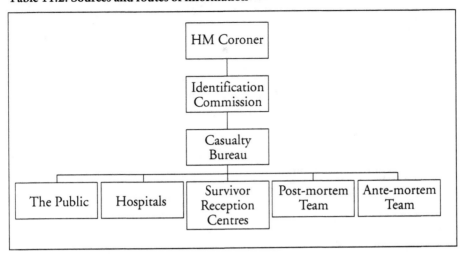

- the ante-mortem team—police officers collecting information from other sources such as passenger lists and questioning relatives as to whether there is anything distinctive such as clothing, jewellery, or medical history about the missing person;[80]
- hospitals receiving casualties;
- survivor reception centres;
- the post-mortem team—who are collating information derived from the examination of bodies at the mortuary, together with anything learnt from the scene.

One aim of the Casualty Bureau will be to classify the inevitable huge numbers of persons reported missing into one of five categories:

- those known to be involved;
- those believed to have been involved;
- those known to frequent that area or means of transport at the relevant time;
- those who commonly use that area or means of transport;
- others not falling into the above categories.

Procedures   **11.30.3**

The intention is that the Commission will formally discuss the progress made on the identification of each individual body. Reports from each of the teams will be

---

[80] This may now include a proactive unit whose sole task is to re-contact those who have earlier reported someone missing and check if they have now turned up. Few people will make the effort required to get through on the phone just to cancel an earlier report but this is actually hugely important for obvious reasons.

given by their representative. Any requests for specific forensic procedures will be made to the coroner, who will make the decision after receiving appropriate advice.

Meetings of the Identification Commission will be held regularly until all the identifications are complete, but are not intended to replace the ongoing liaison between the various teams. However, the coroner is responsible for all matters concerning the bodies and must be made aware of, and give consent for, anything that is to happen to them.

Clarke LJ endorsed the ACPO Emergency Procedures Manual[81] in identifying the role of the Identification Commission as follows:

- liaison with the coroner in formulating identification criteria and evidential requirements;
- confirming the appointment of a supervising pathologist with the coroner;
- controlling the running of the mortuary through the mortuary documentation officer and mortuary duty officer;
- evaluating post-mortem and ante-mortem data;
- compiling identification evidence for the coroner and any other inquiry.

The Commission does not technically make the decision as to whether an individual body is formally identified, this responsibility falls on the coroner.[82] Obviously there is no prospect worse than the wrong body being given to the bereaved and later having to be recovered from them.[83] The coroner should not delegate the decision-making powers in this matter although will be, as noted above, reliant to a great extent on the technical expertise of others.

11.31 The Release of Bodies

It can be argued that one final safeguard to assist in ensuring correct identification lies with the policy for the release of bodies.

It has often been said that no single body should be released to the relatives for funeral until it is firmly established that each victim has been properly identified. An initial identification may be made in good faith and on apparently valid scientific or factual evidence, only for it to be realized later that the situation was

---

[81] Emergency Procedures Manual 2001; Association of Chief Police Officers.

[82] There is an obvious anomaly here between law and necessary practice. The question of identification is one for the inquest, which will generally necessitate a jury in the disaster scenario (although see section 11.33). Although identification will be dealt with at the opening of the inquest prior to release of the body, the resumed inquest will not take place for some time. So there must be a degree of pragmatism by the coroner, who can only hope to ensure that the evidence is such that any jury will agree with the identification at a later time.

[83] A graphic example of this is said to have occurred following the Luxor massacre in November 1997. The bodies of English victims were thought to have been returned to this country but later dental examination found that two had been wrongly identified. See also section 11.32.

not as clear as it appeared and that a better match can be made. Simple errors can occur such as a coffin being wrongly marked. This is a tragedy if the body has already been released and cremated by the wrong family.

However, the author queries whether the changing views of society, and the increasing use of scientific evidence[84] in identification, have now made such a policy less acceptable to the public. Wherever possible, it may still be better to wait and release all the victims at one time but this cannot be a fixed rule; much will depend on how long it will take to identify the last victim. It would be intolerable to hold 30 bodies, that have been identified with some precision, for a month just because one or two remain the subject of investigation. Religious requirements may also be an issue.[85]

It will often be possible for identified bodies to be moved from the temporary mortuary to a suitable place, such as a large undertakers, pending final release. Whilst some degree of security can still be provided there will be better facilities for relatives to view.

Table 11.3. Identification criteria		
Primary	**Secondary**	**Assistance**
fingerprints	distinctive medical	clothing
odontology	deformity	photographs
DNA	marks and scars	body location
unique medical	blood grouping	visual
	physical disease	description
	x-ray[†]	facial mapping*
	jewellery	
	distinctive clothing	

Primary: One feature could be regarded as sufficient in isolation but it would be highly desirable to have at least one secondary item to prevent any suggestion of exhibits being confused.

Secondary: A minimum of three features might normally be required to confirm identity.

Assistance: Not generally regarded as sufficient on their own but may support primary or secondary features.

* Facial mapping may sometimes amount to at least a secondary feature, dependent upon the circumstances.
† X-ray may be a primary feature in certain circumstances.

---

[84] Scientific evidence is, of course, one thing but those involved also have to be sure that the paperwork relating to that evidence is wholly correct.
[85] Some faiths, particularly Moslem and Jewish, wish to bury their dead as soon as possible and find a lengthy delay wholly unacceptable. It will be appropriate to liaise with leaders of relevant faiths at an early stage.

In some circumstances issues of a second post-mortem may arise, as to which see sections 5.11 and 5.12.

11.32   Identification Features

This section considers some of the factors related to established methods of identification. Table 11.3 (above) sets out a suggestion as to how identification features might be used to decide whether a positive match has been established.

DNA profiling. This technique is developing rapidly and in the near future will provide a real solution to mass disaster identification, but at the time of writing is arguably a little too slow and expensive to provide an easy identification in every case.[86]

Extracting a DNA sample from the body part recovered is generally straightforward, if there are sufficient cells. This can be matched against a swab type sample retrieved from a parent or brother/sister. Sometimes a sample of the deceased's own body tissue can be recovered from their home (eg from a hair brush). Some victims may be recorded on the National Criminal Intelligence DNA database but care must be taken to ensure that previously taken samples were obtained under the correct identity.

Useful information about the genetic relationship between victims,[87] the relationship between individual recovered parts or even the total number of dead can also be obtained from DNA profiling.

However, use of DNA profiling can have problems. Some relatives may consider the collection of control samples to be invasive and it is well recognized that DNA results may prove a non-paternal relationship.[88] Clarke LJ goes so far as to suggest that the FLO should approach the mother of the victim in confidence to ask if there is anything she would like to advise regarding lineage, although this of itself may create obvious difficulties.

Quite apart from the issue of expense, the use of DNA profiling might currently only be considered appropriate when other methods are likely to fail.

Odontology. The pattern of fillings, extractions, bridges, and crowns in the average mouth is likely to be unique because of the number of variations possible. Teeth are the most durable part of the human body and will survive many fires.

---

[86] Which is not to say that DNA has not been used successfully, eg with the identification of the 58 bodies found in a container lorry in 2000.

[87] This technique was used for example following the Waco incident.

[88] In theory it could also show a non-maternal relationship but presumably examples of this would be rare. Overall the parental relationship problems can be such that it might be better to first consider recovery of DNA from a comb or toothbrush belonging to the deceased. Medical samples taken during life (eg operative histology blocks or cervical smear materials) may also be available.

However, some younger people may now not have enough dental work to make identification by this method practicable.

Some caution needs to be exercised if it is thought necessary for the jaw of the deceased to be removed for x-ray. The need for any such disfiguring process must be carefully considered on a case by case basis and will only be undertaken as a last resort.[89]

Fingerprints: In theory, identification by fingerprint should present a relatively straightforward solution, provided the prints of the deceased are either on record or can be lifted from other sources.[90] Unfortunately the reality can differ and taking fingerprints from a burnt or bloated body is either difficult or impossible. There are techniques which can assist; occasionally it might be necessary to remove the digit, but again this must be approached with immense caution on a case by case basis and only when all other possibilities have failed.

Physical characteristics: Besides the obvious issues of size, weight, and colouring, victims may have undergone surgery at some time, leaving scars and either missing organs or artificial joints etc.[91] Many surgical prostheses have a serial number. Some tattoos, or a combination thereof, may be unique or nearly so.

X-ray examination: Comparison of ante-mortem and post-mortem films will assist with identification. Variants such as the frontal sinus patterns are unique and an x-ray taken during life may provide evidence of identification equivalent to a fingerprint. Healed fractures, trabecular bone patterns,[92] and other anatomical features can also be unique identifiers. Radiography can also help determine the age of a victim and assess size by proportional methods.

Facial mapping: A computer-assisted method of analysing facial features to compare ante-mortem and post-mortem photographs.

Clothing: Can be distinctive if not burnt, but even then items such as a belt buckle can survive and be easily recognized if sufficiently unusual.

Documents: Will obviously be of great use if not destroyed, but care must be taken to ensure that they *do* relate to that body rather than just being found nearby. It is

---

[89] The presence of dental x-ray equipment on site will virtually remove the need for this. It will also help if the dental examination is undertaken before any reconstruction of the body.

[90] The interior mirror of the deceased's car remains a classic location but the modern equivalent is a favourite CD of the deceased.

[91] Although one victim of the Kings Cross fire had a metal skull plate and remained unidentified.

[92] X-rays, when passing through the body, are attenuated differently, depending on the density of the structure through which they pass. The trabecular bone pattern is a web-like structure which helps to provide strength within the bone. It is of a greater density (though not the greatest) than some of its fellow bone components and therefore shows up on the x-ray 'whiter', so a white web-like structure can be seen amidst varying shades of white, grey, and black.

even possible for an item to be retrieved in close proximity and put into a jacket pocket by a well-meaning rescuer.

Jewellery. Personal effects of this type are sometimes unique or at least uncommon and the details may once have been carefully recorded or even photographed by a jeweller for insurance valuation purposes. Even when single items are not significant, two or three pieces in combination may be a powerful aid. Jewellery is also relatively likely to survive fire and impact.

Exclusion. If two bodies remain unidentified at the end of the inquiry, one being a six foot male and the other a female child, there is not likely to be much doubt about which is which.

Visual identification. This is not generally to be considered dependable in the disaster scenario, indeed Clarke LJ found the evidence suggested that 'this method of identification is notoriously unreliable . . . even where the body is intact and in good condition'. A particular example of this arose following the Luxor massacre of 1997 (see footnotes 67 and 83 of this chapter) but many of those involved in this type of work will know of other instances.

However, a visual identification should not be confused with allowing the relatives to view the body—as to which see section 11.26 above.

Conclusion

11.33 The Inquest and the Public Inquiry

Many large-scale disasters will be the subject of a public inquiry, usually conducted by a senior judge. At first sight the inquiry and the inquest may seem to cover much the same ground but closer examination shows this can be far from correct. Certainly the inquiry will seek to ascertain how the deaths occurred, but this may involve looking at the broad spectrum of the disaster, dealing with the incident as a whole so that individual deceased may never get a mention. An inquest is about individuals.

Unfortunately, this distinction may become blurred in the minds of the public where an inquest is to follow a detailed public inquiry. The inquest is not about issues of blame or guilt[93]—a major difficulty when the expectation of relatives and society as a whole is geared towards a hunt for those responsible for the deaths. The public inquiry is much more likely to have dealt with questions of blame leaving the inquest bafflingly incomplete for those still involved—thus a verdict of anything less than unlawful killing is likely to be called a scandal and a 'whitewash'.

---

[93] Rules 36 and 42; see section 7.02 and 9.12 *et seq.*

However, in March 1997 a Government Working Group on Disasters and Inquests recommended that an inquest should not be required following a fatal disaster if there had been a public inquiry chaired by a judge which adequately established the cause of deaths arising from the disaster.

With effect from 1 January 2000, s 71 of the Access to Justice Act 1999 inserted a new section into the Coroners Act 1988 (s 17A) which requires a coroner to adjourn an inquest[94] when informed by the Lord Chancellor that:

- a public inquiry chaired by a judge is to be held into events surrounding the deaths; and
- the inquiry is likely to constitute sufficient investigation into the deaths.

Whilst the coroner may resume the inquest after conclusion of the public inquiry this would only be in exceptional circumstances.

Certain parts of the Coroners' (Amendment) Rules 1999 make provisions for an inquest resumed in accordance with s 17A. In particular rule 11 provides for admitting the findings of the public inquiry as documentary evidence at the resumed inquest (see section 7.42). There is no requirement for a coroner to summon a jury when resuming an inquest in such circumstances as s 71(5) of the Access to Justice Act 1999 specifically sets aside s 8(3) of the Coroners Act 1988 in this regard.

The coroner is, of course, still required to open an inquest and will take evidence as to the identity and cause of death of each victim before adjourning.

This requirement to defer may be thought similar to the procedures to be followed under s 16 of the Coroners Act where the inquest must be adjourned because a person has been charged with murder etc. (see section 4.39).

It should be noted that these changes apply only to public inquiries chaired by a judge and not all statutory public inquiries, still leaving coroners with the potential for difficult and large-scale inquests following a disaster.

Expectations
11.34

The way that disasters (and issues of identification in particular) are handled has undergone a significant change in recent years, not least with the lessons learnt in this country from the Marchioness and the various rail crashes at the turn of the Millennium. Events in New York on 11 September 2001 also focused minds on the potential for large-scale disasters.[95]

---

[94] This procedure was followed for the first time after the Ladbroke Grove rail crash in which 31 passengers died. It was subsequently used in relation to the death of Dr David Kelly, the Ministry of Defence official whose death was the subject of a public inquiry by Lord Hutton.

[95] See page v.

Whilst demands upon coroners (and others) have thus intensified, the advent of the FLO and SIM[96] should go a long way to ensuring that relatives are treated in the way that society now expects and demands.

Clarke LJ summarized these expectations at the end of his Report:[97]

- provision of honest and, as far as possible, accurate information at all times and at every stage;
- respect for the deceased and the bereaved;
- a sympathetic and caring approach throughout; and
- the avoidance of mistaken identification.

The author would respectfully enlarge upon these by adding that those in positions of authority must consider the impact that any decision made will have on the bereaved.

The coroner is responsible for all issues relating to the bodies of victims until such time as they are released for disposal. The practicalities of mass disaster must be balanced with sensitivity to the needs of the relatives. Indeed, the aim of *all* those dealing with the deceased should be to ensure that, at the end of the day, the relatives feel that time and care has been spent on people rather than 'just bodies'.

Summary

- No authority can plan in isolation for a disaster—regular liaison is essential.
- The coroner has responsibility for all matters to do with the bodies of those killed in a disaster.
- This responsibility must be exercised in co-ordination with the police who will be treating the event as a major crime until the contrary is shown.
- A temporary mortuary may be essential to deal with even a moderately sized disaster in a proper manner.
- The recovery of bodies and the identification of the victims must be handled in a methodical and controlled fashion, preferably by personnel previously trained in such work.

---

[96] Family Liaison Officer and Senior Identification Manager—see sections 11.29 and 11.28 respectively above.
[97] The Marchioness Inquiry (n 2 above) at para 27.4.

12

TREASURE

Treasure Trove is when any gold or silver, in coin, plate or bullion hath been of ancient time hidden . . . whereof no person can prove any property, it doth belong to the King. Nothing is said to be treasure trove but gold and silver.
Coke's Institutes 1644

Historical Perspective   12.01

The early coroner had various legal duties,[1] one of which was establishing whether a valuable object found in or on the ground was treasure trove[2] and thus to be seized for the Crown. Although many of the coroner's duties fell into disuse over the centuries, the obligation to hold an inquest into a find of treasure remains.

Prior to September 1997 there was no specific legislation on the subject[3] and such cases were dealt with under the coroner's common law powers. Treasure trove inquests were heard before a jury. To be declared treasure trove the object had to meet three criteria:

I am most grateful to Mr Vic Round and Ms Lisa Voden-Decker for their help with the revision of this chapter.

[1] See section 1.03.

[2] The phraseology prior to the Treasure Act 1996 was 'treasure trove'. The Act now simply refers to 'treasure'.

[3] Section 30 of the Coroners Act 1988 stated that a coroner should continue to have jurisdiction to inquire into any treasure found in his district, and as to who were the finders, without further specifying any procedure.

- it had to be made substantially of gold or silver;[4]
- it had to have been deliberately hidden with the intention of later recovery;
- the owner or his heirs could not now be identified.

If the find were declared treasure trove by the jury, the coroner took possession of the item on behalf of the Crown. In practical terms this would usually be to the advantage of the finder. The Crown would allow the British Museum (and there-after local museums) an opportunity to acquire the object. If they chose to do so, the finder was given a reward equivalent to the full market value, assessed by an independent committee. Alternatively, if the museums chose not to keep the object(s) then the treasure was returned to the finder.

If the find was not declared treasure trove by the jury, ownership would then be decided under the civil law between the finder and the landowner.

Treasure trove cases were rare, with only about 25 relevant finds being declared each year.[5]

12.02 The Treasure Act 1996

The Treasure Act 1996 (the Act) came into effect on 24 September 1997 and applies only to objects found after this date. The Act provides a basic framework including:

- a criminal offence of failing to report the finding of treasure;
- a detailed definition of treasure.

The Act also makes provision for a detailed Code of Practice (the Code), including guidance to those searching for artefacts. Whilst the Code[6] is approved by Parliament, it does not amount to legislation.

12.03 Requirement to Declare Finds

A person finding an object that he/she believes or has reasonable grounds for believing is treasure must notify the coroner for that district within 14 days.[7] Failure to do so is a criminal offence[8] punishable by up to three months' imprisonment and a fine at level 5 on the standard scale.[9]

---

[4] The find had to be gold or silver that had been tried or refined and not as it appeared in the ground before being mined. J H Baker (ed), *Case of gold and silver mines* (1555) Reports from the lost notebooks of Sir James Dyer (1994, London, Selden Society).

[5] Norfolk was usually the busiest area in this regard with an annual average of about six coin finds.

[6] Revised at the end of 2002. Available on www.culture.gov.uk (cultural property page).

[7] Commencing the day after the find or upon the day on which the finder first believes, or has reason to believe, that the object is treasure.

[8] Triable summarily, ie only before a Magistrates' Court.

[9] Fines are now described as part of a scale so that the maxima may easily be revised from time to time. The current maximum fine on level 5 is £5,000 (as at 31/7/03).

It is a defence for the finder to show that he/she had, and has continued to have, a reasonable excuse for failing to notify the coroner. The Code gives no specific example but indicates a court will take into account whether the finder could have been expected to know that his find was treasure. The parliamentary debate on the Treasure Bill[10] suggested this might apply to a workman digging a trench who came across a valuable find but put it aside and forgot about it because he did not realize it should be reported. It would perhaps be relevant that the workman was digging a trench rather than searching for antiquities.

Definition of Treasure 12.04

By s 1 of the Act the following are to be regarded as treasure:

- *Gold or silver objects (other than coins)*: any object other than a coin containing at least 10 per cent gold or silver by weight of metal and that is at least 300 years old.
- *Gold or silver coins*: coins containing at least 10 per cent gold or silver by weight and that are at least 300 years old. The find must consist of at least two such coins.
- *Other coins*: coins of other metals that are at least 300 years old. The find must contain at least ten such coins.
- *Objects found in association with treasure*: objects found in the same place as, or that had previously been together with, treasure, whether found at the same time or subsequently. There is no requirement for these to be gold or silver, although unworked natural objects will not be treasure.
- *Objects that would have been treasure trove*: any items that would previously have been declared treasure trove but do not fall within the categories given above. In practice this might be objects less than 300 years old, made substantially of gold or silver that were deliberately hidden with the intention of recovery, the owners/heirs being unknown.[11]

The Secretary of State has power under s 2 of the Act to designate other objects considered to be of outstanding historical, archaeological, or cultural importance which are at least 200 years old. The Treasure Designation Order 2002 was made under this provision and extended the definition of treasure to include the following (when found after 1 January 2003):

---

[10] Hansard: 8 March 1996 at 579 and 10 May 1996 at 588.

[11] The Code makes it plain that items in this class will be comparatively rare. Single coins are unlikely to qualify unless there is exceptionally strong evidence to show that they were buried with the intention of later recovery. However (on the authority of the quotation shown at the head of this chapter) the item must also have been hidden 'of ancient times'. There is no definition of what that would now mean and in reality this section may add little to the definition.

- a group of at least two objects (other than coins) from the same find any part of which are base metal (ie any metal other than gold or silver) which are of prehistoric date (ie dating from the Iron Age or any earlier period);
- any object (other than a coin) which is of prehistoric date, and any part of which is gold or silver.

Further guidance on the definition of 'treasure' can be found in paragraphs 5–18 of the revised Code.[12]

12.05 Definition of 'The Same Find'

It will be important for the coroner to decide whether items are part of the same find. This will have relevance both as to the number of coins involved and to objects found in association with treasure. By s 3(4) objects are to be regarded as part of the same find if:

- they are found together; *or*
- they are found in the same place at different times; *or*
- they were found in different places at different times but had been left together and become separated.

By s 3(5), if the circumstances in which objects are found can reasonably be taken to indicate that they were together at some time before being found, they should be presumed to have been left together unless the contrary is shown.[13]

12.06 Items that have been Lost or Ritual Deposits

Because of the previous requirement that the object be hidden with the intention of recovery, it was not possible to declare as treasure trove those items which appeared to have been dropped or lost, or which were votive offerings or ritual deposits.[14] However, s 4(4) now provides that an object may be declared treasure whatever the nature of the place where it was found and whatever the circumstances in which it was left (including being lost or being left with no intention of recovery).

12.07 No Requirement for a Jury

By s 7(4) of the Act, a treasure inquest will be held without a jury unless the coroner orders otherwise. The Code does not set out any guidance as to when this discretion might be exercised.

---

[12] See www.culture.gov.uk (cultural property page).

[13] Dispersal of objects that originally were together might perhaps occur through ploughing of a field, earth works, or building works.

[14] For example, coins buried at a sacred place as a holy offering, or precious items buried with a body.

Procedure on a Find being Made   **12.08**

By s 8 of the Act, a person finding an object that he/she believes or has reasonable grounds to believe is treasure must notify the coroner for that district within 14 days.[15] The coroner will direct the finder either to deliver up the object or take it to a designated museum or archaeological service.[16] The coroner must acknowledge receipt of the *report* of the find in writing. The finder will be given a proper receipt for the find itself by the museum to which he/she is directed. Whilst the finder must declare the site of the find, this will remain confidential.[17]

The museum or archaeological service receiving the find will advise the coroner whether the objects are thought to be treasure (taking advice from the national museums[18] where appropriate) and must advise the national museum if the find is believed to be treasure.

If the items are not thought to be treasure, the coroner may direct the museum to return them to the finder and it will not normally be necessary to hold an inquest. The coroner retains a discretion on this and may nonetheless hold an inquest.

If the items are thought to be treasure, inquiries will be made of the national and local museums as to whether they wish to acquire the objects. If so, there will be a treasure inquest.

Procedure if Objects Disclaimed   **12.09**

If the items are thought to be treasure but the museums do not want them, they may be disclaimed by the Secretary of State under s 6 of the Act. The coroner will not need to proceed with an inquest but must give notice to the occupier and landowner (if different) that the items will be returned to the finder after 28 days. If objections are made, the coroner must ensure the items are retained until agreement is reached or the issue is dealt with in the civil courts. The coroner has no power to make a determination as to title.

---

[15] Commencing the day after the find or upon the day on which the finder first believes, or has reason to believe, that the object is treasure.

[16] A list of museums and archaeological services that can provide a coroner with initial advice on finds has been agreed for the whole of England and Wales. Copies of the list (and Codes of Practice) may be obtained from the Department for Culture, Media and Sport, Cockspur Street, London SW1Y 5DH. See also: www.culture.gov.uk (cultural property page).

[17] And thereafter in public would only be referred to by a four figure grid reference or similar.

[18] The British Museum for objects found in England and the National Museums and Galleries of Wales for objects found in the Principality.

12.10 Procedure at a Treasure Inquest

Section 7 of the Act refers back to s 30 of the Coroners Act 1988:

> 30. A coroner shall continue to have jurisdiction—
> (a) to inquire into any treasure which is found in his district; and
> (b) to inquire who were, or are suspected of being, the finders
> and the provisions of this Act shall, so far as applicable, apply to every such inquest.

By s 9(2) of the Treasure Act, the coroner must take reasonable steps to notify the following of the date, time, and place of the inquest:

- the British Museum or the National Museum of Wales, as appropriate;
- the person who found the treasure;
- the occupier of the land on which the objects were found;
- any other person identified to him by the finder or occupier as interested persons[19] which will include the owner of the land, if different to the occupier.

The revised Code requests that the coroner also informs the local museum and any franchisee under the Crown[20] of the place and date of inquest.

The coroner will have obtained an expert opinion on the objects from the museum or archaeological service concerned. The coroner might also wish to hear oral evidence as to the circumstances of the find although the exact location should remain undisclosed in open court.

Although not specifically set out in the statute, taking into account the definition of treasure and the other requirements of the Act, the purpose of the inquest is to determine (upon the balance of probabilities):[21]

- whether or not the find is treasure;
- who the finder is;
- where the object was found;
- when it was found.

It is not the function of the coroner to decide issues such as landownership, trespass, entitlement to the find or to any reward.

If the find comes within s 1(1)(c) of the Act (an object which if found prior to 24 September 1997 would have been treasure trove) the coroner will also need to determine:

---

[19] The coroner is obliged to make this inquiry of the finder and occupier under s 9(5) of the Act, by s 9(7) 'interested person' includes any person having an interest in the land and will thus include the owner of the land who leases or rents it to the occupier.

[20] Generally the Duchy of Lancaster, the Duchy of Cornwall, and the Corporation of London. The City of Bristol may also hold a treasure trove franchise.

[21] Home Office Circular 44/1977: paras 21 and 29.

- whether the find is made substantially of silver or gold;
- whether it has been hidden from ancient times with the intention of later recovery.

By s 9(6) of the Act the coroner must take reasonable steps to give any interested person an opportunity to examine witnesses at the inquest. However, the revised Code (paragraph 58) indicates that where all parties have indicated that they do not wish to attend the inquest it is sufficient, at the coroner's discretion, to proceed using written evidence only. The recommendation to keep the exact location of the find confidential still applies.

Procedure if the Find is Declared Treasure   12.11

Should the coroner find (on the balance of probabilities) that the objects are within the definition of treasure, arrangements will be made for the item to be delivered to the national museum so that it can be valued by the Treasure Valuation Committee.[22]

The national and local museum, the finder, landowner, occupier, and any Crown franchisee should be informed of the outcome, if not present or represented at the inquest.

The coroner's decision to declare the items treasure can, of course, be subject to judicial review by an aggrieved party.[23]

The objects will be dealt with in accordance with the Code, that is to say they will be offered first to the national museum and thereafter to local museums.

The finder will normally be entitled to a reward equivalent to the full market value of the item although this may be subject to a pre-existing agreement with the landowner to divide any reward.[24] The Secretary of State has power to abate all or some of a reward in certain circumstances set out within the Code. These include:

- if the finder was trespassing;
- the find was not declared at the proper time;
- the full facts were not declared or only part of a find was handed in.

The revised Code indicates that the coroner should keep records of treasure inquests in a standard format.

---

[22] The Committee is drawn from independent experts in the trade to give a valuation on the open market. The Treasure Registrar indicates that coroners sometimes request this information before the inquest but the valuation does not take place until after the hearing.

[23] See section 10.06 *et seq.*

[24] The normal arrangement is for the landowner and the finder to split the reward equally, see para 72 of the Code.

12.12 Speed of Handling Cases

The Code sets out various target times for handling treasure cases:

- where inquest held:
  - from receipt by the coroner or designated museum to payment of ex gratia reward **12 months**
  - from agreement of the valuation by interested parties to payment of the reward **3 months**
- where find is disclaimed before inquest held:
  - from receipt to notification of return[25] **6 months**

Summary

- The Treasure Act 1996 defines treasure in relation to objects found after 24 September 1997.
- Failure to report the finding of treasure is now a criminal offence.
- If an object is not thought to be treasure it will normally be returned to the finder without the necessity for an inquest.
- Even if the find is thought to be treasure, it will normally be returned to the finder without the necessity for an inquest if neither local nor national museums wish to acquire it.
- If the coroner declares the find to be treasure, a reward will normally be paid equivalent to the market value as assessed by an independent committee.

---

[25] The occupier and landowner (if different) should be given 28 days' notice of the intention to return the object.

APPENDIX 1

1997 OPCS Guidance on Referral

1 July 1997

Dear Doctor,

Completion of the medical certificate of cause of death

Prompt and accurate certification of death is essential. It provides legal evidence of the fact and the cause(s) of death, thus enabling the death to be formally registered: the family can then make arrangements for disposal of the body. Death certification also provides the raw data from which all mortality statistics are derived. These are vital for public health surveillance, for resource allocation in the NHS, and for a wide range of research - and thus ultimately for improving the health of the population.

About three-quarters of the 580,000 deaths in England and Wales each year are certified by a doctor, and the remainder by a coroner[1].

The role of the doctor

If you are the attending doctor during the last illness of a person who dies, you have a statutory duty[2] to issue a medical certificate of the cause of death (death certificate). Conversely, if you did not attend the deceased during his or her last illness, you *must not* complete the death certificate.

You must state the cause(s) of death on the certificate to the best of your knowledge and belief. You have a duty to deliver the death certificate to the registrar of births and deaths: in practice, the certificate is often given to a relative of the deceased, then handed to the registrar by the relative (or other informant) who visits the register office to have the death registered.

The role of the registrar of births and deaths

The registrar has a statutory duty[3] to transcribe the cause(s) of death from the death certificate to the official register, nowadays usually a computer database, and to send this information to the Office for National Statistics (previously the Office of Population Censuses and Surveys). It is then coded automatically[4] and incorporated into national mortality statistics. The registrar must also obtain other information from the person who comes to register the death, such as the occupation and place of birth of the deceased. Finally, the registrar has a legal obligation to refer certain deaths to the coroner (see below).

The role of the coroner

The coroner is an independent judicial officer of the Crown who has a statutory duty[5] to investigate the circumstances of certain categories of death for the protection of the public. Thus: *"Where a coroner is informed that the body of a person ('the deceased') is lying within his district and there is reasonable cause to suspect that the deceased (a) has died a violent or an unnatural death; (b) has died a sudden death of which the cause is unknown; (c) has died in prison or in such a place or in such circumstances as to require an inquest under any other Act, then ... the coroner shall as soon as practicable hold an inquest into the death of the deceased ...".*

In fact, the coroner only holds an inquest for some 12% of the deaths he certifies. Coroners often use their discretion[6] to decide that a post-mortem alone provides sufficient evidence of the cause of a sudden death: diseases of the circulatory system account for three-quarters of these deaths[7]. Deaths from accident, poisoning, violence or in prison or police custody are subject to inquest. When the coroner does hold an inquest, he will issue a verdict on the manner of death (eg accident, suicide) as well as certifying the cause(s) of death.

Referral to the coroner

Of the 180,000 or so deaths reported to a coroner each year, 60% are voluntarily referred by a doctor, 2% by a registrar, and the remaining 38% from other sources, mainly the police[1].

Legal aspects

As the law currently stands, there is no statutory obligation for a doctor to report any death to a coroner. The common law duty[8] that requires any person to inform the coroner of circumstances requiring an inquest cannot be enforced by legal sanction. Nevertheless, we encourage you to report all relevant deaths to the coroner. This letter is intended to help you decide whether any given death is reportable.

Referral by the registrar of births and deaths

First, it may help you to know that the registrar is legally obliged[9] to refer a death to the coroner (unless it has already been reported) if it falls, *or appears from the doctor's death certificate to fall*, into one of the following categories:

- the deceased was not attended during his or her last illness by a doctor;
- the registrar has been unable to obtain a duly completed death certificate, or else it appears that the deceased was not seen by the certifying doctor *either* after death *or* during the 14 days before death;
- the cause of death appears to be unknown;
- the registrar has reason to believe the death was unnatural, or caused by violence or neglect, or by abortion, or was in any way suspicious;
- the death appears to have occurred during an operation or before recovery from the effect of an anaesthetic;
- the death certificate suggests that death was due to industrial disease or industrial poisoning.

Referral by the doctor

We would like to encourage the prevailing practice of voluntary referral to a coroner by the certifying doctor. If you judge that the coroner will need to be involved (see Box 1), you can reduce delay in registration of the death by prompt referral. This will also give you an opportunity to explain to the relatives in person the reasons for referral. If you

Box 1

A death should be referred to the coroner if:

- the cause of death is unknown

- the deceased was not seen by the certifying doctor either after death or within the 14 days before death

- the death was violent or unnatural or suspicious

- the death may be due to an accident (whenever it occurred)

- the death may be due to self-neglect or neglect by others

- the death may be due to an industrial disease or related to the deceased's employment

- the death may be due to an abortion

- the death occurred during an operation or before recovery from the effects of an anaesthetic

- the death may be a suicide

- the death occurred during or shortly after detention in police or prison custody.

---

are in doubt about whether to refer a death, contact the relevant coroner's office for advice. When referring a death to the coroner, you should still complete a death certificate unless the coroner advises you not to do so, and indicate on the certificate that you have referred the death.

You should complete the death certificate as accurately as possible. This will reduce the need for referral to the coroner by the registrar, and it will greatly improve the quality of mortality statistics. In particular, you should:

- *avoid* the use of abbreviations, question marks and vague terms such as 'probably';

- *avoid* giving 'old age' or 'senility' as the only cause of death: do so *only* if you cannot give a more specific cause of death *and* the deceased was aged 70 or over;

- *avoid* giving a mode of dying (see Box 2) such as 'heart failure', 'shock' or 'uraemia' unless you also give the underlying causal sequence; *do not* give a mode of dying as the *only* cause on the death certificate.

Box 2

Statements which imply a mode of dying rather than an underlying cause of death:	
Asphyxia	Hepatorenal failure
Asthenia	Kidney failure
Brain failure	Liver failure
Cachexia	Renal failure
Cardiac arrest	Respiratory arrest
Cardiac failure	Shock
Coma	Syncope
Debility	Uraemia
Exhaustion	Vagal inhibition
Heart failure	Vasovagal attack
Hepatic failure	Ventricular failure

The use of the qualification 'acute' or 'chronic' will *not* make these terms acceptable as the sole cause of death.

Registrars may refer a death certified in such terms to the coroner. This will delay registration of the death and may well cause distress to the relatives.

AIDS-related death

There has been publicity[10] about one coroner's view that *"death from AIDS, as a direct consequence of anal intercourse, is - on the balance of probability - 'unnatural', according to the current values of our society, and is proper to put to a jury"*. The phrase 'unnatural death' is not defined by statute, but it has been the subject of a ruling by the Court of Appeal[11]. We have received legal advice, based in part on this ruling, that a death from AIDS should normally be viewed as a death from natural causes. **Therefore, unless there are other grounds for referral to the coroner, a death from AIDS or in an HIV-positive individual** *should not* **normally be referred to the coroner.**

Training video and pocket guidelines

The Office for National Statistics has issued *Death Counts*, a video designed to assist hospital doctors and general practitioners in completing the death certificate. The pack includes pocket guidelines on death certification and referral to the coroner, and test cases that are suitable for individual study or group teaching. An order form is printed overleaf.

Improving the death certificate

Death certificate booklets have been re-issued with fresh guidance (and examples) on how to complete a medical certificate of cause of death.

Yours sincerely,

Professor Michel P Coleman
Deputy Chief Medical Statistician

References

1 Ashley J. & Devis T. Death certification from the point of view of the epidemiologist. *Pop Trends* 1992; 67: 22-28
2 Births and Deaths Registration Act 1953, section 22(1)
3 Births and Deaths Registration Act 1953, section 15
4 Birch D. Automatic coding of causes of death. *Pop Trends* 1993; 73: 1-3
5 Coroners Act 1988, section 8(1)
6 Coroners Act 1988, section 19
7 OPCS. Mortality statistics 1992: England and Wales. Series DH1 no. 27. London, HMSO, 1994, p27
8 R v Clerk, 1702
9 Registration of Births and Deaths Regulations 1987 (Statutory Instrument no. 2088), regulation 41
10 Anon. HIV deaths 'violent and unnatural'. BMA News Review (GP edition), 21 February 1996, p22
11 R v Poplar Coroner *ex parte* Thomas, 1993, QB610

Further copies of this letter may be obtained from:

Pat Hisley
Office for National Statistics, Room C201
Smedley Hydro
Trafalgar Road
Southport   PR8 2HH
　　　(*ONS guidance 1/7/96, revised 1/7/97*)

APPENDIX 2

The *Jamieson* Case

EXTRACT FROM THE JUDGMENT OF BINGHAM LJ

General Conclusions

This long survey of the relevant statutory and judicial authority permits certain conclusions to be stated.

1. An inquest is a fact-finding inquiry conducted by a coroner, with or without a jury, to establish reliable answers to four important but limited factual questions. The first of these relates to the identity of the deceased, the second to the place of his death, the third to the time of death. In most cases these questions are not hard to answer but in a minority of cases the answer may be problematical. The fourth question, and that to which the evidence and inquiry are most often and most closely directed, relates to how the deceased came by his death. Rule 36 requires that the proceedings and evidence shall be directed solely to ascertaining these matters and forbids any expression of opinion on any other matters.

2. Both in section 11(5)(b)(ii) of the 1988 Act and in Rule 36(1)(b) of the 1984 Rules, 'how' is to be understood as meaning 'by what means'. It is noteworthy that the task is not to ascertain how the deceased died, which might raise general and far reaching issues, but 'how the deceased came by his death', a more limited question directed to the means by which the deceased came by his death.

3. It is not the function of a coroner or his jury to determine, or appear to determine, any question of criminal or civil liability, to apportion guilt or attribute blame. This principle is expressed in Rule 42 of the 1984 Rules. The rule does, however, treat criminal and civil liability differently: whereas a verdict must not be framed so as to appear to determine any question of criminal liability on the part of a named person, thereby legitimating a verdict of unlawful killing provided no one is named, the prohibition on returning a verdict so as to appear to determine any question of civil liability is unqualified, applying whether anyone is named or not.

4. This prohibition in the Rules is fortified by considerations of fairness. Our law accords a defendant accused of crime or a party alleged to have committed a civil wrong certain safeguards rightly regarded as essential to the fairness of the proceedings, among them a clear statement in writing of the alleged wrongdoing, a right to call any relevant and admissible evidence and a right to address factual submissions to the tribunal of fact. These rights are not granted, and the last is expressly denied by the Rules, to a party whose conduct may be impugned by evidence given at an inquest.

5. It may be accepted that in case of conflict the statutory duty to ascertain how the deceased came by his death must prevail over the prohibition in rule 42. But the scope

for conflict is small. Rule 42 applies, and applies only, to the verdict. Plainly the coroner and the jury may explore facts bearing on criminal and civil liability. But the verdict may not appear to determine any question of criminal liability on the part of a named person nor any question of civil liability.

6. There can be no objection to a verdict which incorporates a brief, neutral, factual statement: 'the deceased was drowned when his sailing dinghy capsized in heavy seas', 'the deceased was killed when his car was run down by an express train on a level crossing', 'the deceased died from crush injuries sustained when gates were opened at Hillsborough Stadium'. But such verdict must be factual, expressing no judgement or opinion, and it is not the jury's function to prepare detailed factual statements.

7. Cases arise, usually involving the old, the infirm and the senile, where the deceased contributes to his or her own death by a gross failure to take adequate nourishment or liquid, or to obtain basic medical attention, or to obtain adequate shelter or heating. In such a case it may be factually accurate and helpfully descriptive to state that self-neglect aggravated, or preferably contributed to, the primary cause of death. Rarely, if ever, can it be factually accurate or helpfully descriptive to regard self-neglect as the primary cause of death (that is, in the language of the cases, to adopt it as a free-standing verdict).

8. Much of the difficulty to which verdicts of lack of care have given rise appears to be due to an almost inevitable confusion between this expression and the lack of care which is the foundation for a successful claim in common law negligence. Since many of those seeking that verdict do so as a stepping-stone towards such a claim the boundary is bound to become blurred. But lack of care in the context of an inquest has been correctly described as the obverse of self-neglect. It is to be hoped that in future the expression 'lack of care' may for practical purposes be deleted from the lexicon of inquests and replaced by 'neglect'.

9. Neglect in this context means a gross failure to provide adequate nourishment or liquid, or provide or procure basic medical attention or shelter or warmth for someone in a dependent position (because of youth, age, illness, or incarceration) who cannot provide it for himself. Failure to provide medical attention for a dependent person whose physical condition is such as to show that he obviously needs it may amount to neglect.

So it may be if it is the dependent person's mental condition which obviously calls for medical attention (as it would, for example, if a mental nurse observed that a patient had a propensity to swallow razor blades and failed to report this propensity to a doctor, in a case where the patient had no intention to cause himself injury but did thereafter swallow razor blades with fatal results).

In both cases the crucial consideration will be what the dependent person's condition, whether physical or mental, appeared to be.

10. As in the case of self-neglect, neglect can rarely, if ever, be an appropriate verdict on its own. It is difficult to think of facts on which there would not be a primary verdict other than neglect. But the notes to form 22 in the 1984 Rules, although themselves of no binding force, are correct to recognize that neglect may contribute to a death from natural causes, industrial disease, or drug abuse. Want of attention at birth, also mentioned in the notes, may itself be regarded as a form of neglect. A verdict that, for instance, 'the deceased died from natural causes [or industrial disease, or drug abuse] to which neglect contributed' would seem perhaps more apt than a verdict that 'the deceased died from natural causes [or industrial disease, or drug abuse] aggravated by neglect', since 'aggravated' in this context means 'made worse', and in truth the neglect probably did not make the fatal condition worse but sacrificed the opportunity to halt or cure it.

11. Where it is established that the deceased took his own life, that must be the verdict. On such facts, as the applicant in the present case accepted, there is no room for a verdict of neglect (or, as he would have put it, lack of care). It is also inappropriate in such a case, as the applicant also accepted, to describe that cause of death as aggravated by neglect (or lack of care). On certain facts it could possibly be correct to hold that neglect contributed to that cause of death, but this finding would not be justified simply on the grounds that the deceased was afforded an opportunity to take his own life even if it was careless (as that expression is used in common speech or in the law of negligence) to afford the deceased that opportunity. Such a finding would only be appropriate in a case where gross neglect was directly connected with the deceased's suicide (for example, if a prison warder observed a prisoner in his cell preparing to hang a noose around his neck, but passed on without any attempt to intervene).

12. Neither neglect nor self-neglect should ever form any part of any verdict unless a clear and direct causal connection is established between the conduct so described and the cause of death.

13. It is for the coroner alone to make reports with a view to preventing the recurrence of a fatality. The is the effect of Rules 36(2) and 43.

14. It is the duty of the coroner as the public official responsible for the conduct of inquests, whether he is sitting with a jury or without, to ensure that the relevant facts are fully, fairly and fearlessly investigated. He is bound to recognize the acute public concern rightly aroused where deaths occur in custody. He must ensure that the relevant facts are exposed to public scrutiny, particularly if there is evidence of foul play, abuse, or inhumanity. He fails in his duty if his investigation is superficial, slipshod or perfunctory. But the responsibility is his. He must set the bounds of the inquiry. He must rule on the procedure to be followed, His decisions, like those of any other judicial officer, must be respected unless and until they are varied or overruled.

APPENDIX 3

Review of post-*Jamieson* cases

Set out below are the main points from the post-*Jamieson* cases on individual neglect. System neglect is dealt with at section 9.30 *et seq* where *Middleton, Amin*, and *Sacker* are discussed, but there is inevitably some crossover.

Cotton (February 1995)[1]

This case centred on the appropriateness of a decision to move a patient from intensive care into an ordinary ward, whilst on a particular drug. The court held that a gross failure to provide basic medical attention was entirely different from an incorrect clinical judgement.

Two examples were given of where neglect might genuinely be established: a sick patient arriving at the hospital car park and just being left there, or a surgeon leaving a patient in the middle of an operation to go for a round of golf. It was said that the conduct of the hospital staff here was not comparable, being solely a matter of clinical judgement. This, especially where professional opinions differed, was really a matter of negligence and not for the coroner's court.

The decision, and the examples given, are not a reflection of how subsequent case law developed.

Tremble (July 1995)[2]

The deceased was in prison, an officer was informed he was going to kill himself and, despite seeing him standing on the toilet, thought the deceased was not at risk.

It was held that failure to guard against a gesture which had the possibility of going wrong did not amount to neglect. This was not a question of providing medical attention (since he needed none), nor a case of providing something for a person who could not provide it for himself. The court reaffirmed that the crucial consideration will be what the person's condition appeared to be.

Wright (June 1996)[3]

The death occurred after a minor operation, apparently due to an obstruction of the airway whilst anaesthetized. The deceased had been left unattended for a short time in the recovery area and a monitor was said to have failed.

---

[1] *R v Birmingham Coroner ex p Cotton* (1995) 160 JP 123.
[2] *R v South Yorkshire Coroner ex p Tremble* (1995) 159 JP 76.
[3] *R v Surrey Coroner ex p Wright* [1997] 2 WLR 16.

The court emphasized the need for the neglect to be continuous, or at least non-transient, and held that the 'negligent lack of care' alleged in this case did not amount to *Jamieson* neglect.

Broadly consistent with *Cotton*, it can be argued this case has also been overtaken by later decisions. Nonetheless, the requirement that neglect be more than a single isolated mistake was an important marker.

Clegg (December 1996)[4]

A young woman admitted to hospital after an aspirin overdose was not given proper treatment, despite showing the features of severe poisoning. The court held that failure to provide *appropriate* medical attention to a dependent patient in hospital is capable of constituting neglect.

At first sight this appears at total variance with the earlier decisions, there is obviously considerable difference between a 'failure to provide appropriate medical attention' and 'a gross failure to provide basic medical attention'. This may not necessarily mean that the court was intending mere incorrect clinical judgement should amount to neglect,[5] the decision must be interpreted in the exceptional context of that case. It had been accepted that the deceased was 'assessed incorrectly, investigated and monitored inadequately and treated poorly' and that there was a complete failure at every stage to appreciate the importance of the (known) overdose. The apparent inconsistency is easily resolved if the phraseology in Clegg is taken to mean that the court found that there had been a complete breakdown in treatment rather than an incorrect clinical judgement.

Douglas-Williams (July 1998)[6]

Neglect was not the appropriate verdict where the timescale between the deceased first showing signs of distress and his becoming beyond assistance was extremely short (in this case a matter of minutes), as there was no opportunity to provide medical attention. This underlines the need for neglect to be 'non-transient'.

Tristram (October 1999)[7]

The deceased was arrested for being drunk and incapable, he was described as hopelessly drunk. Only a brief and perfunctory search was made. He was examined by a police surgeon but was found fit to be detained. Subsequently a printout from the Police National Computer (PNC) showed markers for 'suicidal' and 'drugs' but this was not followed up. He was subject to routine visits but eight hours later was found dead. The cause of death was multiple drug toxicity.

The court held that it was appropriate to leave neglect to the jury for five reasons:

- The failure to search properly was a breach of the Police and Criminal Evidence Act 1984. In the circumstances the jury would be entitled to characterize this failure as gross.

---

[4] *R v HM Coroner for Wiltshire ex p Clegg* (1996) 161 JP 521. The facts of this case are set out in some detail at section 3.07.

[5] *Jervis on Coroners* (4th supplement to 11th edition) at para 13-36 took the contrary view and suggested that the court in *ex p Clegg* may not have had a report of *ex p Cotton*.

[6] *R v Inner London Coroner (South District) ex p Douglas-Williams* [1999] 1 All ER 344.

[7] *R v HM Coroner for Swansea and Gower ex p Tristram* (2000) 164 JP 191.

- A proper search would have shown medicine bottles, making it obvious that a significant amount of tablets prescribed only that day had gone. Any failure to rush the deceased to hospital at that stage could be characterized as gross.
- When the police surgeon examined the deceased, he had been suffering from multiple drug poisoning. The jury would be entitled to conclude that his failure to detect this by observation or tests was gross.
- The jury were entitled to take the view that failure to act on the PNC printout was gross as it contained information highly relevant to the deceased's condition.
- Throughout the night the deceased had been slowly succumbing to the effects of a fatal drug overdose. Neither police nor the doctor had procured any effective medical treatment for him. The jury were entitled to conclude this was a gross failure of the kind described in *Jamieson*.

The court also found that the coroner's direction to the jury on neglect was erroneous as it referred to a test of whether the police and doctor took reasonable care of the deceased.

This was another case following the *Clegg* line, but goes further and starts to suggest that manifestly incorrect judgement is capable of amounting to neglect. It appears that in examining what the deceased's condition appeared to be, the court was applying an objective test, in other words it was sufficient that those involved *should* have realized he needed attention.

Chief Constable of Staffordshire (July 2000)[8]

The deceased was an alcoholic in police custody. Unknown to anyone he had a history of fits and also had undiagnosed tumours within the brain. His family had contacted the police to explain he might have 'the shakes' but this was not recorded. Next morning there was an episode where he was shaking so badly that he spilled two drinks and was given the third in a container with a lid and a straw. Unaware of the conversation with the family, the custody officer did not conclude the deceased to be ill. An hour later he was placed in the exercise yard with other prisoners who described him as shaking and supporting himself against a wall. He was then left alone for a period during which he fell, apparently due to a fit, and fractured his skull. The jury found that he sustained a head injury from an unrestrained fall in the yard, caused by an epileptic-type fit. Their conclusion was 'accidental death aggravated by neglect'. The police sought judicial review.

The court held that given the information imparted as to the possibility of him suffering the shakes, and his appearance during the tea-spilling episode, there was material upon which a jury could conclude that the deceased ought not to have been left unsupervised in the exercise yard.

On causation, the court found that the 'touchstone' in the present context was the opportunity of rendering care, in the narrow sense that would have prevented the death (also described as the opportunity of doing something effective[9]). There existed circumstances where, if certain steps had been taken, it was at least possible that the death would not have occurred. This established a clear and direct causal connection between the conduct of the police and the death.

Again this amounts to an objective test of the apparent need for medical attention or care—it was not suggested that the police knew that the deceased was at risk, merely that they should have known, or that the risk was there to be appreciated.

---

[8] *R v HM Coroner for Coventry ex p Chief Constable of Staffordshire Police* (2000) 164 JP 665.
[9] See the *Khan* case below.

Scott (February 2001)[10]

The deceased was remanded to prison. Warnings about his mental state, including efforts at self-harm that day, were given from two official sources and his (long) shoelaces had been removed at court. On arrival at the prison he was seen by a doctor for 5–7 minutes. The prison was said to have a substantial amount of knowledge about the deceased's condition but he was placed in a single cell, his laces were returned, and there was no direction for special observations. Subsequently he was found hanging by his laces.

At review, the Prison Service submitted that the medical staff had applied their minds to the prisoner's condition and concluded that he did not appear to be at risk of suicide. It was claimed that reaching a reasonable but erroneous conclusion was very different from *Jamieson* neglect.

The court held that the known facts of mental illness, intent to commit suicide together with actual self-harm, the return of the laces and lack of special observations were sufficient for neglect to go to the jury. There was evidence of a gross failure to provide medical attention when the mental state of the deceased obviously called for such attention.
The court also considered more general matters:

- neglect need not be the sole or predominant cause of death;
- the decision in *Jamieson* was not to be treated as if a statutory enactment, it was part of continually evolving judicial interpretation but did represent a valuable distillation of the case law;
- the view formed by the medical staff (that he was not at imminent risk) was relevant but that of itself did not rule out neglect;
- the court noted that there had been a number of cases where there had been medical attention but where neglect remained a possible verdict;
- omissions on the part of medical practitioners are capable of forming part of the total picture which amounts to neglect.

On causation, the court described the deceased as so mentally ill that he was dependent upon the authorities to care for him and prevent self-harm. In such a case the failure of the authorities to take necessary steps to prevent suicide could be seen as having a direct causal link with the death. This was to be contrasted with the circumstances of the death in *Jamieson* (found not to be neglect).

Touche (March 2001)[11]

This case was primarily concerned with the meaning of 'unnatural' in terms of jurisdiction to hold an inquest. The circumstances are set out, with a discussion of the case, in section 2.20. Nonetheless, there is some relevance to the criteria for neglect as the Court of Appeal suggested that the facts were more than sufficient for a coroner to consider whether the failures amounted to *Jamieson* neglect.

Thus a failure to undertake routine observations and monitoring for a significant time at a recognized critical period (in this case immediately after a caesarean section with spinal anaesthesia) might amount to a gross failure. However, this would not necessarily encompass every omission to monitor where it might arguably have been better to do so, the circumstances here were described as 'astonishing' with the neglect 'starkly apparent'. It

[10] *R (application of Scott) v HM Coroner for Inner West London* 61 BMLR 222.
[11] *R v HM Coroner for Inner London North ex p Touche* [2001] All ER 752.

was claimed that all NHS hospitals routinely monitored such a patient, whereas in this case a private hospital had failed to do so.

Dawson (April 2001)[12]

Following a death in police custody the jury returned a verdict of unlawful killing. At review it was contended that the coroner should also have left 'neglect' to the jury. The court held that the coroner was correct to exercise his discretion (see section 8.33) and not leave every conceivable verdict. There would have been a danger of confusing the jury, particularly on the differences between neglect and unlawful killing.

The court also commented that they did not see any differences in causation between *Jamieson* (clear and direct causal connection) and the general approach in cases of manslaughter by gross negligence (significant contribution—see section 9.37.2). They noted however that other judges apparently took a different view. Nor could the court see the logic in a suggestion that omissions constituting neglect must last for a longer period than omissions constituting gross negligence. The comments on causation in this case were enlarged upon in *Khan* (below).

Marshall (October 2001)[13]

The deceased was arrested by police. It was thought he may have swallowed a quantity of drugs hidden in his mouth. He denied this repeatedly. At the police station immediate arrangements were made for a doctor to attend promptly but the custody officer did not call an ambulance or seek medical advice over the phone. Shortly after, the prisoner admitted swallowing eight grams of crack cocaine and then started to fit. It was agreed that there was little prospect of survival from that point. He died in hospital.

Although neglect was left to the jury it was not returned. The family sought review on the basis of a misdirection to the jury. The application failed but the court said that the jury should have been told that neglect may arise from a serious underestimation of a dependent person's condition. Nonetheless, the coroner correctly made it clear that a mistake could be, but was not necessarily, a gross failure. It might have been better if the coroner had directed the jury to ask whether it was obvious on the facts known to the custody officer that immediate medical attention was required, and if so whether the failure to arrange it was gross.

Nicholls (November 2001)[14]

The deceased was in police custody. When arrested he had been seen to put a bag in his mouth and swallow the contents. This was related to the custody officer but there was disagreement as to whether a police surgeon who saw him was told. He was examined for 25 minutes and denied he had taken drugs that day. He was considered fit to be detained despite signs of opiate intoxication and would be reviewed next morning. He died five hours later from a fatal overdose of heroin. The coroner did not leave neglect for the jury who recorded misadventure. The family sought judicial review.

The court held that there was no precise dividing line between a gross failure to provide basic medical attention and a failure to provide medical attention. The difference is bound

---

[12] *R v HM Coroner for East Riding and Kingston Upon Hull ex p Dawson* [2001] ACD 68.
[13] *R (application of Marshall) v HM Coroner for Coventry* [2001] EWHC Admin 804.
[14] *R (application of Nicholls) v HM Coroner for City of Liverpool* (2002) ACD 89.

to be one of degree, highly dependent on the facts of the particular case. An expert had suggested that 'any doctor acting to a reasonable standard' would have checked the prisoner's respiratory rate after an hour. The court commented that it would regard undertaking or arranging for such checks as capable of falling within the provision of basic medical attention, being neither complex nor sophisticated steps. Another expert had disagreed that such checks were an obvious necessity. The court held that this professional difference was no reason to withhold neglect from the jury, a significant change from Cotton (above).

On causation, it was said that it was important not to read the words in *Jamieson* as if contained in an enactment or to apply them in an over literal manner. It will be a common feature of cases where the neglect alleged is a failure to examine the patient that it will not be possible to know precisely what would have been found had there been an examination. There was no complex chain of events, the court was dealing with the consequences of failing to make a simple check.

This case further narrows the dividing line between neglect and a negligent error of medical judgment. It does not actually infer a test of 'what a doctor acting to a reasonable standard doctor would have done', although comes close to doing so. Nonetheless, this is restricted to basic issues such as reassessing a patient rather than a failure to carry out complex and sophisticated medical procedures.

Khan (March 2002)[15]

The deceased resisted arrested and was noticed to have packages in his mouth which he refused to spit out. As the struggle continued there were indications that a package had burst. At that point an ambulance was called, this was about 8–10 minutes after the start of the incident. The ambulance staff found no signs of life, the cause of death was morphine intoxication. The coroner refused to leave neglect to the jury.

The court reviewed *Jamieson* and the more recent authorities. It was accepted that the question was not whether the neglect was the only cause of death but whether the conduct made a material contribution to the death. But it was still necessary to establish causation on the balance of probabilities, it was not sufficient to say that there was a possibility (or a real possibility) that the deceased's life would be saved by the attention. Causation could be established without showing that the deceased would have survived but only by showing in the alternative that death, although inevitable, was hastened by the conduct in question. Causation cannot be established simply by showing that there was an opportunity to render care, it must be shown to the appropriate standard that care would have been rendered and that it would have saved or prolonged life. Referring to the *Staffordshire* case, the language of doing something effective meant an opportunity of doing something that would probably have been effective.

On the facts, the court held that there was no evidence upon which a reasonable jury could find a sufficient level of fault to justify a verdict of neglect. Any suggestion that an ambulance should be called whenever a suspected drug dealer was known to have packages in his mouth but would not spit them out was 'offending against common sense'. The point at which an ambulance was needed was when the package was believed to have split.

This case gives a very clear decision in terms of causation and is a helpful interpretation of several earlier cases. In short, the inquest must be satisfied on the balance of probabilities that the deceased's life would have been saved or prolonged but for the neglect.

---

[15] *R (application of Khan) v HM Coroner for West Hertfordshire* [2002] EWHC 302 Admin.

Lambourne (July 2002)[16]

The deceased was a young female prisoner with a history of self-harm and disruption. She was on an F2052SH regime and subject to a ten minute watch. She was discovered with a ligature around her neck, this was thought to be a more serious effort at suicide than previous incidents. The doctor examined her and put her on a 15 minute watch with strict conditions. When he saw her the next day it was noted that the risk of self-harm remained high. Later that afternoon a prison officer, apparently unaware of the watch, moved the deceased to another wing. The receiving prison officer ended the 15 minute watch, it remaining unclear how much he knew of the immediate history. The following morning the deceased was found hanging. The coroner refused to leave neglect.

At review the court found insufficiency of inquiry concerning the receiving officer's decision to lift the watch. The court referred to five unanswered questions concerning the apparent failure(s) of the system, primarily on the transfer of information and procedures on stopping the special watch. But it was held that there was sufficient causal connection between the positive act of lifting the watch and the death to justify the issue of neglect being left to the jury.

As the court quashed the inquisition both for insufficiency and for the coroner's refusal to leave neglect 'in either of the ways open', it seems that both *Jamieson* and system neglect were under consideration.

Mumford (October 2002)[17]

The deceased was remanded in custody, he tried to harm himself at court. An F2052SH self-harm form was opened. At the Young Offenders Institute he was seen by a doctor, it was accepted that the findings of this examination were appropriate. The prisoner gave answers that his earlier conduct had been impetuous and that he wanted to sort his life out. In consultation with staff, the doctor removed the deceased's shoelaces but agreed to his request for a single cell and only ordered routine observations. Late in the evening the deceased asked to see a doctor and was told he would have to await the morning, a few minutes later he was found hanging.

It was argued that the cumulative effect of all that was known about the prisoner amounted to system neglect. He should not have been placed in a normal cell and there should have been a system in place to record him as actively suicidal, despite the doctor's subjective findings. The court rejected this saying there was insufficient evidence to leave system neglect for the jury, all that was before the jury was a series of errors, none major, which fell short of *Middleton* system neglect. Had the doctor failed to consider the issues, or posed himself the wrong questions, had the shoelaces not been removed or the intermittent checks been carelessly distanced, the decision might have been different. In the context of this case, the refusal to call a doctor until morning did not amount to neglect.

This is primarily a useful case on system neglect, but some of the judgment also seems relevant to *Jamieson* neglect which, arguably, requires a higher standard of failing than system neglect.

---

[16] *Lambourne v HM Deputy Coroner for Avon* [2002] EWHC Admin 1877.
[17] *R (application of Mumford) v HM Coroner for Reading* [2002] EWHC Admin 2184.

Davies (February 2003)[18]

The deceased was in prison. On admission he was seen by a doctor and prescribed drug detoxification treatment. Due to a mix-up and subsequent change of wing he only received the first dose, no follow up was made. A day or so later (Saturday) he became sick and was told to see the nurse next day. He was worse on the Sunday and was seen by a nurse that night, who told him to attend for treatment the following morning. On the Monday morning he fell from his bed and had to be lifted back on by two officers. It was thought his symptoms were due to drug withdrawal. He was found collapsed about an hour later and died. The cause of death was dehydration consistent with severe diarrhoea and vomiting. The coroner left *Jamieson* neglect to the jury but a verdict of accidental death was returned. The family sought judicial review based on alleged misdirections in the summing-up.

The court held that the *Amin* and *Middleton* cases in the Court of Appeal had not intended to qualify the rigours of the *Jamieson* test in relation to the acts or omissions of an individual. However, a gross failure in accordance with the *Jamieson* test may be found even where an individual has purported to make a clinical decision or diagnosis. Gross failures are not limited to those cases where an individual has failed to take any action at all. The nurse's failure to seek medical assistance was at least capable of constituting neglect even though she exercised her judgement that it was unnecessary. It was wrong to suggest that because the nurse did 'something' that neglect could not be found.

The court also criticized the deputy coroner's reference to the rarity of neglect verdicts[19] saying that to comment on the rarity did not assist in defining neglect to the jury. Nonetheless, the court declined to quash the inquest as it was difficult to see what could be gained, there had been a full inquiry, and recommendations as to improvements in the system had been made.

Metropolitan Police Commissioner (Scott Robbins) (June 2003)[20]

The deceased was held in a police cell over the weekend to be taken back to Cornwall where a warrant was outstanding. He had no history of self-harm whilst in custody but accepted that he taken an overdose five years before. As a result of revealing this he was seen by a doctor who found that there was no continuing risk. No recommendation for special watch or removal of laces etc was made. The deceased was later seen by another doctor for a physical ailment, again no concerns were raised. There had been no indication to the custody staff of depression but the deceased was subsequently found hanging in his cell.

The inquest jury returned a verdict that the deceased had killed himself, contributed to by system neglect. The police sought judicial review.

The court accepted a submission that *Jamieson* formulated three requirements:

- There must be a basis for finding that the deceased's condition was known, or should have been known, to be such that action was necessary.

---

[18] *R (application of Davies) v HM Deputy Coroner for Birmingham* [2003] EWHC 618 Admin.

[19] Apparently quoting from the first edition of this text that 'such cases will be very few and far between'. That was probably true in 1997 when *Jamieson* was to be construed by *Cotton* and *Wright* but the same comment is not to be found in this edition.

[20] *R (application of Commissioner of Police for the Metropolis) v HM Coroner for Southern District of Greater London* [2003] EWHC 1829 Admin.

- There must be a basis for finding that the fact action was not taken amounts to a 'gross' failure. The failure to be demonstrated is not civil negligence but neglect in the sense of failure to provide care.
- There must be a basis for finding that the failure to take action had a clear and direct causal connection with the cause of death. This does not require the neglect to be the sole cause, it extends to contributory factors of some substance (in the sense of more than trivial).

It was also said that provided all the other elements are present, the word 'gross' imports a value judgement and would normally be a jury issue.

In the circumstances of this case the court found no evidence even suggestive of neglect (systemic or otherwise) apart from a failure of three of the four custody officers involved to be familiar with an issued booklet on identifying and dealing with potential self-harm. Even then, this did not provide a causal connection given that a doctor was immediately called and had no recommendation to make. The words 'contributed to by system neglect' were quashed from the verdict.

Although much of this case centres on system neglect, it is also a valuable summary of the current law on *Jamieson* neglect. The question of an objective or subjective test on what the deceased's condition appeared to be is laid to rest—it is sufficient that the deceased's condition 'should have been known'.

APPENDIX 4

Definition of death of a member of the public during or following Police contact for the purposes of reporting by the Police to the Home Office

Category 1: Fatal road traffic incidents involving the police

This definition covers all deaths of members of the public resulting from road traffic incidents involving the police, both where the person who dies is in a vehicle and where they are on foot.

Category 2: Fatal shooting incidents involving the police

This definition covers circumstances where police fire the fatal shots.

Category 3: Deaths in or following custody

This definition covers the deaths of persons who have been arrested or otherwise detained by the police. It also includes deaths occurring whilst a person is being arrested or taken into detention. The death may have taken place on police, private, or medical premises, in a public place, or in a police or other vehicle.

Deaths in the following circumstances are amongst those covered by the definition:

- where the person dies in or on the way to hospital (or some other medical premises) following or during transfer from police detention;
- where the person dies after leaving police detention and there is a link between that detention and the death;
- where the person is being detained for the purposes of exercising a power to stop and search;
- where the death is of a child or young person detained for their own protection;
- where the person is in the care of the police having been detained under the Mental Health Act 1983;
- where the person is in police custody having been arrested by officers from a police force in Scotland exercising their powers of detention under s 137(2) of the Criminal Justice and Public Order Act 1994;
- where the person is in police custody having been arrested under s 3(5) of the Asylum and Immigration Appeals Act 1993;
- where the person is in police custody having been served a notice advising them of their detention under powers contained in the Immigration Act 1971;
- where the person is a convicted or remand prisoner held in police cells on behalf of the prison service under the Imprisonment (Temporary Provisions) Act 1980.

Category 4: Deaths during or following other types of contact with the police

This definition covers circumstances where the person dies during or after some form of contact with the police which did not amount to detention and there is a link between that contact and the death.

Examples of deaths which would be covered by the definition are:

- where the person is actively attempting to evade arrest and the death occurs otherwise than as the result of a road traffic incident;
- where there is a siege situation, including where a person shoots himself or another whilst police are in attendance;
- where the person is present at a demonstration and is struck by a police baton and subsequently dies.

Deaths which follow police contact but which are not linked to that contact would not be covered. For example:

- those attending police stations as innocent visitors or witnesses who are not suspects;
- those which occur in a police vehicle which is being used as an ambulance to transport a dying person to hospital quickly, but not under the circumstances described under Category 3;
- those where police attend the scene of an incident where a person who has not been detained has received fatal injuries.

Notes to the original document

- The above categorizations cannot be considered completely exhaustive. Cases will still have to be considered individually to decide whether and how they should be recorded.
- The term 'police' includes police civilians as well as police officers.
- Deaths involving off-duty police personnel are not included.

APPENDIX 5

Coroners Act 1988

Arrangement of Sections

Coroners

Appointment of coroners

1.—[(1)¹ Coroners shall be appointed—
    (a) for each coroner's district in a metropolitan county, [in a special non-metropolitan county or in]² Greater London or Wales;
    (b) for each coroner's district constituted by an order under section 17 of the Local Government Act 1992 which lies partly in each of two or more non-metropolitan counties;
    (c) for each non-metropolitan county in England [other than a special non-metropolitan county]³ none of which is included in such a coroner's district as is mentioned in paragraph (b) above;
    (d) in the case of a non-metropolitan county in England part of which is included in such a coroner's district as is mentioned in paragraph (b) above, for so much of that county as is not so included; and
    (e) for the City.

(1A) Coroners shall be appointed by the relevant council, that is to say-
    (a) in the case of a coroner's district consisting of or included in a metropolitan district [special non-metropolitan district]⁴ or London borough, the council of that district or borough;

---

¹ Subsection (1) substituted together with subsection (1A); for subsection (1) as originally enacted, by SI 1996/655 r 2(2).
² Words in square brackets inserted by SI 1998/465 r 2(2).
³ Words in square brackets inserted by SI 1998/465 r 2(3).
⁴ Words in square brackets inserted by SI 1998/465 r 2(4).

(b) in the case of a coroner's district consisting of two or more metropolitan districts [special non-metropolitan districts]⁵ or London boroughs such one of the councils of those districts or boroughs as may be designated by an order made by the Secretary of State by statutory instrument;

(c) in the case of a coroner's district consisting of or including a Welsh principal area, the council of that area;

(d) in the case of a coroner's district lying partly in each or two or more Welsh principal areas, such one of the councils of those areas as may be designated by an order made by the Secretary of State by statutory instrument;

(e) in a case falling within subsection (1)(b) above, such one of the councils of the non-metropolitan counties in question as may be designated by order under section 17 of Local Government Act 1992;

(f) in a case falling within subsection (1) (c) or (d) above, the council of the non-metropolitan county in question; and

(g) in the case of the City, the Common Council.]⁶

(2) A relevant council falling within paragraphs (a) or (b) of subsection [(1A)]⁷ above shall not appoint a coroner except with the approval of the Secretary of State; and a relevant council falling within paragraph (b) [(d) or (e)]⁸ of that subsection shall not appoint a coroner except after consultation with the other council or councils in question.

(3) Subject to subsection (2) above, where a vacancy occurs in the office of coroner, the relevant council shall—

(a) immediately give notice of the vacancy to the Secretary of State;

(b) within three months of the vacancy occurring or within such further period as the Secretary of State may allow, appoint a person to that office; and

(c) immediately after making the appointment, give notice of the appointment to the Secretary of State.

Qualifications for appointment as coroner

2.—(1) No person shall be qualified to be appointed as coroner [unless

(a) he has a five year general qualification, within the meaning of section 71 of the Courts and Legal Services Act 1990; or

(b) he is a]⁹ legally qualified medical practitioner of not less than five years' standing [. . .]¹⁰

(2) A person shall, so long as he is a councillor of a metropolitan district [special non-metropolitan district]¹¹ or London borough, and for six months after he ceases to be one, be disqualified for being a coroner for a coroner's district which consists of, includes or is included in that metropolitan district [special non-metropolitan district]¹² or London borough.

[(2A) A person shall, so long as he is a councillor of a Welsh principal area, and for six months after he ceases to be one, be disqualified for being a coroner for a coroner's district which, or any part of which, falls within that area.]¹³

---

⁵ Words in square brackets inserted by SI 1998/465 r 2(5).
⁶ Substituted by SI 1996/655.
⁷ Substituted by SI 1996/655.
⁸ Substituted by SI 1996/655.
⁹ Word substituted by the Courts and Legal Services Act 1990, s 71(2), Sched 10, para 70.
¹⁰ Words repealed by the above, s 125(7), Sched 20.
¹¹ Words inserted by SI 1998/465, r 2(6).
¹² Words inserted by SI 1998/465, r 2(6).
¹³ Inserted by the Local Government (Wales) Act 1994, s 66(6), Sched 16, para 82(3).

(3) A person shall, so long as he is an alderman or a councillor of a non-metropolitan county [in England][14] and for six months after he ceases to be one, be disqualified

(a) [(a) in the case of a county one of which is included in such a coroner's district as is mentioned in section 1(1)(b) above, for being a coroner for that county;

(b) in the case of a county the whole or part of which is included in such a coroner's district as is mentioned in section 1(1)(b) above, for being a coroner for that coroner's district and for so much of that county (if any) as is not so included.][15]

(4) A person shall, so long as he is an alderman of the City or a common councillor, and for six months after he ceases to be one, be disqualified for being a coroner for the City.

Terms on which coroners hold office

3.—(1) The provisions of Schedule 1 to this Act shall have effect with respect to the payment of salaries and the grant of pensions to coroners.

(2) Except as authorised by this or any other Act, a coroner shall not take any fee or remuneration in respect of anything done by him in the execution of his office.

(3) A coroner may resign his office by giving notice in writing to the relevant council, but the resignation shall not take effect unless and until it is accepted by that council.

(4) The Lord Chancellor may, if he thinks fit, remove any coroner from office for inability or misbehaviour in the discharge of his duty.

(5) A coroner who is guilty of corruption, wilful neglect of his duty or misbehaviour in the discharge of his duty shall be guilty of an offence and liable on conviction on indictment to imprisonment for a term not exceeding two years or to a fine or to both.

(6) Where a coroner is convicted of an offence under subsection (5) above, the court may, unless his office as coroner is annexed to any other office, order that he be removed from office and be disqualified for acting as coroner.

Coroners' districts

4.—(1) The Secretary of State may by order divide, amalgamate or otherwise alter the coroners' districts for the time being existing in a metropolitan county [special non-metropolitan county][16] or Greater London; and before making any such order, the Secretary of State shall consult the councils and coroners appearing to him to be affected by the order and such other persons as he thinks appropriate.

(2) The council of a non-metropolitan county [in England][17] may, and shall if directed to do so by the Secretary of State, after complying with such requirements as to notice and consideration of objections as may be prescribed, submit to the Secretary of State a draft order providing—

(a) for such alteration of any existing division of the county into coroners' districts as appears to them suitable; or

(b) where there is no such division, for the division of the county into such coroners' districts as they think expedient;

and the Secretary of State, after taking into consideration any objections to the draft made in the prescribed manner and within the prescribed time, may make the order, either in the terms of the draft submitted to him or with such modifications as he thinks fit.

---

[14] Inserted by the Local Government (Wales) Act 1994, s 66(6), Sched 16, para 82(3).
[15] Words substituted by SI 1996/655, r 2(4).
[16] Words inserted SI 1998/465, r 2(7).
[17] Words inserted by the Local Government (Wales) Act 1994, s 66(6), Sched 16, para 82(4).

(3) If by reason of any order under subsection (2) above it is in the opinion of the Secretary of State necessary that the number of coroners for a non-metropolitan county should be increased,

    (a) the council shall appoint such number of additional coroners for that county as the Secretary of State may direct; and

    (b) section 1(3) above shall apply with respect to any such appointment as if a vacancy had occurred in the office of coroner for that county.

(4) Where a non-metropolitan county [in England][18] is divided into coroners' districts, each of the coroners for that county shall be assigned to one of those districts; and where a non-metropolitan county is not so divided, the following provisions of this Act shall have effect as if the whole of that county were a coroner's district.

(5) Except as provided by this Act, a coroner appointed for or assigned to a coroner's district—

    (a) shall for all purposes be regarded as a coroner for the whole administrative area [in England][19] which includes that district; and

    (b) shall have the same jurisdiction, rights, powers and authorities throughout that area as if he had been appointed as coroner for that area or, as the case may be, had not been assigned to that district.

[(5A) Subsections (2) and (5) above shall not apply to a non-metropolitan county the whole of which is included in such a coroner's district as is mentioned in section 1(1)(b) above [or a special non-metropolitan county].[20]

(5B) In the application of this section to a non-metropolitan county part of which is included in such a coroner's district as is mentioned in section 1(1)(b) above, any reference to subsections (2)(a) and (b), (3) and (4) to a county shall be construed as a reference to so much of that county as is not so included.][21]

(6) The power to make orders under this section shall be exercisable by statutory instrument; and a statutory instrument containing an order under this section shall be laid before each House of Parliament after being made.

(7) An order under subsection (2) above shall be published in the London Gazette and particulars of any order under that subsection shall be published by the council of the non-metropolitan county in such manner as may be prescribed.

(8) In this section 'prescribed' means prescribed by the Secretary of State either by general rules made by statutory instrument or by directions given as respects any particular occasion.

[Coroners' districts: Wales

4A.—(1) The Secretary of State may by order divide, amalgamate or otherwise alter—

    (a) any coroner's district for the time being existing in Wales; or

    (b) any such coroners' districts.

(2) Before making any order under subsection (1) above, the Secretary of State shall consult the councils and coroners appearing to him to be affected by the order and such other persons as he thinks appropriate.

---

[18] Words inserted by the Local Government (Wales) Act 1994, s 66(6), Sched 16, para 82(4).

[19] Words inserted by the Local Government (Wales) Act 1994, s 66(6), Sched 16, para 82(4).

[20] Words inserted by SI 1998/465 r 2(8).

[21] Words inserted by SI 1996/655 r 2(5).

(3) The Secretary of State may, in relation to any area in Wales (the 'review area') direct the council or councils for each Welsh principal area which, or any part of which, falls within the review area to consider any of the following questions—

    (a) whether any alteration should be made in a boundary between coroners' districts which falls within the review area;

    (b) whether a new coroner's district should be created for the whole or any part of the review area;

    (c) whether a coroner's district which falls wholly within the review area should be abolished.

(4) The council or councils to whom such a direction is given shall submit their conclusions to the Secretary of State, together with a statement of their reason for reaching those conclusions.

(5) In making an order under subsection (1) above in a case where he has given a direction under subsection (3) above, the Secretary of State shall have regard to any proposals made to him under subsection (4) above.

(6) Where the Secretary of State intends to give effect to any such proposals without modification, subsection (2) above shall not require him to consult the council or councils who made those proposals.

(7) An order made under subsection (1) above may make such incidental, consequential, transitional or supplemental provision as appears to the Secretary of State to be appropriate.

(8) Except as provided by this Act, a coroner appointed for any coroner's district in Wales—

    (a) shall for all purposes be regarded as a coroner for the whole of Wales; and

    (b) shall have the same jurisdiction, rights, powers and authorities throughout Wales as if he had been appointed as coroner for the whole of Wales.

(9) The power to make orders under this section shall be exercisable by statutory instrument.

(10) Any such statutory instrument shall be laid before each House of Parliament after being made.][22]

Jurisdiction of coroners

5.—(1) Subject to subsection (3) and sections 7 and 13 to 15 below, an inquest into a death shall be held only by the coroner within whose district the body lies.

(2) Subject to subsection (3) and section 13 below, a coroner shall hold inquests only within his district.

(3) A coroner may act as coroner for another district in the same administrative area—

    (a) during the illness, incapacity or unavoidable absence of the coroner for that district; or

    (b) where there is a vacancy in the office of coroner for that district; and the inquisition returned in respect of an inquest held under this subsection shall certify the cause of the coroner's holding the inquest and shall be conclusive evidence of any matter stated in it which falls within paragraph (a) or (b) above.

---

[22] Words inserted by the Local Government (Wales) Act 1994, s 66(6), Sched 16, para 82 (5).

Deputy coroners

Appointment of deputy coroners

6.—(1) Every coroner—
  (a) shall appoint as his deputy a person approved by the chairman of the relevant council; and
  (b) may appoint as his assistant deputy a person so approved.

(2) A coroner may at any time revoke an appointment made under subsection (1) above; but a revocation of an appointment made under paragraph (a) of that subsection shall not take effect until the appointment of a successor to the deputy has been approved by the chairman of the relevant council.

(3) The following, namely—
  (a) every appointment made under subsection (1) above; and
  (b) every revocation of an appointment made under paragraph (b) of that subsection,
shall be in writing under the hand of the coroner; and a copy of every such appointment or revocation shall be sent to the relevant council and be kept with the council's records.

(4) Subsection (1) of section 2 above shall apply in relation to the office of deputy or assistant deputy coroner as it applies in relation to the office of coroner; and subsections (2) to (4) of that section shall apply in relation to, or to persons holding, the office of deputy coroner as they apply in relation to, or to persons holding, the office of coroner.

(5) In this section 'chairman' , in relation to the Common Council, means the Lord Mayor.

Functions of deputy coroners

7.—(1) A deputy coroner may act for his coroner in the following cases but no others, namely—
  (a) during the illness of the coroner;
  (b) during the coroner's absence for any lawful or reasonable cause; or
  (c) at an inquest for the holding of which the coroner is disqualified.

(2) Where a coroner vacates office, his deputy—
  (a) shall continue in office until a new deputy is appointed;
  (b) shall act as coroner while the office remains vacant; and
  (c) shall be entitled to receive in respect of the period of the vacancy the same remuneration as the vacating coroner.

(3) An assistant deputy coroner—
  (a) may act as coroner where the deputy coroner would be entitled to act as coroner but is unable so to act owing to illness or absence for any reasonable cause; and
  (b) where the coroner vacates office, may act for the deputy coroner in like manner while the office of coroner is vacant.

(4) In relation to an inquest or act which he is authorised to hold or to do, a deputy or assistant deputy to a coroner shall—
  (a) have the same jurisdiction and powers;
  (b) be subject to the same obligations, liabilities and disqualifications; and
  (c) generally be subject to the provisions of this Act and the law relating to coroners in the same manner,
as if he were the coroner.

Inquests: general

Duty to hold inquest

8.—(1) Where a coroner is informed that the body of a person ('the deceased') is lying within his district and there is reasonable cause to suspect that the deceased—

    (a) has died a violent or an unnatural death;

    (b) has died a sudden death of which the cause is unknown; or

    (c) has died in prison or in such a place or in such circumstances as to require an inquest under any other Act,

then, whether the cause of death arose within his district or not, the coroner shall as soon as practicable hold an inquest into the death of the deceased either with or, subject to subsection (3) below, without a jury.

    (2) In the case of an inquest with a jury—

    (a) the coroner shall summon by warrant not less than seven nor more than eleven persons to appear before him at a specified time and place, there to inquire as jurors into the death of the deceased; and

    (b) when not less than seven jurors are assembled, they shall be sworn by or before the coroner diligently to inquire into the death of the deceased and to give a true verdict according to the evidence.

    (3) If it appears to a coroner, either before he proceeds to hold an inquest or in the course of an inquest begun without a jury, that there is reason to suspect—

    (a) that the death occurred in prison or in such a place or in such circumstances as to require an inquest under any other Act;

    (b) that the death occurred while the deceased was in police custody, or resulted from an injury caused by a police officer in the purported execution of his duty;

    (c) that the death was caused by an accident, poisoning or disease notice of which is required to be given under any Act to a government department, to any inspector or other officer of a government department or to an inspector appointed under section 19 of the Health and Safety at Work etc. Act 1974;[23]

    or

    (d) that the death occurred in circumstances the continuance or possible recurrence of which is prejudicial to the health or safety of the public or any section of the public,

[he shall proceed to summon a jury in the manner required by subsection (2) above.

    (4) If it appears to a coroner, [before he proceeds to hold an inquest, on resuming an inquest begun with a jury after the inquest has been adjourned and the jury discharged][24] or in the course of an inquest begun without a jury, that there is any reason for summoning a jury, he may proceed to summon a jury in the manner required by subsection (2) above.

    (5) In the case of an inquest or any part of an inquest held without a jury, anything done by or before the coroner alone shall be as validly done as if it had been done by or before the coroner and a jury.

    (6) Where an inquest is held into the death of a prisoner who dies within a prison, neither a prisoner in the prison nor any person engaged in any sort of trade or dealing with the prison shall serve as a juror at the inquest.

Handwritten annotations:
- toxicology required
- Violent / unnatural death
- S-8-
- lying within Coroners jurisdiction

---

[23] 1974 c.37.

[24] Words inserted by the Access to Justice Act 1999, s 71(2).

Qualifications of jurors

9.—(1) A person shall not be qualified to serve as a juror at an inquest held by a coroner unless he is for the time being qualified to serve as a juror in the Crown Court, the High Court and county courts in accordance with section 1 of the Juries Act 1974.[25]

(2) If a person serves on a jury knowing that he is ineligible for such service under Group A, B or C in Part I of Schedule 1 to that Act, he shall be guilty of an offence and liable on summary conviction to a fine not exceeding level 3 on the standard scale.

(3) If a person serves on a jury knowing that he is disqualified for such service under Part II of that Schedule, he shall be guilty of an offence and liable on summary conviction to a fine not exceeding level 5 on the standard scale.

(4) The appropriate officer may at any time put or cause to be put to any person who is summoned under section 8 above such questions as he thinks fit in order to establish whether or not the person is qualified to serve as a juror at an inquest.

(5) Where a question is put to any person under subsection (4) above, if that person—
    (a) refuses without reasonable excuse to answer;
    (b) gives an answer which he knows to be false in a material particular; or
    (c) recklessly gives an answer which is false in a material particular,
he shall be guilty of an offence and liable on summary conviction to a fine not exceeding level 3 on the standard scale.

(6) If any person—
    (a) duly summoned as a juror at an inquest makes, or causes or permits to be made on his behalf, any false representation to the coroner or the appropriate officer with the intention of evading service as such juror; or
    (b) makes or causes to be made on behalf of another person who has been so summoned any false representation to the coroner or the appropriate officer with the intention of enabling that other person to evade such service,
he shall be guilty of an offence and liable on summary conviction to a fine not exceeding level 3 on the standard scale.

(7) A coroner may authorise a person to perform the functions conferred on the appropriate officer by subsection (4) above and references in this section to the appropriate officer shall be construed as references to the person so authorised.

Attendance of jurors and witnesses

10.—(1) Where a person duly summoned as a juror at an inquest—
    (a) does not, after being openly called three times, appear to the summons; or
    (b) appears to the summons but refuses without reasonable excuse to serve as a juror,
the coroner may impose on that person a fine not exceeding [£1000].[26]

(2) Where a person duly summoned to give evidence at an inquest—
    (a) does not, after being openly called three times, appear to the summons; or
    (b) appears to the summons but refuses without lawful excuse to answer a question put to him,
the coroner may impose on that person a fine not exceeding [£1000].[27]

(3) The powers conferred upon a coroner by this section shall be in addition to and not in derogation of any other power which the coroner may possess—

---

[25] 1974 c.23.
[26] Words substituted by the Criminal Justice Act 1991, s17(3), Sched 4, Pt 1.
[27] Words substituted by the Criminal Justice Act 1991, s17(3), Sched 4, Pt 1.

(a) for compelling any person to appear and give evidence before him in any inquest or other proceeding; or

(b) for punishing any person for contempt of court in not so appearing and giving evidence;

but a person shall not be fined by the coroner under this section and also be punished under any such other power.

(4) Notwithstanding anything in the foregoing provisions of this section, a juror shall not be liable to any penalty for non-attendance on a coroner's jury unless the summons requiring him to attend was duly served on him no later than six days before the day on which he was required to attend.

Proceedings at inquest

11.—(1) It shall not be obligatory for a coroner holding an inquest into a death to view the body; and the validity of such an inquest shall not be questioned in any court on the ground that the coroner did not view the body.

(2) The coroner shall, at the first sitting of the inquest, examine on oath concerning the death all persons who tender evidence as to the facts of the death and all persons having knowledge of those facts whom he considers it expedient to examine.

(3) In the case of an inquest held with a jury, the jury shall, after hearing the evidence—

(a) give their verdict and certify it by an inquisition; and

(b) inquire of and find the particulars for the time being required by the [1953 c. 20.] Births and Deaths Registration Act 1953 (in this Act referred to as 'the 1953 Act') to be registered concerning the death.

(4) In the case of an inquest held without a jury, the coroner shall, after hearing the evidence—

(a) give his verdict and certify it by an inquisition; and

(b) inquire of and find the particulars for the time being required by the 1953 Act to be registered concerning the death.

(5) An inquisition—

(a) shall be in writing under the hand of the coroner and, in the case of an inquest held with a jury, under the hands of the jurors who concur in the verdict;

(b) shall set out, so far as such particulars have been proved—

(i) who the deceased was; and

(ii) how, when and where the deceased came by his death; and

(c) shall be in such form as the Lord Chancellor may by rules made by statutory instrument from time to time prescribe.

(6) At a coroner's inquest into the death of a person who came by his death by murder, manslaughter or infanticide, the purpose of the proceedings shall not include the finding of any person guilty of the murder, manslaughter or infanticide; and accordingly a coroner's inquisition shall in no case charge a person with any of those offences.

(7) Where an inquest into a death is held, the coroner shall, within five days after the finding of the inquest is given, send to the registrar of deaths a certificate under his hand—

(a) giving information concerning the death;

(b) specifying the finding with respect to the particulars which under the 1953 Act are required to be registered concerning the death and with respect to the cause of death; and

(c) specifying the time and place at which the inquest was held.

(8) In the case of an inquest into the death of a person who is proved—
  (a) to have been killed on a railway; or
  (b) to have died in consequence of injuries received on a railway,
the coroner shall within seven days after holding the inquest, make a return of the death, including the cause of death, to the Secretary of State in such form as he may require; and in this subsection 'railway' has the same meaning as in the [1842 c. 55.] Railway Regulation Act 1842.

Failure of jury to agree

12.—(1) This section applies where, in the case of an inquest held with a jury, the jury fails to agree on a verdict.

(2) If the minority consists of not more than two, the coroner may accept the verdict of the majority, and the majority shall, in that case, certify the verdict under section 11(3) above.

(3) In any other case of disagreement the coroner may discharge the jury and issue a warrant for summoning another jury and, in that case, the inquest shall proceed in all respects as if the proceedings which terminated in the disagreement had not taken place.

Inquests: special cases

Order to hold inquest

13.—(1) This section applies where, on an application by or under the authority of the Attorney-General, the High Court is satisfied as respects a coroner ('the coroner concerned') either—
  (a) that he refuses or neglects to hold an inquest which ought to be held; or
  (b) where an inquest has been held by him, that (whether by reason of fraud, rejection of evidence, irregularity of proceedings, insufficiency of inquiry, the discovery of new facts or evidence or otherwise) it is necessary or desirable in the interests of justice that another inquest should be held.

(2) The High Court may—
  (a) order an inquest or, as the case may be, another inquest to be held into the death either—
    (i) by the coroner concerned; or
    (ii) by the coroner for another district in the same administrative area;
  (b) order the coroner concerned to pay such costs of and incidental to the application as to the court may appear just; and
  (c) where an inquest has been held, quash the inquisition on that inquest.

(3) In relation to an inquest held under subsection (2)(a)(ii) above, the coroner by whom it is held shall be treated for the purposes of this Act as if he were the coroner for the district of the coroner concerned.

Inquest out of jurisdiction

14.—(1) If it appears to a coroner that, in the case of a body lying within his district, an inquest ought to be held into the death but it is expedient that the inquest should be held by some other coroner, he may request that coroner to assume jurisdiction to hold the inquest; and if that coroner agrees he, and not the coroner within whose district the body is lying, shall have jurisdiction to hold the inquest.

(2) If the coroner who has been requested to assume jurisdiction declines to assume it, the coroner who has made the request may apply to the Secretary of State for a direction designating the coroner who is to hold the inquest.

(3) On the making of an application under subsection (2) above, the Secretary of State—

 (a) shall determine by which coroner (whether one of the two mentioned in that subsection or another) the inquest should in all the circumstances be held; and

 (b) shall direct him to assume jurisdiction or, as the case may be, to exercise his jurisdiction to hold the inquest;

and where a direction is given under this subsection directing a coroner to assume jurisdiction, he, and not the coroner within whose district the body is lying, shall have jurisdiction to hold the inquest and shall hold it accordingly.

(4) Where jurisdiction to hold an inquest is assumed under this section, it shall not be necessary to remove the body into the district of the coroner who is to hold the inquest.

(5) Any request made or agreement given, any application for a direction and any direction under any of the foregoing provisions of this section shall be made or given in writing.

(6) Notice of the making of an application under subsection (2) above shall be given to the coroner who declined to assume jurisdiction and notice of the direction given pursuant to such an application shall be given—

 (a) in a case where the direction is given to the coroner who made the application or the coroner who had notice of it, to the other coroner; and

 (b) in a case where the direction is given to some other coroner, to the coroner who made the application and to the coroner who had notice of it.

(7) On the assumption by a coroner of jurisdiction to hold an inquest under this section, the coroner—

 (a) shall also assume, in relation to the body and the inquest, all the powers and duties which would belong to him if the body were lying within his district (including the power to order its exhumation under section 23 below); and

 (b) may exercise those powers notwithstanding that the body remains outside his district or, having been removed into it, is removed out of it by virtue of any order of his for its examination or burial.

(8) On the assumption of the powers and duties referred to in subsection (7) above by the coroner who assumes jurisdiction to hold the inquest, the coroner within whose district the body is lying shall cease to have any powers or duties in relation to the body or the inquest, notwithstanding that the body remains within his district or comes to be buried there.

(9) It shall be for the coroner who assumes, and not for the coroner who ceases to have, jurisdiction to hold an inquest under this section to pay any fees or other expenses incurred in the course of his duties by the latter coroner before he ceased to have jurisdiction; and any such fees or other expenses shall be accounted for and repaid accordingly.

Inquest where body destroyed or irrecoverable

15.—(1) Where a coroner has reason to believe—

 (a) that a death has occurred in or near his district in such circumstances that an inquest ought to be held; and

 (b) that owing to the destruction of the body by fire or otherwise, or to the fact that the body is lying in a place from which it cannot be recovered, an inquest cannot be held except in pursuance of this section,

he may report the facts to the Secretary of State.

(2) Where a report is made under subsection (1) above, the Secretary of State may, if he considers it desirable to do so, direct a coroner (whether the coroner making the report or another) to hold an inquest into the death.

(3) Where a coroner is directed under this section to hold an inquest, the provisions of this Act and the law relating to coroners and coroners' inquests shall apply with such modifications as may be necessary in consequence of the inquest being one into the death of a person whose body does not lie within the coroner's district.

Adjournment of inquest in [event of criminal proceedings][28]

16.—(1) If on an inquest into a death the coroner before the conclusion of the inquest—

    (a) is informed by the [justices' chief executive for][29] a magistrates' court under section 17(1) below that some person has been charged before a magistrates' court with—

        (i) the murder, manslaughter or infanticide of the deceased;

        (ii) an offence under [section 1 or 3A of the Road Traffic Act 1988 (dangerous driving or careless driving when under the influence of drink or drugs)][30] committed by causing the death of the deceased; or

        (iii) an offence under section 2(1) of the Suicide Act 1961[31] consisting of aiding, abetting, counselling or procuring the suicide of the deceased; or

    (b) is informed by the Director of Public Prosecutions that some person has been charged before examining justices with an offence (whether or not involving the death of a person other than the deceased) alleged to have been committed in circumstances connected with the death of the deceased, not being an offence within paragraph (a) above, and is requested by the Director to adjourn the inquest,

then, subject to subsection (2) below, the coroner shall, in the absence of reason to the contrary, adjourn the inquest until after the conclusion of the relevant criminal proceedings and, if a jury has been summoned, may, if he thinks fit, discharge them.

(2) The coroner—

    (a) need not adjourn the inquest in a case within subsection (1)(a) above if, before he has done so, the Director of Public Prosecutions notifies him that adjournment is unnecessary; and

    (b) may in any case resume the adjourned inquest before the conclusion of the relevant criminal proceedings if notified by the Director that it is open to him to do so.

(3) After the conclusion of the relevant criminal proceedings, or on being notified under paragraph (b) of subsection (2) above before their conclusion, the coroner may, subject to the following provisions of this section, resume the adjourned inquest if in his opinion there is sufficient cause to do so.

(4) Where a coroner adjourns an inquest in compliance with subsection (1) above, he shall send to the registrar of deaths a certificate under his hand stating, so far as they have been ascertained at the date of the certificate, the particulars which under the 1953 Act are required to be registered concerning the death.

(5) Where a coroner does not resume an inquest which he has adjourned in compliance with subsection (1) above, he shall (without prejudice to subsection (4) above) send to the registrar of deaths a certificate under his hand stating the result of the relevant criminal proceedings.

---

[28] Words substituted by the Access to Justice Act 1999, s 71(3).
[29] Words inserted by the Access to Justice Act 1999, s 90(1), Sch 13, para 135.
[30] Words substituted by the Road Traffic Act 1991, s 48, Sched 4, para 40.
[31] 1961 c.60.

(6) Where a coroner resumes an inquest which has been adjourned in compliance with subsection (1) above and for that purpose summons a jury (but not where he resumes without a jury, or with the same jury as before the adjournment)—

    (a) he shall proceed in all respects as if the inquest had not previously been begun; and

    (b) subject to subsection (7) below, the provisions of this Act shall apply accordingly as if the resumed inquest were a fresh inquest.

(7) Where a coroner resumes an inquest which has been adjourned in compliance with subsection (1) above—

    (a) the finding of the inquest as to the cause of death must not be inconsistent with the outcome of the relevant criminal proceedings;

    (b) the coroner shall supply to the registrar of deaths after the termination of the inquest a certificate under his hand stating the result of the relevant criminal proceedings; and

    (c) the provisions of section 11(7) above shall not apply in relation to that inquest.

(8) In this section 'the relevant criminal proceedings' means the proceedings before examining justices and before any court to which the person charged is committed for trial.

Provisions supplementary to section 16

17.—(1) Where a person is charged before a magistrates' court with—

    (a) murder, manslaughter or infanticide;

    (b) an offence under [section 1 or 3A of the Road Traffic Act 1988 (dangerous driving or careless driving when under the influence of drink or drugs)][32] or

    (c) an offence under section 2(1) of the [1961 c. 60.] Suicide Act 1961 consisting of aiding, abetting, counselling or procuring the suicide of another,

the clerk of the court shall inform the coroner who is responsible for holding an inquest into the death of the making of the charge and of the result of the proceedings before that court.

(2) Where a person charged with—

    (a) murder, manslaughter or infanticide;

    (b) an offence under [section 1 or 3A of the Road Traffic Act 1988 (dangerous driving or careless driving when under the influence of drink or drugs)];[33] or

    (c) an offence under section 2(1) of the [1961 c. 60.] Suicide Act 1961 consisting of aiding, abetting, counselling or procuring the suicide of another,

is committed for trial to the Crown Court, the appropriate officer of the Crown Court at the place where the person charged is tried shall inform the coroner of the result of the proceedings before that court.

(3) Where the Director of Public Prosecutions has under section 16(1)(b) above requested a coroner to adjourn an inquest, then, whether or not the inquest is adjourned as a result, the Director shall—

    (a) inform the coroner of the result of the proceedings before the magistrates' court in the case of the person charged as mentioned in that paragraph; and

    (b) if that person is committed for trial to the Crown Court, inform the coroner of the result of the proceedings before that court.

---

[32] Words substituted by the Road Traffic Act 1991, s 48, Sched 4, para 41.
[33] Words substituted by the Road Traffic Act 1991, s 48, Sched 4, para 41.

[Adjournment of inquest in event of judicial inquiry

17A—(1) If on an inquest into a death the coroner is informed by the Lord Chancellor before the conclusion of the inquest that—

    (a) a public inquiry conducted or chaired by a judge is being, or is to be, held into the events surrounding the death; and

    (b) the Lord Chancellor considers that the cause of death is likely to be adequately investigated by the inquiry, the coroner shall, in the absence of any exceptional reason to the contrary, adjourn the inquest and, if a jury has been summoned, may, if he thinks fit, discharge them.

(2) Where a coroner adjourns an inquest in compliance with subsection (1) above, he shall send to the registrar of deaths a certificate under his hand stating, so far as they have been ascertained at the date of the certificate the particulars which under the 1953 Act are required to be registered concerning the death.

(3) Where a coroner has adjourned an inquest in compliance with subsection (1) above, the Lord Chancellor shall send him the findings of the public inquiry as soon as reasonably practicable after their publication.

(4) A coroner may only resume an inquest which has been adjourned in compliance with subsection (1) above if in his opinion there is exceptional reason for doing so; and he shall not do so—

    (a) before the end of the period of 28 days beginning with the day on which the findings of the public inquiry are published; or

    (b) if the Lord Chancellor notifies the coroner that this paragraph applies, before the end of the period of 28 days beginning with the day on which the public inquiry is concluded.

(5) Where a coroner resumes an inquest which has been adjourned in compliance with subsection (1) above—

    (a) the provisions of section 8(3) above shall not apply in relation to the inquest; and

    (b) if he summons a jury (but not where he resumes without a jury, or with the same jury as before the adjournment), he shall proceed in all respects as if the inquest had not previously begun and the provisions of this Act shall apply accordingly as if the resumed inquest were a fresh inquest.

(6) Where a coroner does not resume an inquest which he has adjourned in compliance with subsection (1) above, he shall (without prejudice to subsection (2) above) send to the registrar of deaths a certificate under his hand stating any findings of the public inquiry in relation to the death].[34]

Inquests into road deaths in London

18.—(1) Where an accident occurs within Greater London or the City resulting in the death of a person, and it is alleged that the accident was due to—

    (a) the nature or character of a road or road surface; or

    (b) a defect in the design or construction of a vehicle or in the materials used in the construction of a road or vehicle,

the coroner holding the inquest into the death shall send to the Secretary of State, or to such officer of his as the Secretary of State may direct, notice in writing of the time and place of holding the inquest, and of any adjourned inquest.

---

[34] Inserted by the Access to Justice Act 1999, s 71(1).

(2) An officer appointed by the Secretary of State for the purpose shall be at liberty at any such inquest to examine any witness, subject nevertheless to the power of the coroner to disallow any question which in his opinion is not relevant or is otherwise not a proper question.

(3) In this section 'road' has the same meaning as in [section 182 of the Road Traffic Act 1988].[35]

Medical witnesses and post-mortem examinations etc

Post-mortem examination without inquest

19.—(1) Where a coroner is informed that the body of a person is lying within his district and there is reasonable cause to suspect that the person has died a sudden death of which the cause is unknown, the coroner may, if he is of opinion that a post-mortem examination may prove an inquest to be unnecessary—

(a) direct any legally qualified medical practitioner whom, if an inquest were held, he would be entitled to summon as a medical witness under section 21 below; or

(b) request any other legally qualified medical practitioner,

to make a post-mortem examination of the body and to report the result of the examination to the coroner in writing.

(2) For the purposes of a post-mortem examination under this section, the coroner and any person directed or requested by him to make the examination shall have the like powers, authorities and immunities as if the examination were a post-mortem examination directed by the coroner at an inquest into the death of the deceased.

(3) Where a post-mortem examination is made under this section and the coroner is satisfied as a result of it that an inquest is unnecessary, he shall send to the registrar of deaths a certificate under his hand stating the cause of death as disclosed by the report of the person making the examination.

(4) Nothing in this section shall be construed as authorising the coroner to dispense with an inquest in any case where there is reasonable cause to suspect that the deceased—

(a) has died a violent or an unnatural death; or

(b) has died in prison or in such a place or in such circumstances as to require an inquest under any other Act.

Request to specially qualified person to make post-mortem and special examinations

20.—(1) Without prejudice to the power of a coroner holding an inquest to direct a medical witness whom he may summon under section 21 below to make a post-mortem examination of the body of the deceased, the coroner may, at any time after he has decided to hold an inquest—

(a) request any legally qualified medical practitioner to make a post-mortem examination of the body or a special examination of the body or both such examinations; or

(b) request any person whom he considers to possess special qualifications for conducting a special examination of the body to make such an examination.

(2) If any person who has made a post-mortem or special examination in pursuance of such a request is summoned by the coroner as a witness, he may be asked to give evidence as to his opinion upon any matter arising out of the examination, and as to how, in his opinion, the deceased came by his death.

---

[35] Words substituted by the Road Traffic Act (Consequential Provisions) Act 1988, s 4, Sched 3 para 37(3).

(3) Where a person states upon oath before the coroner that in his belief the death of the deceased was caused partly or entirely by the improper or negligent treatment of a medical practitioner or other person, that medical practitioner or other person—

    (a) shall not be allowed to perform or assist at any post-mortem or special examination made for the purposes of the inquest into the death; but

    (b) shall have the right, if he so desires, to be represented at any such post-mortem examination.

(4) In this section 'special examination', in relation to a body, means a special examination by way of analysis, test or otherwise of such parts or contents of the body or such other substances or things as ought in the opinion of the coroner to be submitted to analyses, tests or other examination with a view to ascertaining how the deceased came by his death.

Summoning of medical witnesses and direction of post-mortem examinations

21.—(1) In the case of an inquest into a death, the coroner may summon as a witness—

    (a) any legally qualified medical practitioner appearing to him to have attended at the death of the deceased or during the last illness of the deceased; or

    (b) where it appears to him that no such practitioner so attended the deceased, any legally qualified medical practitioner in actual practice in or near the place where the death occurred;

and any medical witness summoned under this section may be asked to give evidence as to how, in his opinion, the deceased came by his death.

(2) Subject to subsection (3) below, the coroner may, either in his summons for the attendance of a medical witness or at any time between the issuing of that summons and the end of the inquest, direct the medical witness to make a post-mortem examination of the body of the deceased.

(3) Where a person states upon oath before the coroner that in his belief the death of the deceased was caused partly or entirely by the improper or negligent treatment of a medical practitioner or other person, that medical practitioner or other person shall not be allowed to perform or assist at the post-mortem examination of the deceased.

(4) If, in the case of an inquest with a jury, a majority of the jury are of opinion that the cause of death has not been satisfactorily explained by the evidence of the medical practitioner or of other witnesses brought before them, they may in writing require the coroner—

    (a) to summon as a witness some other legally qualified medical practitioner named by them; and

    (b) to direct a post-mortem examination of the deceased to be made by a practitioner summoned under this subsection, whether or not such an examination has been previously made;

and if the coroner fails to comply with such a requisition, he shall be liable on conviction on indictment to a term of imprisonment not exceeding two years or to a fine or to both.

(5) Where a medical practitioner fails to obey a summons of a coroner issued in pursuance of this section, he shall, unless he shows a good and sufficient cause for not having obeyed the summons, be liable on summary conviction, on the prosecution of the coroner or of any two of the jury, to a fine not exceeding [£1000].[36]

---

[36] Words substituted by the Criminal Justice Act 1991, s 17(3) Sched 4, Pt I.

Removal of body for post-mortem examination

22.—(1) Subject to subsection (2) below, where by the direction or at the request of a coroner, a post-mortem examination of a body is to be made, the coroner may order the removal of the body to any place which may be provided for the purpose either within his district or within an adjoining district of another coroner.

(2) A coroner shall not order the removal of a body upon which a post-mortem examination is to be made to any place other than a place within his district provided by a local authority except with the consent of the person or authority by whom the place is provided.

(3) The removal of a body in pursuance of an order made by a coroner under this section to any place outside his district shall not affect his powers and duties in relation to the body or the inquest into the death nor shall it confer or impose any rights, powers or duties upon any other coroner.

(4) Where a coroner—
   (a) orders under this section the removal of a body to any place outside his district; and
   (b) does not authorise the disposal of the body after examination,
he shall order the removal of the body after examination to a place within his district.

(5) The expenses of any removal ordered by a coroner under this section shall be defrayed as part of the expenses incurred by him in the course of his duties.

(6) In this section—
   'disposal' has the same meaning as in the 1953 Act;
   'local authority' means the council of a [district, London borough or Welsh principal area][37] or the Common Council.

Exhumation of body for examination

23.—(1) A coroner may order the exhumation of the body of a person buried within his district where it appears to him that it is necessary for the body to be examined—
   (a) for the purpose of his holding an inquest into that person's death or discharging any other function of his in relation to the body or the death; or
   (b) for the purposes of any criminal proceedings which have been instituted or are contemplated in respect of the death of that person or of some other person who came by his death in circumstances connected with the death of the person whose body is needed for examination.

(2) The power of a coroner under this section shall be exercisable by warrant under his hand.

(3) No body shall be ordered by a coroner to be exhumed except under this section.

Expenses and returns of inquests

Fees and allowances payable on holding inquest

24.—(1) The fees and allowances which may be lawfully paid by coroners—
   (a) to witnesses and persons summoned to attend as witnesses; and
   (b) to medical practitioners making post-mortem examinations by the coroner's direction or at the coroner's request,
shall be such as may be determined by the Secretary of State with the consent of the Treasury; but nothing in this subsection shall apply in relation to the fees payable in respect of a special examination under section 20 above.

---

[37] Words substituted by the Local Government (Wales) Act 1994, s 66, Sched 16, para 82(6).

(2) A relevant council—

    (a) may from time to time make a schedule of the fees, allowances and disbursements which may be lawfully paid or made by a coroner in the course of his duties, other than fees and allowances to which subsection (1) above applies;

    (b) may at any time vary a schedule so made; and

    (c) shall cause a copy of every schedule so made or so varied to be sent to every coroner concerned.

(3) The Secretary of State may by rules made by statutory instrument prescribe—

    (a) the fees payable to coroners or other persons for furnishing copies of inquisitions, depositions or other documents in their custody relating to an inquest; and

    (b) where in the opinion of the Secretary of State adequate provision is not made for them by a schedule under subsection (2) above, the fees, allowances and disbursements which may be lawfully paid or made by a coroner in the course of his duties, other than fees and allowances to which subsection (1) above applies.

Payments to jurors

25.—(1) A person who serves as a juror in a coroner's court shall be entitled, in respect of his attendance at court for the purpose of performing jury service, to receive payments, at the rates determined by the Secretary of State with the consent of the Treasury and subject to any prescribed conditions, by way of allowance—

    (a) for travelling and subsistence; and

    (b) for financial loss where in consequence of his attendance for that purpose—

        (i) he has incurred any expenditure (otherwise than on travelling and subsistence) to which he would not otherwise be subject; or

        (ii) he has suffered any loss of earnings which he would otherwise have made or any loss of benefit under the enactments relating to national insurance and social security which he would otherwise have received.

(2) The amount due to any person in respect of such service shall be ascertained and paid over to him by the coroner.

(3) For the purposes of this section a person who, in obedience to a summons to serve on a jury, attends for service as a juror shall be deemed to serve as a juror notwithstanding that he is not subsequently sworn.

(4) In this section 'prescribed' means prescribed by regulations made by statutory instrument by the Secretary of State with the consent of the Treasury.

Payment of expenses by coroner

26.—(1) A coroner holding an inquest shall, immediately after the termination of the proceedings, pay—

    (a) the fees of every medical witness;

    (b) the allowance of every juror; and

    (c) all expenses reasonably incurred in and about the holding of the inquest,

not exceeding the fees, allowances and disbursements which may be lawfully paid or made under this Act.

(2) Any fees, allowances or disbursements so paid or made shall be repaid to the coroner in manner provided by this Act.

Accounts to be laid before relevant council

27.—(1) Every coroner shall within four months after paying or making any fees, allowances or disbursements in accordance with the provisions of this Act, cause a full and true account of all fees, allowances and disbursements so paid or made by him under this Act to be laid before the relevant council.

(2) Every account under this section shall be accompanied by such vouchers as under the circumstances may to the relevant council seem reasonable; and the relevant council may, if they think fit, examine the coroner on oath as to any such account.

(3) On being satisfied of the correctness of any such account, the relevant council shall order their treasurer to pay to the coroner the sum due; and the treasurer shall without any abatement or deduction pay that sum—

    (a)   in the case of a metropolitan district or London borough council, out of the general [. . .]³⁸ fund;

    [(aa) in the case of a non-metropolitan district council, out of the general fund]³⁹

    (b)   in the case of a non-metropolitan county council [in England],⁴⁰ out of the county fund;

    [(bb) in the case of the council of a Welsh principal area, out of the council fund]⁴¹

    (c)   in the case of the Common Council, out of the [City fund],⁴²

and shall be allowed that sum on passing his accounts.

(4) In the case of a coroner for a coroner's [district-

    (a)   consisting of two or more metropolitan districts [or special non-metropolitan districts]⁴³ or London boroughs, or

    (b)   which lies partly in each of two or more Welsh principal area,]⁴⁴ [or

    (c)   which lies partly in each of two or more non-metropolitan counties in England,]⁴⁵

the expenses of the councils of those districts, boroughs [areas or counties] in respect of the coroner's service shall be apportioned between those councils in such manner as they may agree or, in default of agreement, as may be determined by the Secretary of State.

Indemnity

[27A—(1) A coroner shall be indemnified by the relevant council (without having to lay before them an account under section 27 above in respect of—

    (a)   any costs which he reasonably incurs in or in connection with proceedings in respect of anything done or omitted in the exercise (or purported exercise) of his duty as a coroner;

    (b)   any costs which he reasonably incurs in taking steps to dispute any claim which might be made in such proceedings;

    (c)   any damages awarded against him or costs ordered to be paid by him in any such proceedings; and

    (d)   any sum payable by him in connection with a reasonable settlement of any such proceedings or claim.

(2) Subsection (1) above applies in relation to proceedings by a coroner only if and to the extent that the relevant council agrees in advance to indemnify him.

---

³⁸ Words deleted by SI 1990/1285.
³⁹ Words inserted by the Local Government Reorganisation (Amendment of Coroners Act 1988) Regulations 1996, SI 1996/655, r 2(6).
⁴⁰ Words inserted by the Local Government (Wales) Act 1994, s 66(6), Sched 16, para 82(7).
⁴¹ Words inserted by the Local Government (Wales) Act 1994, s 66(6), Sched 16, para 82(7).
⁴² Words substituted by SI 1990/1285, art 2, Sched 1, para 9.
⁴³ Words inserted by SI 1998/465, reg 2(9).
⁴⁴ Words inserted by the Local Government (Wales) Act 1994, s 66(6), Sched 16, para 82(8).
⁴⁵ Words inserted by SI 1996/655, r 2(7).

(3) A coroner may appeal to the Secretary of State, or to any person appointed by the Secretary of State for the purpose, from any decision of the relevant council under subsection (2) above.

(4) Any amount due to a coroner under this section shall be paid—
  (a) in the case of a metropolitan or non-metropolitan district council or London borough council, out of the general fund;
  (b) in the case of a non-metropolitan county council in England, out of the county fund;
  (c) in the case of the council of a Welsh principal area, out of the council fund, and
  (d) in the case of the Common Council out the city fund

(5) In the case of a coroner for a coroner's district which—
  (a) consists of two or more metropolitan districts, special non-metropolitan districts or London boroughs
  (b) lies partly in each of two or more Welsh principal areas; or
  (c) lies partly in each of two or more non-metropolitan counties of England
any amount due to the coroner under this section shall be apportioned between the councils of those districts, boroughs, areas or counties in such manner as they may agree or, in default of agreement, as may be determined by the Secretary of State.][46]

Annual returns to be made to Secretary of State

28.—(1) Every coroner shall on or before 1st February in every year furnish to the Secretary of State a return in writing, in such form and containing such particulars as the Secretary of State may direct, of all cases in which an inquest has been held by him, or by some other person acting for him, during the year ending on the immediately preceding 31 December.

(2) Every coroner shall also, as and when required by the Secretary of State, furnish to the Secretary of State returns in relation to inquests held and deaths inquired into by him in such form and containing such particulars as the Secretary of State may direct.

Miscellaneous

Coroner of the Queen's household

29.—(1) The coroner of the Queen's household shall continue to be appointed by the Lord Steward for the time being of the Queen's household.

(2) The coroner of the Queen's household shall have exclusive jurisdiction in respect of inquests into the deaths of persons whose bodies are lying—
  (a) within the limits of any of the Queen's palaces; or
  (b) within the limits of any other house where Her Majesty is then residing.

(3) The limits of any such palace or house shall be deemed to extend to any courts, gardens or other places within the curtilage of the palace or house but not further; and where a body is lying in any place beyond those limits, the coroner within whose district the body is lying, and not the coroner for the Queen's household, shall have jurisdiction to hold an inquest into the death.

(4) The jurors on an inquest held by the coroner of the Queen's household shall consist of officers of that household, to be returned by such officer of the Queen's household as may be directed to summon the jurors by the warrant of the coroner.

---

[46] Inserted by the Access to Justice Act 1999, s 104(1).

(5) All inquisitions, depositions and recognisance shall be delivered to the Lord Steward of the Queen's household to be filed among the records of his office.

(6) The coroner of the Queen's household—

    (a) shall make his declaration of office before the Lord Steward of the Queen's household; and

    (b) shall reside in one of the Queen's palaces or in such other convenient place as may from time to time be allowed by the Lord Steward of the Queen's household.

(7) The provisions of Schedule 2 to this Act shall have effect with respect to the application of this Act and the law relating to coroners to the coroner of the Queen's household.

Treasure trove

30.—A coroner shall continue to have jurisdiction—

    (a) to inquire into any treasure which is found in his district; and

    (b) to inquire who were, or are suspected of being, the finders;

and the provisions of this Act shall, so far as applicable, apply to every such inquest.

Provision of accommodation

31. [The council (whether or not a relevant council) of any of the following, that is to say—

    (a)   a metropolitan district

    [(aa) a special non-metropolitan district]⁴⁷

    (b)   a London borough,

    (c)   a Welsh principal area, or

    (d)   in the case of such a coroner's district as is mentioned in section 1 (1)(b) above, a non-metropolitan county the whole or part of which is included in that coroner's district]⁴⁸

may provide and maintain proper accommodation for the holding of inquests in their area.

Supplemental

Power to make rules

32.—(1) The Lord Chancellor may, with the concurrence of the Secretary of State, make rules for regulating the practice and procedure at or in connection with inquests and post-mortem examinations and, in particular (without prejudice to the generality of the foregoing provision), such rules may provide—

    (a) as to the procedure at inquests held without a jury;

    (b) as to the issue by coroners of orders authorising burials;

    (c) for empowering a coroner or his deputy or assistant deputy to alter the date fixed for the holding of any adjourned inquest within the district of the coroner;

    (d) as to the procedure to be followed where a coroner decides not to resume an adjourned inquest; and

    (e) as to the notices to be given, and as to the variation or discharge of any recognisances entered into by jurors or witnesses, where the date fixed for an

---

⁴⁷ Inserted by SI 1998/465, reg 2(10).
⁴⁸ Words inserted by SI 1996/655, r 2(8).

adjourned inquest is altered or where a coroner decides not to resume an adjourned inquest.

(2) Without prejudice to the generality of subsection (1) above, rules under this section may make provision for persons to be excused service as jurors at inquests in such circumstances as the rules may specify.

(3) The power of the Lord Chancellor under this section to make rules with respect to any matter shall include power—

(a) to prescribe the forms to be used in connection with that matter;

(b) to revoke or amend, or substitute new forms for, any forms which are directed or authorised by or under any enactment to be used in connection with that matter.

(4) The power to make rules under this section shall be exercisable by statutory instrument.

Savings for ex officio coroners and judicial powers

33.—(1) Nothing in this Act shall prejudice or affect the jurisdiction of a judge exercising the jurisdiction of a coroner by virtue of his office.

(2) Nothing in this Act shall prejudice or affect—

(a) the jurisdiction of the Lord Chancellor or the High Court in relation to the removal of a coroner otherwise than in the manner provided by this Act; or

(b) the jurisdiction of the High Court in relation to or over a coroner or his duties.

Application of Act to Isles of Scilly

34.—(1) Subject to subsection (2) below, this Act shall apply in relation to the Isles of Scilly as if those Isles were a non-metropolitan county and the Council of those Isles were the council of that county.

(2) The power conferred on the Secretary of State by section 265 of the [1972 c. 70.] Local Government Act 1972 (application of that Act to the Isles of Scilly) shall include power to make an order providing for regulating the application of this Act to those Isles otherwise than as mentioned in subsection (1) above and such an order may amend or repeal that subsection accordingly.

Interpretation

35.—(1) In this Act, unless the context otherwise requires—

'the 1953 Act' means the [1953 c. 20.] Births and Deaths Registration Act 1953;

'administrative area' means [subject to subsection (1B) below][49] [Wales][50] a metropolitan or non-metropolitan county [in England][51] or Greater London;

'the Common Council' means the Common Council of the City of London and 'common councillor' shall be construed accordingly;

'the City' means the City of London (including the Inner Temple and the Middle Temple);

'Greater London' does not include the City;

'relevant council' has the meaning given by section [1(1A)][52] above.

['special non-metropolitan county; means a non-metropolitan county in which there are two or more local government districts and for which there is no county

---

[49] Words inserted by SI 1996/655, r 2(9)(a).

[50] Words inserted by the Local Government (Wales) Act 1994, s 66(6), Sched 16, para 82(10).

[51] Words inserted by the Local Government (Wales) Act 1994, s 66(6), Sched 16, para 82(10).

[52] Words inserted by SI 1996/655, r 2(9)(b).

council; 'special non-metropolitan district' means a district in a non-metropolitan county;]⁵³

['Welsh principal area' means Welsh county or county borough]⁵⁴

[(1A) In this Act any reference to a council of a non-metropolitan county includes in relation to an area for which there is a district council but no county council a reference to a district council, and any reference to a councillor of a non-metropolitan county shall be construed accordingly.

(1B) In the application of sections 4(5), 5(3) and 13(2) above to a non-metropolitan county part of which is in such a coroner's district as is mentioned in section 1(1)(b) above, any reference in those provisions to an administrative area shall be construed as a reference to so much of that county as is not so included.]⁵⁵

(2) In this Act references to an inquest held with a jury include, and references to an inquest held without a jury do not include, references to an inquest part of which is held with a jury.

Consequential amendments, repeals, transitional provisions and savings

36.—(1) The enactments mentioned in Schedule 3 to this Act shall have effect subject to the amendments there specified, being amendments consequential on the provisions of this Act.

(2) The enactments and instruments mentioned in Schedule 4 to this Act (which include some that are spent) are hereby repealed to the extent specified in the third column of that Schedule.

(3) Where any period of time specified in an enactment repealed by this Act is current at the commencement of this Act, this Act shall have effect as if the corresponding provision of this Act had been in force when that period began to run.

(4) Notwithstanding the repeal by this Act of section 13 of the [1985 c. 51.] Local Government Act 1985—

> (a) any coroner holding office immediately before 1st April 1986 and assigned to a coroner's district in a metropolitan county or in Greater London shall be deemed to have been duly appointed by the relevant council; and
>
> (b) any orders made under section 12 of the [1926 c. 59.] Coroners (Amendment) Act 1926 and in force immediately before that date shall, so far as they affect a metropolitan county or Greater London, have effect as if made under section 4(1) above.

(5) Notwithstanding the repeal by this Act of the [1887 c. 71.] Coroners Act 1887, anything mentioned in subsection (5) of section 45 of that Act which, immediately before the commencement of this Act, was in force by virtue of that subsection shall, except so far as it is inconsistent with this Act, remain in force.

(6) Nothing in this section shall be taken as prejudicing the operation of sections 15 to 17 of the [1978 c. 30.] Interpretation Act 1978 (which relate to the effect of repeals).

Short title, commencement and extent

37.—(1) This Act may be cited as the Coroners Act 1988.

(2) This Act shall come into force at the end of the period of two months beginning with the day on which it is passed.

(3) This Act extends to England and Wales only.

---

⁵³ Words inserted by SI 1998/465, r 2(11).
⁵⁴ Words inserted by the Local Government (Wales) Act 1994, s 66(6), Sched 16, para 82(10).
⁵⁵ Words inserted by SI 1996/655, r 2(10).

SCHEDULES

SCHEDULE 1

SALARIES AND PENSIONS

Coroners' salaries

1.—(1) Subject to the provisions of this paragraph, a coroner shall be paid by the relevant council an annual salary at such rate as may be fixed by agreement between the coroner and the council.

(2) If at any time a coroner and the relevant council cannot agree with respect to any proposed alteration of the rate of his salary—

    (a) the Secretary of State may, on the application of either party, fix the rate of that salary at such rate as he thinks proper; and

    (b) subject to sub-paragraph (4) below, the rate so fixed shall come into force as from such date as he may determine.

(3) In fixing the rate of the salary payable to a coroner under this paragraph, regard shall be had to the nature and extent of his duties and to all circumstances of the case.

(4) A date determined under sub-paragraph (2) above shall be not less than three years from the date when the rate of the coroner's salary as last fixed came into force, unless in the opinion of the Secretary of State the coroner's district has in the meantime been materially altered.

Coroner's pensions

2.—(1) On the retirement, after not less than five years' service, of a coroner—

    (a) who held office as a coroner immediately before April 6, 1978; and

    (b) who did not elect in accordance with article 3(b) of the Social Security (Modification of Coroners (Amendment) Act 1926) Order 1978 that the provisions of the Coroners (Amendment) Act 1926 relating to pensions should not apply to him.

(that is to say, a coroner who is not a pensionable employee for the purposes of the Local Government Superannuation Regulations 1986) the relevant council many, if either of the conditions mentioned in sub-paragraph (2) below is satisfied, grant to him a pension of such amount as may be agreed between him and the council not exceeding the scale contained in paragraph 3 below.

(2) The said conditions are—

    (a) that the coroner has attained the age of sixty-five years;

    (b) that the relevant council is satisfied by means of a medical certificate that the coroner is incapable of discharging his duties whether on mental or physical grounds and that such incapacity is likely to be permanent.

(3) A coroner to whom this paragraph applies—

    (a) shall, at any time after he has completed fifteen years' service and has attained the age of sixty-five years, vacate his office if required to do so by the relevant council; but

    (b) shall, in that case and in the absence of any agreement to the contrary, be entitled to receive the maximum pension which the council is empowered to grant him under this paragraph having regard to the length of his service.

(4) A pension payable to a coroner under this paragraph shall be reduced by the amount of any additional component of his retirement pension (within the meaning of section 6(1)(b) of the Social Security Pension Act 1975) which is payable to him.

(5) In this paragraph 'service' means service, whether before or after the commencement of this Act, as a coroner in the same administrative area; and for this purpose 'administrative area' includes the City.

(6) Notwithstanding the reproduction of article 3 of the Social Security (Modification of Coroners (Amendment) Act 1926) Order 1978 as paragraphs (a) and (b) of sub-paragraph (1) above and of article 4 of that Order as sub-paragraph (4) above—

    (a) those provisions may be amended or repealed; and

    (b) any question as to the validity of those provisions may be determined,

as though they were contained in an order made under section 65 of the Social Security Act 1973.

Scale of pensions

3.—(1) An annual pension not exceeding ten sixtieths of the last annual salary may be granted after the completion of five years' service.

(2) Where the completed service exceeds five years, there may be granted an annual pension not exceeding the aggregate of—

    (a) ten-sixtieths of the last annual salary; and

    (b) an amount; not exceeding one-fortieth of that salary for each completed year's service after five years.

So however that no such pension shall be of an amount exceeding two-thirds of that salary.

(3) For the purposes of this paragraph the last annual salary of a coroner shall be taken to be the salary paid to him in his last completed year of service as coroner, after deducting so much (if any) of that salary as was paid to him with a view to his providing at his own expense for any necessary expenditure in connection with his duties as coroner.

(4) If any dispute arises to the amount to be deducted after sub-paragraph (3) above in computing the last annual salary of a coroner, the dispute shall be referred to the Secretary of State, whose decision shall be final.

Payment of salaries and pensions

4. The salary of a coroner and any pension payable to a person in respect of his service as a coroner shall be deemed to accrue from day to day and, in the absence of agreement to the contrary, shall be payable quarterly.

SCHEDULE 2
CORONER TO THE QUEEN'S HOUSEHOLD

Section 29(7)

1. Sections 1 to 5 of this Act (except subsections (4) to (6) of section 3), sections 6 and 7 of this Act so far as relating to the appointment and functions of assistant deputy coroners and Schedule 1 to this Act shall not apply to the coroner of the Queen's household.

2. Sections 6 and 7 of this Act, so far as relating to the appointment and functions of deputy coroners, shall apply with the necessary modifications to the coroner of the Queen's household as they apply to other coroners and, in particular, with the following modifications, namely—

    (a) that the appointment of a deputy to the coroner of the Queen's household shall be subject to the approval of the Lord Steward of the Queen's household; and

    (b) that copies of such appointments shall be sent to and kept by him.

3. Sections 9 and 32(2) of this Act shall not apply in relation to any inquest held by the coroner of the Queen's household.

4. Section 25 of this Act shall not apply in relation to service on a jury on an inquest held by the coroner of the Queen's household but that shall not affect any entitlement to payment that might otherwise by enjoyed by a juror for service on such a jury.

5. Subject to the provisions of this Schedule and section 29 of this Act, the coroner of the Queen's household shall, within the limits laid down in subsection (3) of that section—

    (a) have the same jurisdiction and powers; and

    (b) be subject to the same obligations, liabilities and disqualifications; and

    (c) generally be subject to the provisions of this Act and the law relating to coroners in the same manner,

as any other coroner.

SCHEDULE 3

CONSEQUENTIAL AMENDMENTS

SCHEDULE 4

REPEALS

APPENDIX 6

The Coroners Rules 1984

1984 No 552

CORONERS

The Coroners Rules 1984

Made—   *9 April 1984*
Coming into Operation   *1 July 1984*

ARRANGEMENT OF RULES

PART I
GENERAL

PART II
AVAILABILITY OF CORONER

PART III
POST-MORTEM EXAMINATIONS

PART IV
SPECIAL EXAMINATION

PART VIII
RECORDS, DOCUMENTS, EXHIBITS AND FORMS

SCHEDULES

The Lord Chancellor, in exercise of the powers conferred upon him by sections 26 and 27 of the Coroners (Amendment) Act 1926[1] and with the concurrence of the Secretary of State hereby makes the following Rules:—

PART I
GENERAL

1. Citation and commencement

These Rules may be cited as the Coroners Rules 1984 and shall come into operation on 1st July 1984.

2. Interpretation

(1) In these Rules, unless the context otherwise requires—

['the 1988 Act' means the Coroners Act 1988];[2]

'appropriate officer' has the same meaning as it has in [section 9 of the 1988 Act];[3]

'chief officer of police' means the chief officer of police for the area in which the coroner's jurisdiction is comprised;

'coroner' includes a deputy and assistant deputy coroner;

'deceased' means the person upon whose body a post-mortem examination is made or touching whose death an inquest is held or the person whose death is reported to the coroner, as the case may be;

'enforcing authority' has the same meaning as it has in section 18(7) of the Health and Safety at Work etc. Act 1974;[4]

'hospital' means any institution for the reception and treatment of persons suffering from illness or mental disorder, any maternity home, and any institution for the reception and treatment of persons during convalescence;

---

[1] 1926 c.59; section 26 was amended by section 2 of the Coroners' Juries Act 1983 (c. 31).

[2] Words substituted by the Coroners (Amendment) Rules 1999: (hereinafter referred to as SI 1999/3325), rule 3(a).

[3] Words substituted by SI 1999/3325, rule 3(b).

[4] 1974 c. 37.

'industrial disease' means a disease prescribed under section 76 of the Social Security Act 1975;[5]

'inquest' means an inquest for the purpose of inquiring into the death of a person;

'legal proceedings' includes proceedings for the purpose of obtaining any benefit or other payments under the provisions of the Social Security Act 1975 relating to industrial injuries or under section 5 of the Industrial Injuries and Diseases (Old Cases) Act 1975;[6]

'pneumoconiosis medical board' and

'pneumoconiosis medical panel' have the same meanings as they have in the Social Security (Industrial Injuries) (Prescribed Diseases) Regulations 1980;[7]

'post-mortem examination' means a post-mortem examination which a legally qualified medical practitioner is directed or requested by a coroner to make under [sections 19 to 21 of the 1988 Act];[8]

'registrar' means a registrar of births and deaths;

[. . .][9]

'special examination' has the same meaning as it has in [section 20(4) of the 1988 Act].[10]

(2) In these Rules any reference to a Rule or Schedule shall be construed as a reference to a Rule contained in these Rules, or, as the case may be, to a Schedule thereto; and any reference in a Rule to a paragraph shall be construed as a reference to a paragraph of that Rule.

3. Revocations and application

(1) Subject to paragraph (2), the Rules specified in Schedule 1 are hereby revoked.

(2) These Rules shall not have effect in relation to any inquest begun before 1st July 1984 or to any post-mortem examination, which, before that day, a coroner has directed or requested a medical practitioner to make; and, accordingly, the Rules revoked by paragraph (1) shall continue to have effect in relation to any such inquest or post-mortem examination.

PART II
AVAILABILITY OF CORONER

4. Coroner to be available at all times

A coroner shall at all times hold himself ready to undertake, either by himself or by his deputy or assistant deputy, any duties in connection with inquests and post-mortem examinations.

PART III
POST-MORTEM EXAMINATIONS

5. Delay in making post-mortem to be avoided

Where a coroner directs or requests that a post-mortem examination shall be made, it shall be made as soon after the death of the deceased as is reasonably practicable.

---

[5] 1975 c. 14; the relevant instrument is SI 1980/377, as amended by SIZ 1980/1493.

[6] 1975 c. 16.

[7] SI 1980/377.

[8] Words substituted by SI 1999/3325, rule 3(c).

[9] Words revoked by SI 1999/3325, rule 3(d).

[10] Words substituted by SI 1999/3325, rule 3(e).

6. Medical practitioner making post-mortem

(1) In considering what legally qualified medical practitioner shall be directed or requested by the coroner to make a post-mortem examination the coroner shall have regard to the following considerations:—

    (a) the post-mortem examination should be made, whenever practicable, by a pathologist with suitable qualifications and experience and having access to laboratory facilities;

    (b) if the coroner is informed by the chief officer of police that a person may be charged with the murder, manslaughter or infanticide of the deceased, the coroner should consult the chief officer of police regarding the legally qualified medical practitioner who is to make the post-mortem examination;

    (c) if the deceased died in a hospital, the coroner should not direct or request a pathologist on the staff of, or associated with, that hospital to make a post-mortem examination if—

        (i) that pathologist does not desire to make the examination, or

        (ii) the conduct of any member of the hospital staff is likely to be called in question, or

        (iii) any relative of the deceased asks the coroner that the examination be not made by such a pathologist,

    unless the obtaining of another pathologist with suitable qualifications and experience would cause the examination to be unduly delayed;

    (d) if the death of the deceased may have been caused by any of the diseases or injuries within paragraph (2), the coroner should not direct or request a legally qualified medical practitioner who is a member of a pneumoconiosis medical panel to make the post-mortem examination.

(2) The diseases and injuries within this paragraph are those in connection with which duties are from time to time imposed upon pneumoconiosis medical boards by Part III of the Social Security Act 1975 and any regulations made under that Act.[11]

7. Coroner to notify persons of post-mortem to be made

(1) Where a coroner directs or requests a legally qualified medical practitioner to make a post-mortem examination, the coroner shall notify the persons and bodies set out in paragraph (2) of the date, hour and place at which the examination will be made, unless it is impracticable to notify any such persons or bodies or to do so would cause the examination to be unduly delayed.

    (2) The persons and bodies to be notified by the coroner are as follows:—

    (a) any relative of the deceased who has notified the coroner of his desire to attend, or be represented at, the post-mortem examination;

    (b) the deceased's regular medical attendant;

    (c) if the deceased died in a hospital, the hospital;

    (d) if the death of the deceased may have been caused by any of the diseases or injuries within Rule 6(2) (other than occupational asthma), the pneumoconiosis medical panel for the area;

    (e) if the death of the deceased may have been caused by any accident or disease notice of which is required by or under any enactment to be given—

---

[11] The relevant instruments and amendments are set out in the footnote to the definition of industrial disease in rule 2(1).

(i) to an enforcing authority, the appropriate inspector appointed by, or representative of, that authority; or

(ii) to an inspector appointed by an enforcing authority, that inspector;

(f) any government department which has notified the coroner of its desire to be represented at the examination;

(g) if the chief officer of police has notified the coroner of his desire to be represented at the examination, the chief officer of police.

(3) Any person or body mentioned in paragraph (2) shall be entitled to be represented at a post-mortem examination by a legally qualified medical practitioner, or if any such person is a legally qualified medical practitioner he shall be entitled to attend the examination in person; but the chief officer of police may be represented by a member of the police force of which he is chief officer.

(4) Nothing in the foregoing provisions of this Rule shall be deemed to limit the discretion of the coroner to notify any person of the date, hour and place at which a post-mortem examination will be made and to permit him to attend the examination.

8. Persons attending post-mortem not to interfere

A person attending a post-mortem examination by virtue of paragraph (3) or (4) of Rule 7 shall not interfere with the performance of the examination.

9. Preservation of material

A person making a post-mortem examination shall make provision, so far as possible, for the preservation of material which in his opinion bears upon the cause of death for such period as the coroner thinks fit.

10. Report on post-mortem

(1) The person making a post-mortem examination shall report to the coroner in the form set out in Schedule 2 or in a form to the like effect.

(2) Unless authorised by the coroner, the person making a post-mortem examination shall not supply a copy of his report to any person other than the coroner.

11. Premises for post-mortems

(1) No post-mortem examination shall be made in a dwelling house or in licensed premises.

(2) Every post-mortem examination shall be made in premises, which are adequately equipped for the purpose of the examination.

(3) Where a person dies in a hospital possessing premises so equipped, any post-mortem examination of the body of that person shall, with the consent of the hospital authority, be made in those premises unless the coroner otherwise decides.

(4) For the purpose of this Rule no premises shall be deemed to be adequately equipped for the purpose of post-mortem examinations unless they are supplied with running water, proper heating and lighting facilities, and containers for the storing and preservation of material.

Part IV
Special Examination

12. Preservation of material

A person making a special examination shall make provision, so far as possible, for the preservation of the material submitted to him for examination for such period as the coroner thinks fit.

13. Report on special examination

Unless authorised by the coroner, the person making a special examination shall not supply a copy of his report to any person other than the coroner.

Part V
Burial Orders

14. Issue of burial order

An order of a coroner authorising the burial of a body shall not be issued unless the coroner has held, or has decided to hold, an inquest touching the death.

15. Burial order where certificate for disposal of body issued

Where a coroner is satisfied that a certificate for the disposal of a body has been issued by a registrar, the coroner shall not issue an order authorising the burial of that body unless the certificate has been surrendered to him; and in such a case he shall on issuing the order transmit the certificate to the registrar and inform him of the issue of the order.

Part VI
Inquests

16. Formality

Every inquest shall be opened, adjourned and closed in a formal manner.

17. Inquest in public

Every inquest shall be held in public:
Provided that the coroner may direct that the public be excluded from an inquest or any part of an inquest if he considers that it would be in the interest of national security so to do.

18. Days on which inquest not to be held

An inquest shall not be held on Christmas Day, Good Friday, or a bank holiday unless the coroner thinks it requisite on grounds of urgency that an inquest should be held on such a day, and no inquest shall be held on a Sunday.

19. Coroner to notify persons of inquest arrangements

The coroner shall notify the date, hour and place of an inquest to—
    (a) the spouse or a near relative or personal representative of the deceased whose name and address are known to the coroner; and
    (b) any other person who—
        (i)   in the opinion of the coroner is within Rule 20(2); and
        (ii) has asked the coroner to notify him of the aforesaid particulars of the inquest; and

(iii) has supplied the coroner with a telephone number or address for the purpose of so notifying him.

20. Entitlement to examine witnesses

(1) Without prejudice to any enactment with regard to the examination of witnesses at an inquest, any person who satisfies the coroner that he is within paragraph (2) shall be entitled to examine any witness at an inquest either in person or by [an authorised advocate as defined by section 119(1) of the Courts and Legal Services Act 1990]:[12]
Provided that—
  (a) the chief officer of police, unless interested otherwise than in that capacity, shall only be entitled to examine a witness by [such an advocate];[13]
  (b) the coroner shall disallow any question which in his opinion is not relevant or is otherwise not a proper question.

(2) Each of the following persons shall have the rights conferred by paragraph (1):—
  (a) a parent, child, spouse and any personal representative of the deceased;
  (b) any beneficiary under a policy of insurance issued on the life of the deceased;
  (c) the insurer who issued such a policy of insurance;
  (d) any person whose act or omission or that of his agent or servant may in the opinion of the coroner have caused, or contributed to, the death of the deceased;
  (e) any person appointed by a trade union to which the deceased at the time of his death belonged, if the death of the deceased may have been caused by an injury received in the course of his employment or by an industrial disease;
  (f) an inspector appointed by, or a representative of, an enforcing authority, or any person appointed by a government department to attend the inquest;
  (g) the chief officer of police;
  (h) any other person who, in the opinion of the coroner, is a properly interested person.

21. Examination of witnesses

Unless the coroner otherwise determines, a witness at an inquest shall be examined first by the coroner and, if the witness is represented at the inquest, lastly by his representative.

22. Self-incrimination

(1) No witness at an inquest shall be obliged to answer any question tending to incriminate himself

(2) Where it appears to the coroner that a witness has been asked such a question, the coroner shall inform the witness that he may refuse to answer.

23. Adjournment where inspector or representative of enforcing authority etc. is not present

(1) Where a coroner holds an inquest touching the death of a person which may have been caused by an accident or disease notice of which is required to be given to an enforcing authority, the coroner shall adjourn the request unless an inspector appointed by, or a representative of, the enforcing authority is present to watch the proceedings and shall, at least four days before holding the adjourned inquest, give to such inspector or representative notice of the date, hour and place of holding the adjourned inquest.

---

[12] Words substituted by SI 1999/3325, rule 4(a).
[13] Words substituted by SI 1999/3325, rule 4(b).

(2) Where a coroner holds an inquest touching the death of a person which may have been caused by an accident or disease notice of which is required to be given to an inspector appointed by an enforcing authority, the coroner shall adjourn the inquest unless the inspector or a representative of the inspector is present to watch the proceedings and shall, at least four days before holding the adjourned inquest, give to the inspector or representative notice of the date, hour and place of holding the adjourned inquest.

24. Notice to person whose conduct is likely to be called in question

Any person whose conduct is likely in the opinion of the coroner to be called in question at an inquest shall, if not duly summoned to give evidence at the inquest, be given reasonable notice of the date, hour and place at which the inquest will be held.

25. Adjournment where person whose conduct is called in question is not present

If the conduct of any person is called in question at an inquest on grounds which the coroner thinks substantial and which relate to any matter referred to in Rule 36 and if that person is not present at the inquest and has not been duly summoned to attend or otherwise given notice of the holding of the inquest, the inquest shall be adjourned to enable him to be present, if he so desires.

26. Request by Chief Officer of Police for adjournment

(1) If the chief officer of police requests a coroner to adjourn an inquest on the ground that a person may be charged with an offence within paragraph (3), the coroner shall adjourn the inquest for twenty-eight days or for such longer period as he may think fit.

(2) At any time before the date fixed for the holding of the adjourned inquest, the chief officer of police may ask the coroner for a further adjournment and the coroner may comply with his request.

(3) The offences within this paragraph are murder, manslaughter or infanticide of the deceased, an offence under section 1 of the Road Traffic Act 1972[14] causing the death of the deceased and an offence under section 2(1) of the Suicide Act 1961[15] consisting of aiding, abetting, counselling or procuring the suicide of the deceased.

27. Request by Director of Public Prosecutions for adjournment

(1) If the Director of Public Prosecutions requests a coroner to adjourn an inquest on the ground that a person may be charged with an offence (whether or not involving the death of a person other than the deceased) committed in circumstances connected with the death of the deceased, not being an offence within Rule 26(3), the coroner shall adjourn the inquest for twenty-eight days or for such longer period as he may think fit.

(2) At any time before the date fixed for the holding of the adjourned inquest, the Director of Public Prosecutions may ask the coroner for a further adjournment and the coroner may comply with his request.

28. Coroner to adjourn in certain other cases

(1) If during the course of an inquest evidence is given from which it appears to the coroner that the death of the deceased is likely to be due to an offence within Rule 26(3) and that a person might be charged with such an offence, then the coroner, unless he has previously been notified by the Director of Public Prosecutions that adjournment is

---

[14] 1972 c. 20; section 1 was substituted by the Criminal Law Act 1977 (c. 45), section 50.
[15] 1961 c. 60.

unnecessary, shall adjourn the inquest for fourteen days or for such longer period as he may think fit and send to the Director particulars of that evidence.

(2) At any time before the date fixed for the holding of the adjourned inquest, the Director of Public Prosecutions may ask the coroner for a further adjournment and the coroner may comply with his request.

29. Coroner to furnish certificate after adjournment

A certificate under the hand of a coroner stating the particulars which under [the Births and Deaths Registration Act 1953][16] are required to be registered concerning a death which he furnishes to a registrar of deaths under [section 16(4) of the 1988 Act][17] shall be furnished within five days from the date on which the inquest is adjourned.

30. Coroner's interim certificate of the fact of death

When an inquest has been adjourned for any reason and [section 16(4) of the 1988 Act][18] does not apply, the coroner shall on application supply to any person who, in the opinion of the coroner, is a properly interested person an interim certificate of the fact of death.

31. Coroner to furnish certificate stating result of criminal proceedings

A certificate under the hand of a coroner stating the result of the relevant criminal proceedings which he furnishes to a registrar of deaths under [section 16(5) or 16(7) of the 1988 Act][19] shall be furnished within twenty-eight days from the date on which he is notified of the result of the proceedings under [section 17][20] of that Act or, if the person charged with an offence before a magistrates' court as mentioned in [section 17][21] of that Act is not committed for trial to the Crown Court, within twenty-eight days from the date on which he is notified under the said [section 17][22] of the result of the proceedings in the magistrates' court.

32. Effect of institution of criminal proceedings

Subject to [sections 16 and 17 of the 1988 Act],[23] an inquest shall not be adjourned solely by reason of the institution of criminal proceedings arising out of the death of the deceased.

33. Coroner to notify persons as to resumption of, and alteration of arrangements for, adjourned inquest

(1) If an inquest which has been adjourned in pursuance of [sections 16 to 17A of the 1988 Act][24] is not to be resumed, the coroner shall notify the persons within paragraph (4).

(2) If an inquest which has been adjourned as aforesaid is to be resumed, the coroner shall give reasonable notice of the date, hour and place at which the inquest will be resumed to the persons within paragraph (4).

---

[16] Words substituted by SI 1999/3325, rule 5.
[17] Words substituted by SI 1999/3325, rule 6.
[18] Words substituted by SI 1999/3325, rule 6.
[19] Words substituted by SI 1999/3325, rule 7(a).
[20] Words substituted by SI 1999/3325, rule 7(b).
[21] Words substituted by SI 1999/3325, rule 7(c).
[22] Words substituted by SI 1999/3325, rule 7(c).
[23] Words substituted by SI 1999/3325, rule 8.
[24] Words substituted by SI 1999/3325, rule 9.

(3) Where a coroner has fixed a date, hour and place for the holding of an inquest adjourned for any reason, he may, at any time before the date so fixed, alter the date, hour or place fixed and shall then give reasonable notice to the persons within paragraph (4).

(4) The persons within this paragraph are the members of the jury (if any), the witnesses, the chief officer of police, any person notified under Rule 19 or 24 and any other person appearing in person or represented at the inquest.

34. Recognizance of witness or juror becoming void

Where any witness or juror who has been bound over to attend at an adjourned inquest, whether without further notice or conditionally on receiving further notice, is notified by the coroner that his attendance at the adjourned inquest is not required or that the inquest will not be resumed, the recognizance entered into by him shall be void.

35. Coroner to notify Crown Court officer of adjournment in certain cases

Where a person charged with an offence within Rule 26(3) is committed for trial to the Crown Court, the coroner who has adjourned an inquest in pursuance of [sections 16 and 17 of the 1988 Act][25] shall inform the appropriate officer of the Crown Court at the place where the person charged is to be tried of such adjournment.

36. Matters to be ascertained at inquest

(1) The proceedings and evidence at an inquest shall be directed solely to ascertaining the following matters, namely—
   (a) who the deceased was;
   (b) how, when and where the deceased came by his death;
   (c) the particulars for the time being required by the Registration Acts[26] to be registered concerning the death.

(2) Neither the coroner nor the jury shall express any opinion on any other matters.

37. Documentary evidence

(1) Subject to the provisions of paragraphs (2) to (4), the coroner may admit at an inquest documentary evidence relevant to the purposes of the inquest from any living person which in his opinion is unlikely to be disputed, unless a person who in the opinion of the coroner is within Rule 20(2) objects to the documentary evidence being admitted.

(2) Documentary evidence so objected to may be admitted if in the opinion of the coroner the maker of the document is unable to give oral evidence within a reasonable period.

(3) Subject to paragraph (4), before admitting such documentary evidence the coroner shall at the beginning of the inquest announce publicly—
   (a) that the documentary evidence may be admitted, and
   (b) (i) the full name of the maker of the document to be admitted in evidence, and
       (ii) a brief account of such document, and
   (c) that any person who in the opinion of the coroner is within Rule 20(2) may object to the admission of any such documentary evidence, and

---

[25] Words substituted by SI 1999/3325, rule 10.

[26] Author's note: The reference here to 'the Registration Acts' is a little puzzling. By the Coroners Amendment rules 1999 (SI 1999/3325) the definition of Registration Acts in rule 2 CR was removed and rule 29 CR was amended to refer to the Births and Deaths Registration Act 1953.

(d) that any person who in the opinion of the coroner is within Rule 20(2) is entitled to see a copy of any such documentary evidence if he so wishes.

(4) If during the course of an inquest it appears that there is available at the inquest documentary evidence which in the opinion of the coroner is relevant to the purposes of the inquest but the maker of the document is not present and in the opinion of the coroner the content of the documentary evidence is unlikely to be disputed, the coroner shall at the earliest opportunity during the course of the inquest comply with the provisions of paragraph (3).

(5) A coroner may admit as evidence at an inquest any document made by a deceased person if he is of the opinion that the contents of the document are relevant to the purposes of the inquest.

(6) Any documentary evidence admitted under this Rule shall, unless the coroner otherwise directs, be read aloud at the inquest.

[37A. Public inquiry findings

(1) Notwithstanding the provisions of Rule 37, at an inquest resumed after having been adjourned pursuant to section 17A of the 1988 Act, the coroner may admit documentary evidence relevant to the purposes of the inquest and containing the findings of the public inquiry to which section 17A(1)(a) refers.

(2) Before admitting such documentary evidence, the coroner shall at the beginning of the resumed inquest announce publicly—
    (a) that the findings of the public inquiry may be admitted,
    (b) the title, date of publication and a brief account of those findings, and
    (c) that any person who, in the opinion of the coroner, is within Rule 20(2) is entitled to see a copy of any such documentary evidence if he so wishes.

(3) Any documentary evidence admitted under this Rule shall, unless the coroner otherwise directs, be read aloud at the inquest.][27]

38. Exhibits

All exhibits produced in evidence at an inquest shall be marked with consecutive numbers and each number shall be preceded by the letter 'C'.

39. Notes of evidence

The coroner shall take notes of the evidence at every inquest.

40. No addresses as to facts

No person shall be allowed to address the coroner or the jury as to the facts.

41. Summing-up and direction to jury

Where the coroner sits with a jury, he shall sum up the evidence to the jury and direct them as to the law before they consider their verdict and shall draw their attention to Rules 36(2) and 42.

42. Verdict

No verdict shall be framed in such a way as to appear to determine any question of—
    (a) criminal liability on the part of a named person, or
    (b) civil liability.

---

[27] Inserted by SI 1999/3325, rule 11.

43. Prevention of similar fatalities

A coroner who believes that action should be taken to prevent the recurrence of fatalities similar to that in respect of which the inquest is being held may announce at the inquest that he is reporting the matter in writing to the person or authority who may have power to take such action and he may report the matter accordingly.

PART VII
SUMMONING OF JURORS AND EXCUSAL FROM JURY SERVICE

44. Summoning of jurors

Subject to the provisions of these Rules, the person to whom the coroner's warrant is issued under [section 8 of the 1988 Act][28] for the summoning of persons to attend as jurors at inquests shall have regard to the convenience of the persons summoned and to their respective places of residence, and in particular to the desirability of selecting jurors within reasonable daily travelling distance of the place where they are to attend.

45. Method of summoning

Subject to the provisions of these Rules, jurors shall be summoned by notice in writing sent by post or delivered by hand and a notice shall be sent or delivered to a juror at his address as shown in the electoral register.

46. Notice to accompany summons

A written summons sent or delivered to any person under Rule 45 shall be accompanied by a notice informing him—

 (a) of the effect of [section 9 of the 1988 Act][29] and Rules 51(1) and 52; and
 (b) that he may make representations to the appropriate officer with a view to obtaining the withdrawal of the summons, if for any reason he is not qualified for jury service, or wishes or is entitled to be excused.

47. Withdrawal or alteration of summons

If it appears to the appropriate officer, at any time before the day on which any person summoned under [section 8 of the 1988 Act][30] is to attend, that his attendance is unnecessary, or can be dispensed with, the appropriate officer may withdraw or alter the summons by notice served in the same way as a notice of summons.

48. Summoning in exceptional circumstances

If it appears to the coroner that a jury will be, or probably will be, incomplete, the coroner may, if he thinks fit, require any persons who are in, or in the vicinity of, the place of the inquest to be summoned (without any written notice) for jury service up to the number needed (after allowing for any who may not be qualified under [section 9 of the 1988 Act][31] and for excusals) to make up such number.

49. Excusal for previous jury service

(1) If a person summoned under [section 8 of the 1988 Act][32] shows to the satisfaction of the appropriate officer or of the coroner—

---

[28] Words substituted by SI 1999/3325, rule 12.
[29] Words substituted by SI 1999/3325, rule 13.
[30] Words substituted by SI 1999/3325, rule 12.
[31] Words substituted by SI 1999/3325, rule 13.
[32] Words substituted by SI 1999/3325, rule 12.

(a) that he has served on a jury, or duly attended to serve on a jury, at inquests held in that coroner's jurisdiction on three or more days in the period of one year ending with the service of the summons on him; or

(b) that he has served on a jury, or duly attended to serve on a jury, in the Crown Court, the High Court or any county court in the period of two years ending with the service of the summons on him; or

(c) that any such court or a coroner has excused him from jury service for a period which has not terminated,

the appropriate officer or the coroner shall excuse him from attending, or further attending, in pursuance of the summons.

(2) In reckoning the days for the purpose of paragraph (1)(a) no account shall be taken of any day or days to which an inquest is adjourned.

50. Certificate of attendance

A person duly attending to serve on a jury in compliance with a summons under [section 8 of the 1988 Act][33] shall be entitled on application to the appropriate officer to a certificate recording that he has so attended.

51. Excusal for certain persons and discretionary excusal

(1) A person summoned under [section 8 of the 1988 Act][34] shall be entitled, if he so wishes, to be excused from jury service if he is among the persons for the time being listed in Part III of Schedule 1 to the Juries Act 1974[35] but, except as provided by that Part of that Schedule in the case of members of the forces, a person shall not by this Rule be exempt from his obligation to attend if summoned unless he is excused from attending under paragraph (2).

(2) If any person so summoned shows to the satisfaction of the appropriate officer or of the coroner that there is good reason why he should be excused from attending in pursuance of the summons, the appropriate officer or the coroner may excuse him from so attending and shall do so if the reason shown is that the person is entitled under paragraph (1) to excusal.

52. Discharge of summons in case of doubt as to capacity to act effectively as a juror

Where it appears to the appropriate officer, in the case of a person attending in pursuance of a summons under [section 8 of the 1988 Act],[36] that on account of physical disability or insufficient understanding of English there is doubt as to his capacity to act effectively as a juror, the person may be brought before the coroner, who shall determine whether or not he should act as a juror and, if not, shall discharge the summons.

53. Saving for inquests held by the coroner of the Queen's household

Nothing in this Part of these Rules shall have effect in relation to any inquest held by the coroner of the Queen's household.

---

[33] Words substituted by SI 1999/3325, rule 12.
[34] Words substituted by SI 1999/3325, rule 12.
[35] 1974 c. 23.
[36] Words substituted by SI 1999/3325, rule 12.

Part VIII
Records, Documents, Exhibits and Forms

54. Register of deaths

A coroner shall keep an indexed register of all deaths reported to him, or to his deputy or assistant deputy, which shall contain the particulars specified in Schedule 3.

55. Retention and delivery or disposal of exhibits

Every exhibit at an inquest shall, unless a court otherwise directs, be retained by the coroner until he is satisfied that the exhibit is not likely to be, or will no longer be, required for the purposes of any other legal proceedings, and shall then, if a request for its delivery has been made by a person appearing to the coroner to be entitled to the possession thereof, be delivered to that person, or, if no such request has been made, be destroyed or otherwise disposed of as the coroner thinks fit.

56. Retention and delivery of documents

Any document (other than an exhibit at an inquest) in the possession of a coroner in connection with an inquest or post-mortem examination shall, unless a court otherwise directs, be retained by the coroner for at least fifteen years: Provided that the coroner may deliver any such document to any person who in the opinion of the coroner is a proper person to have possession of it.

57. Inspection of, or supply of copies of, documents etc

(1) A coroner shall, on application and on payment of the prescribed fee[37] (if any), supply to any person who, in the opinion of the coroner, is a properly interested person a copy of any report of a post-mortem examination (including one made under [section 19 of the 1988 Act][38] or special examination, or of any notes of evidence, or of any document put in evidence at an inquest.

(2) A coroner may, on application and without charge, permit any person who, in the opinion of the coroner, is a properly interested person to inspect such report, notes of evidence, or document.

58. Deputy or assistant deputy to sign documents in own name

Where a deputy or assistant deputy coroner acting for, or as, the coroner signs a document, he shall sign it in his own name as deputy or assistant deputy coroner, as the case may be.

59. Transfer of documents etc to next-appointed coroner

Where a coroner vacates his office by death or otherwise, all documents, exhibits, registers and other things in the custody of the coroner in connection with inquests or post-mortem examinations shall be transferred to the coroner next appointed to that office.

60. Forms

The forms set out in Schedule 4, with such modifications as circumstances may require, may be used for the purposes for which they are expressed to be applicable.

---

[37] See the Coroners' Records (Fees for Copies) Rules 2002 (SI 2002/2401).
[38] Words substituted by SI 1999/3325, rule 14.

SCHEDULE 1
Revocations

SCHEDULE 2
Post-mortem examination report

SCHEDULE 3
Register of deaths reported to coroner

SCHEDULE 4   Rule 60
FORMS

Form 1
Form of declaration of office of coroner

I, A.B., solemnly, sincerely, and truly declare and affirm that I will well and truly serve our Sovereign Lady the Queen and Her liege people in the office of coroner for this county of   , and that I will diligently and truly do everything appertaining to my office to the best of my power for the doing of right, and for the good of the inhabitants within the said county.

Form 2
Warrant to exhume

To: (*insert the names of the Minister and churchwardens or other persons having power of control over the churchyard, cemetery, or other place in which the body is buried*).

Whereas I, A.B., one of Her Majesty's coroners for the   of   am credibly informed that the body of one, C.D., has been recently buried in (*insert the name of the churchyard, cemetery or other place in which the body is buried*), and it appears to me that it is necessary for the body to be examined for the purpose of [my holding an inquest touching the death of the deceased] [my discharging one of my functions in relation to the body or death of the deceased, namely   *insert function*])

I hereby order you to cause the body of the said C.D. to be disinterred for that purpose.

Dated this   day of   19

Signature   ....

Coroner for   ....

Form 3
Warrant to summon jury

To the Coroner's officer and to each and all of the constables of

You are hereby commanded to summon   jurors to appear before me on (*state day of week*) the   (*state date*) day of   19 , at   a.m./p.m. at   (*state place*).

Dated this   day of   19

Signature   ....

Coroner for   ....

Form 4
Summons to juror

To

By virtue of a warrant of A.B., one of Her Majesty's coroners for the　　　　　of
　　　　you are hereby summoned to appear before him as a juror on　　　　　(*state day
of week*) the　　　　　(*state date*) day of 19　, at a.m./p.m. at　　　　　(*state place*) until
you are no longer needed.

You must attend at the time and place shown above unless you are told by the officer
authorised by the Coroner that you need not do so.

Dated this　　　　　day of　　　　19

Signature　　. . . . .
Coroner's Officer/Constable

YOU MUST COMPLETE THE ATTACHED FORM AND RETURN IT TO
(*insert name of officer authorised by the Coroner*) IN THE ENVELOPE PROVIDED
WITHIN THREE DAYS OF THE RECEIPT OF THIS SUMMONS.

WARNING: YOU WILL BE LIABLE TO A FINE IF YOU—
1. refuse to give the information necessary to decide if you are qualified to serve on a jury;
2. deliberately give false information or cause or permit false information to be given;
3. fail to attend for jury service or refuse without reasonable excuse to serve as a juror; or
4. serve on a jury knowing you are not qualified to do so.

Form 5
Notice to accompany summons and reply thereto

This form should be returned in the envelope provided within three days of receiving it.

Surname . . . .

Forename(s) . . . . Date of Birth . . . .

Address . . . .

Telephone number . . . .

(If possible please give a telephone number where you can be contacted between 9 am and
5 pm)

INFORMATION GIVEN WILL BE TREATED IN THE STRICTEST CON-
FIDENCE
YOU ARE QUALIFIED for jury service if you—

(a) are [not less than eighteen nor more than seventy years of age];[39]
(*If you will be under eighteen on or have reached your [seventieth]*[40] *birthday by the date on
which your appearance is required you will NOT be eligible to serve as a juror.*)
(b) are registered as a parliamentary or local government elector;
(c) have lived in the United Kingdom, the Channel Islands or the Isle of Man for a period
of at least five years since attaining the age of thirteen; and
(d) are not one of the persons described in Parts I and II of Schedule 1 to the Juries Act
1974.*

---

[39] Words substituted by SI 1999/3325, rule 15(a).
[40] Words substituted by SI 1999/3325, rule 15(b).

1. Are you QUALIFIED to serve as a juror? Please tick appropriate box.

YES ☐   NO ☐

If you have answered NO to question 1, please answer question 2 and sign the form at the end.

If you have answered YES and wish to apply to be excused from jury service on this occasion, please go on to 3 below and then sign the form at the end.

2. I AM NOT QUALIFIED to serve on a jury because—

3. YOU ARE ENTITLED TO BE EXCUSED if you fall within any of the categories of persons specified in Part III of Schedule 1 to the Juries Act 1974** (although you may serve if you want to).

YOU MAY BE EXCUSED at the discretion of the Coroner or of the officer authorised by the Coroner on grounds such as poor health, illness, physical disability, insufficient understanding of English, holiday arrangements or for any other good reason.

I WISH TO BE EXCUSED from jury service on this occasion because—

(If you are in any doubt as to whether you may be excused from jury service please write to the officer authorised by the Coroner at the address on the front of the summons.)

When you attend as a juror you may be discharged if there is doubt as to your capacity to serve on a jury because of physical disability or insufficient understanding of English.

I HAVE READ THE WARNING IN THE SUMMONS AND THE INFORMATION I HAVE GIVEN IS TRUE.

Signed . . . .

Dated . . . .

* See List 1 attached.
** See List 2 attached.

Form 6
Certificate of attendance

Name of Juror

I hereby certify that the above-named Juror (attended to serve) (served) on a jury at an inquest held before A.B., one of Her Majesty's coroners for   the   of

*on/*from

*to

*Delete as required

[and I further certify that in the opinion of the Coroner it would be reasonable and proper that he/she should be exempt from service on a jury in a coroner's court for a period of years from   ]

Dated this   day of   19

Signature . . . .
Officer authorised by the Coroner.

[Form 7
Form of oath of juror

I swear by Almighty God that I will diligently inquire on behalf of our Sovereign Lady the Queen into the death of C.D. and give a true verdict according to the evidence.

NOTE: If a person wishes to affirm, or swear in Scottish form or in any other form authorised by law, this oath shall be modified accordingly.][41]

Form 8
Summons to witness

To

You are hereby summoned to appear before me on   (*state day of week*)
the   (*state date*) day of   19 , at   am/pm at   (*state place*) to give evidence touching the death of C.D.

Dated this   day of   19

Signature   ....

Coroner for   ....

Form 9
Oath of witness

I swear by Almighty God that the evidence which I shall give shall be the truth, the whole truth and nothing but the truth.

NOTE: If a person wishes to affirm, or swear in Scottish form or in any other form authorised by law, this oath shall be modified accordingly.

Form 10
Direction to medical practitioner to make a post-mortem examination

To

I hereby direct you, in pursuance of [section 19 or 21 of the Coroners Act 1988],[42] to make a post-mortem examination of the body of C.D and to report the result thereof to me in writing.

Dated this   day of   19

Signature   ....

Coroner for   ....

Form 11
Certificate of fine

I hereby certify that I have imposed a fine of   upon E.F. for that he being duly summoned to appear as a juror [witness] at an inquest held before [by] me on the day of   19 .

*did not, after being openly called three times, appear to such summons.
*refused, without reasonable excuse, to serve as a juror.
*refused, without lawful excuse, to answer a question put to him.

*Delete as required

---

[41] Words substituted by the Coroners Amendment Rules 1985 (SI 1985/1414), rule 2.
[42] Words substituted by SI 1999/3325, rule 16.

Dated this   day of   19

Signature   . . . .

Coroner for   . . . .

Form 12
Form of recognizance—witnesses or jurors

G.H. of   acknowledges that he/she owes to our Sovereign Lady the Queen the sum of   , payment thereof to be enforced against him/her by due process of law if he/she fails to comply with the following condition.

Taken before me the   day of   19   .

Signature   . . . .

Coroner for   . . . .

Condition
If the said G.H. [on receiving notice] appears at an inquest touching the death of C.D. to be held on the   day of   next at   or on such other date or at such other place as may be notified to him/her, and there gives evidence [makes further inquiry as a juror] touching the said death, then this recognizance shall be void but otherwise shall remain in full force.

Form 13
Notice of inquest arrangements

To

I hereby give you notice that the inquest touching the death of C.D. will take place on (*state day of week*) the   (*state date*) day of 19   at   am/pm at (*state place*).

Dated this   day of   19

Signature   . . . .

Coroner for   . . . .

Form 14
Coroner's interim certificate of the fact of death

To whom it may concern.

(Name)

of (address)

died on

The precise medical cause of death * was as follows/* has yet to be established.

Dated this   day of   19

Signature   . . . .

Coroner for   . . . .

*Delete whichever is inapplicable.

Form 15
Notice that an inquest which is adjourned in pursuance of [sections 16, 17 or 17A of the Coroners Act 1988][43] will not be resumed

To

I hearby give you notice that the inquest touching the death of C.D. will not be resumed.

Dated this   day of   19

Signature   ....

Coroner for   ....

Form 16
Notice that an inquest which is adjourned in pursuance of [sections 16, 17 or 17A of the Coroners Act 1988][44] will be resumed

To

I hereby give you notice that the inquest touching the death of C.D. will be resumed on (*state day of week*) the   (*state date*) day of   19   at am/pm at (*state place*) [and that your attendance thereat is required].

Dated this   day of   19

Signature   ....

Coroner for   ....

Form 17
Notice that the attendance of a witness will not be required at the holding of an adjourned inquest

To

I hereby give you notice that your attendance at the adjourned inquest touching the death of C.D. to be held on the   day of   19   will not be required.

Dated this   day of   19

Signature   ....

Coroner for   ....

Form 18
Notice that the date, hour or place fixed for the holding of an adjourned inquest has been altered

To

I hereby give you notice that the date/hour/place fixed for the holding of the adjourned inquest touching the death of C.D. has been altered, and that the adjourned inquest will be held on   (*state date and day of week*) at   am/pm at   (*state place*) [and that your attendance thereat is/is not required].

---

[43] Words substituted by SI 1999/3325, rule 17.
[44] Words substituted by SI 1999/3325, rule 17.

Dated this   day of   19

Signature   . . . .

Coroner for   . . . .

Form 19
Certificate of forfeiture of recognizance

I hereby certify that G.H. of   was bound by recognizance taken by me on the   day of   19   , in the sum of   for his appearance at an inquest held at   on the   day of   19   , to give evidence (make further inquiry as a juror) touching the death of C.D., and the said G.H. failed to appear in accordance with the condition of the said recognizance and that the said recognizance is accordingly forfeited.

Dated this   day of   19

Signature   . . . .

Coroner for   . . . .

Form 20
Order to remove body for inquest or post-mortem examination

To (*undertaker or other person as the case may be*)

I hereby authorise you to remove the body of C.D., aged   from

to   before the   day of   19   .

Dated this   day of   19

Signature   . . . .

Coroner for   . . . .

Form 21
Coroner's order for burial

I hereby authorise the burial of the body of C.D. aged   late of   who died at   on   .

Dated this   day of   19

Signature   . . . .

Coroner for   . . . .

Form 22
Inquisition

An inquisition taken for our Sovereign Lady the Queen at   , in the county (*or as the case may be*) of   on the   day of   19   , (and by adjournment on the   day of   19   ) (before and by (1)) me A.B., one of Her Majesty's coroners for the said county (*or as the case may be*), (and the undermentioned jurors,) touching the death of C.D. (a person unknown) (concerning a stillbirth).

The following matters are found:—

1 Name of deceased (if known):
2 Injury or disease causing death:(2)

3 Time, place and circumstances at or in which injury was sustained:(3)
4 Conclusion of the jury/coroner as to the death:(4)
5 Particulars for the time being required by the Registration Acts to be registered concerning the death:

(1)	(2)	(3)	(4)	(5)	(6)
Date and place of death	Name and surname deceased	Sex	Maiden surname of woman who has married	Date and place of birth	Occupation and usual address

Signature of coroner (and jurors)

NOTES

(1) Modify this as necessary according to whether the inquest is held with or without a jury or partly with and partly without a jury.

(2) In the case of a death from natural causes or from industrial disease, want of attention at birth, or dependence on, or non-dependent abuse of, drugs insert the immediate cause of death and the morbid conditions (if any) giving rise to the immediate cause of death.

(3) Omit this if the cause of death is one to which Note 2 applies.

(4) (a) Where the cause of death is one to which Note 2 applies, it is suggested that one of the following forms be adopted:—

C.D. died from natural causes.

C.D. died from the industrial disease of

C.D. died from dependence on drugs/non-dependent abuse of drugs.

C.D. died from want of attention at birth.

(In any of the above cases but in no other, it is suggested that the following words may, where appropriate, be added:

'and the cause of death was aggravated by lack of care/self-neglect'.)

(b) In any other case except murder, manslaughter, infanticide or stillbirth, it is suggested that one of the following forms be adopted:—

C.D. killed himself [whilst the balance of his mind was disturbed].

C.D. died as a result of an attempted/self-induced abortion.

C.D. died as a result of an accident/misadventure.

[CD died in the disaster (*insert name of disaster which was subject of a public inquiry*)][45]

Execution of sentence of death.

C.D. was killed lawfully.

Open verdict, namely, the evidence did not fully or further disclose the means whereby the cause of death arose.

(c) In the case of murder, manslaughter or infanticide it is suggested that the following form be adopted:—

C.D. was killed unlawfully.

(d) In the case of a stillbirth insert 'stillbirth' and do not complete the remainder of the form.

---

[45] Words inserted by SI 1999/3325, rule 18.

APPENDIX 7

The Coroners' Records (Fees for Copies) Rules 2002

2002 No 2401
CORONERS
The Coroners' Records (Fees for Copies) Rules 2002

Made   *18 September 2002*
Coming into force   *1 November 2002*

The Secretary of State, in exercise of the powers conferred on him by section 24(3) of the Coroners Act 1988,[1] hereby makes the following Rules:

1.—(1) These Rules may be cited as the Coroners' Records (Fees for Copies) Rules 2002 and shall come into force on 1 November 2002.

(2) In these Rules 'photocopy' includes a copy produced by xerox machine, photocopier, facsimile, or printed from a computer disk.

2. The fees payable to coroners or other persons for furnishing copies, other than photocopies, of inquisitions, depositions or other documents in their custody relating to an inquest shall be as follows:

(a) for a copy of not more than 360 words, £6.20;
(b) for a copy of not less than 361 and not more than 1440 words, £13.10;
(c) for a copy in excess of 1440 words, £13.10 for the first 1440 words and thereafter 70p for each 72 words or part thereof.

3. The fee payable to coroners or other persons for furnishing photocopies of inquisitions, depositions or other documents in their custody relating to an inquest shall be £1.10 for each page.

4. The Coroners' Records (Fees for Copies) Rules 1997[2] are hereby revoked.

Hilary Benn
Parliamentary Under-Secretary of State

Home Office
18 September 2002

EXPLANATORY NOTE
(This note is not part of the Rules)

These Rules, which replace the Coroners' Records (Fees for Copies) Rules 1997, increase (in line with inflation) the fees payable to coroners or other persons for copies of inquisitions, depositions or other documents relating to inquests.

---

[1] 1988 c. 13.
[2] SI 1997/2544.

APPENDIX 8

Treasure Act 1996

1996 Chapter 24

ARRANGEMENT OF SECTIONS

Meaning of 'treasure'

An Act to abolish treasure trove and to make fresh provision in relation to treasure.

[4 July 1996]

BE IT ENACTED by the Queen's most Excellent Majesty, by and with the advice and consent of the Lords Spiritual and Temporal, and Commons, in this present Parliament assembled, and by the authority of the same, as follows:—

Meaning of 'treasure'

Meaning of 'treasure'. 1.—(1) Treasure is—
  (a) any object at least 300 years old when found which—
    (i)   is not a coin but has metallic content of which at least 10 per cent by weight is precious metal;
    (ii) when found, is one of at least two coins in the same find which are at least 300 years old at that time and have that percentage of precious metal; or
    (iii) when found, is one of at least ten coins in the same find which are at least 300 years old at that time;
  (b) any object at least 200 years old when found which belongs to a class designated under section 2(1);
  (c) any object which would have been treasure trove if found before the commencement of section 4;
  (d) any object which, when found, is part of the same find as—
    (i) an object within paragraph (a), (b) or (c) found at the same time or earlier; or
    (ii) an object found earlier which would be within paragraph (a) or (b) if it had been found at the same time.

(2) Treasure does not include objects which are—
  (a) unworked natural objects, or
  (b) minerals as extracted from natural deposit,
or which belong to a class designated under section 2(2).

Power to alter meaning. 2.—(1) The Secretary of State may by order, for the purposes of section 1(1)(b), designate any class of object which he considers to be of outstanding historical, archaeological or cultural importance.

(2) The Secretary of State may by order, for the purposes of section 1(2), designate any class of object which (apart from the order) would be treasure.

(3) An order under this section shall be made by statutory instrument.

(4) No order is to be made under this section unless a draft of the order has been laid before Parliament and approved by a resolution of each House.

Supplementary. 3.—(1) This section supplements section 1.

(2) 'Coin' includes any metal token which was, or can reasonably be assumed to have been, used or intended for use as or instead of money.

(3) 'Precious metal' means gold or silver.

(4) When an object is found, it is part of the same find as another object if—
  (a) they are found together,
  (b) the other object was found earlier in the same place where they had been left together,
  (c) the other object was found earlier in a different place, but they had been left together and had become separated before being found.

(5) If the circumstances in which objects are found can reasonably be taken to indicate that they were together at some time before being found, the objects are to be presumed to have been left together, unless shown not to have been.

(6) An object which can reasonably be taken to be at least a particular age is to be presumed to be at least that age, unless shown not to be.

(7) An object is not treasure if it is wreck within the meaning of Part IX of the Merchant Shipping Act 1995.

Ownership of treasure

Ownership of treasure which is found. 4.—(1) When treasure is found, it vests, subject to prior interests and rights—

    (a) in the franchisee, if there is one;

    (b) otherwise, in the Crown.

(2) Prior interests and rights are any which, or which derive from any which—

    (a) were held when the treasure was left where it was found, or

    (b) if the treasure had been moved before being found, were held when it was left where it was before being moved.

(3) If the treasure would have been treasure trove if found before the commencement of this section, neither the Crown nor any franchisee has any interest in it or right over it except in accordance with this Act.

(4) This section applies—

    (a) whatever the nature of the place where the treasure was found, and

    (b) whatever the circumstances in which it was left (including being lost or being left with no intention of recovery).

Meaning of 'franchisee'. 5.—(1) The franchisee for any treasure is the person who—

    (a) was, immediately before the commencement of section 4, or

    (b) apart from this Act, as successor in title, would have been,

the franchisee of the Crown in right of treasure trove for the place where the treasure was found.

(2) It is as franchisees in right of treasure trove that Her Majesty and the Duke of Cornwall are to be treated as having enjoyed the rights to treasure trove which belonged respectively to the Duchy of Lancaster and the Duchy of Cornwall immediately before the commencement of section 4.

Treasure vesting in the Crown. 6.—(1) Treasure vesting in the Crown under this Act is to be treated as part of the hereditary revenues of the Crown to which section 1 of the Civil List Act 1952 applies (surrender of hereditary revenues to the Exchequer).

(2) Any such treasure may be transferred, or otherwise disposed of, in accordance with directions given by the Secretary of State.

(3) The Crown's title to any such treasure may be disclaimed at any time by the Secretary of State.

(4) If the Crown's title is disclaimed, the treasure—

    (a) is deemed not to have vested in the Crown under this Act, and

    (b) without prejudice to the interests or rights of others, may be delivered to any person in accordance with the code published under section 11.

Coroners' jurisdiction

Jurisdiction of coroners. 7.—(1) The jurisdiction of coroners which is referred to in section 30 of the Coroners Act 1988 (treasure) is exercisable in relation to anything which is treasure for the purposes of this Act.

(2) That jurisdiction is not exercisable for the purposes of the law relating to treasure trove in relation to anything found after the commencement of section 4.

(3) The Act of 1988 and anything saved by virtue of section 36(5) of that Act (saving for existing law and practice etc) has effect subject to this section.

(4) An inquest held by virtue of this section is to be held without a jury, unless the coroner orders otherwise.

Duty of finder to notify coroner. 8.—(1) A person who finds an object which he believes or has reasonable grounds for believing is treasure must notify the coroner for the district in which the object was found before the end of the notice period.

(2) The notice period is fourteen days beginning with—
  (a) the day after the find; or
  (b) if later, the day on which the finder first believes or has reason to believe the object is treasure.

(3) Any person who fails to comply with subsection (1) is guilty of an offence and liable on summary conviction to—
  (a) imprisonment for a term not exceeding three months;
  (b) a fine of an amount not exceeding level 5 on the standard scale; or
  (c) both.

(4) In proceedings for an offence under this section, it is a defence for the defendant to show that he had, and has continued to have, a reasonable excuse for failing to notify the coroner.

(5) If the office of coroner for a district is vacant, the person acting as coroner for that district is the coroner for the purposes of subsection (1).

Procedure for inquests. 9.—(1) In this section, 'inquest' means an inquest held under section 7.

(2) A coroner proposing to conduct an inquest must notify—
  (a) the British Museum, if his district is in England; or
  (b) the National Museum of Wales, if it is in Wales.

(3) Before conducting the inquest, the coroner must take reasonable steps to notify—
  (a) any person who it appears to him may have found the treasure; and
  (b) any person who, at the time the treasure was found, occupied land which it appears to him may be where it was found.

(4) During the inquest the coroner must take reasonable steps to notify any such person not already notified.

(5) Before or during the inquest, the coroner must take reasonable steps—
  (a) to obtain from any person notified under subsection (3) or (4) the names and addresses of interested persons; and
  (b) to notify any interested person whose name and address he obtains.

(6) The coroner must take reasonable steps to give any interested person notified under subsection (3), (4) or (5) an opportunity to examine witnesses at the inquest.

(7) In subsections (5) and (6), 'interested person' means a person who appears to the coroner to be likely to be concerned with the inquest—
  (a) as the finder of the treasure or otherwise involved in the find;
  (b) as the occupier, at the time the treasure was found, of the land where it was found, or
  (c) as having had an interest in that land at that time or since.

Rewards, codes of practice and report

Rewards. 10.—(1) This section applies if treasure—
  (a) has vested in the Crown under section 4; and
  (b) is to be transferred to a museum.

(2) The Secretary of State must determine whether a reward is to be paid by the museum before the transfer.

(3) If the Secretary of State determines that a reward is to be paid, he must also determine, in whatever way he thinks fit—

    (a) the treasure's market value;

    (b) the amount of the reward;

    (c) to whom the reward is to be payable; and

    (d) if it is to be payable to more than one person, how much each is to receive.

(4) The total reward must not exceed the treasure's market value.

(5) The reward may be payable to—

    (a) the finder or any other person involved in the find;

    (b) the occupier of the land at the time of the find;

    (c) any person who had an interest in the land at that time, or has had such an interest at any time since then.

(6) Payment of the reward is not enforceable against a museum or the Secretary of State.

(7) In a determination under this section, the Secretary of State must take into account anything relevant in the code of practice issued under section 11.

(8) This section also applies in relation to treasure which has vested in a franchisee under section 4, if the franchisee makes a request to the Secretary of State that it should.

Codes of practice. 11.—(1) The Secretary of State must—

    (a) prepare a code of practice relating to treasure;

    (b) keep the code under review; and

    (c) revise it when appropriate.

(2) The code must, in particular, set out the principles and practice to be followed by the Secretary of State—

    (a) when considering to whom treasure should be offered;

    (b) when making a determination under section 10; and

    (c) where the Crown's title to treasure is disclaimed.

(3) The code may include guidance for—

    (a) those who search for or find treasure; and

    (b) museums and others who exercise functions in relation to treasure.

(4) Before preparing the code or revising it, the Secretary of State must consult such persons appearing to him to be interested as he thinks appropriate.

(5) A copy of the code and of any proposed revision of the code shall be laid before Parliament.

(6) Neither the code nor any revision shall come into force until approved by a resolution of each House of Parliament.

(7) The Secretary of State must publish the code in whatever way he considers appropriate for bringing it to the attention of those interested.

(8) If the Secretary of State considers that different provision should be made for—

    (a) England and Wales, and

    (b) Northern Ireland,

or that different provision should otherwise be made for treasure found in different areas, he may prepare two or more separate codes.

Report on operation of Act. 12. As soon as reasonably practicable after each anniversary of the coming into force of this section, the Secretary of State shall lay before Parliament a report on the operation of this Act in the preceding year.

Miscellaneous

Application of Act to Northern Ireland. 13. In the application of this Act to Northern Ireland—

    (a) in section 7—

        (i) in subsection (1), for 'section 30 of the Coroners Act 1988' substitute 'section 33 of the Coroners Act (Northern Ireland) 1959';

        (ii) in subsection (3), for the words from '1988' to 'practice etc)' substitute '1959';

    (b) in section 9(2), for the words from 'British Museum' to the end substitute 'Department of the Environment for Northern Ireland'.

Consequential amendments. 14.—(1) In section 33 of the Coroners Act (Northern Ireland) 1959 (inquest on treasure trove), for 'treasure trove' substitute 'treasure'.

(2) In section 54(3) of the Ancient Monuments and Archaeological Areas Act 1979 (saving for rights in relation to treasure trove) for 'in relation to treasure trove' substitute 'under the Treasure Act 1996'.

(3) In Article 42 of the Historic Monuments and Archaeological Objects (Northern Ireland) Order 1995 (reporting of archaeological objects)—

    (a) after paragraph (10) insert—

        '(10A) This Article does not apply in relation to an object if the person who found it believes or has reasonable grounds for believing that the object is treasure within the meaning of the Treasure Act 1996.';

    (b) in paragraph (11)(a) for 'treasure trove' substitute 'any treasure within the meaning of the Treasure Act 1996'.

(4) Subsections (2) and (3)(b) have effect in relation to any treasure found after the commencement of section 4.

(5) Subsection (3)(a) has effect in relation to any object found after the commencement of section 8.

Short title, commencement and extent. 15.—(1) This Act may be cited as the Treasure Act 1996.

(2) This Act comes into force on such day as the Secretary of State may by order made by statutory instrument appoint; and different days may be appointed for different purposes.

(3) This Act does not extend to Scotland.

INDEX